The Official Book
of the
Irish Setter

by Connie Vanacore

Distributed in the UNITED STATES to the Pet Trade by T.F.H. Publications, Inc., 1 TFH Plaza, Neptune City, NJ 07753; on the Internet at www.tfh.com; in CANADA by Rolf C. Hagen Inc., 3225 Sartelon St., Montreal, Quebec H4R 1E8; Pet Trade by H & L Pet Supplies Inc., 27 Kingston Crescent, Kitchener, Ontario N2B 2T6; in ENGLAND by T.F.H. Publications, PO Box 74, Havant PO9 5TT; in AUSTRALIA AND THE SOUTH PACIFIC by T.F.H. (Australia), Pty. Ltd., Box 149, Brookvale 2100 N.S.W., Australia; in NEW ZEALAND by Brooklands Aquarium Ltd., 5 McGiven Drive, New Plymouth, RD1 New Zealand; in SOUTH AFRICA by Rolf C. Hagen S.A. (PTY.) LTD., P.O. Box 201199, Durban North 4016, South Africa; in JAPAN by T.F.H. Publications. Published by T.F.H. Publications, Inc.

MANUFACTURED IN THE
UNITED STATES OF AMERICA
BY T.F.H. PUBLICATIONS, INC.

This book is dedicated to the Irish Setter, whose love, loyalty, devotion, and beauty have inspired us all.

I would like to acknowledge the participation and contributions made to this book by the Irish Setter Club of America Board of Directors. I especially thank Shirley Farrington, Ken Ruff, Kay Bedeau, Anne Schilling, and Marilee Larson for putting together some sections of the book. I am indebted to Eve Gardner in England, Peter Frost in Australia, and Dave Carey in Canada for their help. Members of the ISCA Health Committee approved the sections on health and care. Sandy Jones provided the pedigrees. Fred Vanacore provided endless homefront support while this work was in progress.

The history was handed down to me through publication of *The New Complete Irish Setter* (Howell Book House, New York), written by E. I. Eldredge and me, which is no longer in print.

To those who so graciously submitted photos, both formal and candid, to brighten the pages of the book, I am truly grateful.

Those breeders and owners who took the time to tell me about their kennel histories deserve special mention, because without their dedication to our breed, we would not have the continuity of a great breed's evolution over the past 25 years.

This has been a group effort, none of which would have been possible without everyone's dedication and love for the Irish Setter.

Connie Vanacore

Table of Contents

Introduction

The Irish Setter is one of the handsomest of all breeds. With his glorious coat, extroverted personality, and elegant bearing, it is little wonder that he draws admiring glances wherever he goes.

The Irish Setter is a sporting dog, bred to find upland birds, to hunt with stamina and initiative, to point, to retrieve if called upon to do so, and to address each task with confidence and enthusiasm. Not all Irish Setters are trained to hunt, but the innate ability is there. It is evident when a four-month-old puppy stealthily stalks a butterfly across a lawn or freezes on point in front of a robin pecking at a worm.

The basic personality of the Irish Setter and his dazzling red coat set him apart from any other breed. There is no mistaking him, whether at home, in the show ring, in the obedience ring, or in the field.

He is Irish to the heart—loving, boisterous, rollicking, carefree, demanding, loyal, and gentle. Because the Irish Setter is what he is, with no pretenses, he is a dog for those who cherish these innate qualities.

In this book, we will present the Irish Setter in all his facets. We will show you in words and pictures the ideal Irish Setter as presented in the official standard for the breed. We will tell you about his accomplishments in the field, in obedience, agility, and conformation, and as a beloved family pet. We will give the reader insights into the care, grooming, and training of the Irish Setter, and we will introduce you to the history of this great breed. You will be able to trace his ancestry and accomplishments through breeders of the past and present.

We hope the reader will find this book about the Irish Setter to be a valuable resource for education and enlightenment about this wonderful breed.

An Irish Setter for everyone.

6

The History
of the
Irish Setter

Beginnings

The origin of the Irish Setter is not definitely known. It is reasonable, however, to suppose that it evolved from older breeds by natural or artificial selection for the purpose of finding and pointing upland game.

Records show that the breed was definitely established as early as 1800, but its history prior to that time relies mainly upon oral tradition, scattered writings, and old sporting prints.

Most historians believe that the foundation stock of the Irish Setter was the setting spaniel, which originated

French 19th-century oil painting of setters on point by P. Tourette.

7

Setter and pointer by G. Muss-Arnoldt.

in Spain and was imported to the British Isles during the period of great cultural exchange between the Spaniards and the Irish. However, there is a difference of opinion as to what crosses were used to create the larger setting dog that led to the Irish Setter. The Bloodhound, Pointer, Irish Water Spaniel, Gordon Setter, English Setter, and their progenitors have been variously named as possible ancestors. As the early-day sportsmen generally kept several breeds in their kennels, it was not unusual for them to interbreed their dogs in order to improve utility in the field.

Whatever crosses were used, the transition from spaniel to setter was apparently very gradual. Sporting illustrations of the period depict setters that resemble spaniels, as in W. Ward's engraving (1806) of G. Morland's painting. A close connection between the breeds is further indicated by the existence in Ireland in about 1770 of a variety of setters called red spaniels (in Gaelic, *modder rhu*).

W. J. Rasbridge, the breed's most renowned historian, expressed his views on the breed's origin in the March 18, 1982, issue of the English magazine, *Our Dogs*. He wrote:

> As I see it, the Irish Setter is one variety of the larger land spaniel, which like the lesser land spaniel, originated in Spain, whence its name. It happened to be a variety that the Irish took to themselves and made their own, probably in the 18th century, so that by the mid-19th century the breed was there to be found at its highest level for work and looks. Ireland became the center from which the breed was disseminated over the rest of the world.

Family strains were established in the early 1700s by English gentry who came to Ireland to acquire land and brought their setting dogs with them. The mixture of the native Irish dogs and the English strains formed the foundation stock for the show and field trial dogs that appeared in the 1860s, according to Mr. Rasbridge. All

Two setters and a pointer by G. Muss-Arnoldt.

Irish Setters listed in the first stud book in England came direct or at one or two removes from Ireland.

By 1800, setter type had become so well established that it is easy to recognize the Irish Setter in artwork of that era. During those formative years, breeders gradually refined their stock from red-and-white or black-and-white to the pure red dog that we know today. From 1780 to 1850, Irish families took special pride in the purity of their own strains of setter and in the number of years they had possessed them. Many of the royal families of Ireland, such as the Marquis of Waterford, Lord Clancarty, Lord Angelsey, Lord Lismore, Lord Dillon, Lord Rossmore, Lord Forbes, Lord Howth, Sir Frances H. Loftus, Sir George Gore, Earl of Enniskillen, and many others, developed their own lines of pure red setters. John G. King was known at the time as the father of the breed, and Harry Blake Knox was the first to speak of the breed as the "Irish Red Setter."

The distinguishing mark of the Irish Setter through the years has been its color, which is likened to that of a freshly opened horse chestnut burr. It has been variously described

Portrait of Toledo Blade, a tri-colored setter, by Edmund Osthaus.

9

as red, mahogany, chestnut, blood-red, and, indeed, almost every shade between yellow and brown during its formative years. According to Mrs. M. Ingle Bepler (whose Rheola Kennels in England were established in the late 1890s), three distinct color strains were known in early Ireland. Solid red predominated in the north, the particolored red-and-white in the south and west, and an attractive "shower of hail" variety along the northwest coast. "Shower of hail" setters were typical of the breed in points and color, but were sprinkled with uniform, quarter-inch, white spots about an inch apart.

Color was long a bone of contention among breeders, some claiming red as the proper color and others insisting upon red-and-white, although both strains probably originated from much the same parent stock.

The Dublin bench shows of 1874 and 1875 had separate classes for red and red-and-white setters. Both varieties were described by Anna Redlich in *Dogs of Ireland* (1949). Even as late as 1964 in Ireland, the red-and-white blood was occasionally infused with that of the solid reds to improve style and head carriage, according to their breeders. Today, the breeds are totally separate and have developed distinct styles, temperaments, and gaits.

The first dog show was held in the town hall at Newcastle-on-Tyne in England on June 28th and 29th, 1859. It was for pointers and setters only and drew 60 entries. Next came shows at Birmingham, Leeds, Manchester, and London, which included other breeds as well as gun dogs. There was considerable uncertainty about what constituted true type in Irish Setters, each owner claiming that he alone possessed the ideal dog.

Bob

Major Hutchinson's "Bob," whelped in 1859 and shown four years later, was described in one reference as "a wide-fronted, thick-shouldered Suffolk cart horse," and in another reference as "good all over, formed in exact proportion, and with substance as well as symmetry."

Plunket

The celebrated Irish Setter field trial winner, Plunket, whelped in 1868, combined two English strains, that of Robert LaTouche and Hutchinson. He was sired by Plunket's Beauty out of Macdona's Grouse. Grouse was a daughter of Hutchinson's Bob and was bred by the

Portrait of Leda, an early setter, by Percival Rousseau.

Portrait of Plunket, the celebrated field trial winner of the late 1800s.

Honorable D. Plunket. Although Plunket was small and bitch-like, he possessed speed, endurance, and exceptional style on point. Macdona sold Plunket to R. Purcell Llewellin of English setter fame, who exported him to America, where he was used to improve American stock.

Ch. Palmerston

In the 1870s, the dog that was most influential in establishing the type of Irish Setter from which the modern show dog has evolved was born. He was Ch. Palmerston, and although his date of birth is in dispute, he came into the possession of J. M. Hilliard in 1874. Palmerston had been owned by Cecil Moore, a solicitor in Omagh, one of the founders of the Irish Setter Club in Dublin, and a gentleman who had more to do with the drafting of the standard for the club than anyone else. The story, according to Rawdon Lee, writing in 1893, was that "Mr. Moore, finding Palmerston a rather delicate dog for field work, though most persevering and with an excellent nose, ordered his man to drown him. He did not want anyone to use him for shooting purposes, as he'd passed his prime. Mr. Hilliard met the poor old dog on the way to what was expected to be his watery grave and begged Mr. Moore to give him the dog. Mr. Moore relented, on condition that Mr. Hilliard would keep him for show purposes only." The story may be apocryphal, but Mr. Hilliard acquired the dog and began to show him in 1875. In June of that year, Palmerston won the championship at Belfast and then at Cork. He was sent to London to be used at stud and died in 1880. Palmerston was described by Rawdon Lee as an "immense dog, 64 pounds, and with an abnormally long and narrow head." The size does not square with descriptions of him as delicate for field work, as categorized by Mr. Moore, but he was 23 1/2" at the shoulder and was a deep, dark, blood-red. He had a slight snip of white on his forehead, which came to be known as the Palmerston snip. Some of his descendants carried a broad blaze on the foreface, which eventually was characterized as a fault.

After his death, Palmerston's head was mounted and hung in the entrance of the Waldorf Astoria Hotel in New York, where Mr. Hilliard's son was manager. It was taken down in 1918 and passed into the hands of the Irish Setter Club of America (ISCA). It was never seen again, and one report states that it was thrown away by the person into whose custody it had been placed.

Only a few of Palmerston's sons and daughters came to America. One of the best known of them was Rose, imported by Dr. William Jarvis in 1877. It was Dr. Jarvis who discovered the nick between the Palmerston and the Elcho strains that had a profound effect upon Irish Setter history in America.

The Irish Setter in America

In order to obtain a true picture of the early history of the Irish Setter in America, one should consult the first volume of the 1878 *National American Kennel Club Stud Book*. Only sporting dogs were registered then, an English Setter called Adonis being Number One and Admiral 534 being listed as the first Irish Setter. The first registrants were not uniform in color or type, with everything listed from solid red to red-with-white, red-with-black, or even lemon-colored.

Only imported Irish Setters or their progeny could be registered as Irish Setters. The American strains were referred to as Native Setters and were classified in a separate section called "Cross-Bred and Other Setters." The explanation for this was that, "Owing to the indefinite character of some pedigrees, it was impossible to decide to what breed certain dogs belonged. They were included in the present class to save discarding them altogether."

On January 26, 1876, a bench show was held at the Exposition building in Chicago with classes for imported red or for red-and-white Irish Setters and their progeny. There were similar classes for native red or red-and-white setters that were called Irish. It was under these conditions in the decade following 1870 that the Irish Setter gained a foothold in America. Many dogs that made history were then imported from Ireland and England. Because they were evidently superior to our native setters in type and certainly in purity of blood, they more or less set the standard of the era.

One of the first importations was Plunket, famous as a field and bench dog in England. Although he sired more than a score of litters from bitches in this country, only a few of the resulting offspring made names for themselves, perhaps because of the paucity of bench and field events at that time. Many of his puppies carried considerable white, either as a frill on the chest and feathering or on the feet.

Charles H. Turner and Elcho

In the fall of 1875, Charles H. Turner, guiding spirit of the St. Louis Kennel Club, imported Sullivan's Rose, Erin, Frisk, and Elcho. Erin won the Greenwood Plate Trophy for Irish Setters at the Memphis Field Trial of 1876. Although he was an excellent dog afield, he had a bad temper and once attacked his trainer, who had to knock the dog down with a fence rail in self-defense. Erin sired Bob, represented as the "best snipe dog that ever lived," and Duck, noted for her outstanding show record. She was defeated only once.

From left to right, Ch. Elcho and Ch. Rose.

Ch. Berkley.

Unquestionably, the greatest bench-winning bitch of her time was the imported Lou II, who won first at three Westminster shows and was widely exhibited with her famous son, Berkley. Her pedigree traces back to the early days in Ireland when some of the setters were unnamed, instead being designated as "Lord Lismore's dog" or "Delaney's bitch."

Mr. Turner imported Elcho from J. C. Cooper of Limerick, Ireland. He was whelped on May 1, 1874, and was considered by his trainer, Robert S. Greenhill, to be the the best "first season" dog he ever had. Elcho was the first Irish Setter to become a bench champion in America. He won prizes in Chicago, St. Louis, New York, and Boston. That was no mean feat when the only way of travel was by rail or horse-drawn wagons, and journeys to shows lasted several days. Elcho was the best Irish Setter of his period in America, not only because of his own record, but because of the success of his progeny on the bench and in the field. He was regarded as a great producer and was often referred to as "The Prince of Stud Dogs." He sired 7 field trial winners among the more than 50 bitches brought to him. His litters included 30 bench

PLATE IX.

BERKLEY (RED IRISH SETTER. WHELPED JULY 10, 1876.)

OWNED BY MR. A. H. MOORE, PHILADELPHIA, PENN.

	LOO II.					ELCHO.		
Nuttall's MAYBE.		Mr. Clendening's GROUSE.			NELL.		CHARLIE.	
					NANCE.	HEATHER.	JUNO.	PAT.
Mr. Nuttall's MAYO.	Mr. Walsh's CHANCE.	Mr. Clendening's BLANCHE.	Mr. Clendening's BURROW II.		LOO.	DANE	INA.	GROUSE.
Mr. Nuttall's JUNO.	Mr. Corbet's YORK.	Capt. Ponsonby's Dog.	Lord Langford's Bitch.	Mr. Hughe's RUBY.	Mr. Clendening's FAG.	QUAIL. BONE.		
Mr. Corbet's Bitch.	Mr. Fox's Dog.	Mr. Corbet's FAN.	Capt. Berkeley's DASH.	Mr. Veitch's VINO.	Mr. Clendening's HARRY.			
	Mr. Corbet's KATE.			Mr. Corbet's GROUSE.				

BERKLEY, whelped July 10, 1876, bred by St. Louis Kennel Club, won the following prizes:

Hampton, Iowa, 1877, Second prize, Puppy Stakes, nineteen entries.

St Louis 1878, First prize, Open Class; also following specials: best Brace with his dam Loo II; best Pair with Loo II; best Kennel with Loo II; best Setter of any age or breed bred in America; best Setter bred in the United States.

Boston, 1878, Champion prize; also specials, best Pair with Loo II; best kennel with Loo II, &c.

New York, 1878, Champion prize.

St Paul, Minn., 1878, Champion prize.

Philadelphia, 1879, Champion prize; also special for best Irish Setter Dog.

Champion prize St. Louis 1879.

Special for best Irish dog 1879.

Special with Duck for best brace 1879.

Champion prize, New York 1880.

Pedigree of Berkley.

show winners. He imparted quality, symmetry, and refinement to his puppies, characteristics that predominated for several generations and continue in the best Irish Setters today.

Elcho was said to have possessed a very dark red coat, a clean-cut, 11-inch head, well-placed ears, lean neck, good shoulders, deep chest, and properly curved quarters. He measured 24 inches at the shoulder and weighed 56 pounds.

Dr. William Jarvis and Elcho

In the spring of 1877, Dr. William Jarvis, Claremont, New Hampshire, acquired Ch. Elcho and kept him for many years as his own private shooting dog. Dr. Jarvis, in addition to being a successful breeder and importer of Irish Setters, was a sportswriter of high merit. He was a dentist by profession, as well as a judge of Irish Setters for more than a quarter of a century. He imported Rose (Palmerston-Flora) and Noreen (Garryowen-Cora) from Ireland. The matings of these two Palmerston bitches to Elcho gave America its finest Irish Setter foundation stock.

The Elcho-Rose mating was repeated nine times and the Elcho-Noreen mating five times.

The best known of Ch. Elcho's 197 puppies from 51 different dams was Ch. Elcho, Jr. Writers of the day acclaimed him the foremost individual of his breed in the United States, a statement confirmed by his show record. He was exhibited at more than 40 shows, ranging from the puppy class in Boston in 1882 to Irish Setter Specials in Chicago in 1891, without a single defeat. He was an upstanding, rangy dog of harmonious proportions, in which the "extreme limit of refinement" had been attained. He produced five bench champions, and even though he was not a field trial winner, he was a good shooting dog. Elcho, Jr. died in 1891.

Ch. Glencho, a litter brother to Ch. Elcho, Jr., was ranked high among influential sires of the day, producing puppies by 55 bitches.

The 1880s saw a rapid rise in popularity of the Irish Setter, both on the bench and afield, chiefly due to the Elcho-Palmerston bloodlines. There was still a preference to import stock from the British Isles, many of which went

PLATE XIV.

ELCHO & ROSE *(CHAMPION RED IRISH SETTERS).*

OWNED BY DR. WM. JARVIS, CLAREMONT, N. H.

ELCHO.

NELL. CHARLIE.

NANCE. HEATHER. JUNO. PAT.

LOO. DANE. INA. GROUSE.

QUAIL. BONE. RHUE. DERG.

ELCHO was born May 1st, 1874, and bred by J. Oppenheimer, St. Petersburg, Russia, and his blood combines the strains of Lord Waterford's and Marquis of Ormande's kennels. He was named after the Elcho Challenge Shield, by R. S. Greenhill, of the Irish Rifle Team, who once owned him, and has won the following prizes :

Second Irish Setter Class, Dublin, 1875.
First Imported Class, Chicago, 1876.

First Champion Class, St. Louis, 1876.
First Special Stock Dog Prize, St. Louis, 1876.
First Imported Class, Baltimore, 1877.
First Special for best brace of Setters, with Loo II., Baltimore, 1877.
First Champion Class, Boston, 1877.
First Special Champion Medal for best Setter, Boston, 1877.
First Champion Class, St. Louis, 1878.
First Stock Dog Class, St. Louis, 1878.
First Capelle's Special Stock Dog Prize, St. Louis, 1878.
First Jaccard's Special for best Irish Dog or Bitch, St. Louis, 1878.
First Stock Dog Class, Boston, 1878.
"Elcho" has not been exhibited since.

ROSE.

Cecil Moore's FLORA. CHAMPION PALMERSTON.

SOPHY. Jephson's DASH. Cecil Moore's KATE. Cecil Moore's GROUSE.

Cecil Moore's KATE. Cecil Moore's GROUSE. Mr. Trumble's bitch. Cecil Moore's SHOT.

Harrington's SOPHY. Evan's GROUSE.

Mr. Lloyd's KATE. Evan's SHOT.

Hazard's BELL. Hazard's GROUSE.

ROSE was born Nov., 1874, and bred by Cecil Moore, Esq., Ullardmore Dalkley, Ireland. She traces back authentically through the kennels of Mr. Moore, Capt. McDonald, husband of the Countess of Antrim, Mr. Lloyd, Mr. Evans and Mr. Hazzard, to the Earl of Enniskillen, bred about 1796.

Rose has won the following prizes—only times exhibited :
First, Belfast, Ireland, 1876.
Second, Cork, Ireland, 1876.
First, Bristol, England, 1877.
Second, Detroit, U. S. A., 1879.
First, St. Louis, U. S. A., 1879.
First Special for best Irish bitch, St. Louis, U. S. A., 1879.

Pedigree of Ch. Elcho and Ch. Rose.

back to the Palmerston strains and were of Irish origin. One of the influential dogs to be brought over was a famous field trial dog, Muskerry, bred by J. Gibbons Hawkes of Kenmore, Ireland. Muskerry and his imported sons contributed ruggedness and field ability to the Palmerston-Elcho strain in America.

The Law Strain

In the 1890s, a new strain of Irish Setters was developed that was known at the Law strain, the fountainhead of which was Ch. Ben Law, whelped in 1896 and owned by Charles A. Gale of Rutland, Vermont. Ben's three-year bench show career was not a straight string of victories, but he did win at Westminster in 1901. He sired 60 dogs out of a dozen bitches, producing many important champions. The most prolific and influential son of Ben Law was Ch. Pat Law, siring 160 offspring. He was owned by Walter McRoberts of Peoria, Illinois, and had a great influence over a 40-year period in the Midwest.

The Law setters were great shooting dogs. They were the choice of market hunters in the early 1900s and excelled on prairie chickens. They were bold, rugged, sturdy, tireless, and possessed of sure bird-finding ability.

Otto Pohl, a druggist and sportsman in the Midwest, established a great reputation at field trials and bench shows. In 1909, he bought Ch. Drug Law and Ch. Pat-A-Belle from Walter McRoberts and trained both dogs for prairie chicken and quail shooting. Pohl also brought over an English Field Trial dog, Morty Oge, who figures in the pedigrees of many American-bred dogs of the day. Morty Oge was a large, coarse, dark mahogany dog with a wide head. He was not successful on the bench but was superb in the field. The 17 bitches bred to him produced many good bird dogs throughout the Midwest. His second import in 1914, Ch. Rheola Clanderrick, was from Mrs. M. Ingle Bepler. This dog won his championship easily and was widely used at stud. The Clanderrick name persisted for more than 40 years.

The Irish Setter in the East

In the East at the same time, Joseph and Thomas Wall of Montreal, Chicago, and then Brooklyn, New York, established the Lismore line of Irish Setters. Also in the East, the brothers Louis and S. A. Contoit established the St. Cloud kennels on the Elcho-Noreen foundation. Louis Contoit claims to have owned at least 5,000 Irish Setters over a period of 40 years. The Contoit brothers were among the first to establish a modern strain of Irish Setters by linebreeding. They mated several sisters to the same sire and then crossed the offspring. They usually retained the bitches and sold the males. Outstanding among their early sires were Ch. St. Cloud III and Ch. St. Cloud Fermanagh, both important producers of beautiful type.

The Early 20ᵗʰ Century

In the decade following World War I, there was an unprecedented increase in the number and popularity of Irish Setters. At least 200 of them were imported from Canada and the British Isles, with the result that interbreeding the divergent strains led to wide variations in breed size and type. Before the decade had passed, however, a new, stylish, streamlined Irish Setter that was destined to set the type of the modern dogs emerged from this "melting pot." The old Law strain was on the decline, while the Boyne family originated by J. A. Carbery of Drogheda, Ireland, started to ascend.

Palmerston

Dr. John D. DeRonde (Palmerston Kennels) of New York City kept approximately 60 dogs at his country estate and sold setters as far west as California. Mary Pickford, the famous movie star, owned one of his breeding. Dr. DeRonde was a judge and president of the ISCA. His first big winner was a Canadian import, Tyrone Larry, a dark red, 56-pound dog that became an American and Canadian champion despite a plain head and straight stifles. He sired more than 140 offspring, many of which were successful at shows and field trials.

St. Val / Knocknagree

About 1909, the kennel prefix St. Val appeared in the names of excellent Irish Setters that carried the early Lismore and St. Cloud bloodlines. The profile of one of these dogs adorns the bronze medal of the ISCA, which

continues to this day. The kennel was owned by Warren Delano, Jr., and after his death, his daughter, Miss Laura Delano of Rhinebeck, New York, continued the strain under the Knocknagree prefix beginning in 1923.

Milson

The Milson prefix, which played an important role in Irish Setter history, was used by Sidney H. Sonn of Harrison, New York from 1923 until 1930. He started with a puppy, Milson Peggy (Ch. Lismore Freedom ex Ch. Swifty Holden). She was a favorite at shows but made her mark as the dam of several outstanding dogs, all sired by Ch. Higgins Red Pat.

About 1930, the Milson bloodlines were transferred to Harry Hartnett, a breeder and professional handler, later to the Caldene Kennels of Dr. Jay Calhoon, and subsequently to the Knockross Kennels of Welrose (Slim) Newhall.

Of the Cloisters

Edwin M. Berolsheimer, President of Eagle Pencil Company, founded a kennel of Irish Setters using "of the Cloisters" as a suffix. His estate atop the cliffs at Tarrytown, New York, was the inspiration for the name. All his dogs were trained hunting dogs as well as show dogs, and until his death in 1949, Mr. Berolsheimer championed the cause of Irish Setters in the field. He owned the first American Kennel Club (AKC) Irish Setter Field Champion, Elcova McTybe. Several McTybe setters followed in his footsteps. Elcova McTybe was bred and trained by Elias C. Vail, a prominent Irish Setter trainer whose dogs competed both at shows and at field trials.

Ch. Bergniel Red Helmet

Another dog of importance during the 1920s was Ch. Bergniel Red Helmet (Lord Lismore II ex Bergniel Guri), a consistent show winner from 1923 to 1928. He is best known as the sire of seven champions, among which were Emily Schweitzer's Ch. Verbu Red Mollie and several champions by Ch. Kenridge My Dear, bred by C. C. Stillman, a gentleman who popularized the Morgan horse in America. Ch. Kenridge My Dear had four litters by Ch. Bergniel Red Helmet.

Ch. St. Cloud's Fermanagh III

Another dog of importance to the breed was Ch. St. Cloud's Fermanagh III, shown under the colors of Mrs. Cheever Porter of New York City by Henry Hartnett. He was ancestor to her famous dogs, Ch. Milson O'Boy and Ch. Rosecroft Premier. Although Mrs. Porter maintained few of the dogs she owned, she enabled the best to be shown and bred, thus influencing the breed in lasting ways.

William Cary Duncan

One of the most unique personalities in Irish Setter affairs for more than a quarter century was William Cary Duncan. He loved all three of the setter varieties and enjoyed hunting and trialing with his dogs. His profession was writing musical comedies for Broadway, and his dogs were his great relaxation. Mr. Duncan was the Irish Setter delegate to the AKC for 20 years prior to his death in 1945. He was also the breed correspondent for the *AKC Gazette* and he was the dog editor for *Outdoor Life* magazine. His best known Irish Setter was Ch. Elcova's Admiration, which he acquired from Elias Vail.

Higgins

The 1920s saw no less than 30 Boyne dogs imported from Ireland and England, plus many other less influential strains. In 1923, William W. Higgins of Charleston, West Virginia, imported from J. A. Carbery a small, dark mahogany, profusely coated Irish Setter named Higgins' Paddy of Boyne (Eng. Ch. Terry of Boyne ex Dora of Boyne). Although Paddy did not compete in shows or field trials, he became famous as a sire and exerted a great influence on the breed. He was bred to 16 bitches, but the nick that proved to be exceptional was his four litters by Craigie Lea Mona (Ch. Lismore Freedom ex Clare II.) Mona was a relatively large, solid red bitch of excellent conformation, although she was never shown. Six great champions resulted from those matings: Ch. Higgins' Red Pat, whelped 4/26/24; Ch. Higgins' Red Coat, whelped 9/30/27; Sister A.C.F., whelped 9/30/27; Ch. Barney of Boyne, whelped 5/30/28; Ch. Rose of Sharon II, whelped 5/30/28; and Ch. Patricia of Boyne, whelped 2/1/29.

At one time, Ralph and Irene Hallam of Chicago owned all six champions together with their sire and dam, one of the greatest aggregations of Irish Setters ever assembled in one kennel. Many believe that Red Pat was the best Irish Setter that ever lived. It was Red Coat, however, who made the greatest impact as the sire of 30 champions. The progeny of Paddy and Mona dominated the show honors in America for a quarter of a century. As the generations progressed, the bloodlines blurred, but nearly every American Irish Setter has some of this pair's bloodline in his ancestry.

The strain possessed certain outstanding qualities that we value today—clean, arched necks flowing into beautiful shoulders, depth of chest, and lovely eye and ear placement. Refinement of breed type exemplified by thin lips and ear leather, chiseling of the muzzle, and domed occiputs characterized these dogs. They were slow in developing, usually requiring more than 18 months to mature, but they did not grow coarse with age.

Ch. Higgins' Red Pat's remarkable show record of 24 Bests in Show, 43 Group Firsts, and 74 Bests of Breed brought the Irish Setter into the public eye. A wonderful showman and campaigner, Pat traveled thousands of miles in his career, from his debut at Westminster in 1926 to his farewell appearance at that show six years later. He won Best of Breed at the 1926 AKC Sesquicentennial show in Philadelphia and Best in Show at the first Morris & Essex Kennel Club show in 1927, an event of historic importance in the dog world. Red Pat died of cancer in the veterinary hospital at the University of Pennsylvania on July 9, 1932.

Ch. Higgins' Red Coat was also an outstanding show dog but did not amass the wins that his brother did. He did garner a Best in Show and placed twice in the group at Westminster and three times at Morris & Essex. In 1931, he was transferred to Dr. Frederick Neilson, who owned the Rosecroft Kennels, and the last eight years of his life were spent at Harry Hartnett's Milson Kennels. He died in July, 1939. He is credited with 220 registered get from 39 bitches, representing 45 litters. Several of his offspring figure prominently in the ancestry of Irish Setters today.

The history of the 1930s is dominated by the Ch. Higgins' Red Coat family. Among the most important were the lines from his three sons: Ch. Milson O'Boy, Ch. Kinvarra Son of Red Coat, and Ch. Redwood Russet of Harvale.

Ch. Milson O'Boy

Ch. Milson O'Boy (Ch. Higgins' Red Coat ex Milson Miss Sonny), owned by Mrs. Cheever Porter, was one of the greatest show dogs of all time. Those who saw him never forgot him. In a five-year period, he accumulated 11 Bests in Show, 46 Group Firsts and 103 Best of Breed awards. He was Best in Show at Morris & Essex in 1935, defeating 3,175 dogs of 73 breeds. He died at the age of 13 on June 29, 1945, having spent several years in retirement with his mistress. He sired 163 puppies in 41 litters. Among his outstanding get were Ch. Milson Top-Notcher and Ch. Milson O'Boy II.

Knightscroft

Ch. Milson O'Boy II was the foundation sire for the Knightscroft Kennel of Joseph and Henrietta Knight. They bred him to several Milson bitches and produced, among others, Ch. Rosecroft Premier (Ch. Milson O'Boy II ex Rosecroft Fern), given to Frederick Neilson. The Knights bred 37 champions and flourished from 1932 until Henrietta Knight's death in 1963.

Ch. Rosecroft Premier was acquired by Mrs. Cheever Porter and, in addition to a fine show career, was the sire of such influential dogs as Ch. End O'Maine Luckalone, owned by Hollis Wilson of Amherst, Wisconsin. End O'Maine dogs served as foundation stock for many kennels. Joyce Nilsen's Thenderin Kennels traces back to him through Ch. Kinvarra Portia.

Dr. Jay W. Calhoon

When Harry Hartnett dispersed his kennel because of poor health in 1944, the breeding stock was transferred to Dr. Jay W. Calhoon, Uhrichsville, Ohio. He bred a variety of bloodlines and successfully preserved the Milson lines, which were subsequently carried on by Slim Newhall. The sire, Ch. Caldene Mick O'Boy, was his foremost stud dog, but in 1960, Mick's son, Knockross O'Boy, carried on the family through his 36 champion offspring. Knockross

Ch. Milson O'Boy, one of the greatest show Irish Setters of all time. Owned by Mrs. Cheever Porter.

Portrait of Ch. Milson Top-Notcher, from the Milson Kennels.

O'Boy had 14 points toward his championship but accidently became blind in one eye and was withdrawn from the show ring. His progeny included Mrs. Betty Crawford's Ch. Knockross Ruby and Emily Schweitzer's Chs. Verbu Erin and Verbu Maureen. Ruby was bred to Ch. Draherin Irish Regardless 4 times and produced 21 champions. Among them were Ch. Shannon's Shawn of Erin, Ch. Shannon's Erin, Ch. Major O'Shannon, and Ch. Shannon's Laird Shane.

Tyronne Farm

Another breeder who contributed many years of his life to the progress of the Irish Setter was Jack A. Spear, Tyronne Farm Kennels, of Tipton, Iowa. In 1934, Jack purchased Jordan Farm Nancy and Ch. Tyronne Farm Joan from the Jordan Farm Kennels of Bolivar, New York. At the same time, he purchased Ch. Tyronne Farm Jerry from Maurice Baker and, in 1935, he bought the famous producing dam and lovely show bitch, Ch. Ruxton's Mollie O'Day from E. D. Levering. Mollie, first bred at 7 years of age, had 5 litters and 35 puppies in her lifetime. Those litters produced 14 champions, including both bench and field winners. One successful nick was achieved when Jack bred Mollie to Ch. Kinvarra Kermit, owned by Lee Schoen of Darien, Connecticut. That litter, whelped on February 13, 1939, contained six champions.

Tyronne Farm dogs had their own particular style and were prominent in the show ring for 30 years, winning 50 or more championship titles and at least 50 Best in Show awards. Ch. Tyronne Farm Clancy, the top-winning Irish Setter for 1949, won 19 Bests in Show, including Morris & Essex in 1950. Several of Jack's dogs were sold to breeders in various parts of the US, where they served as foundation stock for other kennels. Ch. Tyronne Farm Malone II, owned by Kinvarra Kennels, had an impressive effect on the breed that extended for several generations. On the West Coast, Ch. Tyronne Farm Malone through Ch. Seaforth Dark Rex and Ch. Innisfail Color Scheme CD made a great contribution. Approximately 75 percent of the California Irish Setter show dogs had his bloodlines. Webline, Enilen, County Clare, Lismoro, Glendee, and other kennels trace back to Malone.

Kinvarra

Lee Schoen, founder of Kinvarra Kennels, was a prominent judge, breed historian, and successful author of animal stories. He was successful in the New York City wholesale fur business and was a president of the ISCA. Lee, one of the foremost authorities on the breed in the world, chose Kinvarra as his kennel name from a list of 500 possibilities, scientifically by vote, as though he sensed it would have future significance. The name (said to mean "community of kin") is that of a town in County Galway. It was registered by Lee in 1932, several years after he began to raise Irish Setters and three years after the first of a flow of importations that continued, except for the interruption of World War II, for nearly half a century.

The most important of Lee's early imports was the bitch Borrowdale Yseult of Kinvarra. She was not much over 23 inches in height, dark, lustrous, and beautiful to watch in the field. When bred to the successful show dog, Ch. Kinvarra Son of Red Coat, she produced the small but elegant Ch. Kinvarra Craig. From these three dogs came a line of champion descendants that carry on today in most of the breed's enduring kennels.

A steady stream of champions came from this kennel in the 1930s, '40s, and '50s. The last included Ch. Kinvarra Bootsie, not only an excellent brood matron but a successful field trialer as well.

In 1934, Lee imported the bitch Ch. Kinvarra Mollie of Gadeland for E. I. "Ted" Eldredge (Tirvelda). Ted was 14 years old at the time and asked Lee to select a bitch for him that he considered suitable for American competition. Under an agreement in which the bitch's first sire and best puppy in the litter would go to Lee, he chose Mollie. For that first and most notable litter, Mollie was bred to Craig. In a litter of 14, Lee narrowed his choice down to two males. At a loss as to which one to take, he closed his eyes and reached for the dog destined to become one of the all-time Irish Setter greats—Ch. Kinvarra Kermit. The other, Tirvelda Barrymore, became the only one in that outstanding litter that did not amount to much.

Kermit, beautifully proportioned and well-coordinated, with an extremely gay and friendly disposition, won several Bests in Show, but it is as a sire that he made his greatest impact. Bred to bitches that Schoen astutely thought would make a contribution to the breed, Kermit sired 29 champions—an incredible figure, considering that a major portion of his progeny reached showable ages during World War II, when very few dog shows were held.

All of the Kinvarra dogs were field-trained and were put through basic obedience.

Kilkara

Kinvarra formed the basis of Kelly Fox's Kilkara Kennel, now of Prospect, Kentucky. Kelly owned Mollie's brother, Ch. Kinvarra Raglan CD, Ch. Kinvarra Flicker, and other excellent dogs.

Thenderin

Another Kinvarra bitch that had enormous influence was acquired by Joyce Nilsen of Thenderin Kennels. She was Ch. Kinvarra Portia—the dam, when bred to Ch. End

O'Maine Luckalone, of Ch. Thenderin Brian Tristan. Whelped on St. Patrick's Day in 1948, Brian Tristan was purchased by James R. and Mary Fraser. As a young dog, he was most unmanageable and willful, but as he matured he became obedient and personable. He turned into a strong, sound Irish Setter. During his career from 1950 to 1954, Brian won 10 Bests in Show, 23 Sporting Groups, and 61 Bests of Breed. He topped the group at both Westminster and the International Kennel Club show in Chicago in 1953. It was as a prepotent sire of 30 champions that Brian made his most important contribution to the breed. The high quality of Irish Setters in America, particularly in the Midwest, can be attributed in no small part to Ch. Thenderin Brian Tristan. Am. Can. Ch. Cherry Point Brask, Ch. Esquire of Maple Ridge, Ch. Headliner the Flaming Beauty, and Ch. Michael Bryan Duke of Sussex are good illustrations of this quality.

Redwood

Another branch of the Red Coat family was headed by Ch. Redwood Russet of Harvale (Ch. Higgins Red Coat ex Ch. Redwood Rita). Redwood was the prefix of Lewis H. Starkey, who lived in New York and later moved to Pasadena, California. Russet was shown on the West Coast from 1936 to 1939 and was seldom defeated in the breed during his career. At the 1946 Specialty Show of the Irish Setter Club of Southern California, 50 of his sons and daughters appeared in he ring with the old dog as a "living pedigree" exhibition.

The 16 champions sired by Russet represented Crosshaven, End O'Maine, Kendare, Waterford, Hollywood Hills, and other kennels in the West and Midwest. He was given to Ted Eldredge and spent the last seven years of his life at Tirvelda.

Crosshaven

Ward Gardner of Walla Walla, Washington, started his Crosshaven Kennels in the early 1930s with two well-bred bitches, Ch. Lady Mac of Shanagolden (a California blend) and Ch. Ruxton's Shannon of Boyne. In 1937, the latter whelped a litter of 11 puppies by Redwood Rocket that included 6 champions. One of them, Ch. Sally O'Bryan of Crosshaven, was said to be the first of the heavily coated Irish Setters. Sally was the top-winning bitch in America in 1939. Runner-up was her litter sister, Ch. Stardust of Crosshaven. Both bitches were bred to Ch. Russet of Harvale, a double cross to Ch. Higgin's Red Coat. Sally produced Ch. Faig-a-Baile of Crosshaven, later owned by Ted Eldredge, while Stardust was the dam of Ch. Kleiglight of Aragon and Ch. Molly of Crosshaven.

Aragon

Ch. Kleiglight of Aragon (1939–1952), one of the truly great Irish Setters, was owned by H. Jack Cooper, Franklin Park, Illinois, who bred and showed dogs for more than 40 years. Although Cooper had numerous Irish Setters, as well as many other breeds, the imported dog Ch. Golden Dawn of Gadeland O'Aragon was the most important. He was a winner at the big English shows, including Crufts, and upon his arrival in the US, raced to his American championship in eight weeks under seven different judges in 1932. He was the sire of 253 offspring in 73 litters, some the result of repeat matings. He was the grandsire of Ch. Kinvarra Mollie of Gadeland, the foundation bitch for Tirvelda. On Father's Day, June 19, 1938, 37 of Dawn's sons and daughters gathered at Aragon Kennels to pay their respects to him. More than 300 people stopped by during the afternoon to witness an informal bench show of his non-champion get.

Kleiglight, or "Pete," as he was called, was the prolific sire of 595 registered offspring in 131 litters from 94 bitches. The 30 champions that he sired carried the names of Beauty, Knocknagree, and others. His bloodlines had a pronounced effect on Midwestern Irish Setter strains. Pete died of a stroke in 1952. His owner and breeder, Jack, died the following year, and the kennel was continued by Jack's widow, Ethel Cooper. Jack's son, Dick, followed in his father's footsteps, becoming a successful professional handler of many Irish Setters, including one of the top-winning Irish, Ch. Starheir's Aaron Ardee. During his illustrious career as a handler, he was most closely associated with the Salilyn English Springer Spaniels of Mrs. Julia Gasow of Troy, Michigan.

Runwild

Virginia Hardin of Runwild Kennels in Northbrook, Illinois, is another Irish Setter breeder whose career spanned many generations. She obtained her first dog when she was eight years old in 1915. He was Duke of Aragon from Jack Cooper's kennel. Her first show was in 1930, when she showed Duke, now 14 years old, to a second-place ribbon. Her first real show dog was Rheola Norna of Duck Puddle. At that time, she was introduced to obedience by Emily Schweitzer and to show handling by Dick Cooper. Her first obedience dog was Verbu Christopher Oogh, UD. She also began to run her dogs in the field. Runwild Kennels was registered in 1947

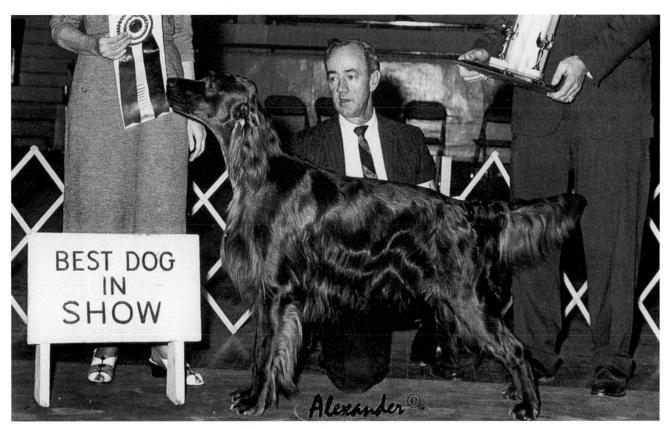

Ch. Runwild Finnagain winning Best In Show. Owned by Virginia Hardin.

with Ch. Runwild Fin McCoul CD and Ch. Runwild Alannah CD. Alannah, bred to Ch. Charles River Color Sargeant, began a long line of Runwild champions, the most famous of which was Ch. Runwild Fiona, owned by Robert Bridell. Virginia was a licensed AKC handler from 1940 to 1976. Virginia continued to be active in Irish Setter affairs, as president of the ISCA from 1979 to 1981 and as a director for many years.

Verbu Christopher Oogh UD, Runwild Kennel's first obedience champion. Owned by Virginia Hardin.

Ch. Runwild Kilkenny winning First Field Trial Dog at the Irish Setter National Specialty in 1977. Owned by Virginia Hardin.

Tercor

Harold Correll, holding professional handler license number one from the AKC, was a loyal supporter and occasional breeder of Irish Setters under the Tercor prefix. At one time, he owned Ch. Knightscroft Patty Boyne and Ch. Faig-a-Baile of Crosshaven. In his 35-year career, he handled 500 dogs to their championships, among them Ch. Charles River Color Sergeant, Ch. Knightscroft Symphony, and Ch. Phantom Brooks Burgundy. He was known as a great raconteur and a fierce competitor in the ring. His kennels were in Bernardsville, New Jersey, where he died of a heart attack at the age of 65 on August 8, 1965. His son, Terry Correll, carried on for a while but then retired and moved west.

John Downs

An import, Ch. Red Sails of Salamagundi, was brought to America, where he eventually ended up at the kennels of John Downs and later Mrs. Alan Ryan. As a complete outcross he contributed sound rear quarters, impressive style, and exceptional spirit to his progeny. He was the sire of Color Sergeant. John Downs continued his strain in the East with Ch. Charles River Streamliner.

Other Breeders

Other breeders in the 1940s and '50s were Hayden and Lois Martin of Sunny Acre Irish Setters in Gary, Indiana; Eldon McCormack of Yakima, Washington, who owned Ch. Cherry Point Brask, II; Doris Swain (Laurel Ridge) of Canton, Massachusetts; and Leslie and Helen Walsh of Monrovia, California.

In the '60s, Dr. James and Phyllis Wilson of Milltown, Wisconsin, bred Cherry Point Setters. He raised litters from Milson, Red Barn, Tyronne Farm, and others. The Wilsons bred their Ch. End O'Maine Encore to Ch. Thenderin Brian Tristan, producing the famous Am. Can. Ch. Cherry Point Brask. Ernest and Virginia Lewis of Pacific Palisades, California, owned the great Ch. Innisfail Color Scheme CD, prepotent sire of 25 champions. He had a tremendous influence on the breed on the West Coast.

Others active in the 1960s were George Glassford, who bred dogs under the Tuxedo prefix in Ohio and William and Loretta Golden of Pacific Palisades, who owned Ch. Webline Mi-Golden Flame CD (Ch. Innisfail Color Scheme CD ex Ch. Knightscroft Erin McCuhl). In 1963, Flame whelped the Golden litter with musical names, sired by Ch. Thenderin Chaparal Cayenne. They were Symphony, Crescendo, Lyric, and Jubilee CD. The last, Ch. Webline Golden Jubilee CD, became one of the top sporting dogs during his career.

Nial and Marie Koonts bred and owned several Irish Setter champions from Midwest stock. Both are now judges. Another Midwesterner who was important in several lines was Jack Funk, whose dogs all carried the "Flaming Beauty" suffix. The most famous dog in his kennel was Ch. Headliner the Flaming Beauty (Ch. Thenderin Brian Tristan ex Ch. Larrie of Tidewater.)

Muckamoor

Ann and Peter Buck owned the Muckamoor Kennels in Plover, Wisconsin, with a combination of Knightscroft and Kinvarra breeding. The most successful litter was that sired by Muckamoor Michael McGuire ex Ch. Weblyn Masterpiece, a bitch leased from Lee Prescott. From this litter came Ch. Muckamoor Marty McCuhl, who died early but left 15 champions, one of which was

Ch. Muckamoor Candia Audie. Several Midwest and Northwest kennels used Muckamoor dogs as their foundation stock.

Banshee

The Banshee Irish Setters of Ivan and Lenore Klapper, established in 1947, were based on Knightscroft and Red Barn lines. The beautiful-headed Ch. Knightscroft Lady Vogue CD was their foundation bitch. Ivan was the president of the ISCA for 12 years, and although they are no longer breeding, the Klappers, based in Gardiner, New York, maintain their interest in the breed.

Wolfscroft

Dr. Wolfgang A. Casper started in Irish Setters in 1946. His first dog was a Knightscroft bitch, Knightscroft Dixie Belle. She was outcrossed to an English import, Ch. Brynmount Maydorwill Brandison, to produce the first Wolfscroft litter. Dr. Casper was best known for reorganizing the Eastern Irish Setter Association (EISA) in 1948. He was president and later an honorary life member. He was active in the sport and, in 1960, founded the Combined Setter Clubs of America, whose annual show is a highlight for fanciers of the three setter breeds. Wolfgang died at the age of 80 in March 1982. During the first part of his career in dogs, he shared his interest with his wife, Anne. After her death, he married Denise, who carries on the Wolfscroft name with a particular interest in obedience.

Webline

The Webline Kennels, owned by Dick and Madeline Webb, was originally formed in 1953 as a partnership between Dick and Avril Roslyn and named Weblyn. To avoid confusion, Weblyn and Webline is a continuous breeding line. Four dogs, Ch. Knightscroft Erin McCuhl, Ch. Innisfail Color Scheme CD, Ch. Thenderin Margevan Minstrel, and Margevan's Dawn, were the first owned by Weblyn. Color Scheme sired a total of 12 litters and produced 29 champions. Erin McCuhl whelped one litter of four with four champions resulting. Dawn whelped two litters with four champions.

One of the significant results of the Color Scheme-Erin mating was Ch. Weblyn Mystic Mark, Ch. Weblyn Madrigal, Ch. Weblyn Mi-Golden Flame, and Ch. Weblyn Masterpiece. These, in turn, produced about 40 champions, including several top-winning Irish, such as Ch. Webline Rio Hondo (Madrigal), Ch. Webline Wizard of Macapa (Mark), and Ch. Webline Golden Jubilee (Flame).

Webline never owned more than four adult Irish Setters at one time, and their breeding program was limited to no more than two litters in any one year. Despite, or perhaps because of, this policy, they have been honored with many awards from the ISCA. Dick was also honored as a recipient of the E. I. Eldredge Memorial Award in 1988. Dick was a popular professional handler for many years and is now a Sporting Dog judge.

Some of their Best in Show and Specialty winners were Ch. Innisfail Color Scheme CD, Ch. Weblyn Limelight CD, Ch. Webline Zingaro, Ch. Webline Golden Jubilee CD, Ch. Webline Mystic Mark, Ch. Webline Rio Hondo, Ch. Webline Fame and Fortune, Ch. Webline Free 'n Easy, and Ch. Royal Oak's Fortune's Fella.

Innisfail

Another important kennel in California from the mid-1940s until the 1970s was that of Roy and Nedra Jerome. They owned the Innisfail name, which contained a combination of the most illustrious kennels in the country. Their most famous dog was Ch. Innisfail Color Scheme CD, one of the last of their breeding who turned out to be one of the biggest winners. He was Ch. Innisfail Flashback's Design, eight-time Best in Show winner, owned by Dr. Selma Stoll. Nedra was a gifted artist and Roy was a popular lecturer on canine anatomy and gait. Roy died in the 1970s.

Westwind

The Westwind Kennels were established in 1942 when Luz and Clyde Holvenstot bought a bitch puppy, Knightscroft Magic (Ch. Milson O'Boy II ex Ch. Rosecroft Kitty Kelly) from Joe and Henrietta Knight. Bred to Ch. Knightscroft Fermanagh, Magic produced their foundation stock, and over 30 years, crosses to Ch. Caldene Mick O'Boy and Knockross O'Boy produced a number of champions, among them South American and Spanish champions. Westwind was particularly noted for its beautiful bitches, among them Ch. Westwind Scarlet Fandango, Ch. Westwind Scarlet Arabesque, and Ch. Westwind Scarlet Cascade. A dog that Luz purchased from Slim Newhall was bought as a young dog by Bernie and Wilma Baron. He became Ch. Westwind Scarlet Gay Blade. Luz was a judge of all sporting breeds and a fine painter and sculptor. She created more than 30 different bronzes of setters, done in the classic lost wax process. She is currently retired and lives and paints in Vancouver Island, British Columbia.

Red Barn

The Red Barn Kennels of William B. and Marion Neville in Blauvelt, New York, was one of the largest in the US. Established in the 1940s on foundation stock from Knightscroft and others, their influence was widely felt

21

Luz Holvenstot with a group of Westwind dogs in the 1940s.

Ch. Harmony Lane's Risin'O'The Moon winning Best of Opposite Sex at nine-and-a-half years of age. Owned by Jeanette Long.

over a period of 30 years. Ch. Knightscroft Primrose, a double cross to Ch. Milson O'Boy II, produced Ch. Red Barn Rosabelle UDT. In 1952, the Nevilles obtained Ch. Kendare Red Dawn, who became the sire of 13 champions, among them Ch. Boxley Holly Anne. She was the dam of five champions in 1953, including Am. Can. Ch. Red Star of Hollywood Hills CDX, Red Barn Red Stardust, Royal Charm, Royal Holly, Royal Talisman, and Redstar Talent Scout. Talisman and Red Star of Hollywood Hills CDX were used extensively by Red Barn and other kennels. Barry Neville died in 1979, and Red Barn reduced its breeding program dramatically over the next few years. In the late 1980s, Red Barn's breeding program was revived in partnership with Paula and Karolynne McAteer, prominent breeders today.

Merryborne

Jeanette Long of Merryborne Kennels in Columbia, South Carolina, began in 1967 with Ch. Harmony Lane's Risin'O'The Moon, a Ch. Conifer's Lance granddaughter. Over the years, she has produced several champions from four litters carrying the Merryborne name.

Ch. Tirvelda Sybil, one of the foundation bitches of Tirvelda Kennels.

Tirvelda

Many of the kennels reported in this history section have had common ancestors whose progeny continue today in the bloodlines of many current dogs. Among the most prominent of these are the dogs of Tirvelda. Because Ted Eldredge was a major breeder for 50 years and had such a strong influence on the breed and on the people within the Irish Setter fancy, it is appropriate to expand on his biography. As noted in the Kinvarra section, Ted acquired his first Irish Setter in 1934 from Lee Schoen. She was a bitch of such prepotent type that one of his bitches 40 years later resembled her almost exactly. She was shown by Harold Correll to her championship, undefeated in the classes.

A series of disasters almost wiped out the budding Tirvelda line until 1957, when Ted imported Ch. Hartsbourne Sallyann of Tirvelda from Eileen Walker in England. Sallyann was bred to Ch. Kinvarra Malone, who was the great-great grandson of Mollie of Gadeland. The Malone-Sallyann matings produced Ch. Tirvelda Sybil and Ch. Tirvelda Nutbrown Sherry. All the Tirvelda dogs trace to one of those two bitches, but it was Sherry that became a noted dam of record.

Ted bred more than 100 champions, including one of the top-producing dams in breed history, Ch. Tirvelda Nutbrown Sherry. One of Sherry's sons, Ch. Tirvelda Michaelson, is the second leading sire in the breed. Sherry was bred to Ch. Michael Bryan Duke of Sussex and produced a litter of 11 puppies, 10 of which finished their championships. One died of heartworm complications and the others went on to become significant in the history of the modern Irish Setter. They were Ch. T. Michael Bryan, Ch. T. Michele, Ch. T. Cathy O'Rinn, Ch. T. Nor'wester, Ch. T. Michaelson, Ch. T. Rick O'Shea, Ch. Earl of Harewood, Ch. T. Kensington Red, Ch. T. Barrabas, and Ch. T. Val O'Rinn.

The two sires that were most important were Ch. Tirvelda Michaelson and Nor'Wester. Nor'Wester was a 26-inch dog with a flat, heavy, dark coat. He had started off in a kennel in the Northwest but did not do well there, so Ted brought him back to the farm in Virginia. Once he matured, he went out on the show circuit with Michele Leathers Billings and in a short period of time won 21 Sporting Groups and 3 Bests in Show. He went to live the rest of his 14 years at the home of Ed and Helen Treutel in New Jersey, where he became an important sire for their Tirvelda bitches.

Michaelson was initially sold to a man about whom Ted had reservations, which turned out to be well founded. About a year later, he set out to look for the dog and found him after a long, circuitous search through puppy mills, backyards, intermediaries, and shady characters. The dog was emaciated and sick, but after spending three months in a veterinarian's care, "Mike" was finally returned to Tirvelda. Michele Billings finished him in two weeks, and he retired as the King of Tirvelda, sire of 50 champions, until his death at the age of 14 in 1976.

Earl of Harewood also started out with an inauspicious beginning, but ended up with Dave and Ruth Wilson of Wilson Farms kennels, where he was

Ch. Tirvelda Michaelson ROM, bred by Ted Eldredge of Tirvelda Kennels.

23

the personal hunting dog of Dave and the sire of 20 champions.

Ch. Tirvelda Michael Bryan produced one important bitch, Ch. Tirvelda Sabrina, when he was bred to his aunt, Ch. Tirvelda Sybil. Sabrina was bred to Ch. Legend of Varagon UDT to produce Ch. Tirvelda Tambourlane and Ch. Tirvelda Maidavale. Maidavale was one of the most beautiful of the Tirvelda bitches, and when bred to Ch. Tirvelda Rustic Duke, a younger full brother to Sherry and Sybil, she produced Ch. Tirvelda Queen Mab, Ch. Tirvelda Court Jester, and President Richard Nixon's dog, King Timahoe.

Mab was bred to Ch. Tirvelda Michaelson to produce Ch. Tirvelda Telstar and several other important offspring, including Tirvelda Samaria. She died in an accident before she could be shown, but she produced one litter for Meadowlark Kennels that proved to be some of the foundation stock for Rose Marie Ross.

Telstar was the sire of Am. Can. Ch. McCamon Marquis, twice a National Specialty winner and the top Irish Setter in 1977 and 1979. He retired from American competition with 157 Group Firsts, a record for the breed at that time. He became top Irish Setter in Canada in 1981, shown by his breeder Sue Korpan (now Susan McCamon) of British Columbia. During his career in the states, he was shown by George Alston and co-owned by Lillian Gough.

Tirvelda dogs served as the foundation stock for many kennels in the 1970s and '80s, and their descendants blended with other lines to form the Irish Setter that we see today.

Ted Eldredge was ISCA's delegate to the AKC from 1968 until 1985 and served as a director of the AKC for two terms from 1976 until 1984. He died on March 13, 1985.

Sportmirth

Ed and Helen Treutel of Sportmirth Irish Setters bought a five-month-old bitch from Tirvelda in 1965. Thus began an all-consuming hobby that led the Treutels into all facets of the Irish Setter fancy. The puppy became Am. Can. Ch. Tirvelda Best Regards CD (Ch. Charles River Streamliner ex Ch. Tirvelda Nutbrown Sherry). She was owner-handled to ISCA's Best Bitch Award in 1967 and 1968. Bred only twice to Ch. Tirvelda Nor'Wester, she produced four champions and several other pointed offspring. From the first litter, the most important was Ch. Tirvelda Valentine, who followed her dam's record as Best Bitch in 1970 and 1971. A brother, Ch. Tirvelda Sportin' Life CD, was the sire of ISCA's Best Bitch in 1973, Ch. Kimberlin Kyrie, owned by Claire Andrews.

Ed was president of the ISCA from 1976 to 1978 and served on its board of directors for 15 years. He was instrumental in establishing the versatility programs for the field. Both Helen and Ed were active in the EISA—he as president, she as secretary—and he was the guiding force behind EISA's first Independent Specialty in 1969.

Ch. Tirvelda Telstar ROM, an important Tirvelda sire.

Sportmirth Evergreen Brian CD VC taking Best of Winners at Twin Brooks Kennel Club in 1980. Owned by Ed and Helen Treutel.

Am. Can. Ch. Tirvelda Best Regards CD, winner of the 1967 and 1968 ISCA's Best Bitch award and dam of four champion offspring. Owned by Ed and Helen Treutel.

Ch. Tirvelda Valentine, daughter of Tirvelda Best Regards and winner of the ISCA's Best Bitch award in 1970 and 1971. Owned by Ed and Helen Treutel.

Ed was a world-renowned trumpet player and teacher at the Juilliard School of Music in New York for more than 50 years. Ed died on October 17, 1997, and Helen followed him in April 1998.

Varagon

On the West Coast, the Varagon Kennels of Ray and Valerie Gonsor were a major influence for 20 years, beginning in 1958 with their first litter, which produced Ch. Maveric of Varagon CDX. Their breeding program was founded on Innisfail with Ch. Innisfail Best Regards CDX. Her offspring included Am. Mex. Ch. Crimson Satan of Varagon CDX, Ch. Enchantment of Varagon, Ch. Legend of Varagon, and Ch. Flashback of Varagon. Enchantment was bred to Ch. Michael Bryan Duke of Sussex to produce Ch. Donamar Bold Echo of Varagon, many of whose get are found in pedigrees primarily in California and other Western states today. Special note should be taken of Ch. Legend of Varagon, who was acquired by Renee Taylor in California. Determined to have a show dog, Renee traveled the Western hemisphere with "Trofi," putting 13 titles on him during his successful showcareer. He became Am. Mex. Can. Ch. Legend of Varagon UDT PR PU, Can. CDX. He sired 12 American and 17 Canadian champions, including two Best in Show sons, Ch. Danalee Bright Legend and Can. Ch. Julerin Image of Trofi. Legend appears in the background of many Irish Setters today.

Both Ray and Valerie retired from breeding and showing to become judges. They both judged at ISCA National Specialties. They both have since passed on.

Glendee

Another kennel of recent history, which ceased operations with the death of one of the partners, was the Glendee Kennels of Thorne and Myra Harris. Glendee Kennels was born with the purchase of Tyronne Farm Midnight Flash in 1961, followed by Tyronne Farm Midday Flame. The Flash-Flame litter was born in 1962 and produced Glendee's first homebred champions, Sir Michael Galway of Glendee and Ch. Glendee's Duke of Wicklow. Flame was bred to Ch. Tyronne Farm Rex to produce Myra's most famous show dog, Ch. Glendee's Bourbon on the Rocks CD. A Tyronne Farm bitch, Ch. Tyronne Farm Gloribee produced 5 litters for Glendee with 12 champions from 4 sires. In 1976, Glendee acquired a daughter of Ch. Candia Indeed, Ch. Rossel Bridie Rose. She finished her championship easily and was bred to Am. Can. Ch. McCamon Marquis. That produced the "jewel" litter containing Ch. Glendee's Diamond in the 'Ruff, Ch. Glendee's Stone Cutter, Ch. Rossel Rosalee, and Ch. Charlton Oriental Jade. Stone Cutter was sold to a breeder in Brazil, where he was used at stud successfully. Oriental Jade never had a litter but was an outstanding show bitch for her owner, Susan Kilbey.

Fleetwood Farms

The Fleetwood Farms Kennels of Hugh and Virginia Rumbaugh started with Aragon and Tyronne Farms breeding in the 1950s. Their best-known dogs were the result of a mating of Ch. Fleetwood Farms Noreen to Ch. Thenderin Brian Tristan. Known as the "car" litter because the puppies were born in a car, the litter contained Chs. Fleetwood Farms Sixty Special, Coupe de Ville, and Sedan de Ville. Coupe de Ville went to the Merry Dell Kennels of Mary Lou Hobbs. Bred to Ch. Draherin Irish Chieftain, she produced the beautiful bitch Ch. Merry-Dell's Autumn Glory. A son of Sixty Special, Ch. Fleetwood Farm Brougham was bred to Ch. Shannon's Susie Starlet, owned by Joe and Lorraine Weick. That litter produced Ch. Starheir's Aaron Ardee, who during his long show career defeated more than 70,000 dogs. He was used extensively at stud and was extremely influential in subsequent generations of Fleetwood Farms dogs.

Hugh Rumbaugh died in the mid-1990s. Virginia died in 1998. Fleetwood Farms continues under the guidance of Patricia Jesson.

Verbu

Emily Schweitzer of Verbu Kennels acquired her first Irish Setter in 1923. The dog was Glencho Ruddy Oogh. In 1930, she purchased Verbu Red Mollie (Ch. Bergneil Red Helmet ex Palmerston Mollie Bawn) at the age of five and showed her to her championship.

Emily was among the pioneers in obedience in America. She put advanced titles on most of her show dogs, and many of them acquired field champion points as well during the 1950s and '60s. In 1972, Emily had her first field champion, trained by Jake and Sally Huizenga of Salinas, California. She was Ch. Duffin Miss Duffy CD VC. In 1978, some 55 years after the arrival of Glencho Ruddy Oogh, there was a new triple winner—Ch. Verbu Katie Oogh CD VC with 8 field trial awards.

Emily never allowed anyone to breed to her dogs, nor did she sell puppies, so that her valuable lines were never

Ch. Verbu Maureen, a wonderful example from Verbu Kennels. Owned by Emily Schweitzer.

From left to right, two pioneers of the breed, Ms. Virginia Hardin and Miss Emily Schweitzer.

accessible outside her kennel. She felt that breeders are too careless in selling their dogs and that many animals suffer as a result. Therefore, no Verbu dog was ever put in a position where a change of circumstance could endanger him.

Emily has been dedicated to the Irish Setter her whole life, and now, in retirement, she still maintains a keen interest in the progress of the breed. In 1988, she was the recipient of the E. I. Eldredge Memorial Award, the highest honor ISCA offers.

Draherin

Draherin, one of the truly great kennels of all time, was started by a young girl in her teens in 1948. A six-month-old son of Ch. Pinewood High Hat and End O'Maine Refrain, obtained from Hollis Wilson of End O'Maine, was the first Irishman to be owned by Lucy Jane Myers. With this acquisition, an illustrious chapter in Irish Setter history commenced.

Almost immediately, Lucy Jane bought a puppy from Jane Ridder, a friend of the Myers and niece of Laura Delano of Knocknagree kennels. The dam, Sue of Witchwood, was straight Knocknagree breeding. The puppy became the first dog to bear the Draherin kennel name, Draherin Mahcree O'Rhue, the first Draherin Canadian and American champion, the first Draherin Best in Show winner, the second CDX Draherin titleholder, and the 30th champion offspring of his famous sire, Ch. Kleiglight of Aragon.

For bitches, Lucy Jane went to the Thenderin Kennels

of Athos and Joyce Nilsen. Lucy Jane had seen Hollis Wilson handle Thenderin Brian Tristan in the Open Class at the 1948 Minneapolis show. That dog so captivated her that she was hooked on Irish forever. From Thenderin she obtained the 13-month-old bitch, Thenderin Elixir. "Lucy" was her name, and lucky she certainly was, because all the famous Draherin dogs descended from her.

After some false attempts to breed Lucky, she finally came into whelp after being bred to Brian Tristan. From this breeding came Ch. Draherin Centurian CD, a dog whose influence can be found in the pedigrees of some of the Irish in the Pacific Northwest. Another became Ch. Draherin Coronado. He was owned by Floyd Crosley of Shamrock Kennels in Nebraska, and his blood can be found in dogs from that area.

Two bitches from the Brian Tristan ex Elixir litter made lasting contributions to the breed. Draherin Coronation was the granddam of Am. Can. Ch. Draherin Billy Boy, the sire of Dr. Robert Helferty's Best in Show winner, Ch. Kelly Shannon O'Deke. The second bitch from the litter was Draherin Coronet, who became the foundation bitch of Glen Cree kennels. Coronet, through her daughter, Glen Cree High Time (when bred to Ch. Draherin County Leitrim) produced Am. Can. Ch. Draherin Bachelor Boy, owned by the late Cmdr. Thomas Threlkeld. Bachelor Boy broke all Canadian records by winning close to 70 Bests in Show. High Time was also the dam of Glen Cree Bridey Murphy and Glen Cree Merriment. The latter was an important dam for Rose Ross' Meadowlark Kennel.

Elixir's third litter was sired by Ch. Tyronne Farm Malone II. In it were two brothers destined to go down in Irish Setter history as two of the most influential sires. These were Ch. Draherin Irish Regardless and Ch. Draherin Irish Chieftain. They can be found in the pedigrees of almost every top winner and producer from the early 1960s to the present, further extending the contribution to the breed of type and temperament of their great granddam, Ch. Kinvarra Mollie of Gadeland, the English import selected by Lee M. Schoen to be the foundation for Tirvelda.

Still another litter out of Elixir by Patrick Red Jacket, a dog that Lucy Jane purchased for $75 and that had 14 points before his untimely death, produced the great Best in Show bitch, Ch. Draherin Echo of Elixir.

Irish Regardless was bred four times to Betty Crawford's Ch. Knockross Ruby, and together they produced 19 champions. These included a number of Best in Show winners, the most famous being Am. Can. Ch. Shannon's Erin and Ch. Major O'Shannon.

Lucy Jane elected to own Ch. Shannon's Erin because

he was a son of Autumn Artistry and because of his attitude and flair. He became a top show dog, shown first by Lucy and then by Dick Webb. He won the breed at Westminster in 1967 and 1968 and placed fourth in the Group both times. But it is as a sire of top-quality offspring that he lives on. Among the most notable are Ch. Draherin Questionnaire and Ch. Draherin King's Ransom. The latter can be found in many pedigrees throughout the country today.

Echo of Elixir, half-sister to Regardless and Chieftain, was bred to Innisfail Color Scheme. Only two puppies survived from that breeding, but the bitch became Ch. Draherin Annie Laurie, Lucy Jane's favorite. The male survivor was Ch. Draherin Autumn Artistry.

Annie Laurie was an exceptionally prepotent dam. From four litters came 13 champions, the most notable of which were Ch. Draherin Party Doll and Ch. Draherin Pandora. Also, by Ch. Draherin's King's Ransom, she produced Ch. Draherin Marietta, owned by Winy Arland.

Annie's brother, Artistry, was a strapping, overdone dog but beautifully balanced, with a glorious head and powerful body. He was a great sire of many champions, but the one destined to be the most influential was Ch. Draherin County Leitrim, whose dam was Ch. Yorkhill's County Kerry II.

Leitrim was the sire of Am. Can. Ch. Draherin Bachelor Boy. He produced six champions in one litter for Bryfield Kennels of Bob Field in Arizona and four more out of Warren Ellis' Ch. Webline Venus. For Mary Olich (Nie) he produced Ch. Glenavan Sensation and Ch. Glenavan Hallelulia.

Two others from this family deserve special mention: Ch. Draherin Echo's Guy and Ch. Draherin Echo's Hope, foundation animals for Sally Reese's Candia Kennels. The most famous of the Candia dogs, heavily linebred on Draherin, was Winy Arland's Ch. Candia Indeed, top sire in the history of the breed.

The nick between Draherin and Tirvelda in various forms has been repeated through the generations and has produced outstanding animals in both lines that can still be found today.

Although Lucy Jane is semiretired from breeding and showing, she remains a vital part of the breed, and her influence can be felt through both Canadian and American breeders today.

Charlton

Another breeder who is no longer active but who played an enormous part in the development of the breed as we know it today was Mrs. Thomas Arland (Winy). She and Lucy Jane Myers together defined the Irish Setter of the 1970s and '80s. Her first champion was purchased from Lucy Jane. He became Am. Can. Ch. Charlton's Tory of Tipperary. Other prominent dogs at Charlton were Ch. Draherin Ivy Leaguer, Ch. Shannon's Empress, Ch. Candia Fatima, and Ch. Draherin Marietta. One dog stood out above all others at this kennel. He was Ch. Candia Indeed ROM, who Winy acquired in a trade for an English Cocker Spaniel puppy. Although he died of bloat at the age of eight, he has remained the leading sire in the breed. "Indeed" combined the lines of Tirvelda and Draherin. His sire was Ch. Bayberry Kinkaide, a dog of Tirvelda lines ex Ch. Candia Fatima, a Draherin-bred bitch. Almost every line in the US contains some of the bloodlines tracing back to Ch. Candia Indeed.

Many of the kennels that began as long as 50 years ago are still active, and their stories continue in the chapter *Irish Setters Today.*

Irish Setters Today

Throughout the history of the great kennels that have led to the Irish Setters we see today, one is struck by the interweaving of bloodlines and the overlapping of generations. The lives of the great breeders span generations. Some are still active and others still influence the breed through the stock that they have produced. Although Kinvarra or Knightscroft do not appear in the immediate past of most of today's kennels, they remain nonetheless in the back of many important pedigrees.

Much has changed since the days of the great kennels of the past. For example, their brood bitches were just that. It was not uncommon to breed an outstanding bitch five, six, or seven times, well into her eighth or ninth year. Today, breeders do not use their breeding stock in that manner. A bitch may produce two, three, or four litters in her lifetime, and this tends to limit the influence she may have on the breed. However, our top-producing bitches can hold their own with any of those in the past. The measure is quality, not quantity. Today, there are few big kennels. The majority of Irish Setters are homebodies, in company with two or three bitches and perhaps one stud dog. Our gene pool has contracted over the past 25 years, as Irish Setters have gone from a ranking of Number 3 in popularity in the AKC stud book in 1974 to Number 60 in 1999.

This decrease in registrations is both good and bad for the breed. Those breeders who are active at the end of the century are truly dedicated to the breed. They try to choose their breeding stock carefully and are unwilling to take the chances that some of the great kennels of the past could afford to do. When a breeder maintained a dozen bitches and several stud dogs, if one mating did not turn out, there was always another combination to try. Today, with so many lines interwoven, it is difficult to find the occasional outcross, because the top sires of the past two decades have many common ancestors.

Among the Irish Setter fanciers of today, there are both familiar names and newcomers, some of whom will be around for the next quarter century. Some will breed an occasional litter, show one or two dogs, and be gone. Others will become the mainstay of our breed far into the 21st century.

This chapter is organized alphabetically by the name of the owners, and as many of the active breeders over the last quarter of the 20th century as possible are included.

Claudia Aaron-Sneed and Laura Terbeeck, *Aralyn*–Wilmington, NC

Claudia obtained her first Irish Setter in 1978, and her first three dogs were all from Knockross breeding. She co-owned several dogs with Cynde and Dennis Sporre (Blueprint), who trace back to Tirvelda, and in 1993 bought two bitches sired by Ch. Tirvelda Once Upon A Time. One was Ch. Quailfield Unforgettable (Ch. Tirvelda Once Upon A Time ex Ch. Quailfield Red Hot Business) and the other was Ch. Kenobi Chasin' The Magic (Ch. Tirvelda Once Upon A Time ex Ch. Kenobi Awsum Summer Breeze), who finished with three majors.

Both of these bitches were bred in 1997, and both litters have offspring pointed from the puppy class. Aralyn Castle Hook (Am. Can. Ch. Blueprint Cardinal Rules ex Ch. Quailfield Unforgettable) is owned by Mike and Joanne Wright, Raleigh, North Carolina. Aralyn Legend

(Ch. Quailfield Business BIV Pleasure ex Ch. Kenobi Chasin' The Magic) is co-owned by Claudia and Joan Staby. Claudia's daughter, Laura, has shown Irish since her junior days and owns Aralyn Carrick-On-Suir and Aralyn Autumn Damask.

Claire Andrews, *Kimberlin*–N. Scituate, RI

Claire acquired her first purebred dog, an Irish Setter bitch, in 1947. At that time, she showed actively in both conformation and obedience. The first two dogs obtained their UDT titles and perfect scores during their careers. They were Lady Velvet of Hillcrest UDT and Ch. Kimberlin Brian Boru UDT. In a limited breeding program, she has consistently produced winning stock.

Her foundation bitch, Ch. Shawnlea's Gayla, was purchased from Miss May H. Hanley. Her pedigree was predominantly Knightscroft and Charles River. This bitch

proved herself by winning the ISCA's coveted Golden Leash award in 1961. She was the dam of Am. Can. Bda. Ch. Kimberlin Encore, who in 1964 began his illustrious career by going Best of Breed and Third in the Group at Westminster. Encore also won the Golden Leash in 1964.

In 1971, Ch. Kimberlin Cara (Ch. Celou's Lex McCrory ex Ch. Shawnlea's Gayla) was listed as top-producing dam. Bred to Ch. Tirvelda Sportin' Life, Cara produced Am. Bda. Ch. Kimberlin Kyrie, who was the Number One Irish Setter bitch for 1973. During her career, Kyrie was entirely breeder-owner-handled and was the winner of 11 Sporting Groups. Cara, bred to Ch. Danalee Bright Legend, produced Ch. Kimberlin Keela, who also won the Golden Leash in 1974.

In 1981-82, a dog by Ch. Thenderin William Muldoon ex Am. Bda. Ch. Kimberlin Kyrie, Ch. Kimberlin O'Killea of Top'O, owned by Sam and Barbara Topliss, was a top

Ch. Shawnlea Gayla, the foundation bitch for Kimberlin Kennels and winner of the 1961 ISCA Golden Leash Award, with owner Claire Andrews.

Ch. Kimberlin Kyrie, Number One Irish Setter Bitch in 1973, shown here winning Best of Breed under judge Maxwell Riddle with owner Claire Andrews.

Ch. Kimberlin Of Thee I Sing taking Winners Bitch at the 1992 National Specialty under judge Robert Forsyth with owner Claire Andrews.

contender on the West Coast. He came east and won Best of Breed and Group Third at Westminster in 1982.

In 1988, Ch. Kimberlin Killian (Ch. Tioga Tegan to Kimberlin ex McCamon Kimberlin Belle) was Winners Dog at the National Specialty in Oakland, California. In 1992, his daughter out of Ballycroy Kimberlin Autumn, Kimberlin Of Thee I Sing, was Winners Bitch at the National Specialty in Oregon. "Spangle" finished her championship within a month and was awarded the Golden Leash for that year.

At the 25th anniversary National Specialty in Rhode Island in 1997, Ch. Kimberlin Out of the Blue (Kimberlin Keebler ex Ch. Kimberlin Kyla) captured Winners Dog and an Award of Merit. That same month, Claire celebrated her 50th year with Irish Setters and was awarded the coveted E. I. Eldredge Memorial Award.

Two of her dogs have earned VC titles, and three have earned their Junior Hunter titles, all breeder-owner-handled.

Claire continues to breed and show selectively, building on her firm foundation of success. She is also a licensed judge of Irish Setters and has officiated at the National Specialty.

Am. Can. Ch. Lyn Erin Rhythm 'N Blues with owner Linda Acquavella.

Linda Acquavella, *Lyn Erin*–Moriches, NY

Linda's first Irish Setter arrived in 1974, but it was not until she acquired Ch. Draherin Leading Man from Lucy Jane Myers in 1980 that she became interested in breeding and showing. Ch. Lyn Erin Trace O'Thunder was purchased from Dr. Robert Helferty and Ruth Cordes in 1976. Bred to Leading Man, she produced Am. Can. Ch. Lyn Erin Rhythm 'N Blues, Ch. Lyn Erin Diamonds Are Forever, and Ch. Kimberlin Katydid. Leading Man was bred to another bitch purchased from Lucy Jane, Draherin Niadh, to produce Ch. Lyn Erin Midnight Blue, Ch. Lyn Erin Chances Are, and Am. Can. Ch. Lyn Erin Memory. "Tracy" and Niadh are the foundation of all of Linda's line, and all subsequent generations descend from these two bitches.

Ch. Lyn Erin Rhythm 'N Blues, when bred to Devlin Scarlett O'Hara (purchased from Mary Diesem), produced Chs. Lyn Erin Almost Autumn, Arfin' Annie, and Abbey

Ch. Lyn Erin Almost Autumn. Owned by Linda Acquavella.

Road. In 1994, Valerie Gervais from British Columbia sent down Kulana Quillan (Ch. Lyn Erin Midnight Blue ex Ch. Kulana Mystique), who finished his title at 22 months with all majors. Quillan comes full circle, because Linda's original Draherin dogs are included in his pedigree. From Ch. Kulana Quillan and Ch. Lyn Erin Almost Autumn she has Lyn Erin Almost Heaven and Lyn Erin My Blue Heaven.

In 1998, Linda has started a new line with the acquisition of two bitches. Saxony Hearts Desire, bred by Jean Roche, and Bryn Myrddin Merriment, although one of her bitches is sired by Jean Ryan's Scottish import, Ch. Sametsuz Ard-Righ.

Linda is proud of the fact that each dog that carries the Lyn Erin prefix has always been owner-handled to all titles and wins.

Cecily Barker, *Arab Irish*–Olivette, MO

Cecily's involvement with Irish Setters began in 1967 with a puppy bred from Ch. Rascal O'Farrell and a bitch from both field and show-accomplished lines. She was Scarlett O'Brennan CD. Scarlett proved to be a challenge to train because she was too clever, but she managed to earn her CD and several show points. She was a wonderful mother and produced litters by Ch. Squire Sean of Essex, Am. Can. Ch. Candia Big Red, and Ch. Glendee's Bourbon on the Rocks. She is the dam of Ch. McKelvey's Shawn of Windsor (owned by the McKelveys), Ch. Arab Irish Sunshine Patriot (Carol Rentz), and Argentine Ch. Mr. Beau Jangles. Candia Big Red joined the Barker family in 1970 and lived out his days with them. All present Arab Irish dogs go back to Scarlett, Big Red, and Bourbon on the Rocks. In recent times, they have been heavily linebred on Ch. Courtwood Marxman.

In 1987, the McKelvey's Shawn was given to Cecily, and she was bred to a dog with a strong field trial background. She produced Shawn's Red Roman, trained for the field by Jack McKelvey and Hugo Kosmel. He ended up with a family in Montana, and at the age of 11, the owners gave him back to Joan McKelvey and Cecily to live out his days in a warmer climate. Cecily decided to take Roman for one last field expedition and entered him in a local field trial. Handled by 15-year-old Tommy Ruff, Roman won first place, a fitting finish for a great gun dog.

In 1986, Cecily bred Arab Irish Lakefield Erin to Ch. Honeyrock St. Louis Cardinal to produce Ch. Arab Irish Jayne Mansfield. Jaynie was bred twice to produce seven champions to date, making her an ROM. Her first litter was by Ch. Seregon Second Edition ROM. The second was by Ch. Sunnyhill Wings of the Wind. All the Arab Irish are entered in conformation, hunt tests, and field trials, because Cecily believes that all Irish should be useful gun dogs as well as beautiful pets.

Judy and Tom Baumgartner, *Northern Oaks*–New London, WI

Judy and Tom acquired their first Irish Setter from Sue Hahnen in 1991. She became Ch. Courtwood Laurel Oak in 1993. They also acquired Ch. Rockherin Crimson N'Clover, Ch. Pin Oak Traveler, and Kenobi Karri N' The Force. All are owner-handled by Judy.

Pete Bauer and Judy Corbett-Bauer, *Cherokee*–Alexandria, MN

The first Cherokee Irish Setter arrived in 1966, when Pete moved from his native New York to Minnesota armed with a degree in elementary education. After meeting Lucy Jane Myers, he purchased Draherin Gaelic Chieftain from her, followed by Draherin Serenade (Ch. Draherin King's Ransom ex Ch. Draherin Echo's Hope). Chieftain and Serenade produced three champions, one of which was Am. Can. Ch. Cherokee Serenades Refrain ("Teddy"). Fran Behne bred her Ch. Jadestar Crystal Clear to him in

Am. Can. Ch. Tapnar Cherokee Kinsman. Owned by Pete Bauer and Judy Corbett-Bauer, Cherokee Kennels.

1985. Pete took one of the puppies, which became Ch. Tapnar Cherokee Kinsman. At the St. Louis National Specialty in 1986, he was Winners' Dog. His son, Ch. Lucky Morn's Dan Eze Debonair UD CGC was Best of Winners in 1992 at the National Specialty in Portland, Oregon. Two of Kinsman's grandchildren, Ch. Avon Farm's Cat Ballou, co-owned with Jan Smith, and Ch. Carousels Look Out World, are current residents with the Bauers. They also co-own Ch. Farpoint Cherokee Dreamer with Susan Miller. Judy Bauer is a successful breeder of English Cocker Spaniels under the Jaybriar prefix. Pete is a judge of Irish Setters and English Cocker Spaniels.

Martin and Barbara Sue Bellin, *Bellin Farms*—Setauket, NY

The Bellins have owned, loved, and shown Irish Setters in conformation and obedience for 30 years. Their first Irish and matron was Beauty Belle of Echo Hill. She was bred to Ch. Seaforth's Echo of Dark Rex and later to Ch. Starheir's Aaron Ardee, owned by Fleetwood Farms. Currently, they own Fleetwood Farms Copyright and Ch. Thenderin Olympic Flame. The Bellins breed occasionally, their dream being to breed the very best Irish Setters and perhaps one day to find that "quixotic ideal Irish Setter in our litter."

Renette Berggren, *Cairncross*—Longmont, CO

Renette began her association with Irish Setters in spirit when she was 12 years old. That was 1963, and she was captivated, as so many others were at the time, with the movie *Big Red*. She obtained her first Irish Setter while working as kennel help at the age of 17 for the famous handlers, Larry and Alice Downey of Libertyville, Illinois. From them, she bought a young male, Thompson, and showed him to his championship. From then on, she was hooked.

In 1971, she purchased her second dog as a show prospect from Michael Johnson (Kilgary Irish Setters) of Colgate, Wisconsin. This was Ch. Kilgary Aman. He became the foundation stud dog for Cairncross, as well as the bedrock of O'Kerri, Rossan, and Tramore kennels. He was a wonderful, laid-back, big-moving, healthy dog. After his death, Renette purchased O'Kerrie's Autumn

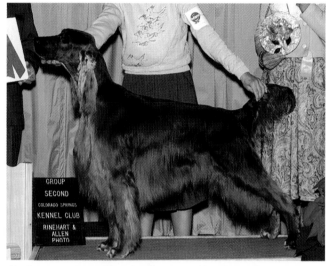

Ch. Cairncross Second Wind, ROM. Owned by Renette Berggren.

Ecstasy (a Kilgary Aman granddaughter) and Rossan's Xanadu (a Kilgary Aman daughter). These two bitches became the foundation for Cairncross, and the combination of their offspring has proven to be the most successful in her breeding program. Xanadu was the product of Aman bred to a Beaverbrook bitch. This combined the Draherin influence on the sire's side with Tirvelda on the dam's side. Ecstasy brought the Aman influence to both sides of the pedigree.

Ch. Rossan's Xanadu produced BIS and BISS Ch. Cairncross Second Wind ROM when bred to Ch. O'Kerrie's Armagh. Similar to his grandfather, Aman, in

Ch. Kilgary Aman, foundation dog for Cairncross Kennels as well as many other lines. Owned by Renette Berggren.

Ch. Rossan Xanadu, one of the foundation bitches for Cairncross Kennels. Owned by Renette Berggren.

Five generations of Cairncross Irish Setters.

type and temperament, he has proven to be an excellent show dog and a very good sire. Bred to Ch. O'Kerrie's Autumn Ecstasy, he produced three champions, Cairncross Deja Voodoo, Cairncross Skyline Fantasy, and Cairncross Scarlett O'Wind. Deja Voodoo was bred to Ch. Pompei's First Class to produce Ch. Cairncross Sierra Classic, Ch. Cairncross Silverado, Am. Can. Ch. Cairncross Forerunner, and Am. Can. Ch. Cairncross Kenworth.

Renette maintains a small kennel of six to eight dogs and breeds about one litter a year. She also handles professionally.

Sherrie Lyn Bercklin-Morgan, *Shambrio*— Caledonia, WI

Shambrio Kennels was established in 1974 by Sherrie Lynn and Craig Morgan with the purchase of a bitch, Bromsdales Breezin Bi. In 1988, they obtained Ch. Chandar's Symphony of Shambrio from Donna Long, who after a whirlwind career, finished her championship at 21 months with 4 majors. She was bred in 1991 to Ch.

Ch. Chandar Symphony of Shambrio. Owned by Sherrie Lyn Bercklin-Morgan.

Ch. Shambrio's Naughty But Nice shown with co-owner Amy Batzner.

Saxony's Evening Reflections. Of the eight puppies in the litter, five finished their championships. One of these was kept by Shambrio, Ch. Shambrio's Naughty But Nice, co-owned by Amy Batzner. Bred late, she produced six puppies by Ch. Wingfield Outback Tryst in 1998.

Sherrie Lyn has also bred and raised numerous English Cocker Spaniel champions and has owned and shown English Setters and German Shorthaired Pointers. She has added a Petit Basset Griffon Vendeen to the mix. She is a licensed AKC judge and also judges junior showmanship, in which her daughter, Amanda, is active.

Ruth and Kate Berman, *Wenvarra*–Potomac, MD

Ruth and Bill Berman bred their first bitch, a Ch. Kinvarra Redstone daughter out of a Wendover import, to Ch. Kinvarra Malone in 1966. That litter produced two group and specialty winners that became the foundation of the Wenvarra line. During the 1970s, they also acquired the beautiful Ch. Spiretop Sorceress, who attained her championship in a little over one month.

Kate Berman with Ch. Tirvelda Seanafield Jacinth.

The Bermans have maintained a small group of dogs, each shown to its championship, and have bred only one or two litters from each generation. Their litters by Ch. Tirvelda Distant Drummer and Ch. Santera Tamberluck CD produced particularly outstanding dogs, and of six puppies produced by Ch. Wenvarra Sea Witch bred to Ch. Meadowlark's Vindicator, two of the three that were shown became champions by the age of two.

The kennel became a family affair when daughter Kate began to show in conformation and junior showmanship at the age of ten. As a teenager, she acquired and finished Ch. Tirvelda Seanafield Jacinth, as well as several of their homebreds. In 1987, Kate was ranked first among sporting dog junior handlers and third among all junior handlers in the country.

Kate and Ruth are continuing the breeding and showing program started so many years ago. At the time of Bill's death in 1998, the Bermans were awaiting the arrival of a litter by Saxony's Emerald Heart out of Ch. Wenvarra Wind Dancer, the eighth generation of Wenvarra dams.

Barbara Bernhardt and Jane Towell, *Erinmhor*–Silver Spring, MD

Barbara grew up with English and Irish Setters because her father kept them in the 1930s, '40s, and '50s. Barbara accompanied him on hunting expeditions and acquired great respect for the Irish as a hunting companion. In the 1960s, Barbara moved to Washington, DC, and in 1973 acquired an Irish Setter, the start of several generations of Erinmhor dogs. Her first champion was a daughter of Am. Can. Ch. McCamon Marquis, who became Ch. Rainbow Maggy May. Maggy's son, Ch. Fieldstone Erinmhor Tribute ("Hooley") was a group winner and ranked Number Nine Irish Setter before his third birthday. Presently, seven Irish share their home with Barbara and Jane. Both are active members of the Potomac Irish Setter Club and the ISCA. Barbara served as president of the Potomac for five terms and has been a Board member of the ISCA for nine years. She chaired the 1997 ISCA National Specialty in Rhode Island. Barbara is retired from the Catholic University of America and plans to spend more time with her Irish in obedience and hunting tests.

Lorraine and Emily Bisso, *Pendragon*–Metairie, LA

Lorraine grew up in the company of the Irish Setter owned by her uncle, and in 1964, she obtained her first dog, Ch. Hil-Mor's Duke of Sheelin, a son of Ch. End O'Maine Pat Hand out of Tirvelda Maureen O'Beauhart. He was part of Hollis Wilson's last litter. Sheelin finished easily with a Best of Breed and Group Third over top specials. Sheelin was Lorraine's "juniors dog." After graduating college, Lorraine bought a bitch, Tara Hill Reflection (Ch.

Tirvelda Telstar ex Rockherin Rebecca) from Beurmann and Elizabeth Brewbaker. Reflection was a half-sister of Am. Can. Ch. McCamon Royal Burgundy, foundation of McCamon Kennels.

She was the dam of both bench and field champions. Bred to a McCamon dog, she produced Ch. Pendragon Witch of the Woods, owned by Emily Schweitzer. By Ch. Briarwood's Blazing Sunset, she produced the Best of Breed winners Ch. Pendragon Merry Monarch and Ch. Pendragon Merry Maker, also owned by Emily Schweitzer. Reflection was ISCA's Field Matron in 1986, because the bitches owned by Ms. Schweitzer were field champions as well as bench champions. Emily Bisso is now showing in juniors, following her mother's path, with Reflection's great-grand-daughter, Ch. Pendragon Independence. Emily has qualified twice for junior competition at Westminster and has piloted "Annie" to a Best of Breed and group placements. Lorraine is a licensed AKC judge and has served several terms as President of the Irish Setter Club of New Orleans. She is Vice President of the ISCA and has been National Show Chairman twice. She feels that "beyond balance and smooth fit both standing and in motion, an Irish Settter should have an innate elegance coupled with a love of fun, a long, lean, chiseled headpiece and a correct, flat coat. There is nothing more beautiful than an Irish in whose eyes the 'look of eagles' dances with glee."

Tom and Beth Bray, *White Oak*–Easley, SC

Tom and Beth have loved Irish Setters since their introduction to the breed in 1969. However, it was not until the 1980s, with the purchase of Charlar Mademoi-selle Montana, that they became involved with dog shows and breeding. She was bred to Ch. Airechta's First Remembrance, and three puppies were kept from the litter, one of which, Ch. White Oak Charlar's Destiny, is their first homebred champion. Montana was bred again in 1997 to Ch. Scarlly's Proudly We Hail and produced ten puppies that will be White Oak's future.

Cecilia Brewer, *Cymbeline*–Alamogordo, NM

The first show Irish to come to Cecilia was Fleetwood Farms Lady O' the Sun in 1981. Because Cymbeline means "Lady of the Sun" in Gaelic, that became Cecilia's kennel name. At about the same time, she met Jan Smith of Jadestar Kennels, who became her mentor and co-breeder of her litters. She acquired Jadestar Devon Blueprint from Jan. She was her first champion and foundation bitch, combining Tirvelda and Draherin lines. When bred to Ch. Jadestar Excaliber, she produced Cecilia's first homebred champions, the future of her kennel. She is interested in conformation and agility and plans to continue to breed occasionally.

Following in her mother's footsteps, Emily Bisso wins Best Junior Showman in 1997 with Ch. Pendragon Independence.

Helen Calvin with Bryfield's Rookie of the Year.

Helen Calvin, *Bryfield*—Cave Creek, AZ

Bryfield Kennels had its beginning in 1956, when Robert Field and his wife, Mary, purchased their first setter, Brydie. They became enchanted with the breed and selected two outstanding puppies that became the foundation for Bryfield stock, Ch. Candia Fawn and Ch. Candia Eve. Fawn's great showmanship and spirit, style, and soundness made her a favorite both in and out of the ring. She was an excellent producer, with six champions in one litter. Eve consistently stamped her get with dark, heavy coats, dark eyes, and strong, driving hindquarters. She, too, is the dam of numerous champions.

Robert was a professional handler and showed his Bryfield dogs as well as others throughout the Southwest and California. He retired from handling to become an AKC-licensed judge. Among his many assignments, he was invited to judge the Irish Setter Club National Specialty in 1991. His wife, Mary, died in May 1992, and he remarried in 1995. His wife, Susan, shares his love for the breed.

The second chapter in the Bryfield story belongs to Helen Calvin. In 1987, she went to the Fields to buy a puppy for her husband, Bill. After many years of mentoring by the Fields, she took over the breeding and handling of Bryfield dogs. Helen brought several new lines into the Bryfield strain: Meadowlark, Charlton, and Cairncross were added. Together, Helen, who lives in Cave Creek, Arizona, and Robert, who resides in Phoenix, plan to continue the kennel as it was since its inception five decades ago.

Patrice Clawson, *Ballymera*—Avon, NY

Patty Clawson chose the kennel name, Ballymera, because it is the place in Ireland where St. Patrick tended his master's sheep. She became interested in Irish Setters at the age of five when she saw them at shows where she went with her father to show Pointers.

Many years later, married and settled, she purchased two bitches from Rose Marie Ross of Meadowlark Kennels. They became Am. Can. Ch. Meadowlark's

Am. Can. Ch. Meadowlark's Whisperin' Breeze ROM, dam of more than 12 champions. Owned by Patrice Clawson.

Whisperin' Breeze ROM (Ch. Meadowlark's Masterful ex Meadowlark's Wyndchimes) and Am. Can. Ch. Meadowlark's Rainbow N'Roses (Am. Can. Ch. Meadowlark's Muir Woods ex Meadowlark's Magic Genie). The two bitches were quite different in personality and appearance. Breeze was full of mischief and never-ending energy. "Molly" was elegant and beautiful. Her sole desire in life was to be at Patty's side.

Breeze was bred four times, the first three to Am. Can. Ch. Quailfield Mak'n Business. In those 3 litters she produced more than 12 champions. Two of those were Best in Show dogs—Am. Can. Ch. Ballymera's Stormin' Norman and Ch. Jewelset's Made For You. Norman won Best of Breed at the 1996 Irish Setter Club National Specialty in Las Vegas under British judge Peter Edwards. At the same show, his younger full brother, Ch. Ballymera's Ridin' The Wind, was Best of Winners. Breeze's fourth litter was by Ch. Quailfield's Successful Business. These youngsters still have their careers ahead of them.

Molly was bred to Ch. Meadowlark's Vindicator to produce Ch. Ballymera's First N'Finest, Ch. Meadowlark's Bewitched and Ch. Ballymera's First Edition. Ballymera's First Encounter, sold to Julie Waters and Kim Velletri (Jewelset), produced several champions when bred to Breeze's son, Ch. Jewelset's Made In The Shade. Molly was also bred to Ch. Quailfield Mak'n Business to produce Ch. Sunshine's Heart of Ballymera and Ballymera's Heart of Gold. Several offspring from both these bitches have been bred and have produced typey, sound get. Breeze has produced beautiful movement and Molly has produced elegance and type.

Jeri Colella, *Hazelhill*—Fulton, NY

Jeri began her involvement with Irish Setters in 1967 at the age of 13 with the purchase of Jeri's Scarlet Redbird. Redbird was a wonderful field dog and helped to lay the groundwork for Jeri's love of the breed. It was not until 1981, with the purchase of Ramblin'Red Indianfire from

Am. Can. Ch. Ballymera's Stormin' Norman, Best of Breed winner at the 1996 Irish Setter National Specialty. Owned by Patrice Clawson.

Ch. Hazelhill Sweet Cakes winning Best in Sweepstakes in 1987. Owned by Jeri Colella.

Ch. Quailfield Successful Magic. Owned by Jeri Colella.

Anne Marie and Randy Kubacz, that she became committed to conformation and breeding. Indianfire never finished but was pointed—but more important, she was a devoted and loving companion and a true ambassador of the breed. She was bred twice and was the dam of three champions, the most notable of which is Ch. Hazelhill Sweet Cakes.

Sweet Cakes was a very balanced and sound bitch and distinguished herself during her career in the classes with multiple breed wins. She was bred only twice and from her first litter produced two dogs of note. The first is Ch. OTCh. Hazelhill Shining Star UDX MH, owned by Tom and Candace Macalusco of Long Beach, California, the only triple-titled Irish Setter in breed history. The second dog from that litter is Ch. Hazelhill Sugarshack. He is proving to be a sire of note. When bred to Ch. Quailfield Red Hot Business, he produced a litter of eight, of which four have finished. They are Am. Can. Ch. Quailfield Stylish Success, Ch. Quailfield Successful Magic, Ch. Quailfield Successful Business, and Am. Can. Ch. Quailfield Sure Fire Success.

Hazelhill typically maintains 10 or 12 Irish at any time. Jeri breeds a litter every two years, on average, and prides herself on breeding dogs that are balanced, sound and healthy. Her "Annie" (Indianfire) lived to be 15 years old, with never a sick day. She seems to have passed this healthy constitution to her daughter, grandchildren, and great grandchildren. Jeri x-rays all her dogs for hip dysplasia and breeds for correct, balanced angles, front and rear. Having started with field dogs, Jeri wants her Irish to capable of going into the field for a day's hunting. In order to do that, they must be balanced and sound.

Nancy and Dr. William Curtis Conner, Jr., *Tainaron*–Montague, MA

Tainaron was established in 1969 with the purchase of a Ch. Tirvelda Nor'wester daughter, who was a half-sister to Ch. Tirvelda Valentine, owned by the Treutels. She became Ch. Tainaron Saffron Replica CD. When bred to Ch. Tirvelda Earl of Harewood, she produced three champions: Tainaron Charisma, Tainaron Chances Are, and Tainaron Executive Privilege. Saffron was important to the Conners in another way because she provided them with an introduction to E. I. "Ted" Eldredge, who became a friend and mentor. On visits to Ted's farm, they met many of the Tirvelda champions and fell in love with Ch. Tirvelda Michaelson. All their breeding stock from Saffron on relates back to Tirvelda.

The Conners have endeavored to put international titles on their dogs, as well as American titles in conformation, hunting tests, and obedience. Am. Can. Ch. Meadowlark Drury Lane Am. Can. Bda. CD was their first adventure showing outside the United States. In 1975, their goal of acquiring a Ch. Tirvelda Michaelson daughter was realized when they purchased Am. Can. Ch. Meadowlark Nuance. Bred twice, in the first litter she produced Ch. Tainaron Mr. Minstrel. When bred to Ch. Meadowlark's Intrepid, she produced Am. Can. Bda. Bah. P.R. Dom. Rep. So. Am. Ch. Tainaron Masterstroke, who was shown and finished in six countries while winning sporting groups in five of them. "Mr. Brown" proved to be an important stud dog for Tainaron, producing many champions and hunt test winners from a variety of bitches. In addition to Masterstroke, Earl of Harewood, and Intrepid, the Conners have used the following stud dogs: Ch. Tirvelda Middle Brother, Ch. Shawnee Sundance, Ch. Rendition Erin of Sunny Hills, Ch. Seregon Second Edition, Ch. Avon Farms Wall Street, Ch. Herihunda Sailaway Americup, Ch. Tainaron Harbour Master, Ch. Cucuhullain Good Fortune ROM, and Ch. Tainaron Racing Silks CD. Several of these have been used twice on different bitches.

Among the bitches Masterstroke was bred to, in addition to the Conners' own, were Am. Can. Seregon Second Nature ROM, Windntide Love On the Rox CDX, Honeyrock St. Louis Angeline, Ch. Herihunda Sailaway Marina, Fld. Ch. Blue Time Lemonade, and Ch. Coppertop Prizzie Returns. All of these have produced champion get, and their offspring have also produced many champion, obedience, and hunting-titled dogs.

Curt and Nancy consider temperament and health to be paramount to their breeding program. In conformation, they emphasize and value fronts, shoulder angulation, strong bodies (especially backs and legs), pretty or handsome heads, feminine bitches, and masculine males. In personalities, they look for intelligence, sense of humor and mischievousness, willingness to please and learn, and "birdiness." Nancy's most cherished dogs over the years have been the ones "who never failed to make me smile every day." The Conners try to breed dogs that are capable of giving a lifetime of joy and love.

Debbie Contardi, *Triskelion*—Longmont, CO

Triskelion Irish Setters began in 1971 with a pet-quality Irish Setter bitch named Shamrock's Red Velvet CDX. As a novice with a rambunctious puppy, Debbie was able to find training help through Lt. Colonel J. T. and Marguerite LeSeur, who were the parents of Peggy Wampold from Massachusetts.

Debbie has owned Irish Setters and Brittanys over the last 25 years, and in 1994 she purchased her first show-quality Irish Setter, Estrella Miss Demeanor, from Jeanette Holmes. Since then she acquired Ramblin'Red Viva Maria (Ch. Ramblin'Red Kildavan ex Rebellion's September Morn) from Anne Marie and Randy Kubacz; Ch. Token's Wiffenpoof Song, the first champion for Triskelion (Ch. Liafail London Pride ex Ch. U-UD Token's Talk of the Town UD, co-owned and bred with Kay Bedeau of Token Kennels); and Soraj Sandpiper O'Triskelion (Ch. Cucuhullain Good Fortune ROM ex Ch. Estrella Sand 'N' Sable), bred by Jeanette Holmes and Carol Newman.

All of Debbie's dogs are well rounded and attend conformation, obedience, and agility classes.

Craig Cooper, *Chamberlayne*—Lynnwood, WA

Craig received his first Irish Setter as a gift from his parents in 1976. He usually keeps six to eight dogs, enabling him to maintain focus on the quality of each individual dog that is produced. He keeps a senior stud dog, a junior stud dog, two brood bitches and show animals that include those currently on the show circuits and puppies-in-training.

Craig's foundation bitch came from Lorelei Windhorn and Scott Thompson (Sallynoggin Kennels). She was Ch. Charlton's Thistledown, whose predominant bloodline traces back to Ch. Candia Indeed. She produced five important champions from two litters for Chamberlayne. The most noted were Am. Braz. Ch. Chamberlayne's Masquerade (top-producing sire in Brazil), and Ch. Chamberlayne Think of Me, the only dam in the history of the breed to produce three successive ISCA Golden Leash Award winners. Her breeding to Ch. Kinvale Evergreen Destiny produced Ch. Chamberlayne's Big Easy and Ch. Chamberlayne's Echo of Kinvale. When bred to Ch. Kinvale Send In the Clowns, she produced the top-winning bitch, Am. Can. Ch. Chamberlayne's Sassafrass, co-owned with Mike Sicora. These are the foundation of Craig's current breeding program.

Ch. Charlton's Thistledown, foundation bitch for Chamberlayne Kennels. Owned by Craig Cooper.

Am. Can. Ch. Chamberlayne's Big Easy. Owned by Craig Cooper.

Craig believes that the most important attribute of the Irish Setter is versatility. Without question, he says, the Irish is the most reliable, aristocratic, and versatile of all sporting breeds. His goal is to produce dogs "that will make a contribution of some nature: show, field, obedience, or simply as a personal companion."

Bob and Patty Cowie, *Kinloch*—Chesapeake, VA

Bob and Patty owned an Irish Setter at the time of their marriage in 1978 but obtained their first two show bitches from Penny Nunnally of Scarlly in 1979. These half-sisters, Ch. Scarlly's Fiddle DeeDee and Ch. Scarlly's Sailing Silhouette, along with Ch. Kintyre's Midnight Flyer, obtained from Tom and Barbara Johnstone in 1981, formed the foundation for Kinloch.

Various combinations of these dogs produced four champions, but wanting to keep the type they liked while adding new blood, the Cowies purchased a puppy from Mike and Kathy Landon. She was Trendsetter's Steppin' Out. "Julia Sugarbaker" finished in under two months at barely two years of age and was bred to Ch. Meadowlark's Vindicator. The Kinloch "Cross" litter produced five champions, with another on the way. After maternity leave, Julia returned to the ring as a special and won 8 groups, 4 specialty shows, and 2 ISCA National Specialty Awards of Merit. She finished her show career in 1994 as Number Seven Irish, owner-handled.

Another important addition was Ch. Kinloch's Ruby Tuesday. A Scarlly-Meadowlark cross, she was linebred to Ch. Tramore Simply Smashing and to Ch. Saxony's Evening Reflections. Two have finished from the first litter and one from the second—Ch. Kinloch's On The Edge, who finished with four specialty majors.

A new purchase with similar bloodlines, Kintyre's Diva of Kinloch (Ch. Quailfield Mak'n Business ex Ch. Scarlly's Love Potion No. Nine), co-owned with breeder Barbara Johnstone, had an outstanding puppy career. Also new at Kinloch was a litter by Ch. Ballymera's Stormin' Norman ex Ch. Kinloch's Maltese Cross, co-bred with Charmaine Timm.

Currently Patty continues to work with the Scarlly-Meadowlark combination to achieve the look she wants. Of particular importance are correct planes with good depth of muzzle on a long, lean head, a dark eye, elegance with substance, hard toplines, and good angulation and soundness, with notable reach and drive. They breed primarily to provide themselves with dogs to show because that is their first love. They have produced 11 litters and 17 champions in 19 years.

Ch. Trendsetter's Steppin' Out, dam of five champions and winner of eight Group Firsts, four specialty shows, and two ISCA National Specialty Awards of Merit. Owned by Bob and Patty Cowie.

Wendy, Matt, and Tracy Czarnecki, *Bright Star*—Petaluma, CA

Wendy's first Irish Setter arrived in 1972, the first dog she ever owned, from a litter bred from two undistinguished parents. She took the pup home at 6½ weeks, picking her because she was the most active. She became Field Ch. Lady Ribbon Bright Star CD, the foundation of Bright Star Setters. At about 11 months of age, Ribbon was introduced to her first bird, quite by accident, by a Gordon Setter trainer named Norm Sorby, owner of Springset Kennels. He was a hunter and thought perhaps Ribbon might have some potential. She proved to be a natural, and in 1973 was sent to Irish Setter breeder and trialer Bill Eichenberger for training. It was there that Wendy learned about Dual Champions and set herself the goal of breeding and owning one.

Ribbon was a very special dog—not much to look at, but in the field she had excellent run and range and a superb nose. Her manners were exceptional. She was extremely intelligent, eager to please, and easygoing at home. Ribbon was bred to a Varagon dog, Varagon Nitehawk Bright Star JH VC. From that litter came Sidney of Bright Star, who was bred to Ch. Rendition Buckingham Bear. She tore a cruciate ligament before she was able to achieve either show or field titles. However, she was bred to Ch. Candy K's Wizard of Oz in 1988. From that litter came Am. Can. Ch. Scarlet Victory Bright Star, Am. Can. CD JH VC ("Nike").

Dual Ch. AFC Cordon Bleu Bright Star JH, the 17th Dual Champion Irish Setter and first Irish to earn the title of Amateur Field Champion. Owned by Wendy, Matt, and Tracy Czarnecki of Bright Star Setters.

Nike was bred to Am. Can. Ch. Lyn Erin Midnight Blue in 1993. In that litter of 12 came DC/AFC Cordon Bleu Bright Star JH. "Tempe" was the 17th Dual Champion Irish Setter and the first to have earned the title of Amateur Field Champion as well. It took 25 years and 5 generations to finally realize Wendy's dream of producing a dual champion.

Tempe's litter brother, Am. Can. Ch. Rhythm N'Blues Bright Star JH, is another on the dual pathway. After finishing his show titles in 1997, he began running in senior field trial stakes.

Joy's second litter in 1989 was by Ch. Rusticwood's Olympic Medalist CD and produced FC AFC World Class Wynn Bright Star MH ("Aspen") and Olympic Victory Bright Star ("April"). Aspen whelped three litters sired by Ch. Blue Time Drummer Boy, Ch. Kulana Quillan, and Am. Can. Ch. Rhythm N'Blues Bright Star JH. One daughter is a Junior Hunter and is pointed in Canada. April's most notable offspring is Am. Can. Ch. Strike It Rich Bright Star JH (sired by Rhythm N'Blues).

Bright Star prides itself on the livability of their Irish Setters, as well as their intelligence, trainability, calmness, and good nature. They strive to produce beautiful and physically sound dogs, free of known genetic defects, structurally able to work a full day in the field. They have bred ten litters since 1977, with backgrounds tracing to Varagon, Rendition, Candy K, Draherin, and Rusticwood. Bright Star is a family endeavor. Matt, a retired US Air Force officer, works as a computer systems network

Am. Can. Ch. Scarlet Victory Bright Star Am. Can. CD JH VC. Owned by Wendy, Matt, and Tracy Czarnecki.

engineer and handles the dogs in the field. Daughter Tracy has handled more than 30 dogs to AKC and CKC championships. She participates in obedience and some field competition. Wendy is a writer for dog publications and, at the same time, she maintains her kennel of between 12 and 20 dogs, 5 to 8 of which are Irish Setters. She also owns Gordon Setters, which she shows and trials.

Ann R. Daniel, *Villa–Dan*–Batavia, OH

Ann and Ervil Daniel owned Irish Setters beginning in 1957. Their first champion was Ch. Daniel's Misty Morn CD. Bred to Am. Can. Ch. Major O'Shannon, she produced Ch. Tuxedo Comanche Majorette, owned by Dr. Robert Helferty.

Ch. Villa Dan Vallejo with owner Ervil Daniel.

The Daniels were among the first Irish Setter breeders to test-mate all their dogs and breed only dogs that cleared the test-matings for progressive retinal atrophy (PRA). They were instrumental in helping others test-breed by setting up a network to supply dogs and in establishing the Irish Setter Genetic Registry, which continues to register dogs that were test-mated and that have been cleared of PRA through DNA testing.

An important bitch for Villa-Dan was Am. Bda. Ch. Villa-Dan Stacey Shine Bright ROM. She was an outstanding producer as well as a successful show dog. Bred to Am. Can. Ch. Santera Tamberluck CD, she produced a litter of seven champions. Among her offspring were Best in Show Ch. Villa-Dan Vallejo and Ch. Villa-Dan Darth Vader.

Ervil passed away in 1998.

Ken and Debbie Davis, *Emerald Isl's*–Royal Oak, MI

Ken and Debbie received their first Irish as a gift in 1981 and subsequently decided to purchase a dog and a bitch that combined two lines they admired, McCamon and Rockherin. From Regalaire Kennels they acquired Regalaire Reigning Princess and Regalaire Classic Tribute. Both finished their championships with specialty wins. Classic Tribute also became a Junior Hunter. Their foundation bitch was Emerald Isl's Carrousel, who hated the show ring but produced quality puppies. They have also acquired Rockerin Center Stage from the Wheatleys. She finished her championship easily and is part of their limited breeding program. Most of their dogs are linebred, but they occasionally outcross a litter, striving to breed closely to the standard with health and temperament as very important goals for their puppies.

Jeff and Peggy Davis, Brentwood, CA

Both Jeff and Peggy are active in the Irish Setter Club of the Pacific, since their acquisition in 1992 of a puppy that became Ch. Willowhill Windchime. Jeff enjoys hunting, which he did with their first Irish Setter and with their current dog, Prentiship Split Decision. They hope to continue their activities in co-ownership with Cindy Stafford and Karen Holmes, both California breeders.

Ch. Willowhill Windchime, winning Best of Breed at the Irish Setter Club of the Pacific Specialty in 1998. Owned by Jeff and Peggy Davis.

Elaine and Michelle DeChambeau, *Beaubriar*–West Bridgewater, MA

The first Irish owned by the DeChambeau family was a bitch of Irish breeding sired by Ch. Celou's Rex McCrory, owned by Louis Iacobucci. Their first litter and the first to carry the Beaubriar name was Beaubriar's Windsong Lady CDX Can. CD, a combination of their original bitch,

Pinecrest's Carrageen Rhu CD, bred to a Thenderin dog, Innisfree Gallant Lad, in 1975. She was an outstanding obedience dog and the first Irish shown by daughter Michelle in junior showmanship. They next obtained Ch. Windscent Whisper CD VC from Sid Marx and Joyce Nilsen (Thenderin). Her sire was Ch. Thenderin William Muldoon. Whisper was handled exclusively by Michelle, who finished her in 1983 with a Group First.

The DeChambeaus added two males of significance to their breeding program, Am. Can. Ch. Ronita Rainmaker (Am. Can. Ch. Candia Indeed ex Ch. Redwhiskey's Maidavictory) in 1980 and Ch. Thenderin Attribute (Ch. Thenderin Goin' The Distance ex Ch. Ronita California Dreamin'). Both of these dogs were purchased because they combined the best qualities and bloodlines of the great dogs of the past that the DeChambeaus had come to admire and respect.

Ch. Thenderin Attribute. Owned by Elaine and Michelle DeChambeau.

Ch. Thenderin Attribute, when bred to Am. Can. Ch. Ronita Rainmaker in 1984, produced their first homebred champions, Ch. Beaubriar's Comin' Attraction and Ch. Beaubriar's Sneak Preview JH. A repeat breeding in 1986 produced Ch. Beaubriars Double Agent JH and Ch. Beaubriars Double Feature JH. Both of these youngsters went on to become the first Irish Setter bitches in New England to obtain their Junior Hunter titles. One of Elaine's most cherished memories is of

Ch. Beaubriar's Sneak Preview JH. Owned by Elaine and Michelle DeChambeau.

Attribute winning the Brood Bitch class at the age of eight at the 1989 National Specialty with those notable offspring.

Sneak Preview and Double Feature have proved to be successful brood bitches for Beaubriar. Sneak Preview was bred to Am. Can. Ch. Meadowlark's Wyndjammer to produce Ch. Beaubriars Moonstruck. Double Feature was bred to Am. Can. Ch. Devlin's North Star (a Wyndjammer son) in 1992 to produce Ch. Beaubriar Bewitched, owned by Pat Kenwell; Ch. Beaubriars Mystic Trance, owned by

Ch. Beaubriar's Magic Connection. Owned by Michelle DeChambeau.

Ch. Beaubriar's Casual Affair taking Best of Winners at the Harrisburg Kennel Club. Owned by Elaine and Michelle DeChambeau.

Saxony's Snow in August winning Best Puppy. Owned by Elaine and Michelle DeChambeau.

Jan Newport; Ch. Beaubriars Sorceress; and Ch. Beaubriars Fantasia, owned by the DeChambeaus. The next generation brought Ch. Beaubriars Magic Connection, bred to Mystic Trance to produce Ch. Beaubriars Casual Affair, a bitch that finished with four majors in 1999. Magic Connection produced several outstanding youngsters when bred to Ch. Beaubriars Sorceress.

Additions to Beaubriar in 1999 were two puppies from Jean Roche's Saxony Kennel, Saxony's Wild Irish Rose (Ch. Copperleigh's Tegan O'Balcaire ex Ch. Saxony's Creme de la Creme) and Saxony's Snow in August (a male by Ch. Meadowlark's Monarch ex Ch. Saxony's Southern Nights).

The family has belonged to the ISCA and the Irish Setter Club of New England since 1975 and they hope to "be as blessed in the future with good dogs and good fortune as we have in the past."

Ch. Kintyre's Debutante finished her championship at 15 months of age and was in the top ten of the breed her first year in competition. Owned by Norbert and Nena Dee.

Ch. Camelot's Stardust winning Best of Breed at the Maryland Kennel Club in 1987. Owned by Norbert and Nena Dee.

Norbert and Nena Dee, *Camelot*—Leesburg, VA

The Dees purchased their first Irish Setter in 1973, and their foundation bitch, a Ch.Major O'Shannon daughter, Shane's Irish Taradee CD in 1975. "Tara," whose bloodlines were a combination of Draherin and Knockross, was bred in 1978 to Ch. Meadowlark's Masterpiece, producing Chs. Camelot's Cloud Chaser and Camelot's Cover Girl. Further breeding with Scarlly bloodlines produced Chs. Camelot's Starstruck and Stardust.

Ch. Camelot's I Love Lucy (a Taradee daughter) was bred to Ch. Meadowlark's Vindicator to produce Ch. Camelot's Risky Business and Fatal Attraction. Ch. Camelot's Signature (a Taradee great-granddaughter), bred

to Risky Business, produced Ch. Camelot's City Slicker, their current top producer. Camelot then added the Quailfield bloodlines to their breeding program by obtaining a Ch. Quailfield Mak'n Business daughter, Ch. Kintyre's Debutante, from Johnstone's Kintyre Kennel. "Debra Ann" finished at 15 months, and in her first year as an owner-handled special by Nena was in the top ten in breed and group competition.

The Dees maintain, on average, 10 Irish, and they breed a litter about every 18 months. They consider the most important attribute in an Irish Setter to be temperament, and in show-quality dogs they look for correct movement first, then balance and showmanship.

They are members of the Potomac Irish Setter Club, which Norbert served as president. He is a member of the board of directors of the ISCA.

Linda and Martin Dick, *Sandcastle*—Westhampton, NY

After many years of owning Irish Setters as companions, the Dicks' lives changed in 1993 when Ch. McDerry's Lil Miss Understood ("Chloe") joined their household (Ch. Cucuhullain Good Fortune ROM ex Ch. McDerry's Becky Thatcher JH). Their "beginner's luck" stood them in good stead, because Chloe became a specialty and group winner and Best of Opposite Sex at the 1996 National Specialty in Las Vegas. In 1997, she was bred to Am. Can. Ch. Cucuhullain Eternal Knight, her great-uncle. Of the three girls and one boy in the litter, the boy, Sandcastle Knight Eternal, finished his championship at two years of

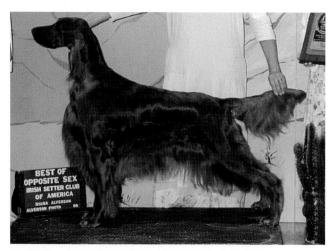

Ch. McDerry's Lil Miss Understood winning Best of Opposite Sex at the 1996 National Specialty in Las Vegas, Nevada. Owned by Linda and Martin Dick.

Am. Can. Ch. Devlin's Windsong of Tara Am. Can. CD. Owned by Mary and Lee Diesem of Devlin Kennels.

Ch. Sandcastle Knight Eternal. Owned by Linda and Martin Dick.

Am. Can. Ch. Devlin's Northstar winning Best of Breed at the Northwestern Connecticut Dog Club. Owned by Mary and Lee Diesem.

age, and one of the girls is also a champion. It is the Dicks' intention to continue the tradition of their ancestors by linebreeding future generations.

Mary and Lee Diesem, *Devlin*—Rexford, NY

Devlin Kennels was started with the purchase of Onesquethaw Tracie Devlin from the kennels of Orpha Clemons in Selkirk, NY. Devlin was named for the Irish revolutionary Bernadette Devlin. Tracie was by Ch. Tirvelda Michael Seamus ex Ch. Onesquethaw Kate O'Finn, whose background was Red Barn. She was the mother of Can. Ch. Devlin Autumn Blaze O'Hara UD and Can. Ch. Devlin Michael Sean O'Hara UD. Both mother and offspring were obedience trained, as all Devlin dogs have been since. Camelot's Sunny Sinclair CDX was another well-known obedience dog. In Canada, where the

Diesems were entered in both conformation and obedience, Sunny dived into the St. Lawrence River to retrieve his dumbbell, which he had accidentally flipped off the bank. He began swimming toward the American shore, and after many tense moments and shouts from the crowd on the Canadian side, he returned, shook himself off, and went into the building to the Open ring, where Mary meekly handed a very wet leash to the steward. Sunny proceeded to obtain his third CDX leg, proving his excellent heeling with the wet paw prints on the matting. After a quick blow dry, he went into the breed ring and won Winners Dog. When Sunny was killed by a car, cards and letters arrived from all over Canada and the US. His is the only dog portrait still to hang in Mary's bedroom.

Another important dog for Devlin was Am. Can. Bda. Ch. Devlin's Tamber Glow, Am. Can. UD. Bda. CDX (Ch. Santera Tamberluck ex Can. Ch. Devlin's Rebecca's Brandy). Tamber sired many puppies for Devlin.

Some other dogs of note at Devlin are Am. Can. Ch. Devlin's Windsong of Tara CD ROM and Am. Can. Ch. Devlin's Northstar, a top winner on both sides of the border. Mary is a judge of several sporting breeds in addition to all setters and is also an obedience judge. She and Lee also raise English and Gordon Setters. She wrote, "Our dogs are the stars of our lives, the laughs we needed, the reasons for our being, the purpose for our lives, and perhaps God's greatest blessings to us. To all our animals, thank you for your love, and for showing us, by your sensitivity and affection, how we, and other people, should care for and love each other."

Duane and Jackie Drummond, *Jamonds–* Carthage, IN

Jamonds was established around 1974 with the purchase of a young male from Charlene Legan, Ch. Charnel's Chuker D. Indeed. He and all of the important dogs from this kennel trace back to Ch. Candia Indeed ROM. Two bitches have made a big impact on their breeding

program. The first was Mandolin Star Struck (Ch. Charlton's Moon Lover ex Daragins Kimber Dee). Bred to Ch. Blueprint Kachina Doughboy, she produced Jamonds' first champion. Their other foundation bitch is Ch. Mandolin Tough Enough (Ch. Seregon's Second Edition ex Mandolin Spring Trilogy). Tough Enough, bred to Ch. Cucuhullain Dr. Seuss, produced Ch. Jamonds Bostonian. A once-in-a-lifetime dog, he is what the Drummonds want a dog to be. The other important male they have produced is Ch. Jamonds Call the Play (Ch. Rusticwoods Running Mate ex Ch. Jamonds Just Because).

Building on this foundation, they try to breed a litter about every two years that can function in all phases of the sport, obedience, agility, field, and show, and still be great family pets.

Ch. Jamonds Call the Play winning an Award of Merit at the 1998 Irish Setter Club of America National Specialty. Owned by Duane and Jackie Drummond.

Ed Dubrowsky, *Redbramble*–Melville, NY

The first Redbramble Irish were Clancy and Colleen, which the Dubrowskys bought in the early 1970s and which lived to be more than 16½ and 15½ years of age. They provided the family with many years of pleasure in the field and three litters. By 1988, the last of that combination was gone and they began anew, based on outcrossed bloodlines, because Ed feels that outcrossing is the key to good health. They imported some dogs from Ireland and also acquired Rumraisin On the Line CGC TDI CD JH from Debra Hamilton's Rumraisin kennels. In 1999, they bought a pup from Canadian stock, blending Crosshaven and Shangrila lines. In the last ten years, they have imported three bloodlines from Ireland

Ch. Jamonds Bostonian winning Best of Breed at the Western Irish Setter Club Specialty in 1995. Owned by Duane and Jackie Drummond.

Ch. Redbramble Barkis Is Willing. Owned by Ed Dubrowsky of Redbramble Kennels.

and England and combined these with some of the best American stock for what they hope will be a lasting contribution to the breed in field and conformation.

Judy Eaton and Maralee Eaton Martin, *Chantilly*–Rock Hill, SC

Judy's first Irish was a pet acquired from Tirvelda in 1977. At the time, Saint Bernards were their primary breed. After several years, they bought a Ch. Candia Indeed daughter, but luck was not with them, as the bitch and a whole litter of puppies were lost to parvo. Meanwhile, Chantilly became known for English Cocker Spaniels, which continued to be their main interest until Judy decided she could live no longer without an Irish Setter. Her most notable success in the breed has been with a dog bought from Jean Roche's Saxony Kennel, Ch. Saxony's Sympatico. He had a fine show career,

culminating in an Award of Merit at the 1996 National Specialty. At the same show, a bitch that she purchased from Gail Miller, Ch. Analainn's Cat Dancing, also won an Award of Merit. A Sympatico son, Ch. Saxony's Chevron Flight, is the current winner at Chantilly. Bred to Cat Dancing, she has the "Glory" litter, and in 1998, she purchased from Rose Ross's Meadowlark Kennel Ch. Meadowlark's Heaven Sent, who will also be bred to Chevron Flight. Judy continues to breed and show English Cockers in addition to the growing family of Irish Setters.

Laura Edwards, *Rosette*–Dublin, OH

Ch. Courtwood Silver Wings, a top ten Irish Setter for three years and sire of five champion get. Owned by Laura Edwards.

Laura's start in Irish began in 1971 when she purchased an Australian-bred bitch while she was living on the island of Guam. Although not a good show dog, "Bluesette" was accomplished in obedience and served as Laura's education in showing and breeding.

In 1984, back in the states, Laura became acquainted with Susan Hahnen of Court-wood Kennels and was able to purchase a puppy that became Ch. Courtwood Silver Wings ("Solomon"). He had a distinguished show

Ch. Analainn's Cat Dancing winning Best of Breed at the Lumberton Kennel Club in 1995. Owned by Judy Eaton.

Ch. Courtwood Book Cover, sire of four champion get. Owned by Laura Edwards.

career, handled by Laura to a rating in the top ten Irish Setters for three years. He produced five champions, all from Courtwood linebred bitches.

In 1985, Laura added Ch. Courtwood Book Cover (Ch. Courtwood Manuscript ex Courtwood Mystic Morn). "Emily" was bred only once, to Silver Wings, to produce four champions. Laura next acquired Courtwood Tail Wind (Ch. Courtwood Grand Hotel ex Ch. Courtwood Bag O'Tricks). He finished at 23 months with 3 majors, a Best in Sweepstakes and a Best Puppy in Specialty.

Most recently, Laura and Sue Hahnen co-bred a litter with the Drummonds (Jamond) sired by Ch. Courtwood Grand Hotel ex Ch. Jamond's Naturalizer. Of that litter, Laura has kept Courtwood All Smiles.

Laura, who used to travel extensively with the airlines, has turned her dog interests into useful products for dog owners. Her collapsible grooming tables are eagerly sought after, and she is designing a state-of-the-art grooming box for showgoers.

Dick and Shirley Farrington, *Shawnee—Riverside, CA*

The story of the Farringtons' journey in Irish Setters began in 1969, when Dick was out driving with a friend and came upon a sign by the side of the road advertising Irish Setter puppies for sale. Shirley was not thrilled when the little bundle of red fur came into the house, because she was just recovering from surgery. As "Patrick" methodically spent the first year destroying their beautiful backyard and lawn, Shirley threatened to sell him any number of times, but Patrick stayed. He became an obedience school dropout, but at a puppy match he won Best in Match and they were hooked.

In 1971, they purchased a show bitch from Pat Haigler (Rendition). She became Am. Can. Ch. Rendition's Indian Summer ROM. "Shauna" and Shirley learned together in the show ring. When Shauna was a little over two years of age, they entered two very large shows. She

Three beautiful champions from the Shawnee Kennels of Dick and Shirley Farrington (from left to right): Rendition Indian Summer ROM, Shawnee Indian Sonnet ROM, and Shawnee Sundown.

Ch. Shawnee Pipedream O'Charlton ROM, the only dog to win Best of Breed at two consecutive National Specialties in 1980 and 1981. He was also the Number One Irish Setter in 1981 and the sire of 40 champion get.

won both, for two five-point majors in less than 24 hours. That was probably the biggest thrill Shirley has ever had showing Irish Setters. Shauna was specialed very little, but she made her mark as a top-producing dam with 11 champion get.

Her first litter was sired by Ch. Candia Indeed ROM in 1974. That litter produced Am. Can. Ch. Shawnee Sundown and Am. Can. Ch. Shawnee Sundance. Both dogs had good careers—Sundown on the West Coast and Sundance in the East.

Shauna's repeat breeding to Ch. Candia Indeed produced the "Indian" litter of five champions, two of which were ROM dams: Ch. Shawnee Indian Sonnet ROM and Ch. Shawnee Indian Breeze CD ROM.

The third litter by Indeed produced the "Prairie" litter, including Chs. Prairie Scout, Prairie Sage, Prairie Wildfire CD, Prairie Challenge, and the most famous of the litter, Ch. Shawnee Pipedream O'Charlton ROM. Piper was a top-ranked Irish Setter in 1981 and was the only dog to win Best of Breed at two consecutive National Specialties in 1980 and 1981.

In 1980, Ch. Shawnee Indian Meadow was bred to Ch. Meadowlark's Anticipation ROM. From that breeding came Am. Can. Ch. Shawnee Night Lace ROM, ("Lacey") who surpassed her grandmother's record, producing 13 champions. Five of those came from the "Western" litter, sired by Ch. Brookfield Frontier Drifter, a son of Ch. Shawnee Indian Sonnet ROM.

Lacey was bred next to Draherin Pied Piper to produce Am. Can. Ch. Worcath's Northern Dancer, a multi-group winner in Canada. She was then bred to Ch. Ramblin' Red Kildavan, producing the "Midnight" litter, and her last litter was a repeat to Ch. Brookfield Frontier Drifter. Two puppies resulted from that litter, both champions.

In recent years, the Farringtons have bred on a very limited basis, but they continue to build on their foundation stock. They are currently showing Shawnee Sandia Serenade and Shawnee Teddi Bear, who represents five generations of Shawnee breeding and is a great-great-great-granddaughter of Indian Summer.

At the same time that Indian Summer was making her mark on the breed, Shirley purchased a bitch from Lucy Jane Myers of Draherin Kennels that became Am. Can. Ch. Draherin Illumination. Bred only once, she established a related line for Shawnee that carries on through Ch. Shawnee Winter Smoke CD CGC TDI, who is the sire of Ch. Shawnee Santa Fe Country, a current contender.

The Farringtons have produced more than 50 champions, many of them owner-handled. It has been a unique experience, they say, one not to be missed for anything. They fondly remember "the love of so many redheads and the lasting friendships that were formed. There have been many ups and downs, joy and heartache, but we would not have missed one moment."

Shirley and Dick have both been active in the Irish Setter Club of Southern California. Shirley is the immediate past president of the ISCA.

Elizabeth Fleming, *Sunstrand*–Frankfort, IN

Elizabeth grew up with Irish Setters, which her grandfather owned for hunting. Her first two were rescue dogs that she took through obedience training, becoming heavily involved with that aspect of the sport. Her first obedience competitor was Huguley's O'Brian Shannon Boy Am. UDT Can. CDX in 1975. She also got involved in tracking, judging obedience, and teaching training courses.

In 1981, she branched out into conformation, with a young dog of Redheather stock, Ch. Sunstrands

Ch. Sunstrands Padderson, bred and owned by Elizabeth Fleming.

Padderson. In 1988, she acquired Draherin Irish Lace, who was bred to Padderson. Offspring of these carry on the early foundation stock that included Beaverbrook Prelude (Bayberry Southerner ex Wilson Farm Dove of Kincora). Elizabeth continues to breed offspring of Beaverbrook and Draherin lines.

Elizabeth was among the early fanciers to test-breed litters in order to clear breeding stock against progressive renal atrophy (PRA) before the DNA blood test was available. All of her dogs are DNA tested and their hips are x-rayed and OFA-certified before being bred. She strives for beautiful heads and proper structure. She credits her Irish for seeing her through difficult personal tragedies, and she is grateful to those who helped her learn about the breed, especially Lucy Jane Myers. She is pleased that much of her original stock came from Draherin lines. Elizabeth belongs to several obedience clubs, the Western and Indianapolis Irish Setter clubs, the 4-H Club of Kokomo, and the ISCA.

Bruce and Mary Foote, *Vermilion*–Magnolia, TX

Bruce obtained his first pet Irish Setter in 1971, but it was not until 1991, with the purchase of Ch. Rusticwoods Song of Hawaii (Ch. Quailfield's Mak'n Business ex Ch. Rusticwood's Made In Heaven) from Carolyn Roche that the Footes became seriously involved with breeding and showing. He holds the record for the most specialty show wins for an Irish Setter in the history of the breed, with 31 wins. He also won Awards of Merit at four National Specialty shows (1995-98) and was ranked as Number Two Irish in 1997.

In 1992, they purchased another show dog, Ch. Meadowlark's Renaissance (Ch. Meadowlark's

Am. Can. Ch. Meadowlark's Eyecatcher, one of the foundation bitches of Mary and Bruce Foote's Vermilion Kennels.

Masterful ex Ch. Meadowlark's Made In the USA), and from 1991 to 1994 they purchased several bitches, all of Meadowlark breeding.

Among the most notable of these is Am. Can. Ch. Meadowlark's Eyecatcher (Ch. Meadowlark's Vindicator ex Meadowlark's Solitaire), who became a group and specialty winner. She was bred to Renaissance to produce Ch. Vermilion's Tuxedo Junction in 1995. In 1997, she was bred to Ch. Quailfield's Mak'n Business to produce two youngsters currently being shown by the Footes.

Their other Meadowlark bitches, Irish Lace and Impetuous, bred either to Song of Hawaii or one of the Quailfield dogs, have produced the next generation for Vermilion. The Footes strive to breed Irish Setters that love to show yet are a pleasure to live with, are healthy, have breed type, and are well balanced and beautiful to behold. They maintain 14 Irish at their home.

Roberta Foy, *Red Fire*–Moscow, ID

Roberta's love of Irish Setters began in 1962 when she and her husband, Vail, purchased a puppy as a hunting companion. She became Am. Can. Ch. Red Fire Deirdre CD (Ocavan Red Flash ex Draherin Quest for Treasure). All Irish Setters owned by the Foys descend from Deirdre. Roberta lost her husband in 1991 but continues her interest in the breed. Currently, she owns Ch. Red Fire Star O'the County Down CD CGC ("Gay"). Bred to Ch.Tainaron Racing Silks CD, she produced two pups. One was killed in an accident. The other, Red Fire Hialeah, is currently being shown and will be bred to carry on the Red Fire line. Both bitches provide a link to the past and hope for the future. Roberta says they are first and foremost beloved companions, sharing her life as have all their predecessors.

Ch. Rusticwoods Song of Hawaii holds the breed record of 31 specialty show wins. He also won Awards of Merit at four National Specialties and was ranked the Number Two Irish Setter in 1997. Owned by Mary and Bruce Foote.

Ch. Red Fire Star O'the County Down CD CGC. Owned by Roberta Foy of Red Fire Kennels.

Ch. Saxony Tiger Lily winning Best American Bred Bitch at the 1990 ISCA National Specialty. Owned by Aileen Frazier.

Aileen Frazier, *Witchwynd*–Spring Valley, CA

Aileen purchased her first Irish in the early 1970s. He epitomized all that was wrong with the breed at the height of its popularity, but she loved him anyway. Through his breeder, she was exposed to the world of dog shows, clubs, and obedience. Eventually, she teamed up with Pam Dahl to purchase a Ch. Candia Indeed daughter, Kyla. She was bred once to Rendition Country Charlie. Pam kept the bitches and Aileen kept two dogs from the litter, Ch. Witchwynd Tell England and Ch. Witchwynd Foreign Correspondent. Also in the litter were Ch. Timmara Spellbound, Ch. Timmara Arabesque, and major-pointed

Ch. Witchwynd Tell England. Owned by Aileen Frazier.

Timmara Notorious, who took up residence with Jan (Stevenson) Krohne, who became Aileen's closest friend. A litter sired by Ch. Witchwynd Foreign Correspondent ex Redheather Flicker O'Fire, co-bred with Alvina Pacione, produced Ch. Witchwynd's Heart's On Fire, Witchwynd Wildest Heart, and Redheather Rejoicing Heart, owned by Martha Murphy in Dallas. Ch. Witchwynd Tell England was bred only to two bitches and the mating to Witchwynd Wildest Heart was wildly inconsistent. The breeding to Ron and Vicki Larmour's Sierra Lyn Christmas Star gave them Ch. Sierra Lyn Expect the Best, who figured in the foundation of Sierra Lyn setters, and Sierra Lyn Best Friend, pointed but with utter disdain for the show ring. Her one litter produced the current Ch. Witchwynd March Madness, now in obedience.

Oversize has been a problem for Witchwynd, but the introduction of Ch. Saxony Tiger Lily (Ch. Scarlly's Red Hot ROM ex Ch. Saxony Midnite Forgetmenot) has enabled Aileen to provide some moderation in size and bone when she was bred to Ch. Rusticwoods Made To Party. She also owns Beckery Field of Dreams, bred by Holly Kruse, sired by Ch. Jemini Sundance Kid ex Ch. Rendition Beckery Brigid CD NA CGC, through which flows the blood of her original dogs. In combining the strengths of both families, her goal is to produce a typey, more moderate dog that is smart, sweet, a wonderful companion, and a good representative of the breed.

Carol and John Furman, *Carrageen*–Gray, ME

It was either fate or in the genes, for Carol's mom had an Irish Setter when she was growing up—a son of Terence of the Cloisters. When Carol chose a puppy after she was married, it was an easy choice. They acquired their first Irish in 1974 and their first show-quality dog in 1979—Ch. Robi Lee's Hartigan O'Deegan CDX. They purchased their foundation bitch, Trademarx Cinnamon Rose CD (Ch. Hallmark Jameson ex Ch. Redwhiskey's Kiss Me Kate), in 1981. Since then, they have been active in both conformation and obedience, with limited breeding. Their current hopeful is Carrageen One Last Dance (Ch. Jewelset's Made N The Shade ex Carrageen's Colleen Corigan).

Celeste and Jack Gavin, *Gabhantyr*–Morriston, FL

Gabhantyr means "land of the Gavins" in Gaelic, and what could be more appropriate for an Irish Setter kennel name? In 1967, Celeste bought her foundation bitch, Tirvelda Brengwain ("Gwen") and a dog who turned out to be a significant force, not only for Celeste but for the breed, Am. Can. Ch. Tirvelda Hunter's Moon ROM (Ch. Tirvelda Michaelson ex Ch. Rockherin Rebecca), co-owned with Ted Eldredge. "Treve" was the first dog Celeste ever put a point on, her first champion, and her first Best in Show and specialty winner. He was the sire of 20 champions, including a Winners Bitch at the 1978 and 1983 Nationals and Winners Dog and Best of Opposite Sex at the 1990 National. He was also the sire of two Best in Show dogs from one litter as well as a Westminster Group winner.

When Treve was bred to Gwen, two champions were produced. Gwen bred to Rockherin Merri Chris produced Am. Can. Ch. Tirvelda Sprig of Gabhantyr, who became a multiple Best in Show winner, won Best of Breed at the 1978 National Specialty, and won Best of Breed at the 1979 Combined Setter Specialty—the only bitch to win both shows.

Ch. Tirvelda Sprig O'Gabhantyr, a multiple Best in Show, Best of Breed, and specialty winner. Owned by Celeste and Jack Gavin.

Celeste's greatest contribution to the breed is not as a breeder but her ability to bring to the forefront top dogs that have made an impact on the breed.

After Treve, Celeste purchased Ch. Shawnee Pipedream O'Charlton ROM from Winy Arland (Ch. Candia Indeed ROM ex Ch. Rendition Indian Summer ROM). He became the Number One Irish in 1981 and the only dog to win two consecutive National Specialties, in 1980 and 1981. He was the sire of 40 champions, grandsire of Ch. Meadowlark's Vindicator ROM, and great-grandsire of Ch. Meadowlark's Wyndjammer ROM.

After Piper retired, Celeste obtained Ch. Meadowlark's Wyndjammer ("Rhett") from Rose Ross (Ch. Courtwood Marxman ex Meadowlark's Aviance). He became

Ch. Tirvelda Hunter's Moon ROM, one of Jack and Celeste Gavin's first champions and sire of 20 champion get.

Ch. Meadowlark's Wyndjammer ROM, Number One Irish Setter in 1987 and sire of 67 champion get, shown here on the day he retired.

Ch. Meadowlark's Vindicator ROM concluded his show career with six all-breed Bests in Show, 40 Group Firsts, and many specialty wins. He is also the sire of 81 champions, making him the number-two sire in the history of the breed.

Ch. Kennlee In A Heartbeat, a multiple Group and Best in Show winner. Owned by Cindy Geiser.

Number One Irish in 1987. He was the sire of 67 champions, including many Best of Breed winners.

Finally, in 1989, Celeste obtained Ch. Meadowlark's Vindicator ROM, also from Rose Ross (Ch. Meadowlark's Intrepid ex Meadowlark's Magical Mirage). Before coming to Celeste, Vindicator ("Jamie") was campaigned by Nick Theodose and handled by George Alston to Number One Irish in 1988, winner of the 1988 National Specialty show, and Group Third at Westminster. Under Celeste's guidance, he was Number One Irish Setter in 1989. Jamie concluded his career with 6 all-breed Bests in Show, 40 Group Firsts, and many specialty wins. He is the sire of 81 champions with more being shown, making him the Number Two sire in the history of the breed. He is the sire of seven all-breed Best in Show winners, both in the United States and Canada. He is the only dog to sire both Winners Dog and Winners Bitch at the National Specialty (1993), out of a Wyndjammer daughter. He is the double grandsire of the top-winning Irish Setter in the history of the breed, Ch. Pompei's The American Way, a bitch bred, owned, and handled by Annette Isydorek Pusey.

Both Vindicator and Wyndjammer are behind almost all of the top dogs in the country in the last decade, which also puts ex Ch. Shawnee Pipedream O'Charlton, ROM behind them.

Their most recent addition is Saxony's Pocantino Hills.

Cindy and Dr. John Geiser, *Insight*–Lacon, IL

Cindy has owned Irish Setters since the age of ten, when she persuaded her parents to buy one. Over the next 15 years, the family was never without an Irish pet. In 1988, Cindy met Penny Nunnally and purchased Scarlly's Tonites

the Knight from her. He finished his championship easily before the age of two. In 1996, the Geisers entered into partnership with Shirlee Murray (Kennlee) and Patti Hunsicker to co-own a bitch that became a specialty and group winner, Ch. Kennlee In A Heartbeat. In 1997, she was bred to Ch. Kennlee Treasure Bay to produce the first dog to carry their kennel name, Insight's Made U Look, a dog with a promising show career.

Jim and Nancy Godbey, *Pin Oak*–Westmoreland, NH

The first Irish purchased by the Godbeys was Ch. Shangrila Wyndchime (Ch. Meadowlark's Wyndjammer ex Shangrila Silhouette), whom they obtained from Lynne Mehring in 1988. Bred to Ch. Rossan's Raz-Ma-Taz (Ch. Cloverleaf's Ascendant ex Ch. Rossan's Afternoon Delight) in 1990, she produced the top-winning, Best in Show, specialty, and group winning Ch. Pin Oak Vicksburg JH. The second litter for Wyndchime was to Ch. Orchard Farm Kelsey (Ch. Meadowlark's Vindicator ROM ex Ch. Orchard Farm Close Encounter) owned by Mary Klinck. From this litter came Ch. Pin Oak Robert E. Lee JH, a Best in Show, specialty, and group winning dog. In both these successful endeavors they were guided by Dennis and Mary Laturie, knowledgeable Irish Setter handlers in the Midwest.

The Godbeys keep a small number of dogs at their place in the country. They have bred only four litters and, on

Four beautiful Irish from the Pin Oak Kennels of Nancy and Jim Godbey (from left to right): Am. Can. Ch. Pin Oak Vicksburg JH, Ch. Shangrila Wyndchime ROM, Ch. Pin Oak Heart A Fire, and Ch. Pin Oak Robert E. Lee JH.

average, breed no more than every two years. Presently, six Irish reside at Pin Oak. In addition to Wyndchime, Robert E. Lee, and Vicksburg are Ch. Pin Oak Heart A Fire, a Lee son out of a Meadowlark bitch, and two youngsters sired by Ch. Castlebar Country Statesman out of Vicksburg.

The attributes that the Godbeys consider to be most important in their breeding program are temperament, balance, and the ability of their Irish to perform as sporting dogs.

Tina Gradowski, *Glenaubry*–Hoffman Estates, IL

Tina's start in Irish Setters began when she was a teen, but her entry into the world of shows and obedience began with the purchase of Am. Can. Ch. Cloverleaf's Windsong. Bred to Am. Can. Mex. Int. Ch. Lucky Morn Avant Garde CD, she produced her first homebred champions: Glenaubry Captain Kirk and Glenaubry Enterprise. Next, she tried obedience with Ch. Lucky Morn Dragon Heart CDX CGC, co-owned with Jan Ziech. Currently, two additional hopefuls reside with Tina: Deep-Vu Celtic Dragon and Rockherin Dragon Star.

Leta and Wendell Graham, *Kaerdon*–Port Orchard, WA

The first Irish to come to the Graham household arrived in 1972, but it was not until 1981 when they purchased a puppy from Meadowlark Kennels that they became involved with the sport. Ch. Meadowlark's Mai'Tai (Ch. Shawnee Pipedream O'Charlton ROM ex Meadowlark's Moonlight Magic) became Kaerdon's foundation bitch, along with another acquired later, Ch. Meadowlark Love Boat. All their dogs are DNA tested or genetically clear of PRA.

Ch. Kaerdon's Broker's Tip, sire of 10 champion get. Owned by Leta and Wendell Graham.

One of Kaerdon Kennels' foundation bitches, Ch. Meadowlark Love Boat. Owned by Leta and Wendell Graham.

Ch. Courtwood Town Hall NA CGC taking Best of Winners at the Combined Specialty Club Show of Greater Milwaukee. Owned by Debbie and Dan Griese.

In 1986, they bred Tai to Am. Can. Ch. Camelar the Curragh CD, which produced the "stock" litter: Chs. Kaerdon Broker's Tip, Stock Broker, Ticker Tape, and Shareholder. Am. Can. Ch. Kaerdon's Broker's Tip bred to Love Boat produced three American and Canadian champions. Broker's Tip has produced 10 champions to date. His Love Boat son, Ch. Kaerdon MadHatter, has produced nine champions and two Junior Hunters. Love Boat was bred to Ch. Paterjay Meadowlark's Arglin, owned by Anna Jones, to produce Ch. Paterjay Kaerdon's Sent W'Love.

Leta continues to breed and show from her foundation stock. In 1997, she was approved to judge Irish and English Setters and Junior Showmanship. She and Wendell have been members of the ISCA since 1977 and members of the Irish Setter Club of Seattle. Wendell has been president of the Seattle club numerous times.

Dan and Debbie Griese, Savage, MN

Debbie and Dan acquired their first Irish Setter in 1974 and several years later began their interest in showing, obedience, and agility. Ch. Courtwood Barrier Reef CGC (Ch. Ballingarry Phantom Jet CD ex Ch. Courtwood Silver Slippers) was Debbie's greatest teacher in both conformation and her latest endeavor, obedience. They also own Ch. Courtwood Town Hall NA CGC (Ch. Courtwood Grand Hotel ex Ch. Courtwood Bag O'Tricks

CD). Debbie says he is probably the most "fun dog" she will ever own. Always happy and rarin' to go, he excels at agility and placed first in Novice A at the 1998 National Specialty.

Susan Griffiths, *Kerry–Eire*–Derby, NY

Susan's involvement with Irish began in 1970, and in 1976, she bred her first litter from her foundation bitch, Ch. Danalee Cover Girl (Ch. Danalee Bright Legend ex Danalee Keynote of Shanderin), who was tightly linebred on Varagon. Cover Girl was bred to Ch. Candia Indeed ROM to

Ch. Danalee Cover Girl, an influential foundation bitch for Susan Griffiths' Kerry-Eire Kennels.

Ch. Kerry-Eire Revolutionary ROM, Number One Irish Setter and Number Two Sporting Dog in 1980. Owned by Susan Griffiths.

produce two individuals that have had a great influence on the breed. The first, Ch. Kerry-Eire Little Rebel ROM CD VC was a top-winning bitch and a natural achiever in obedience and field. Her offspring by Ch. Courtwood Summer Forecast ROM produced Ch. Kerry-Eire Heaven Only Knows CD and Ch. Kerry-Eire Stairway T'Heaven CD. The former is the foundation stud of Kathy Whiteis' Sunshine Kennels and the latter is the foundation bitch for Carolyn Roche's Rusticwoods Kennels.

The second important dog from the Cover Girl ex Indeed breeding was Ch. Kerry-Eire Revolutionary, the

Number One Irish and Number Two Sporting Dog for 1980. Bred only a few times, his mating to Ch. Liafail Sea Urchin, owned by Frances Robinson of Bermuda and Paula McAteer, continues to have a significant impact on the breed. The "Bermudian" litter contained Ch. Kerry-Eire Coral Charm ROM VC and Ch. Red Barn Revolutionary Star ROM, owned by Karolynne McAteer.

Coral Charm was bred first to Ch. Kerry-Eire Heaven Only Knows CD, producing four champions and a bitch retained by Susan, Kerry-Eire Sealed With A Kiss. She has used her to continue the Varagon-Innisfail-Indeed bloodlines. Coral Charm's next litter to Ch. Meadowlark's Vindicator produced six champions. The most famous of these is Ch. Quailfield's Mak'n Business, owned by Patricia Nagel, a top winner in the United States and Canada and a significant sire. Charm's last breeding was to Ch. Liafail London Pride, producing three champions, including Ch. Kerry-Eire Tap Dancin' and Ch. Kerry-Eire Cakewalk. The latter was bred to Ch. Rockherin Shangrila At Last, who is a Mak'n Business son.

Susan believes that the most critical measure of the Irish Setter is not the standing picture, but should be found in an exquisite, flowing gait that is consistent within itself front to rear and effortlessly sustained over territory and time. She feels that a good breeder has incredible patience, has spent years loving and studying Irish Setters, is a responsible risk-taker, and never breeds for the instant winner. The Irish Setter, she says, "should be a joyous and functional companion, beautiful to look at, never tiring the eye. Thus, it must be healthy, intelligent, and versatile in all arenas of work and play."

Mark and Janet Grimsley, *Rediron*–Stafford, VA

In 1992, the Grimsleys purchased a finished bitch from Rose Ross (Meadowlark). She was Ch. Meadowlark's Royal Cabernet CD. They also acquired from Rose a

Ch. Kerry-Eire Coral Charm ROM VC, an influential dam for Kerry-Eire Kennels. Owned by Susan Griffiths.

Ch. Meadowlark's Beam-Me-Up, the first Rediron Kennels champion. Owned by Janet and Mark Grimsley.

littermate dog, Meadowlark's Beam-Me-Up, who became their first champion. In 1995, Royal Cabernet was bred to Ch. Meadowlark's Irish Monarch. Co-breeders were Rose Ross and Ivy Frank, Irish Monarch's owner. Three puppies were retained by the Grimsley, with the two bitches in the litter starting their show careers with the Rediron prefix.

Claudia and Ron Grzych, *Grainuaile*–Fenton, MI

A foundation bitch from Milesian Kennels in Michigan in the late 1970s started Claudia and Ron in obedience and conformation. Their purchase of a puppy that became Am. Can. Ch. U-CDX Shangrila Country Squire Am. Can. CDX TT began their career in both facets of the sport. Bred to Can. Ch. Milesian Heart A'Fire, the litter contained Canadian and Bermudian champions and obedience-titled dogs. When bred to Ch. Rusticwoods Olympic Medalist ROM, several American and Canadian champions and obedience-titled dogs resulted.

Craig and Pat Hackenberg, *Castlebar*– Park Ridge, NJ

The Hackenbergs began in 1972 in the obedience ring, and their first show dog was obtained from Ted Eldredge of Tirvelda Farms. Ted was their mentor and best friend, and he guided them throughout his life. They also credit George and Mary Ann Alston, professional handlers, with teaching them how to present and groom their dogs. Their first dog from Ted was an 18-month-old that became Ch. Tirvelda Final Ruling. They then took Ch. Tirvelda Skylark and bred her to Ch. McCamon Marquis to produce the first Castlebar champion, Ch. Tirvelda VIP of Castlebar, owned by Jane Wille. They then leased Ch. Sardonyx Canadiana and co-bred her to Ch. McCamon

Marquis. From that litter came the Hackenbergs' foundation bitch, an outstanding show dog and dam, Am. Can. Ch. Sardonyx Castlebar Witsend ("Petals"). When bred to Ch. Meadowlark's Vindicator, Petals produced six champions, including Ch. Castlebar Command Presence. Command Presence ("Opie") was Number Two Irish Setter for 2 consecutive years, winning more than 100 Bests of Breed, specialties, and groups. He was the First Award of Merit at the National Specialty in 1994. Opie has produced 11 champions to date, plus 2 tracking dogs, 7 Junior Hunters, 3 dogs with CD obedience titles, and 1 dog with a CDX. Two are working toward their agility titles.

Ch. Castlebar Command Presence was the Number Two Irish Setter for two consecutive years, winning more than 100 Bests of Breed, Group, and Specialty titles. Owned by Pat and Craig Hackenberg.

Opie's sister, Ch. Castlebar Garden Party ("Tulip"), co-owned with Dale Hood, is a top-winning bitch. When linebred on Vindicator, she produced two champions of note, one of which is a Junior Hunter.

Opie, bred to Ch. Castlebar Forever Yours (Ch. Meadowlark's Top Gun ex Am. Can. Ch. Sardonyx Castlebar Witsend), produced Ch. Castlebar Country Statesman, still a young dog that finished easily and is proving to be a good stud dog for Castlebar.

Ch. Sardonyx Castlebar Witsend, foundation bitch for Pat and Craig Hackenberg's Castlebar Kennels.

Ch. Castlebar Country Statesman taking Winners Dog at the 1997 Harrisburg Kennel Club Show. Owned by Pat and Craig Hackenberg.

Susan Hahnen, *Courtwood*–St. Paul, MN

There is no question that one of the most important kennels to emerge during the past 25 years is that of Sue Hahnen of Courtwood Kennels. She started in 1967 with a bitch that did not quite measure up and so never finished, but in the early '70s, she bought an 18-month-old bitch that became Sue's foundation and an influential force in the breed. She became Am. Can. Ch. Shannon Kelly O'Green ROM (Sir Patrick of Alpine Meadows ex Citadel

An influential force in the breed and the foundation bitch for Susan Hahnen's Courtwood Irish Setters, Am. Can. Ch. Shannon Kelly O'Green ROM produced 14 champions.

Daybreak O'Tipperary). She had a successful show career, but her main contribution was in the whelping box. Bred four times to Ch. Candia Indeed ROM, she produced 14 champions. The litters were named for the seasons: Spring, Summer, Fall, and Winter. The Spring litter was the best known, with 8 out of 10 finishing. Two prominent males were Ch. Courtwood Spring Son and Ch. Courtwood Spring Venture. From the Summer litter

Sire of 69 champions, Am. Can. Ch. Courtwood Summer Forecast ROM won 15 Bests in Show, 26 specialties, and multiple group titles throughout his career. Owned by Susan Hahnen.

came Am. Can. Ch. Courtwood Summer Forecast ROM ("Simon"). He finished his championship at 12 1/2 months, owner-handled, and went on to win 15 Bests in Show, 26 specialties, and multiple groups. After retiring from active competition, he won 7 specialty shows from the Veteran class in one year. Simon is the sire of 69 champions.

A Simon son, Ch. Charlton's Moon Lover ROM ("Schindler"), was an influential sire in Sue's breeding program. His dam was a Varagon Afterglow daughter. Six champions came from the breeding of Ch. Courtwood Spring Flare to Moon Lover. This was the "Bright" litter. It contained Am. Can. Ch. Courtwood Bright Idea, who was Best of Opposite Sex at the 1984 National Specialty. Ch. Courtwood Summer Magic was also bred to Moon Lover to produce the influential sires Ch. Courtwood Marxman and Ch. Courtwood Manuscript ROM.

Courtwood Mystic Morn (sire and dam were Indeed offspring) was bred to Ch. Courtwood Manuscript ROM, and produced a litter of five champions, the "book" litter. Ch. Courtwood Book Cover, owned by Laura Edwards, produced four champions from one litter by Ch. Courtwood Silver Wings, also owned by Edwards. Courtwood Winter Love was bred to Moon Lover, producing the "dark" litter. Dark Stockings was the dam of Ch. Courtwood Milestone (Aschenbrenner) and Ch. Cherry Bounce Courtwood.

Another important dam for Susan came from the "bright" litter. She was Ch. Courtwood Bright Ruby ROM. When bred to Ch. Charlton's London Fog (a double Indeed grandson), she produced the "silver" litter, of which six finished. Ch. Courtwood Silver Chalice (David and Jani O'Flynn) was Best of Breed at the National Specialty in 1990. His brother, Silver Wings, was owner-handled and a multi-group and specialty winner in 1988. Ruby's second litter, the "golden" litter, produced three champions. Ch. Courtwood Golden Gate is the sire of 19 champions. One of his daughters, Courtwood Endearment Am. Can. CDX, produced Ch. Courtwood Easy Living AX, the first agility-titled Irish Setter, owned by Linda Schindler. Ch. Courtwood Silver Slippers produced two litters, the "bay" litter and the "ba" litter, which in turn produced eight champions. Ch. Courtwood Bandanna ROM came from the second litter.

Carol Rentz and Sue co-bred Courtwood Amazing Grace (tightly linebred on Indeed and Kelly) to Ch. Pompei's Touch of Class. From this breeding came Ch. Courtwood Grand Hotel ("Donald"), sire to date of 17 champions. His first litter from Bandanna resulted in seven champions, among them Henrietta, Heart & Soul, Heavy

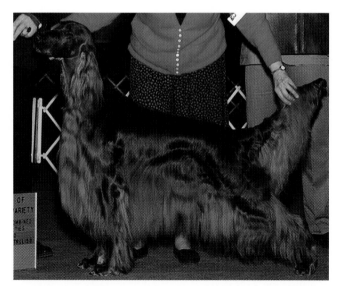

Ch. Courtwood Golden Gate, sire of 19 champion get. Owned by Susan Hahnen.

Ch. Courtwood Grand Hotel, sire of 17 champion get. Owned by Susan Hahnen.

Ch. Courtwood Bandanna ROM taking Best of Winners at the Cyclone County Kennel Club in 1992. Owned by Susan Hahnen.

Ch. Courtwood Inn Keeper taking Best of Winners at the 1997 Lake Minnetonka Kennel Club Show. Owned by Susan Hahnen.

Rains, Halls O'Ivy, Hyacinth-Blue, and High Sierra. Bred to Bandanna's litter sister, Ch. Courtwood Bag O'Tricks, he produced Ch. Courtwood Town Hall, Courtwood Tail Wind, and Courtwood Tin Whistle.

Sue leased Donald's litter sister, Ch. Edenderry Grace Note, and co-bred her with Carol Rentz to produce the "rain" litter when bred to Ch. Courtwood Heavy Rains ("Thompson").

Donald's daughter, Ch. Courtwood Halls O'Ivy, was co-bred to Ch. Meadowlark's Irish Monarch. Three of

the six offspring in that litter are finished. Sue received one male, Ch. Courtwood Inn Keeper, and Sue is using him on some of her bitches that are closely related to Donald.

Sue breeds no more than one litter a year and sometimes less, but her advice and counsel has enabled co-owners and co-breeders to produce 108 champions for Courtwood, as of early 1999. Sue's astute eye and knowledge of her lines and breeding possibilities ensure that figure will rise as time goes by.

Pat and Frank Haigler, *Rendition*–Fullerton, CA

In 1967, the Haiglers acquired their first Irish Setter, and they were immersed in the show world shortly thereafter. Through Barbara LaVoie of Michigan, they were able to purchase Ch. Tyronne Farm Rendition (Ch. Sir Michael Galway of Glendee ex Lady Kerrybrooke) and his sister, Ch. Michael's Patti O'Shea. The male provided their kennel name and the bitch, Patti, was their first champion and foundation bitch. Patti was bred to Ch. Shannon's Erin ROM to produce the Sunny Hills litter. In that litter was Ch. Rendition Erin of Sunny Hills, known as Erin II, an important sire for Meadowlark, and Ch. Rendition Tippi of Sunny Hill. Tippi was bred to Ch. Candia Indeed ROM three times and produced many champions.

In 1972, the Haiglers acquired Am. Can. Mex. Ch. Draherin King's Ransom ROM from Lucy Jane Myers. It was a thrill for them to be able to own such a great show, stud, and companion dog. He was campaigned to three Bests in Show and many specialty and group wins.

In 1974, an Erin II daughter, Rendition Jennifer, was bred to Ch. Candia Indeed ROM. That litter produced Am. Can. Mex. Ch. Rendition Chantilly Lace. She was a top-winning show dog in 1976 and 1977. Upon retirement, she was first bred to Ch. Rendition St. Patrick and then to Ch. Shawnee Pipedream O'Charlton ROM. A great producer of champions, she lived to be 15 years old.

In 1981, they bred Am. Mex. Ch. Rendition Patrick (Mex. Ch. Rendition Country Charlie ex Rendition Apple Ginger, a Piper-Chantilly Lace daughter). Patrick was an outstanding show winner, with five Bests in Show, more than 30 specialty wins, and many Group Firsts. Their third "Patrick" proved to be a lucky name for them.

The last to finish was Ch. Rendition Mercedes Benz (Ch. Rusticwoods Song N Dance Man ex Rendition Pretty Woman). "Ben" finished with all specialty majors and many sweepstakes wins.

Rendition stock has been the bedrock of many kennels throughout the United States. Among them are Ch. Rendition Irish Inspiration ROM and Ch. Rendition Razzle Dazzle ROM, foundation for the Scarlly Setters of Penny Nunnally; Ch. Rendition Wild Poppy ROM, owned by the Alexanders and dam of the top-winning bitch, Ch. Arista's Finest Rose; and Ch. Rendition Indian Summer ROM, foundation for the Farringtons' Shawnee kennels.

Debra Hamilton, *Rumraisin*–Armonk, NY

Although Debra had owned three beloved Irish Setters since 1973, it was not until 1986 that she acquired her first show dog, Ch. Ramblin'Red Quincidence from Anne Marie and Randy Kubacz. "Quincy" (Ch. Ramblin'

Ch. Ramblin'Red Quincidence. Owned by Debra Hamilton of Rumraisin Kennels.

Red Kildavan ex Ch. Ramblin' Red Lorelle) was the beginning of Debra's successful show and breeding career and of a lasting friendship with the Kubacz family. In 1991, Quincy was bred to Ch. Red Barn Top O' the Line (Ch. Kimberlin O'Killea Of Top 'O ex Ch. Red Barn Revolutionary Star ROM). This was the first Rumraisin litter, named for one of Debra's original dogs, Raisin in the Sun CD, a dog rescued from a puppy mill. This litter produced Ch. Rumraisin on the Q.T. ("Violet").

A litter sister to Violet, Rumraisin on the Run, owned by Sandra Smith, was bred to Ch. Cucuhullain Good Fortune ROM in 1995, producing Ch. Rumraisin Sorcerer, who was finished exclusively from the Bred by Exhibitor class.

Ch. O'Dandy's Caitlin O'Balcaire winning Best of Opposite Sex at the Longshore-Southport Kennel Club in 1996. Owned by Debra Hamilton.

In 1996, Debra acquired Ch. O'Dandy's Caitlin O'Balcaire (Ch. Cucuhullain Good Fortune ROM ex Ch. Balcaire Paprika). She was previously owned by Col. Malcolm and Elizabeth Spaulding, but the couple needed to place her because of illness in the family. Caitlin was bred in 1997 to Ch. Courtwood Heavy Rains, owned by Sue Hahnen and Mary Thompson. Twelve puppies were born in that litter, some of which Debra hopes will provide a bright future for Rumraisin.

Lynn Hayes, *Connall*–Brattleboro, VT

Lynn bought her first Irish Setter in 1970 as a companion, but the acquisition of a puppy from Kate Seymour in 1986 marked her introduction to dog shows, performance events, and breeding. The puppy became Am. Can. Ch. Cucuhullain Eternal Encore JH CD VC CGC, affirming her belief that Irish are a versatile breed. He was the winner of two National Specialty Awards of Merit. Her foundation bitch, Ch. Cucuhullain Good Morning, continues Lynn's association with Kate. Two litters and a planned third litter are all linebred on Ch. Candia Indeed ROM.

Michael D. Heasley, *Pella*–Newell, WV

Pella Kennels started in 1984 with the purchase of a foundation bitch, Highland Durin Class Act (Ch. Kingscourt Franklin Durin ex Ch. Durin's Daily Double) bred by Carmen Hufstetler. Bred to Stoneypoint Loriens Quest, she produced Ch. SKCh. Pella's Fire From Heaven CD VC CGC. Although "Flame" never saw a bird until he was $8\frac{1}{2}$ years old, he now has three legs toward his Junior Hunter title and one VC field pass.

Ch. Pella's Prince of Thieves, pictured here winning Group First to finish his championship. Owned by Michael Heasley.

Mike also purchased a puppy that became Ch. Lorien's Special Delight CD CGC (Ch. Rusticwoods Olympic Medalist ROM ex Loriens Southern Starflower) from Barbara Wollenhaupt. She has been bred three times to Ch. Meadowlark's Midnight Special, Ch. Rusticwood Party Animal, and the last litter in 1996 to Ch. Quailfield's Mak'n Business. This was the "crime" litter, with Ch. Pella's Prince of Thieves finishing easily in Hawaii and several others becoming pointed.

Pella strives to build a complete Irish Setter; a combination of structural soundness, breed type, trainability, bird sense and, above all, a loving temperament with an outgoing devil-may-care attitude.

Teresa and Howard Hike, *TaraMac*– Port Orchard, WA

TaraMac was founded in 1991 with the purchase of Ch. Kaerdon's Twilight Serenade JH (Ch. Kaerdon's MadHatter ex Am. Can. Ch. Kaerdon's Ticker Tape) from

Ch. Kaerdon's Twilight Serenade JH winning Best of Breed in 1996. Owned by Teresa and Howard Hike.

Leta Graham. At the same time, they acquired Ch. Saxony's Laurentide Ice (Ch. Scarlly's Road Runner ex Ch. Saxony's Uptown Tangerine). A new addition is Meadowlark's Top Hat N'Tails (Ch. Meadowlark's Masterful ex Meadowlark's Outrageous). Their first litter (Ch. Kaerdon's Grand Masterpiece ex Ch. Kaerdon's Twilight Serenade JH) has several promising youngsters, and their second litter (Meadowlark's Top Hat N'Tails ex Mijeans Fax It To Kaerdon) is also on its way. A small kennel, TaraMac breeds only when there is a need for a new puppy. Teresa is active in Irish Setter rescue and is chair for the Irish Setter Club of Seattle's Rescue Program.

From left to right: Ch. Charlton's Indeed I Do, Am. Can. Ch. Charlton's London Fog, and Fancy Free Summer Savory. Owned by Jeanette Holmes.

Jeanette Holmes, *Estrella*–Paradise, CA

Jeanette grew up in the 1950s, immersed in the horses and dogs bred and shown by her neighbors in Sacramento, California. Finally, in the 1970s, she acquired a puppy, realizing her dream of owning an Irish Setter. During those years, at the height of Irish popularity, it took more than 80 bitches to make 5 points in California. Jeanette was fortunate to have the friendship and guidance during those early years of showing of the professional handler Tom Tobin and breeder and professional handler Carole Lewis. Jeanette decided to become a professional handler, a vocation that she maintained full-time until recently and now pursues on a smaller scale. In about 1980, she acquired her foundation bitch, Ch. Charlton's Indeed I Do, from Winy Arland. "Tulip" was four years old when she came to Jeanette. She was quite a character—full of herself, with heartwarming antics, and always a true and faithful friend. Tulip was bred four times—twice before Jeanette got her, once to Ch. Courtwood Cavalier, and once to Ch. Shawnee Pipedream O'Charlton ROM. Three Charlton champions resulted from those matings.

She was then co-bred with Winy Arland to Candy K's Redford and Am. Can. Ch. Charlton's London Fog. From the latter breeding, Ch. Rebellion Brother Love was produced. Tulip's fourth litter by Ch. Meadowlark's Gingerbread Man produced three champions for Jeanette. At the time, she was using the prefix Fancy Free, and those offspring were Ch. Fancy Free Peg O'My Dreams CD, Ch. Fancy Free Tap Dance Kid, and Ch. Fancy Free Camelot. Jeanette used three different prefixes, lastly adopting "Estrella," which was originated by her husband at the time, Paul Holmes. They currently both use that prefix for their individual kennels. Among recent champions produced by Jeanette are the obedience and conformation-titled dogs of Kay Bedeau, Token's Unsinkable Molly B UDT, Ch. Token's Talk of the Town CDX, and several Estrella champions. She has bred approximately 12 litters and co-bred 5 since 1969.

The attributes that she considers most important in an Irish Setter are intelligence, outgoing and sweet nature, stable and steady temperament, breed type, balanced structure, and good health. The Irish Setter must have that "rollicking" personality that gives its companions joy and makes one laugh.

Paul Holmes, *Estrella*–Big Fork, MT

Paul, the other half of Estrella Irish Setters, started in 1967 by attending a dog show and deciding he would rather show dogs than teach school. It took ten years to get a handler's license from the AKC (a requirement in those days that was abandoned about 1974). His first Irish was Candia Encore in 1969, but she was not show quality. He went next to Ted Eldredge to purchase a Ch. Shannon's Erin daughter, Tirvelda Topaz. When bred to Bob and Pat Robinson's Erin grandson, Ch. Portrait O'King's Challenge, she produced Ch. Tirvelda Estrella McMuffin.

They acquired Ch. Shawnee Indian Breeze CD from the Farringtons, a bitch that became their top producer, co-bred with Dawn Stafford. Bred to Tapnar

Ch. Shawnee Indian Breeze CD, top producer for Paul Holmes' Estrella Irish Setters.

Ballaghderreen and Ch. Courtwood Summer Forecast ROM, she produced two influential males for Estrella, Estrella Jiminy Cricket and Ch. Estrella Instead.

Currently, Ch. Estrella Candlestick and her daughter Estrella Victoria's Secret reside at Paul's, and are his hopefuls for the future.

Dale Hood, *Ruxton*–Towson, MD

In 1970, while attending her first show, Dale met Mary Ann Foxwell of Foxfyre Irish Setters. She introduced Dale to the world of show dogs and dog shows. From a breeding of Neerb's Scarlet Tara to Ch. Mos'n Acre Wilson Farm Harvest, Dale co-owned a bitch who was to become her first champion. Ch. Foxfyre's Scarlet Ember CD was a breed-winning and group-placing bitch at a time when male specials were Best of Breed winners 95 percent of the time.

Several exceptional bitches later (Dale only keeps bitches), including Ch. Rockherin Follow the Sun, she acquired a puppy from Craig and Pat Hackenberg of Castlebar Irish Setters that became Ch. Castlebar's Garden Party ("Tulip"). Tulip is the litter sister of Ch. Castlebar Command Presence (Ch. Meadowlark's Vindicator ex Ch. Sardonyx Castlebar Witsend). Tulip is identical to her mother, whom Dale truly adored. Tulip was bred twice. The first litter, by Ch. Quailfield Mak'n Business, produced Ch. Ruxton Larkspur, retained by Dale, and Ch. Ruxton Sweet Jasmine JH CD, owned

Ch. Castlebar's Garden Party winning Best of Breed at the 1992 Delaware County Kennel Club. Owned by Dale Hood and Craig Hackenberg.

Ch. Castlebar Ruxton Olympia, a Group and Best in Show-winning bitch, won Best of Breed at Westminster and took Group Third in 2000. Owned by Dale Hood and Craig Hackenberg.

by Christine Miller, J. Murter, and Therese Fila. Tulip's second litter was by Ch. Ballymera's Stormin' Norman (Ch. Quailfield Mak'n Business ex Ch. Meadowlark's Whisperin' Breeze). A bitch, Ch. Castlebar Ruxton Olympia, co-owned with Craig Hackenberg, finished at two years of age with 17 major points. She started her show career in 1999 with the co-ownership of Ron Readmond, handled by Greg Strong, and has become a Group and Best in Show-winning bitch. "Daisy" won the Breed at Westminster and took Group Third in 2000. Another bitch, Ruxton's Olympic Memories, owned by Therese Fila, has three majors toward her championship.

Catheryne and Thomas Houston, *Daventry–* North Little Rock, AR

Catheryne's first Irish arrived in 1978. For some time the Houstons concentrated on obedience, but when living in

Ft. Worth, Texas, they purchased a show bitch from Roy and Shirlee Murray (Kennlee). Subsequently, they returned to Kennlee and bought a puppy that became Ch. Kennlee Treasure Hunter (Ch. Ballymera's Stormin' Norman ex Ch. Kennlee Sugarshack). From Patty Clawson (Ballymera) and Vicki and Ron Larmour (Sierra Lyn), they obtained two bitches, Ballymera's Close to Daventry (Ch. Quailfield Mak'n Business ex Ch. Ballymera Hurricane) and Sierra Lyn Airtight Alibi (Ch. Sunshine's Remember When ex Ch. Sierra Lyn White Diamonds). They also purchased a puppy dog that they co-own with the Larmours, Sierra Lyn Boomer.

Carol and Fran Huegen, Utica, NY

Carol and her husband Fran, although they have had many Irish Setters over the years, have only recently joined the ranks of showgoers. Their two Irish presently shown are Valley View's Xmas Carol and Kenobi's Magnum Force.

Kenobi's Magnum Force (left) and Valley View Xmas Carol (right) enjoy a day in the field. Owned by Carol and Fran Huegen.

Jim and Judy Huffman, *Brefney*–Greendale, WI

The Huffmans became seriously interested in the fancy in 1981 when they received their first show dog, Ch. Namar's Concept, a loving but willful dog that amused bystanders with his antics in obedience. Their second champion was Shangrila New Moon Rising, a daughter of the top-winning bitch, Ch. Shangrila Moonshadow. Two of their dogs were lost in an unfortunate accident when they were exposed to pesticides sprayed on a motel lawn. Currently, they own Ch. Shangrila Twelfth Hour, whom they lovingly call "the Queen." A youngster, Ch. Kerry-Eire Kachina, is their hope for the future.

Diana Hunter, *Carrollton*–TX

Diana has had dogs most of her life and has been around all types of animals, because she is a third-generation circus performer. She did a trapeze act and assisted in other performers' bareback riding and dog and pony acts. She obtained her first Irish Setter bitch in 1976 and a male in 1977. He became Am. Can. Ch. Flashback's Rustic Shadow. In 1982, the once-in-a-lifetime dog entered her life from the kennel of Susan Griffiths. He was Am. Can. Ch. Kerry-Eire Hallelulia CDX UKC CDX Can. CD. "Shane" always gave his all in whatever was asked of him. He was followed by Ch. Hallelulia's Heir Apparent CD Can. CD UKC CD CGC, a rollicking personality and a free thinker. Both father and son have been featured as models.

Am. Can. Ch. Kerry-Eire Hallelulia CDX UKC CDX Can. CD. Owned by Diana Hunter of Carrollton Kennels.

Kazuko Imai, *Merry Kids*–Tokyo, Japan

Merry Kids began in 1989 with the purchase of Am. Ch. Cherokee Storm Fury (Ch. Windwood's Night Hawk ex Ch. Beaverbrook Shayne Seranade). A bitch, she was bred to Kazuko's next purchase, Ch. Kenora Roman Gladiator

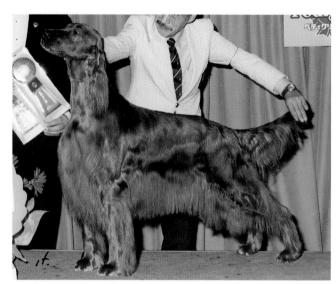

Am. Jpn. Int. Ch. Shadyview's Just Me Again winning Best in Group at the 1997 FCI Asian International Dog Show. Owned by Kazuko Imai.

(Ch. Tramore North to Alaska ex Allegiance Baccara). Both of these animals are group winners in Japan, and they have produced two litters containing Japanese and Spanish champions. In 1995, good fortune smiled on Merry Kids with the arrival of Ch. Shadyview's Just Me Again (Ch. Regalaire Music Man ROM ex Ch. Windwood Merry Mockingbird). She is a Japanese, Asian, and International champion. She has been bred twice, to Spanish Ch. Bramblebush Th'heir Apparent (Ch. Arab Irish Monte Hall ex Bramblebush Sweet Little Lies), producing a number of Japanese and International champions and group winners. Kazuko uses only American-bred dogs to further her breeding and showing interests.

Bonita Marie Ingram, *Winfree*–Salem, NJ

Bonnie began Winfree in 1980, naming it in admiration of the beauty and majesty of Irish Setters as they run in the fields "free as the wind." She bought Fleetwood Farm's Royal Delight, who was an intelligent, loving, and patient friend for 16 years. In 1988, Bonnie got Ch. Meadowlark's Carina from Rose Ross. Her fun-loving showmanship and exceptional movement made her an easy champion, now a favorite in her later years in the Veterans Class. Carina was bred to Ch. Meadowlark's

A family portrait—mother Ch. Meadowlark's Carina (left) and daughter Ch. Winfree She's Like the Wind (right). Owned by Bonita Marie Ingram.

Vindicator and produced Ch. Winfree's She's Like the Wind in 1992. In 1995, Carina was bred to Ch. Meadowlark's Irish Monarch to produce Winfree's Colors of the Wind and Winfree's Magic Carpet Ride.

The spirit of the Irish Setter continues to inspire and support Bonnie in her journey through life. She thanks God for the joy they have brought to her heart.

Bob Iversen, Crystal, MN

Bob's pride and joy was Ch. Courtwood Book Mark, one of the "book" litter bred by Sue Hahnen (Am. Can. Ch.Courtwood Manuscript ROM ex Courtwood Mystic Morn). All five in the litter finished, and all lived long and healthy lives. Born in 1985, "Mark" lived until 1998.

Linda Jacobelli, *Ohkom Farms*—Forbes Road, PA

Linda purchased her first show Irish and her first show dog from Joe and Gerry Lee (Kenobi Kennels). He became Ch. Kenobi Awsum Ominous Sky (Ch. Villa-Dan Darth Vader ex Ch. Rockherin Neesa of Kenobi ROM). From the Lees she bought a bitch, Kenobi Beyond Believing CGC. When bred to Ominous Sky, she produced Ch. Ohkom Born To Be Wild CGC. Bred to Am. Can. Ch. Captiva's Ride With the Wind, she produced the "Berry" litter in 1997. The first to finish was Am. Can. Ch. Ohkom Goldenberry. Others are pointed in the US and Canada, and one, Okhom Zoomberry, is a Junior Hunter.

Ch. Courtwood Book Mark, Bob Iversen's pride and joy.

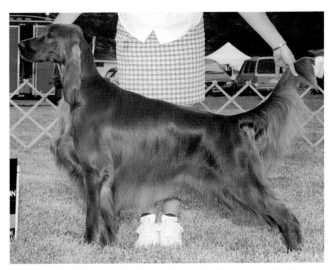

Am. Can. Ch. Ohkom Goldenberry. Owned by Linda Jacobelli of Ohkom Farms.

Fleetwood Farms champions winning Best Team at the 1981 ISCA National Specialty (from left to right): Ch. Fleetwood Farm HMR Drednought; Fleetwood Farm Aaron Ardee; High Regards King of Fleetwood; and Ch. Fleetwood Farm St. Patrick. Owned by Patricia Jesson.

Patricia Jesson, *Fleetwood Farms*–Akron, OH

Fleetwood Farms began in 1942, and its early history is found in this book. In 1976, Pat purchased her first show Irish, a dog that became Ch. Fleetwood Farms Free Spirit. Virginia Rumbaugh invited Pat to work with the Irish of Fleetwood to show-train them for their handler, Dick Cooper, and in 1981, she moved to Fleetwood Farms to learn about breeding and raising dogs and responsibly continuing the Fleetwood Farms bloodline. She became involved in showing some of the dogs as braces or teams at local shows. At one time, she showed a team of four Best in Show sons of Ch. Starheir Aaron Ardee, a feat never before accomplished in the breed. In 1989, they added new bloodlines to Fleetwood, and Pat continues to raise and show dogs with that prefix.

Jean Johnson and Joanne Holmberg, *Mi Jean*–Vancouver, WA

Mi Jean Kennels began in 1973 in Alaska. Their first dog died of bloat at 18 months, and they turned to Kilgary bloodlines for their next Irish. She was Ch. Killarney's Kerika CD. They also bought Ch. Palomar's Shamrock of Saraval. Bred together, this pair produced Ch. Mi Jean's Classic Example. They

Ch. Mi Jean's Every Now and Then. Owned by Jean Johnson and Joanne Holmberg of Mi Jean Kennels.

Ch. Mi Jean's I Fooled Ya winning an Award of Merit at the 1999 Irish Setter Specialty. Owned by Jean Johnson and Joanne Holmberg.

Kintyre Kennel's first homebred champion, Ch. Kintyre's Sugar and Spice. Owned by Barbara and Tom Johnstone.

bought Ch. Tramore Jester O'Mi Jeans from Ginny Swanson of Tramore Kennels. Classic Example bred to Shamrock produced Ch. Mi Jean's Abracadabra. "Abby" was bred twice, the first time to Ch. Chamberlayne's Masquerade to produce a litter of three champions. She was then bred to Ch. Tramore Rich N Famous to produce the next generation for Mi Jean, including the bitch Ch. Mi Jean's Every Now and Then, first to Ch. Mi Jean's Dignitary and then to Ch. Donegan's Denim Genes. From this came a dog who embodies the rollicking personality of the Irish, Ch. Mi Jean's I Fooled Ya. Current litters are descended from him.

Tom and Barbara Johnstone, *Kintyre*– Sunbury, OH

Kintyre began in 1971 with the purchase of the Johnstones' first Irish Setter as a family pet. Persuaded to show, they become totally involved and decided to buy a show-quality bitch. They began with Tirvelda bloodlines and produced their first homebred champion, Ch. Kintyre's Sugar and Spice. Bred to Ch. Scarlly's Showboat ROM, she produced four champions. Her daughter, Ch. Kintyre's Spice is Nice, was bred to a Showboat son, Ch. Scarlly's Show 'Nuf, to produce three champions. They continued to breed within the Scarlly lines and in 1994, purchased a bitch, Ch. Scarlly's Love Potion No. Nine, whom they bred to Ch. Quailfield's Mak'n Business in 1996. Three of this litter finished easily in 1998. They were Ch. Kintyre's Deal Me In; Ch. Kintyre's Debutante, owned by Norb and Nena Dee; and Ch. Kintyre's Decidedly So. A repeat of this breeding took place in 1998.

The Johnstones have always tried to make their involvement with dogs family-oriented. They have raised five children and have six grandchildren. All are animal lovers, and their daughter, Kathy, is a natural handler who competed in junior showmanship and is still involved with the dogs.

They have strived to breed for quality, not quantity, and breed only every several years. Their family moved several times during Tom's career as an engineer, and in each place they belonged to local Irish Setter clubs. Now

Ch. Kintyre's Decidedly So taking Best of Winners and Best of Opposite Sex at the 1998 Northeastern Indian Kennel Club Show. Owned by Barbara and Tom Johnstone.

retired, he has resumed handling dogs. They continue to meet and make new friends while enjoying the camaraderie of the many people they have met in their travels over the years.

Anna Jones, *Paterjay*–Pittstown, NJ

Anna's introduction to Irish Setters was through the obedience ring in 1971. By 1979, she entered the breed ring with foundation stock purchased from Rose Ross (Meadowlark) and Pat Haigler (Rendition). From Rose she purchased a dog, Ch. Meadowlark's Honesty O'Padian, and a bitch, Meadowlark's Mint Julep. This combination produced the "A" litter, Ch. Paterjay Meadowlark's Adare and Arglin. From Pat, she purchased a dog, Ch. Rendition Tumbleweed, and a bitch, Ch. Rendition Peppermint Patti CD, who was bred twice. The first litter, by Paterjay Meadowlark's Ardagh, produced Paterjay Rendition Brinara. Her next litter by Ch. Meadowlark's Mischief Maker resulted in Ch. Paterjay Cill Dara.

Ch. Meadowlark's Honesty O'Padian. Owned by Anna Jones of Paterjay Kennels.

In 1990, a breeding of Ch. Paterjay Meadowlark's Arglin to Ch. Meadowlark's Love Boat, owned by Leta Graham of Kaerdon Kennels,

Ch. Paterjay Meadowlark's Arglin taking Best of Winners at the Tuxedo Park Kennel Club in 1987. Owned by Anna Jones.

A valuable stud dog and top-winning showman, Ch. Meadowlark's Fire 'N Rain is shown here winning an Award of Merit at the 1994 Westminster Kennel Club show. Owned by Anna Jones and Walter Hackos.

resulted in Anna keeping a stud puppy, Ch. Paterjay Kaerdon's Sent W'Love. The offspring of Cill Dara and Sent W'Love are currently in the ring.

Ch. Meadowlark's Fire 'N Rain, bred by Rose Ross and co-owned with Walter Hackos, proved to be a valuable stud dog as well as a top-winning show dog for Anna. He was bred to Brinara to produce the "D" litter of Derryveagh, Derreen, and Drinagh. He has also sired litters for Claire Andrews (Kimberlin) and for Leigh and Anne Marie Hearn (Pendoric in Australia). A breeding to an Australian bitch resulted in several Australian champions.

A new addition at Paterjay is a bitch from Bob and Brenda Gibson of Canada, Hilloch Will O'Wisp of Paterjay, who will add a new dimension to Anna's breeding program.

Sandra Jones, *Dreamtime*–Damascus, MD

Sandy grew up around Irish Setters, obtaining her first in 1973. Her first real show dog and her first champion was purchased from Gloria Askins, Ch. Legacy Grand Master. She also bought a puppy from Sue Griffith's Kerry-Eire Kennels. In 1987, Sandy purchased Cloverleaf's Rebecca from Linda Ratkovich. Sandy asked Linda for a nice puppy that she could finish by the time the dog was about three years old. Rebecca became her foundation bitch. She turned out to be fourth pick in the litter, but as it happened, that wasn't bad, because four bitches and one dog finished out of that litter. Rebecca became a champion at 20 months of age. Sponsored by Mrs. Arthur

Warner and handled by George Alston, Rebecca won 5 Bests in Show and 15 specialties. She retired from the show ring in 1991, when George retired from handling.

Another sister in Rebecca's litter, Ch. Cloverleaf's Who's That Girl, owned by Annette Izydorek Pusey, went on to become a Best in Show bitch. They are possibly the only littermate Best in Show Irish Setter bitches ever produced. Who's That Girl was the foundation of Pompei Kennels.

Ch. Cloverleaf's Rebecca, foundation bitch for Sandra Jones' Dreamtime Kennels.

Ch. Dreamtime April Magic JH, Sandra Jones' first homebred champion.

Rebecca produced seven puppies from two litters. In the first litter was Ch. Dreamtime April Magic JH ("Kathleen") by Ch. Meadowlark's Show Stopper. By Ch. Tramore Never Say Never, she produced Chs. Dreamtime Cutting Edge and Dreamtime The Magic Is Back.

Kathleen was Sandy's first homebred champion. Bred to Ch. Camelot's City Slicker in 1995, she produced a litter of 13. Two are finished (Chs. Star Attraction and Mr. Sandman) and others are pointed. Her second litter by Ch. Ballymera's Stormin' Norman in May 1998 is just getting started.

Charlotte Kay, *Aintree*–North Ft. Myers, FL

Charlotte has had at least one Irish Setter in her life since 1973, when her husband rescued their first dog while he was attending the Auburn School of Veterinary Medicine. Her first outstanding dog was Ch. Elvatowne Thunderstruck, who finished his championship with two Group Firsts. At the time, she also obtained Rendition Country Kate from Pat Haigler. Those two produced six puppies, all of which became champions. Her second important dog was Ch. Lyn Erin Chances Are, acquired from Linda Acquavella. "Chance" was not only a multiple group and specialty winner but had the personality, intelligence, and temperament of a lifetime. Charlotte feels a debt of gratitude to Linda and Ernie Acquavella, Judy Fritkin (Elvatowne), and Lucy Jane Myers, whose Draherin dogs are behind all of her dogs. She has become involved in obedience and rescue, and these activities have brought a great deal of pleasure, knowledge, and new experiences.

Ch. Lyn Erin Chances Are, a multiple group and specialty winner. Owned by Charlotte Kay.

Charlene R. Kickbush, DVM, and Tom Greer, *BrambleBush*–Bishop, GA

Charlene received her first Irish Setter in 1972 as a birthday present and within two years had her first show-quality and foundation bitch, Palomar's Molly Dew Indeed, a daughter of Ch. Candia Indeed ROM ex Ch. Palomar's Rollingbay Molly. Molly was bred and owned by Lauralea and Tom Conlon, who were Charlene's mentors and friends until Laurie's death.

In 1981, Charlene acquired a puppy that was to become Ch. Windermere Marrakesh Express CD, sired by Ch. Ash-Ling Celebration (Ch. Draherin King's Ransom ex Glenavan Taste O'Honey). "Katie" was bred to Express to produce her first homebred litter in 1982. These were linebred on Draherin and Courtwood bred to her basic Bayberry stock. In the 1980s, she continued to concentrate on Charlton and Draherin. One of her most successful combinations was that of Ch. Arab Irish Monte Hall, bred by Cecily Barker and co-owned with Charlene, to Ch. BrambleBush Autumn Design. This gave them Ch. BrambleBush Irish Design, owned by Ken and Mary Pooler; Ch. BrambleBush Unfrkblvbl, co-owned and handled by Ronelle Willadsen; and BrambleBush On A Wing 'N A Prayer.

BrambleBush has also produced some excellent hunting and obedience dogs: BrambleBush Famous Shamus MH, owned, trained, and handled by Nina Johnson of Houston, Texas; and BrambleBush Dakota O'Malley UDX CGC, owned and trained by Pattie Beddows of Tequesta, Florida.

Charlene believes that her success in breeding has been the result of a sound foundation and the goodness of those people who had a working knowledge of pedigrees. She has strived to breed dogs in which form follows function. Her success in presentation and handling came from two people—Ronelle Willadsen, who always made things right, especially when the pressure was just too much, and her husband, who became a part of BrambleBush in 1988 and brought a professional handler's perspective to the program so that tunnel vision was never tolerated by either one.

Charlene is a director of the ISCA.

Margaret Korzeniowska, *Tramperus*–Des Plaines, IL

From a beginning in Poland in 1979, where she competed successfully in five countries with her foundation bitch, Ch. Pl. CAC CACIB Jun Rysi Wykrot, she was able to produce excellent field and show-titled dogs. While in Poland, she became an FCI judge of pointing breeds and a director of the English Breeds Section at the Pointing Dogs Club.

In 1981, Margaret moved to the US and soon thereafter purchased Ch. Regalaire Strike Up the Band (Ch. Regalaire Music Man ROM ex Regalaire Blush With Pride) and his daughter by McCamon Irish Cream, Regalaire Lady Guinevere from Barbara Riegle. Strike Up the Band was bred to her Polish import, Ch. Tramperus Sharon, thus starting a new American and Polish line.

Holly Kruse, *Beckery*–Philadelphia, PA

Holly's family always had an Irish Setter, but it was not until she got Kerry in 1976 (Summit Rise Marauder ex Modder Rhu) that she attempted an entrance into the show ring. Kerry hated the whole thing and ended up on the couch for the next 13 years. He was instrumental, however, in getting Holly involved in club affairs and developing the interest to go further. She found that she liked the Rendition dogs and purchased a puppy from Pat Haigler (Candy K's Redford ex Ch. Rendition Honey Bee) in 1981. He became Ch. Rendition Wind Voyager CGC ("Tristan") and was her devoted companion through high school, college, graduate school, the deaths of both her parents, and many other events in her life, good and bad. Tristan passed away just short of his 14th birthday in 1995.

When Tristan was 12, Holly got Rendition Beckery Brigid from Pat Haigler (Ch. Rusticwoods Song 'N Dance

Ch. Regalaire Strike Up the Band. Owned by Margaret Korzeniowska of Tramperus Kennels.

Ch. Rendition Beckery Brigid CD NA CGC. Owned by Holly Kruse of Beckery Kennels.

Man ex Rendition Pretty Woman). A conformation champion and CD-titled, Brigid's great love is agility, at which she excels.

Holly also owns Paterjay Emain Macha from Anna Jones and two puppies from a litter out of Brigid bred to Ch. Jemini Sundance Kid, a dog linebred on old Rendition stock.

Holly started an all-setters discussion list on the Internet in 1994, called "setters-L." Currently, it has a subscription of about 1,000 people. Its purpose is to share knowledge and information on all aspects of owning one or more of the setter breeds. Holly is also the author of the official Internet FAQ on Irish Setters, an information service for anyone wanting to have accurate breed facts presented by someone who has been in the breed her whole life.

Anne Marie, Randy, and Peter Kubacz, *Ramblin' Red*–Jackson, NJ

In 1968, Anne Marie and her siblings bought an Irish Setter as a Christmas present for their parents. While walking the dog in Prospect Park in Brooklyn, she met Marjorie Martorella (now an AKC Best in Show and Sporting and Hound judge), who encouraged her to show her pet, Kerry. He became Shannon's Kerry of Windsor UD, and the story of how he became an obedience-titled dog would give anyone hope. Kerry was everything that gave Irish a bad reputation in the '60s. He took advantage of his novice owners until they finally contacted his breeder, who referred them to a private obedience trainer. In one lesson, Kerry was performing beautifully. Kerry enjoyed learning the exercises, which Anne Marie taught him from a book she took out of the library. When she began to train him for CDX work, she didn't own any jumps, so she covered lawn chairs with sheets to simulate them. When she attempted to train at the Poodle Obedience Training Club in Queens, they required a reference letter from her former club because they did not want a "crazy Irish" disrupting their classes. Kerry went on to attain his UD with very high scores, including one all-breed High In Trial. He was also a member of the Eastern Irish Setter Association scent hurdle team in the 1970s.

Anne Marie's real hope for a top-notch obedience dog was Kerry's daughter, Kerrianne Kelenn of Kells CD. One day when Kelenn was 3½ months old, she was watching Anne Marie train Kerry. When Anne Marie said "heel," Kelenn came to heel position and sat, so she was included in training sessions. She finished her CD easily before she was mature and knew all the CDX exercises, but Anne Marie did not want her jumping at full height until she was old enough. Anne Marie began to do field work, and there she met Randy. Kelenn was bred to Ch. Derrinraw's Sir Michael, and shortly after her puppies were born, she

Purchased from a pet shop, AFCh. Galway's Red Disappointment CD was Randy Kubacz's first Irish Setter.

became ill. She died after six days in intensive care. Anne started to work her daughter, Avelle, in obedience, but memories of Kelenn were too painful. She completed Avelle's CD but stopped after that and never competed in obedience again.

Randy purchased his first dog in a pet shop, and while walking, he met a member of the Irish Setter Club of Long Island, Bob Fitch, who encouraged Randy to join. He became interested in obedience and field, and his dog, Shannon, went on to become Field and Amateur Field Champion Galway's Red Disappointment CD.

Ch. Ramblin'Red Kildavan, Best of Breed at the 1987 ISCA National Specialty and the 1989 Westminster Kennel Club show, Number One Irish Setter in 1998, and multiple Best in Show winner. Owned by Anne Marie and Randy Kubacz.

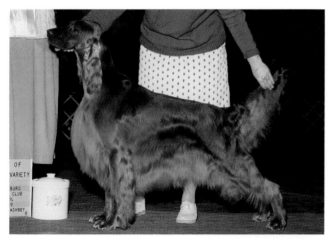

Am. Can. Ch. Ramblin'Red Fortune Teller, Best of Breed at the ISCA National Specialty in 1997, Number One Irish Setter and Number Five Sporting Dog in 1998, and Best of Breed at the Westminster Kennel Club show in 1999. Owned by Anne Marie and Randy Kubacz.

Ch. Ramblin'Red Phaegan, Best of Breed at the Westminster Kennel Club in 1990 and multiple group and specialty winner. Owned by Anne Marie and Randy Kubacz.

Anne Marie and Randy were married in 1975, and both were active trialers. Their most successful field dog was National Ch. National Red Setter Ch. Field and Amateur Field Ch. Ramblin'Red Banshee. Banshee won the ISCA's first National Field Trial Championship.

Meanwhile, Anne Marie became increasingly interested in the show ring and finished her first champion, Ramblin'Red Avelle CD VC. Bred to Ch. Draherin King's Ransom ROM, Avelle produced Ch. Ramblin'Red Guinevere and Ch. Ramblin'Red Glingael ROM. "Gael" was Randy's first owner-handled champion. While Guinevere was the more successful show dog, Gael was the better producer. Her son, Ch. Ramblin'Red Kildavan was Best of Breed at the 1987 National Specialty and at Westminster in 1989. He was a multiple Best in Show winner and Number One Irish Setter in 1988 with the co-ownership of Nat and Gloria Reese. Another of her offspring, Ch. Ramblin'Red Phaegan, won two Awards of Merit at National Specialties, was Best of Breed at Westminster in 1990, and was a multiple group and specialty winner.

Another Avelle daughter, Ramblin'Red Iaslinn ROM, produced ten champions, including five when leased to Kate Seymour of Cucuhullain Irish Setters. Her grandson, Ch. Cucuhullain Good Fortune ROM, is currently one of the top sires in the breed.

Linebreeding on Kildavan and Phaegan produced Ch. Ramblin'Red Verran and Ch. Ramblin'Red Vanara. Vanara, a specialty-winning bitch, produced Ch. Ramblin'Red Xhilaration, co-owned with Dr. Eileen McDonald, who is proving to be a good producer for Nightn'gael. Bred to Good Fortune, Vanara produced Ch.

Ramblin'Red Fortune Teller, who won Best of Breed at the ISCA National Specialty in 1997. "Gypsy" is a multiple Best in Show, specialty, and group winner. In 1998, she was Number One Irish Setter and Number Five Sporting Dog. In 1999, she won Best of Breed at Westminster.

Another Gael daughter, Ramblin'Red Rhiannon, produced Ch. Windstar's Valiant Cavalier, co-owned and

Peter Kubacz with Ch. Ramblin'Red Vanara winning First in Junior Showmanship in 1997.

co-bred with Karen Schwartz, who was Anne Marie's first breeder-owner-handled Best in Show winner.

Peter Kubacz was born in 1984 and shares his parents' avid interest in showing dogs. He has qualified for Westminster Junior Showmanship every year since he became eligible at the age of 10. He made it to the finals in 1997 and in 1998 placed second in finals competition. He also represented the US at the World Dog Show in Helsinki, Finland, in 1998. At age 12, he handled his dog, Ch. Ramblin'Red Zoom, to his championship. He was the top Junior in the country in 1999.

The Kubaczs have been fortunate to own two other Irish Setters that have enhanced their breeding program. Ch. Saxony's Evening Reflections, co-owned with Jean Roche, came to them as a Best in Show winner, but he had been ill and required intensive medical attention

Ch. Saxony's Evening Reflections, Randy Kubacz's first owner-handled Best in Show winner, winner of Best of Breed at the ISCA National Specialty in 1994, and Best of Breed and Group Second at Westminster in 1994.

before returning to the show ring. He rebounded to become Randy's first owner-handled Best in Show winner, winner of Best of Breed at the ISCA National in 1994, and Best of Breed and Group Second at Westminster in 1994.

Ch. Summerset's Special Deal, linebred on Kildavan, Glingael, and Guinevere, was a specialty and group winner obtained as a puppy from Debra Roig and Susan Reyes. She was co-owned with Bob and Marge McKay and became their new foundation when they returned to active participation in the sport.

Anne Marie was the recipient of the E. I. Eldredge Memorial Award from the ISCA in 1995. She is also the only person to handle a national field trial winner and two National Specialty winners.

The Kubaczs credit many people with helping and influencing them. Lucy Jane Myers of Draherin was open and helpful when Anne Marie was trying to begin her foundation. She also relied on Pat Haigler, whom she met when she bred to Ch. Draherin King's Ransom, to give her advice on breeding good temperaments. Two people stand out who have helped them achieve the skills in presenting and conditioning dogs. George Alston's handling clinics have given each of them the edge to compete with the best and not lose their composure. Both Randy and Anne Marie have taken the course eight times, and Pete has already taken it three times. Celeste Gavin was wonderful about helping them in their early years to condition and groom their dogs.

The goal at Ramblin'Red is to breed healthy companions that can compete at any level and to help newcomers who need the same kind of assistance they received at the start.

Linda Kumanchik, *Tameron*–Sanford, FL

Linda's family has owned Irish Setters since 1964. Her own involvement began in 1975 with a bitch of Gala Glen breeding and a rescued Irish male, who, though a challenge to train, eventually got his UD degree.

Their Gala Glen bitch was bred to Ch. Dunholm Clancy of Durin and then to Ch. McKendree's Bold Venture to produce Ch. Tameron's Touch of Velvet CD and Tameron's Three Times a Lady CD.

Linda's daughter, Julie, entered the ring when she was 3½ and has since shown many Irish and Cocker Spaniels in the breed ring.

Linda is involved in Irish Setter and Cocker Spaniel rescue and with pet therapy dogs. Irish Setters are ideally suited to be therapy dogs, Linda says, because of their loving, generous, and cheerful spirit.

Ch. Erinfyr Heat of the Night. Owned by Cathy Faas and Mary and James Lamphier.

Ch. Erinfyr Cormac, a group-winning dog that produced specialty and group winners. Owned by Mary and James Lamphier.

James and Mary Lamphier, *Erinfyr–*Winchester, VA

Erinfyr Setters began in 1976 with a graduation present to Mary. "Megan" was such a wild creature that she was immediately enrolled in obedience school. The instructor told the entire class how untrainable Irish were, so, of course, they were "forced" to graduate in the top of the class. At the same time, Mary discovered the world of dog shows. Ted Eldredge was a valuable mentor for the novice exhibitor. He provided the Lamphier's first show dog, Tirvelda Brynmount Ariana CD. She became their foundation bitch, producing several champions, among them Ch. Tirvelda Erinfyr Faelte. Faelte produced Ch. Erinfyr Brendhan CD and Ch. Erinfyr Brianna CD ROM. Brianna was bred three times, first to Ch. Meadowlark's Intrepid to produce Ch. Erinfyr Virginia Gold Cup. Bred to Ch. Powderhorn's Stars and Stripes, she produced Ch. Erinfyr Seannache, Ch. Tirvelda Erinfyr Seamus, and Erinfyr Sile. Her last breeding was to Ch. Erinfyr Cormac to produce Ch. Erinfyr Heat Lightning, Ch. Erinfyr Heat of the Night, and Ch. Erinfyr Star Heat.

Brendhan sired only two puppies by Gala Glen Roberta—Ch. Erinfyr Caoimhe and Ch. Erinfyr Cormac. Cormac was a group-winning dog that produced specialty and group winners. After 20 years of breeding, the Lamphiers decided they needed to add to their breeding program and did so with Ch. Heatherwood's Sweet Crimson and Seregon First Lady. Young hopefuls that descend from these bitches have been bred to their stud dogs.

Kathleen and Michael Landon, *Trendsetters–*Louisburg, NC

"Blarney" (Ch. Costa Brava's Clearly Blarney) entered the Landons' lives in 1976. He was soon followed by his half-brother, "Ryan" (Ch. Costa Brava's Diplomat). Both of

The foundation for Trendsetters Kennels (from left to right); Ch. Scarlly's Road Runner ROM at 11 years of age and Ch. Legacy's Summer Surprise at 9 years of age. Owned by Kathleen and Michael Landon.

these were of Tirvelda breeding. Deciding that one more wouldn't hurt, they purchased "Lenny" (Ch. Scarlly's Road Runner ROM). They weren't looking for a bitch, but as things happen, "Super," (Ch. Legacy's Summer Surprise ROM) was looking for an owner. Blarney, Lenny, and Super became the foundation of Trendsetters. Blarney sired two litters, producing six champions. Super earned her ROM with 11 champions, and Lenny produced 19 champions. All Trendsetters' dogs go back to one or more of these three.

Ryan was Winners Dog at the 1982 National Specialty under breeder-judge Ray Gonsor, one of their most exciting wins. The following year, Lenny was Best of Winners at the 1983 National Specialty under Dick Webb, another breeder-judge. National Specialties were always lucky shows for Kathleen, as several others placed in large classes at successive nationals.

Nothing could top Lenny's Best of Breed from the Veteran's class at the 1989 National Specialty under Barbara Heller. Kathleen says, "I wish for everyone who loves an Irish Setter the pure joy of having your heart at the end of the lead, as I did that day. The icing on the cake—the victory lap in the classic Morgan Roadster, courtesy of Bill Conner, was the most fun I've ever had at a dog show."

The Landons are proud of all the dogs they have bred, but the most successful from a show standpoint is Ch. Trendsetters' Steppin'Out, owned and shown by Bob and Patty Cowie. She gave them Breeders of the ISCA Best Bitch award for 1994, and they are grateful to the Cowies for campaigning her.

Now into their fourth generation of homebred champions, the Landons plan to continue breeding a litter only every couple of years. Their grand ambition is to breed primarily for themselves and to be proud of what they breed.

Ron and Vicki Larmour, *Sierra Lyn*–Ramona, CA

Sierra Lyn Irish Setters began in 1977 when Vicki purchased her first pet from a family member. Her first show Irish came from the originator of Rusticwoods Setters, Ann Miller. He was Ch. Rusticwoods Lovers Moon ("Romeo"). Ch. Brookfield Frontier Glory ("Kate") followed and later came Powderhorn's Fourth of July and Ch. Challenge Never Been Kissed. Their first homebred champion was Ch. Sierra Lyn Fame and Glory. They have produced many champions from this foundation stock, the most recent being Sierra Lyn's Academy Award ("Oscar").

The Larmours have attended National Specialties since 1986 and are active in the Irish Setter Club of San Diego.

Linda and Doug Lenehan, *Ballingarry*–Des Moines, IA

Linda purchased her first Irish from former breeder Christine Lawrence in 1966. That six-week-old puppy became Ch. Sherry's Kelly of Brian Adair CDX. Linda has bred only three litters, the most notable of which

Ch. Ballingarry Phantom Jet CD, a group and specialty winner. Owned by Linda and Doug Lenehan.

was that of her bitch, Ch. Cloverleaf's Forevermore, to Ch. Courtwood Golden Gate. Six finished from the Ballingarry "Jet" litter including Phantom Jet CD, I'm Jetsetter CD, Jetaway, Jet Stream, Jet Eire, and Jet Star. Phantom Jet, I'm Jetsetter, and Jetaway were specialty and group winners. Phantom Jet (dog) and Jetaway (bitch) have produced specialty and group winners. The Lenehans hope to carry on the Ballingarry name with Ch. Courtwood

Ch. Ballingarry Jetaway. Owned by Linda and Doug Lenehan.

Country Song, Phantom Jet's great-great-granddaughter.

Ione Lienke, *Bellaire*–Andover, MN

Ione started in Irish Setters in 1976 with a pet she purchased for ten dollars from a local breeder. Not of great show quality, he was nonetheless a prized companion. Deciding to enter the world of shows, she acquired a Ch. Courtwood Summer Forecast daughter and Ch. Charlton's Moon Lover daughter. Neither of these finished, and she bought Ch. Hallmark's Changing Leads from Eileen Miller, Bonnie Jo Hall, and Gail Tannenhaus. After a successful career, he went to live in Mississippi with Karen Christensen.

Ione was compelled to be without a dog for several years, but recently she went back to Sue Hahnen and purchased Ch. Courtwood Tin Whistle (Ch. Courtwood Grand Hotel ex Ch. Courtwood Bag O'Tricks). This bitch is a littermate to Ch. Courtwood Town Hall and Ch. Courtwood Tail Wind.

Marge Lippman, Ridgewood, NJ

Marge adopted her first Irish Setter, "Rusty," while she was still in high school. He was an abused dog with six months to live. With Marge's good care, he lived to be 12 years old and was her best friend. Because of Rusty, Marge became interested in rescue, and in the past 28 years, she has been able to place 1,107 Irish in new homes.

When Rusty died, she was given another rescue, "Brandy," who lived for 13 years. She then obtained Brandy's Autumn of Gabhantyr Am. Can. CD from Celeste Gavin. He was her companion for 17 years.

Marge was finally ready for her first show dog in 1994 and purchased from Nancy Conner (Tainaron) a puppy that became Am. Can. Ch. Tainaron Harbor Lights CGC. For Marge, Alex is a once-in-a-lifetime dog because the experience of showing him was new and wonderful.

Am. Can. Ch. Tainaron Harbor Lights CGC winning Group First at the Tioga County Kennel Club in 1998. Owned by Marjorie Lippman.

Her twin goddaughters, Lauren and Debbie Schwartz, started in junior showmanship at the age of 14. They both worked for top handlers, qualified for Westminster, and were ranked among the top juniors. Now in college, they will show dogs on their vacation and summer breaks. They showed Alex to several of his numerous breed and group wins. They feel that dog shows have contributed to their education in sportsmanship and responsibility. Marge is justly proud of her two charges.

Donna Long, *Chandar*–West Columbia, SC

When Donna was 13 years old, neighbors moved in across the street that would profoundly affect her life. They were mother and daughter dog fanciers, and from them she received her first show dogs, Doberman Pinschers and Miniature Pinschers. After she saw and purchased her first Irish, however, it was as if no other breed existed. Her first Irish were of pet quality, but she waited and eventually purchased from Laurie Conlon of Palomar Setters her foundation bitch, Palomar's Joy of Chandar ROM. Joy was also the dam of Ch. Chandar's Jillian ROM. Joy gave her offspring sound Irish temperaments and movement, along with "lots of angles," which Donna believes an Irish needs. Donna has bred 32 champions to date, including group and specialty winners.

Palomar's Joy of Chandar CD CGC, foundation bitch for Donna Long's Chandar Kennels.

Donna believes that her success has been the result of following a breeding plan, linebreeding, and using dogs that she believes fit the standard with pedigrees that complement and consolidate that ideal. She likes to look at the entire dog, but winning or popularity is not a prerequisite. She bred to Ch. Shawnee Pipedream O'Charlton ROM before he had his first point and did the same with Ch. Killary's Bert Reynolds. Draherin Pied Piper and Rendition Big Apple never attained their championships, but each produced three champions when bred to Chandar bitches. She has heavily linebred on Ch. Candia Indeed ROM with great success. She credits her foundation bitch, Joy, and Ch. Shawnee Pipedream O'Charlton ROM, her foundation stud dog, with giving her puppies soft, sweet temperaments.

Recently, Donna began working her Irish in the field, and she finds this endeavor to be especially rewarding. Not only are they doing what they have been bred for, but she says, "We are in the great outdoors, and it is wonderful! The dogs and I both love it! It is amazing to me, that after five generations of not considering this aspect of Irish Setters in my breeding program, they are still 'bird dogs.'"

Earl and Patricia Long, *Bretmoor*–Haymarket, VA

Earl and Pat have had Irish Setters for many years. Their most notable dog was acquired from Ted Eldredge. He is Ch. Tirvelda Instant Replay UD. After several years'

Ch. Tirvelda Instant Replay UD. Owned by Earl and Patricia Long.

absence from the show ring, they bred a litter with Joe and Gerry Lee by "Bret" out of Ch. Kenobi Chasin' The Tides. Several of these young dogs are in the show ring under the Bretmoor prefix.

Wendy Loyns, *Souvenir*–Manteca, CA

Souvenir began in 1978 with the purchase of an eight-week-old puppy that later became Ch. Rendition

Souvenir's Counterfire CD taking Best of Winners at the Camellia County Kennel Club in 1995. Owned by Wendy Loyns.

Sha's Confidence (Ch. Ash-Ling Celebration ex Renditon Siobhan). "Shea" was bred to Brookfield Frontier Warrier (Ch. Kilgary Dungannon ex Ch. Shawnee Indian Sonnet). All the puppies in this litter were lost to parvo except one bitch that became Ch. Souvenir's Canadian Mist CGC. Her first litter, by Ch. Rebellion's Lumberjack, produced four champions. In 1988, she was leased to Rebellion Kennels and bred to Ch. Rebellion's Ring of Fire. From this litter, Wendy kept Ch. Souvenir Flags R Flying, her choice to carry on her line. She was bred to a Ch. Scarlly's Showboat grandson in 1997, and this litter is currently being shown.

Wendy also participates in obedience. Her Ch. Souvenir's Canadian Mist CGC earned her first leg on a CD title when she was 11 years old. She was 12 when she won the second leg, but unfortunately she did not live to complete her title. Two other Souvenir dogs who are CDs are Ch. Souvenir's Country Bumpkin and Souvenir's Counterfire. Souvenir's Patriot CD JH VC is owned by May Jean Ralph.

Donna Jo Lyles, *O'Deryn*–Pahrump, NV

In 1986, Donna became a member of the ranks of Irish Setter owners with the arrival of Windhaven's Kellee by Design CD CGC and in January 1988, another bitch joined the household. She is Am. Can. Int. Ch. Eirecrest Dark Jewel Am. Can. CD CGC (Ch. Auburn War Eagle ex Ch. Redheather Marquis Diamond). She was bred to Ch.

Two O'Deryn champions (from left to right); Am. Can. Ch. Eirecrest Dark Jewel Am. Can. CD CGC and Am. Can. Int. Ch. Kaerdon's O'Deryn ASCA CD Am. Can. CDX FD CGC. Owned by Donna Jo Lyles.

Kaerdon's Broker's Tip and to Kaerdon's Token of Love, both owned by Leta and Wendell Graham. These two litters contained several conformation and obedience winners. Retained by Donna and co-owned with the Grahams is Am. Can. Int. Ch. Eirecrest Kaerdon's O'Deryn ASCA CD Am. Can. CDX FD CGC. He has many group placements in Canada, and in 1996 was the top obedience Irish Setter in Canada. He is the sire of several pointed puppies and a multiple High In Trial dog, O'Deryn's Shadowman Am. Can. U-CD, owned by Bonnie Henry. A sister, O'Deryn's Something In Red CD CGC received two High In Trial awards on her way to her CD. She has several points in the US and Canada.

Patricia Lyons, MD, *Seanpat*–Glen Mills, PA

This kennel is based on the premise that the Irish Setter is a versatile breed and that any given individual should be able to perform competently as a pet, show dog, hunting dog, and obedience dog. Therefore, good health, soundness, intelligence, and outgoing temperament are of primary importance and must be considered an integral part of Irish Setter type.

Seanpat Kennels began in 1972 with the purchase of Patricia's Sean, a dog from Knockross and Rawlinscroft breeding that was never shown. He was known as "Sean Patrick," hence the kennel name Seanpat, because he is always first in their hearts.

In 1982, Pat bought a 16-week-old puppy from Mabel Coulter in Northern Ireland. She was from English Cornevon and Wendover lines and grew up to become Ch. Lurgavon Meagan Seana UD SH VCX. When bred to Ch. Kerry-Eire Gaelic Treasure JH, "Meagan" produced Ch. Seanpat Blair JH, Ch. Seanpat Brian JH, Ch. Seanpat Breeze of Autumnfyre CD, and Seanpat Beagan CD JH VC.

When bred to Ch. Lucky Morn Avant Garde CD, owned by Jan Ziech, she produced Ch. Seanpat Carlin, Ch. Seanpat Conchobhar, Seanpat Clasagac JH, and Seanpat Clancy CD.

In addition to Meagan, Hallmark Regency Ribbons CD, VC and Ch. Lurgavon Overture of Seanpat CD JH VC ("Kevin") joined the breeding stock for Seanpat. Kevin came from Ireland in 1984, obtained his titles easily, and produced Ch. Seanpat Anluan CD JH when bred to Regency Ribbons. Kevin's grandchildren are currently campaigning in all three areas.

Claire Marx, *Trademarx*–Windham, ME

Claire bought her first two Irish Setters from Betty Lowell of Maine. The first was Can. Ch. Tamarack O'Casey CDX, Can. CD. He was a wonderful introduction for Claire to the world of Irish Setters. Her second Irish became Can.

Ch. Tamarack Copy O'Casey Am. Can. CD VC. Her third was Can. Ch. McDerry's Gibson Girl Am. Can. CD VC.

Since those early beginnings, Claire has owned 15 Irish, of which 7 had VC titles. Her foundation bitch was Bda. Ch. Trademarx Kaison Am. Can. CD VC TT (Ch. Hallmark Jameson ex Ch. Redwhiskey's Kiss Me Kate), co-bred with Mary Dash. She was bred to Ch. Robi Lee's General Mac, her half-brother, to produce Am. Can. Ch. Trademarx Bold Elegance CD VC TT and Can. Ch. Trademarx Gaela Celebration CD VC TT. The latter, bred to Ch. Cucuhullain Eternal Encore CD JH produced Am. Can. Ch. Trademarx Stein Song and Trademarx Eternal Gaelwind CD. Claire also owns a son and daughter by Stein Song.

Claire is a believer in the versatile Irish Setter, and she enjoys all aspects of the breed. She is active in rescue and is the rescue coordinator for the Irish Setter Club of New England.

Amy Maxwell, *Tapestry*–Fairfax Station, VA

Tapestry's foundation bitch, Ch. Quinniver's Premiere (Ch. Rossan's Raz-Ma-Taz ex Rockherin Quinn) was purchased from Pam Schaar in 1988. A beautiful, elegant bitch, "Kelsey" finished her championship and was bred to Ch. Meadowlark's Vindicator. From a litter of four, three finished their championships: Ch. Tapestry's Royal Hue, owned and handled by Amy; Ch. Tapestry's Royal Vision, co-owned with Fran Jacoby, Amy, and Pam Schaar; and Ch. Tapestry's Changing View, owned and handled

Ch. Quinniver's Premiere, foundation bitch for Amy Maxwell's Tapestry Kennels.

by Amy. Changing View was bred to Ch. Quinniver's Intermezzo (Ch. Rossan's Raz-Ma-Taz ex Rockherin Quinn). This combination has produced several promising young dogs.

Ch. Tapestry's Royal Hue left his mark on the breed as the sire of a number of exquisite animals. Bred to Ch. Dunholm Militza's Prize Girl, owned by Roger and Tracy McNeal, he produced three champion littermates that are currently being shown successfully by their owners.

The essence of Tapestry's breeding program is elegance, soundness, and soft, sweet expressions.

Laurice Mays, *Carousel*–Tualatin, OR

Carousel Irish Setters was created in 1987 with the purchase of a puppy from Leslie Russell that became Ch. Avon Farm Carousel CD JH. "Katie" produced three litters on which Laurice's breeding program is based. Her first litter was by Ch. Avon Farm Wall Street to produce Ch. Carousel's Stage Struck JH. Her second litter by Ch. Lyn Erin Midnight Blue produced Ch. Carousel Don't Look Now, Ch. Carousel Look Out World, and Carousel's Take A Good Look. Her last litter was to Avon Farm Balboa Park to produce Ch. Carousel's Play For Keeps.

Stage Struck was bred once to her nephew, Ch. Avon Farm Mr. Debonair, to produce three outstanding bitches,

Ch. Carousel's Don't Look Now JH taking Best of Winners at the 1997 Dog Fanciers Association of Oregon. Owned by Laurice Mays.

Marti (Donnell) and Gwen Mazanetz, *Calmarra*–Menomonee Falls, WI

The foundation for Calmarra was laid when the Mazanetz family purchased a show puppy in 1976 for their 12-year-old daughter, Marti, who was active in 4-H, junior showmanship, and obedience with a pet Irish Setter. The new addition became Am. Can. Ch. Kimberlin Rockets Red Glare CD. He was Marti's junior show dog as well as

Ch. Avon Farm Carousel CD JH, foundation bitch for Laurice Mays' Carousel Irish Setters.

Ch. Carousel's Rave Review, Carousel's Paws for Applause, and Carousel's Standing Ovation.

Ch. Carousel's Don't Look Now was bred in 1998 to Ch. Jamond's Call the Play, and a litter of two promising puppies was born. Take A Good Look was bred to Ch. Avon Farm Just George to produce Carousel's By George, major pointed from the puppy class.

Am. Can. Ch. Calmarra Encore to Kimberlin CD, a multiple group winner and sire of several American and Canadian champions. Owned by Marti and Gwen Mazanetz.

a successful showman. Bred twice to Ch. Shawnee Indian Red Dove, owned by Carol Rossi, four champions and two pointed offspring resulted. All carried the Calmarra prefix.

The most significant for Calmarra was Am. Can. Ch. Calmarra Encore to Kimberlin CD. He was a multiple group winner and sired several American and Canadian champions.

With limited breeding, Calmarra has produced 16 champions and a number of obedience degrees. Marti is currently showing two great-granddaughters of Encore.

Karolynne McAteer, Briarcliff Manor, NY

Over the course of the last two decades and for the past four generations, all dogs and litters bred and shown by Karolynne trace back to the mating of Am. Can. Bda. Ch. Liafail Sea Urchin, acquired from Dr. and Mrs. W. McCrory of Liafail, out of their English Brackenfield bitch bred to Ch. Kerry-Eire Revolutionary. The get were born in Bermuda, since Lia was co-owned by Paula McAteer (Karolynne's parents were then living on the island) and Frances E. Robinson of Bermuda.

Of the 12 puppies born of that mating, 6 became American champions, and several were triple champions. Two from that litter are of particular note: Ch. Red Barn Revolutionary Star ROM, co-owned by Karolynne and Paula McAteer and Marion Neville, founder of Red Barn Kennels; and Ch. Kerry-Eire Coral Charm ROM, owned by Susan Griffiths.

Both "Star" and "Corey" were successful show champions, but they made their greatest contribution in the whelping box. Both received ISCA's awards as Litter of

the Year, Dam of the Year, and Matron of the Year. Corey's contribution is found in the profile of Susan Griffith.

Star was bred twice. Her litters were whelped by Marion Neville at Red Barn, and all her get carry the Red Barn prefix. Her first mating to Ch. Kimberlin O'Killea Of Top'O produced six American champions. Karolynne kept two, Ch. Red Barn Top O'the Line and Ch. Red Barn Molly Pitcher JH CGC ROM. Molly became a top producer, a National Specialty Award of Merit winner, a group and multiple breed winner, and Karolynne's introduction to the field. Her antics and good nose helped to put to rest the issue that "breed dogs couldn't find a bird to save their souls."

Also from Star's first litter, Marion Neville kept Ch. Red Barn Bright Beacon for herself. He was among the top-ten ranked Irish Setters during his campaign.

Ch. Red Barn Ranger Walker taking Best of Winners at the Wallkill Kennel Club in 1999. Owned by Karolynne McAteer.

Ch. Liafail Lyra taking Best of Winners at the Ox Ridge Kennel Club in 1997. Owned by Karolynne McAteer and Dr. and Mrs. McCrory.

Ch. Red Barn Revolutionary Star ROM received the ISCA award for Litter of the Year, Dam of the Year, and Matron of the Year. Owned by Karolynne and Paula McAteer and Marion Neville.

Star's second litter with Ch. Scarlly's Red Hot ROM produced another six champions. Star returned to the show ring as a veteran, retiring with the honor of Best in Veteran Sweepstakes at the National Specialty in Oregon in 1992.

Molly was bred twice. The first litter was by Ch. Liafail London Pride, owned by Dr. and Mrs. McCrory, to produce five champions. Her second litter was by Ch. Castlebar Command Presence, owned by the Hackenbergs, and assured her ROM status. From this litter came Ch. Red Barn Wild Colonial Boy, owned by Dr. Helene O'Connor. Bred to Marion Neville's Ch. Red Barn Valley View Velvet, Karolynne acquired a puppy, who in 2000 became Ch. Red Barn Ranger Walker. This dog provides her with the fourth generation of her breeding. She also co-owns Ch. Liafail Lyra with the McCrorys, a Coral Charm granddaughter.

Karolynne looks to Star as her ideal—a bitch of wonderful type and elegance, correct size, and with movement that set her aside from others. Karolynne says she had "so many" breed attributes and a wonderful, soft expression connected to correct planes. Apart from the obvious desire to have a beautiful body with sound movement, Karolynne wants open, welcoming temperaments that are so much a part of being an Irish Setter. She breeds a litter once every three years or so and keeps no more than three dogs at home—as she says, "No more would fit on the bed!"

Jeri Lynn McClure and Dixie Demorest, *Stoneypoint*–Hartford, IL

Dixie and Jeri met in 1970 when they both attended obedience classes with their Irish Setters. They became friends immediately, brought together by their love of the Irish. They joined the Edwardsville Illinois Kennel Club and immediately became involved in club affairs. Realizing that they did not have show-quality animals, they went to Bill and Patsy Brooks of Bayberry Kennels for their first show puppy. Bayberry Buccaneer finished his championship easily, and there was no looking back.

Their first litter was the result of a breeding to a bitch from Cecily Barker of Arab Irish to Ch. Rendition Erin of Sunny Hills in 1973, producing three champions. Their foundation bitch was bred by Louise DeShon, Valley View Ingenue, a double Michael Bryan Duke of Sussex granddaughter. Their first three litters were sired by Ch. Shannon's Erin sons. From that beginning they have more than 30 champions, all breeder-owner-handled.

Their first top-winning bitch was Ch. Stoneypoint's Ruff Stuff, whelped in 1980. Bred to Ch. Caitlin Excellent Choice, a dog of Courtwood breeding, their first Best in Show dog resulted. He was Ch. Stoneypoint's Ruff Ryder.

Ch. Stoneypoint's Storm Trooper winning Best of Breed at the 1992 Heart of America Kennel Club show. Owned by Jeri McClure.

Also in the litter was Ch. Stoneypoint's Ruffian and Stoneypoint's Genuine Risk, who was lost to bloat.

Ruffian was bred to Ch. Courtwood Marxman in 1986 to produce another Best in Show winner, Ch. Stoneypoint's Stormy Weather and Ch. Stoneypoint's Storm Trooper. Jeri and Dixie considered Stormy Weather, a bitch, to be one of their best, but she never was able to be bred. Storm Trooper produced several champions, including four bitches from his mating to Ch. Stoneypoint's All That Jazz. Ch. Stoneypoint's All That Pizazz was in the top ten in 1993 and 1994. Ch. Stoneypoint's All the Glory ROM produced the ISCA's litter of the year awards in 1994 and 1995 when bred to Ch. Meadowlark's Top Gun. Seven champions resulted from that mating. Stoneypoint's newest star is Ch. Stoneypoint's The Magician.

Dr. Eileen McDonald, *Nightn'gael*– New Rochelle, NY

After purchasing two Irish Setters as pets in the early 1970s, Eileen fell in love with Ch. Derrinraw's Sir Michael, owned by Ellen Reilly Passage, whom she saw at a show. In 1975, she bought a young son of Michael, bred to Am. Bda. Ch. Kimberlin Kyrie, from Claire Andrews. He became Ch. Kimberlin Brian's Song. Although he was bred and produced champions, Eileen's circumstances prevented her from continuing to breed and show for several years. In 1992, Eileen was given another Kimberlin dog and shortly thereafter purchased a bitch from the Kubaczs, who became Ch. Ramblin'Red Xhilaration, "Lara" (Ch. Castlebar Command Presence ex Ch. Ramblin'Red Vanara).

Ch. Ramblin'Red Xhilaration, a multiple group and specialty winner. Owned by Dr. Eileen McDonald.

Lara was a successful show bitch, with multiple specialty wins and group placements. Bred to Ch. Cucuhullain Good Fortune ROM, she produced the youngest Irish Setter ever to finish. He is Am. Can. Ch. Nightn'gael Ramblin'Red Kian, who finished at seven-and-a-half months of age. Littermates Ruset, Ciara, and Brook also finished easily. A subsequent breeding to Ch. Courtwood Heavy Rains, owned by Mary Thompson and Susan Hahnen, has produced several promising youngsters.

Eileen names Claire Andrews, Ellen Passage, and Ellen's mother as mentors in her early years of showing, because they helped her develop a philosphy about the dog "game," as well as imparted years of knowledge. She has also had a successful relationship with Anne Marie Kubacz in breeding and showing Lara's offspring. She plans to continue building on her foundation stock to produce occasional litters, with a focus not just on aiming for the the "great one," but producing consistently sound animals that will bring years of joy to both showgoers and pet owners.

From left to right: Nightn'gael Ramblin' Red Ronan CD, winning Winners Dog, and Am. Can. Ch. Nightn'gael Ramblin'Red Kian, winning Best in Sweepstakes. Owned by Dr. Eileen McDonald.

Pat and Carol McGarry, *Windntide*– Normandy Park, WA

This kennel was established in 1970, and because individual attention is a priority with the McGarrys, they have bred just 6 small litters in 27 years. They generally maintain three or four adult dogs. Nonetheless, they consider themselves blessed with a continuous line of extraordinary bitches. Their foundation bitch, Am. Can. Ch. Dunbrook Enchantment ("Tawny") was acquired at eight weeks of age from Jay and Kellie Zirkle. When bred to Am. Can. Ch. Tirvelda Hunter's Moon, she produced the group and specialty-winning Ch. Windntide Sophistication ("Roxy"). Roxy was Best of Winners at the sixth National Specialty show and Best of Opposite Sex at the

eighth. Bred to Ch. Dunbrook Love Is Blue, she produced Ch. Windntide Hot Cross Buns ("Bunny"), who was Best of Winners at the 16th National Specialty. Roxy, when bred to Ch. Meadowlark's Masterpiece, produced Ch. Windntide Cordial on the Rox ("Sophia"), the dam of group and specialty winning Ch. Windntide Sandcastle ("Sandy").

Four individuals from the McGarrys last litter (Ch. Windntide Sandcastle bred to Ch. Kaerdon's MadHatter) are currently being shown. Among the most promising is Windntide Making Waves, a Best of Breed, group, and specialty-winning bitch from the classes.

Over the years, the McGarrys' philosophy and goals have remained unchanged. Their primary reason for owning Irish Setters is for their companionship. They thoroughly enjoy their active, athletic, humorous nature and the treasured friendships they have formed through them. Of paramount importance is producing dogs that are of sound health and temperament while maintaining the highest conformation quality. They feel very strongly about the issues of irresponsible breeding and pet overpopulation. In keeping with those concerns, they have enjoyed rising to the challenge of consistently having top-winning dogs while producing very few individuals.

Bob and Marge McKay, *Morrigan*–Mahwah, NJ

The McKays' first Irish came to them in 1969 through a friend of Marge's who had bred her bitch, Red Barn Bourbon Holiday to Ch. Red Barn Duke of Sussex, owned by Marion Neville. Starting in obedience classes, the McKays were persuaded to enter a show. In 1971, Bob handled his first dog to their first points, a major. The dog became Ch. McKay's Red Baron CD and the start of an addicting hobby.

Ch. Windntide Cordial on the Rox. Owned by Carol and Pat McGarry.

Ch. Windntide Sandcastle winning Best of Breed in 1997 as a veteran. Owned by Carol and Pat McGarry.

Ch. Summerset Special Deal, a multiple Best of Breed, group, and specialty winner. Owned by Marge and Bob McKay and Anne Marie Kubacz.

Ch. Morrigan's Red Skye At Night winning Best of Breed or Variety at the Penn Ridge Kennel Club in 1997. Owned by Marge and Bob McKay.

Their most memorable win with "Red" was when he was chosen Best of Opposite Sex at the first ISCA National Specialty under renowned English judge, J. W. Rasbridge.

The McKays took a hiatus from active participation in the show ring while their son, Kevin, was growing up, but in 30 years they have finished six champions and four CD titles. Their foundation bitch, acquired from and co-owned with Anne Marie Kubacz, is Ch. Summerset Special Deal, "Katie" (Ch. Kinvale Send In The Clowns ex Summerset Elfin Mischief). Katie is a multiple Best of Breed, group, and specialty winner. Now, as a veteran, she has been Best Veteran in Show. Her first litter, sired by Ch. Ramblin' Red Verran, produced Ch. Ramblin' Red You're the One ("Conor") and Ramblin' Red Yuletide Magic, a champion in Japan and pointed in the US. From her second litter by Ch. Courtwood Heavy Rains came the group-winning Ch. Morrigan's Red Skye At Night, with others in the litter pointed.

The McKays' goal in breeding is to improve the quality of each generation and to do everything possible to place their puppies with loving and responsible owners.

Norma McKendree, *McKendree*–Jacksonville, FL

The family purchased their first Irish Setter in 1965, guided by Norma's childhood love for the breed. She was a bitch of Red Barn breeding, called Cindy, and upon the suggestion of a friend, Norma went to her first show. She arrived in high heels with four children in tow, but despite her lack of knowledge, Cindy won occasionally and the children showed her in junior showmanship.

Norma decided to raise Irish Setters, and the family moved to the country to accommodate their growing interest. Upon further advice, Norma contacted Ted Eldredge, who advised breeding their bitch to Ch. Tirvelda Michaelson. Thus began McKendree Kennels.

Their most famous dog was Ch. McKendree's Bold Venture ("Stanley"). Shown in his early career by daughter Jan, he was sponsored by Mrs. Cheever Porter and in 1975, 1976, and 1977, he was Number One Irish Setter, handled by Jane Forsyth.

Harold passed away in 1999, and Norma continues her interest in the breed. She has bred litters primarily for herself, keeping one or two from a litter. She believes that the best compliment to a breeder is the people that buy a pet and return ten years later for another because the first was so dear. She says, "The greatest part of all this, of course, are our beautiful redheads, but next are all the friends we have met through all the years of showing."

Velma McMullen, *Interlude*–Toledo, OH

The song "When Irish Eyes Are Smiling" had a special meaning to Velma's late husband, Bill, because it reminded him of his love of Ireland and Irish Setters. In 1970, Bill and their son voted to buy one of the red dogs, and McMullen's Kelley O'Shannon CD became part of their lives. Velma took Kelley through obedience to her CD title in three shows, and although Kelley was fully capable of going on to advanced obedience, Velma decided to enter the conformation ring.

In 1975, she purchased a bitch from Rose Ross of Meadowlark Kennels that became Ch. Meadowlark's Katy of Misty Morn, the dam of three champions when bred

Ch. Meadowlark's Katy of Misty Morn. Owned by Velma McMullen of Interlude Kennels.

Ch. Meadowlark's Captured Dream, winner Best of Opposite Sex at the ISCA National Specialty in 1994. Owned by Velma McMullen.

Interlude's Sonata, the future foundation bitch of Interlude II. Owned by Rosanna I. Porter.

to Ch. Rendition Erin of Sunny Hills: Ch. Interlude's Antrim Heir, owned by Susan Hoffman Fry; Ch. Interlude's Apollo, owned by Velma and sponsored during his career by Dr. Robert Helferty to numerous breed and group placements; and Can. Ch. Interlude's Apache Warrior, owned by Bob and Nancy Pressler. Two others in the litter were pointed. Next bred to Ch. Meadowlark's O'Brian, owned by Velma, Katy produced Ch. Interlude's Betty Boop.

Next to arrive from Meadowlark was Ch. Meadowlark's Captured Dream, Best of Opposite Sex at the National Specialty in 1994. Her first litter by Am. Can. Ch. Meadowlark's Mischief Maker, owned by Dave and Peggy Wampold, produced Ch. Meadowlark's Accolade, owned by Maggie and Wayne Ford (Herihunda), and Ch. Meadowlark's Advocate, owned by Bobbie Hartman of Lafayette, California. Others, including Meadowlark's Avalon, owned by the Wampolds, are currently being shown.

The second litter from Captured Dream, sired by Ch. Quailfield Mak'n Business, produced the "musical" litter, which is just getting started.

Velma wrote, "The love I have for my breed is as deep as my soul. My breedings have been few, but I am more interested in the quality that I produced. When selecting a male I look for one that will complement my brood bitch in temperament, health, and conformation, in that order of importance. I spend time researching the get of potential mates. Among the conformation attributes I feel are most important are movement, smooth shoulders and top line, expressive eyes, and the crowning glory of a nice headpiece. Finally, I admire a beautiful silhouette that exemplifies our breed."

She will be "passing the torch" of her kennel name to Rosanna I. Porter of Toledo, Ohio, owner of Ch. Interlude's Sonata, whom she hopes will become the foundation for Interlude II. Velma plans to apply for her judging license and will breed only occasionally.

Roger and Tracy McNeal, *Militza*–Glen Allen, VA

Tracy's first Irish was a rescue from the local pound, a wonderful family pet that greatly influenced her interest in the breed. After losing her in 1987, she purchased a bitch from John Savory of Dunholm Kennels. Honeyrock Militza of Dunholm became her foundation bitch. She was bred to Ch. Dunholm Kildare, a son of Ch. Meadowlark's Anticipation ROM, to produce Ch. Dunholm Militza's Prize Girl.

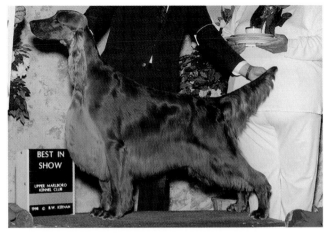

Ch. Militza's Tell Me No Lies, multiple Best in Show and group-winning bitch. Owned by Tracy and Roger McNeal.

Prize Girl, bred to Amy Maxwell's Ch. Tapestry's Royal Hue (Ch. Meadowlark's Vindicator ex Ch. Quinniver's Premiere) produced the "Tell Me" litter. From this litter came the Best In Show and group-winning bitch, Ch. Militza's Tell Me No Lies. Her brother, Ch. Militza's Tell Me Why, finished his championship in March 1999 with two specialty majors. A sister, Ch. Militza's Tell Me Later, is co-owned with Denise Hall. Tracy feels that this litter has been a blessing for her, and she hopes they will continue the success of their small kennel.

Caren McWeeny and Mary Dash, *McDerry–Plympton, MA*

McDerry Irish Setters was established in 1967 as the family effort of Mary, Arlie, and Susan Dash. Their strongest foundation bitch proved to be Ch. Redwhiskey's Kiss Me Kate. She was bred three times and produced six champions. It was Kiss Me Kate, bred to Ch. Hallmark Jameson, that produced Ch. McDerry's Jaimie Girl, an important bitch in many ways because she cemented the long-term partnership of the Dash family and Caren McWeeny. Jaimie Girl was bred to Ch. Courtwood Manuscript ROM, producing Ch. McDerry's National Jubilee JH. This bitch was bred to Ch. Courtwood Golden Gate to produce Ch. McDerry's Becky Thatcher JH.

In 1990, Mary and Caren purchased from Kate Seymour the dog that is now a leading sire in the breed, Ch. Cucuhullain Good Fortune ROM. "Devon" was awarded ISCA's Best Sire honors in 1996 and 1997. The introduction of Aus. Am. Ch. Quailmoor Jamaican Rum, bred to Ch. McDerry's Almost Illegal, has provided an exciting future, strong in type and temperament. McDerry's recent litter is sired by Devon out of his granddaughter, McDerry's Ain't Misbehavin'. They are hopeful that the potential of these youngsters will be realized.

Ch. McDerry's Becky Thatcher JH ROM taking Winners Bitch at the 1990 Irish Setter Club of New England show. Owned by Mary Dash and Caren McWeeny.

Ch. Cucuhullain Good Fortune ROM was awarded the ISCA's Best Sire honors in 1996 and 1997. Owned by Mary Dash and Caren McWeeny.

Ch. McDerry's Jaimie Girl. Owned by Mary Dash and Caren McWeeny.

Littermates from Lynne and Bill Mehring's Shangrila Kennels; Ch. Shangrila Moon Shadow (left) and Ch. Shangrila Majestic Galaxy (right).

Bill and Lynne Mehring, *Shangrila*–Highland, MI

Shangrila Kennels began in 1967 with the arrival of Ch. Red Cedars Prince Michael UD and Ivor Glen Katherine Colleen. These two dogs were worked in show, field, and obedience. Mike was bred a few times until the Mehrings realized they were too inexperienced to do it right. Colleen was bred to FCh. Cinnamon O'Delgado to produce their first field champion, Shangrila Maggie O'Casey. She was the beginning of the field line. The last of that line was Shangrila Nighthawk.

In 1973, Lynne purchased a bitch puppy from Betty Crawford for show and as a possible brood bitch. She was Ch. Shannon's Scarlet Urchin. Scarlet's only litter was by Tirvelda Eamon of Gabhantyr, but one of that litter became Ch. Shangrila Scarlet O'Hara ROM, with eight champions from two small litters. When bred to Tara Hill's Harvest Moon, she produced Ch. Shangrila Moon Shadow, a multiple Best in Show bitch with top ranking in 1985 and 1986. That litter also contained a top sire, Ch. Shangrila Stargazer, as well as Ch. Shangrila Eclipse of the Moon and Ch. Shangrila Majestic Galaxy. Next bred to Ch. Shangrila Southern Crown CD (Tara Hill's Harvest Moon ex Milesian's Merry Maura), she produced Ch. Shangrila Carte Blanche, Ch. Shangrila Country Squire

CDX, Ch. Shangrila Chrystal Candi, and Ch. Shangrila Carrousel.

Lynne purchased Milesian Merry Maura at two years of age, and she produced four champions. Her son, Ch. Shangrila Southern Crown CD, was bred four times and produced ten champions. Moonshadow was not a

Ch. Rockherin Shangrila At Last. Owned by Lynne and Bill Mehring.

The culmination of 30 years of breeding, Ch. Shangrila Annie Laurie JH is shown here winning Best of Opposite Sex at the Irish Setter Club of Michigan in 1998.

prolific whelper, producing only two champions. However, one of her daughters, Shangrila Silhouette, produced Shangrila Wyndchime ROM.

In 1989, I purchased a bitch from the Wheatleys that became Ch. Rockherin Shana of Shangrila. Bred to Ch. Rossan's Raz-Ma-Taz, she produced three champions. In 1992, she acquired from the Wheatleys Ch. Rockherin Shangrila At Last ("Luke"). When bred to Shana, he produced two bitches, Ch. Shangrila Dreams of Jade and Ch. Shangrila Annie Laurie JH.

Annie Laurie is the culmination of 30 years of breeding and a dam of 5 champions from her first litter, with promising youngsters in the second. Annie is training for her advanced hunting certificates and possibly for field trials. Annie was raised, trained, and is now shown by co-owner Martina Friedeberg. Her litter by Ch. Rusticwoods Song of Hawaii is still young.

Ch. Shangrila Kiss Me Kate (Ch. Dunholm Clancy of Durin ex Shangrila Autumn Harvest) was bred to Ch. Seregon Second Edition to produce Ch. Shangrila Candle in the Wind ("Bridie"). Bred to Luke, she produced five champions, the "Sweet" litter.

Ch. Shangrila Sweet Alyssum (Raz-Ma-Taz ex Shana) produced Karen Lynch's Kellyglen litter, co-owned with Lynne.

No matter the size of the animal, Lynne says, an Irish Setter must be elegant, yet substantial. Balance, movement, and good fronts are most important in her breeding program. She tries to breed intelligent animals without losing the deviltry that so stamps the Irish. She credits her success to the bloodlines of Tirvelda, Shannon, Meadowlark, and Rockherin Kennels, but she says, "Without the many good friends and associates I have made in the fancy, it would mean little."

Mary Merlo, *Evergreen*–Mastic Beach, NY

The foundation of Evergreen Kennels began in 1978 with the purchase of Mary's first show bitch from Joan and Ernie Viola and Dana Haskell's Kinvale Kennels. Ch. Kinvale Royal Irish (Am. Can. Ch. Courtwood Spring Son ex Ch. Kinvale Majorette of Kendel CD) became her founding brood bitch. Using the expertise of one of her mentors, Susan Hahnen, she bred Royal Irish to Ch. Charlton's Moon Lover ROM (Ch. Courtwood Summer Forecast ROM ex Can. Ch. Kinsale's Charlton). This combination produced Ch. Evergreen Promises Promises, Winner's Bitch at the 1986 National Specialty, Ch. Evergreen Poetry in Motion, and Ch. Evergreen Personal Best.

A four-generation portrait of Evergreen Irish Setters—Ch. Evergreen Best Kept Secret CD, daughter (top left); Am. Can. Ch. Evergreen Chase the Clouds JH CGC, grandson (top right); Ch. Evergreen Personal Best, great-granddam (bottom left); and Evergreen Kinvale Can Do, great-granddaughter (bottom right). Owned by Mary Merlo.

Personal Best was bred twice. Her first litter was by Ch. Courtwood Golden Gate (Ch. Rossan's Raz-Ma-Taz ex Ch. Courtwood Bright Ruby). That produced Ch. Evergreen Best Kept Secret CD, who was bred to Ch. Cucuhullain Good Fortune ROM. The only male in that litter, Am. Can. Ch. Evergreen Chase the Clouds JH CGC, was an Award of Merit winner at the 1997 and 1998 ISCA National Specialties. He is multiple group and specialty winner.

Personal Best was linebred to Ch. Kinvale Send in the Clowns (Ch. Kinvale Evergreen Destiny ex Meadowlark's Mystique). This resulted in three champions out of six puppies: Ch. Evergreen Belle of Panda Sham, Ch. Evergreen Be a Clown, and Ch. Evergreen Butter Brickle.

Continuing to linebreed on Courtwood and Kinvale, Ch. Kinvale Royal Irish was bred to Ch. Courtwood Manuscript ROM (Ch. Courtwood Moon Lover ROM ex Ch. Courtwood Summer Magic). This produced a litter of two, and the male became Ch. Kinvale Evergreen Destiny ROM, a multiple group and specialty-winning dog. A repeat of that breeding produced another two puppies, one of which is Ch. Evergreen Return Engagement. Return Engagement was bred twice, first to Ch. Kinvale RSVP to Panda Sham and then to Ch. Evergreen Be a Clown. Both of these litters produced champions, one of which was Ch. Evergreen Sweet Sensation.

The litter from the breeding to Ch. Evergreen Chase the Clouds JH is just beginning to perform. Evergreen Kinvale Can Do won ten Bests in Sweepstakes during her puppy career.

It is Mary's conviction that the Irish Setter should possess balance, both standing and in motion. The parts must flow into one another, without causing the eye to break at any particular area. She is a firm believer in linebreeding the best that one can obtain. She says, "By choosing animals that exhibit the conformation and temperament so desired in the Irish Setter and linebreeding on those desired traits, one should produce animals of that same quality."

Am. Can. Ch. Evergreen Chase the Clouds JH CGC. Owned by Mary Merlo.

Cheryl Mika, *O'Kerrie*–Monee, IL

Cheryl had three mentors in her life with dogs. The first was her mother, Lois, who came from a dog family that went back to the late 1800s. She was involved with Boston Terriers and Chow Chows, as were her parents and her maternal grandparents. She taught Cheryl patience and kindess and that whether it is the Best in Show winner or the ugliest dog, they all deserve respect and love.

Next came Larry Downey, an Irish Setter breeder and professional handler. He graded her litters and taught her to look at the whole, not pieces. Larry stressed learning about the breed because it is a breeder's responsibility to be educated. He told Cheryl that the most critical person in evaluating your dogs is you. He also advised her that show dogs are athletes and conditioning them is an art.

Her other important mentor was Bernie Baron, past president of the ISCA and subsequently its delegate. Bernie's wit and honesty immediately drew Cheryl to him when they met at a National Specialty. He reinforced Larry's commitment to education. Cheryl felt that Bernie always had time for her questions, problems, and joys.

Cheryl purchased her first Irish Setter in 1969. Sired by Larry Downey's Ch. Blayneywood Country Squire ex Ch. Shawn's Erin McCarthy, Erin's O'Kerrie McCartney had 12 points but was spayed because she had cancer.

Three bitches were important to Cheryl's breeding program: O'Kerrie's Kismet was bred twice to Ch. Kilgary Aman to produce Ch. O'Kerrie's Cherry Cherry CDX and Ch. O'Kerrie's Sweet Surrender. Full sisters, they solidified her type so that to this day, she can spot an Irish that is descended from one of them.

Two stud dogs have played a vital role in Cheryl's line and in the lines of others, primarily in the Midwest. They are Ch. O'Kerrie's Armagh ROM and Ch.O'Kerrie's State Trooper, who was Winners Dog at the 1990 National Specialty.

Cheryl keeps between eight and ten adults at her home. She says, "I may not breed the most or the best Irish Setters but those I do have brought joy to me and to others."

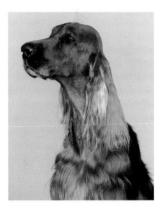

Ch. O'Kerrie's Armagh ROM, an influential stud dog in the O'Kerrie line. Owned by Cheryl Mika.

Barbara Miller, *Windkist*–Berthoud, CO

Barbara dreamed of owning an Irish Setter since she was a child, and in 1972, married and living in Colorado, she finally fulfilled that dream with the purchase of her first, Em Of My Heart. Although Em was her successful introduction to dog shows, Barbara lost her to bloat at the age of three. Barbara has never been without one or more Irish since then, but it was not until

Ch. Swashbucklers Olympic Special. Owned by Barbara Miller of Windkist Kennels.

Tramore Analainn's Darby came into her life that she was able to breed her Ch. Swashbucklers Olympic Special to her, and in 1998 her first, long-awaited litter arrived. She kept four from the litter to help her go forward.

Barbara has a rescue Irish, Brianna, that is one of the seniors in the Irish household, which also contains Swashbucklers Costly Kisses and a Brittany, "Hershey." Barbara says, "I am rich with red dogs. My dream turned into a Super Dream. Maybe the longer you wait the better it gets? At Windkist, the Irish Setters are 'Kist' by the 'Winds' of love."

Sharon Miller, *Willowfenn*–Fawn Grove, PA

Sharon bought her first Irish Setter puppy from the Fleetwood Farms Kennels of Virginia Rumbaugh. She was Fleetwood Farms Crimson Katie Am. Can. CD. Sharon bred both Katie and her daughter Can. OTCh. Fleetwood Farms Crimson Hope UD back to dogs of Fleetwood Farms, resulting in many obedience-titled dogs. One of them was Fleetwood Farms Crimson Faith UD, Can. CD. Faith was High in Trial at the 1985 National Specialty. She also bred Faith's sister, Fleetwood Farms Crimson Dawn Am. Can. CD, to Ch. Palomar's Skyrocket Corcaigh Am. CDX, Can. CD. This was the first Willowfenn litter and produced her first homebred champion, Am. Can. Ch. Willowfenn's Crimson Charity. Two other obedience-titled dogs came out of that litter, Willowfenn's Princess Daisy CD CGC, the first Irish to receive a CGC title. Daisy is owned by Charlotte and Danielle Prosics.

Sharon Miller's first homebred champion, Am. Can. Ch. Willowfenn's Crimson Charity.

Willowfenn's Christopher St. UD is owned by Evelyn and Daniel Kearon, the first Irish to achieve all his obedience titles within six months.

Sharon then bred Charity to Am. Can. Ch. Hallmark Art O'Dressage Am. Can. CD twice. From those breedings came many obedience titleholders and Ch. Willowfenn's Crimson Liam CD; Ch. Willowfenn's Truly Fair CD, owned by Marge Arnett; Ch. Willowfenn's Shasta Daisy CD CGC JH, owned by the Prosics; and OTCh. Willowfenn's Abbington Square UDX, owned by Daniel and Evelyn Kearon. In 1977, she co-bred a litter with Evelyn from grandchildren of Charity and Art O'Dressage.

Many Willowfenn dogs have been used in commercials and ad campaigns through the years.

Susan Miller, *Farpoint*–Sedalia, CO

In 1974, Susan acquired her first Irish Setter, a good obedience dog that served as Susan's demonstration dog for the obedience classes she taught. In 1988, she

Can. OTCh. Fleetwood Farm's Crimson Hope UD conquers the bar jump in the utility class. Owned by Sharon Miller.

Ch. Tramore Physical Attraction CD CGC, Susan Miller's first show-quality bitch.

94

Ch. Farpoint Tramore Work of Art winning Best of Opposite Sex at the Texas Combined Specialties Association in 1998. Owned by Susan Miller.

purchased a bitch of show quality from Ginny Swanson of Tramore Irish Settters. She became Ch. Tramore Physical Attraction CD CGC ("Hannah") (Ch. Tramore Never Say Never CDX ex Am. Mex. Ch. Tramore Joy of Allegiance). In 1993, Hannah was bred to Ch. Cairncross Second Wind. Only one puppy resulted from this union, Ch. Farpoint Miller Time.

Next, Susan purchased a puppy that became Ch. Tramore Uptown Girl (Ch. Saxony's Evening Reflections ex Ch. Tramore Kiandra). She was bred twice to Ch. Tramore Yours Truly, producing nine puppies in the first litter and eight in the second litter born in 1996, of which two are finished and others are pointed.

In 1992, Susan took another puppy of Tramore breeding, who became Ch. Farpoint Tramore Work of Art (Ch. Tramore Rich N Famous ex Ch. Cairncross No Excuses). She had a successful show career and in 1996, was bred to Ch. Farpoint Miller Time. Four have completed their championships, with others pointed.

Farpoint plans to continue with selective breedings of the new generation, both linebreedings and an occasional outcross. Susan aims to maintain high standards and quality in her selections.

Lisa Moore, *Deep Vu*–Tucson, AZ

Lisa's introduction to dog showing came from Jan Smith of Jadestar Kennels. In 1988, she met Jan Ziech and from her obtained her first show puppy, which became Ch. Lucky Morn Dann Eze Debonair UD. "Dann E" was Best of Winners at the 1992 National Specialty. In 1991, Lisa obtained a half-sister, who became Ch. Lucky Morn Thief of Hearts CDX, and in 1993, she acquired a field-bred puppy from Dennis Hidalgo, Firefly's Flash Dancer, who won the Puppy Stake at the National Field Trial in 1994 and the Futurity in 1995. Currently, Lisa has a litter by Ch. Analainn's Thyme Worthy ex Thief of Hearts. This is the first Deep Vu litter, named for a family hunting lodge.

Ch. Lucky Morn Dann Eze Debonair UD, Best of Winners at the 1992 ISCA National Specialty. Owned by Lisa Moore.

Dennis and Sue Murphy, *Redscent*–Brighton, CO

Dennis and Sue started their affair with the Irish Setter in 1980, working in field and obedience. In 1984, they acquired their foundation bitch from Barbara Riegle of Regalaire Kennels, who became Ch. Regalaire Royal Burgundy. Bred twice to Ch. Regalaire Music Man ROM, she produced Ch. Regalaire Strike Up the Band, Ch. Redscent Jack Daniel, Ch. Redscent Brandy Alexandra, Ch. Redscent Southern Eagle, and Ch. Redscent Tug on My Heart.

Sue and Dennis continued the next generation, breeding Brandy Alexandra to Ch. Regalaire McCamon Motown twice, in 1994 and 1996, producing two champions to date, with more being shown. Her third litter was by Ch. Regalaire Music O'the Moon.

From left to right: Ch. Regalaire Royal Burgundy; Ch. Regalaire Music Man; Ch. Redscent Jack Daniel; Ch. Redscent Brandy Alexandra; Ch. Redscent Tug on My Heart; and Ch. Redscent Southern Eagle at the 1992 Irish Setter Club of Colorado Specialty. Owned by Sue and Dennis Murphy of Redscent Kennels.

Redscent looks forward to continuing this strong and healthy line that Barbara Riegle and their foundation bitch have entrusted to them. They have also enjoyed the life and friends that this "crazy dog world has blessed them with."

Kathleen Murphy, *Weathervane*–Newington, CT

Weathervane originated as a small family kennel in Connecticut in the late 1970s. The philosophy guiding the kennel was and continues to be to provide the best for the dogs, whether they win in the ring or not.

Their first success was their Can. Ch. Kinvarra Weathervane Am. Can. CD. His loving and gentle personality won them over and opened the door for the males that followed. He was joined by Can. Ch. Nightn'gael Amber Cascades.

Can. Ch. Kinvarra Weathervane Am. Can. CD. Owned by Kathleen Murphy of Weathervane Kennels.

Following the death of their dearly loved Cloverleaf's Chariot of Fire Am. Can. CD, Sue Hahnen sent them a male sired by Ch. Courtwood Grand Hotel ex Ch. Courtwood Bandanna ROM. He became Ch. Courtwood

Heart 'N Soul, the seventh in his litter to finish, handled by Anne Marie Kubacz.

In 1996, Kathleen received the second Nightn'gael dog from Dr. Eileen McDonald, from whom their first dog came so many years ago. He became Ch. Nightn'gael Ramblin'Red Ruset (Ch. Cucuhullain Good Fortune ROM ex Ch. Ramblin'Red Xhilaration).

Kathleen hopes to continue with offspring from these beautiful and sound males.

Ch. Courtwood Heart 'N Soul taking Winners Dog at the 1998 Irish Setter Club of New England Specialty. Owned by Kathleen Murphy.

Roy and Shirlee Murray, *Kennlee*–Roanoke, TX

Kennlee was started in 1973 by Shirlee, who never considered herself a big breeder. Her goal has remained constant through the years; to improve on each breeding and keep one for herself to finish. She started with Thenderin lines and added Scarlly lines to it. She has bred more than 50 champions to date.

Ch. Kennlee Sunny Days ROM was a great producing bitch. Bred to Ch. Scarlly's Show'Nuf ROM the litter contained seven champions, among them Ch. Kennlee Speshal E'Nuf and Ch. Kennlee Silver Dollar Speshal, the latter owned by Patty and Henry Hunsicker.

Both Roy and Shirlee are professional handlers. Shirlee handled Ch. Meadowlark Top Gun to three Bests in Show and then bred him to Ch. Scarlly's Highway to Heaven. Shirlee also handled Ch. Scarlly's Spitfire ("Mary Lou") to Number One Irish Setter Bitch for several years. She was co-owned with Penny Nunnally and bred to Ch. Rosewood Anakin Skywalker, a linebred Scarlly dog owned by Shirlee. Five of the litter were important for Shirlee and for other kennels: Ch. Kennlee Love Me Tender, Ch. Scarlly's Love Potion No. 9, Ch. Scarlly Love of Kennlee, and Ch. Scarlly Kennlee Love Affair.

Ch. Kennlee Treasure Bay winning an Award of Merit at the 1998 ISCA National Specialty. Owned by Shirlee and Roy Murray and Patti and Henry Hunsicker.

Love Me Tender was bred to a daughter of Sunny Days to produce Ch. Kennlee Sugarshack. Sugarshack, in turn, was bred to Ch. Ballymera's Stormin' Norman to produce the "Treasure" litter. Ch. Kennlee Treasure Bay, co-owned with the Hunsickers, was First Award of Merit at the 1998 National Specialty. Treasure Bay's daughter by Ch. Donegan's Kennlee Devil is Due, Ch. Kennlee Duenotunderestimate, also co-owned with the Hunsickers, was also an Award of Merit winner in 1998.

Shirlee credits the first love of her life, Brynlaw Country Star, with making all her success possible.

Patricia Nagel, *Quailfield*–Angola, NY

In 1970, Patti brought home a rescue Irish Setter, Brad's Red Lad, for her son. He was tops in 4-H with her daughter, Wendy, and all during those years, the family worked in obedience and junior showmanship.

In 1984, she bought her first show-quality bitch from Sue Griffith. She became Ch. Kerry-Eire Special Treasure, and after finishing her championship, handled by Patti's nephew, Ken Wall, she was bred to Ch. Sunshine's First Rate. From that litter came Ch. Quailfield McCalls, a beautiful bitch that was a multiple group and specialty winner.

When Patti decided on the direction her breeding program would go, she leased from Sue Griffith Ch. Kerry-Eire Coral Charm ROM. She bred Corey to Ch. Meadowlark's Vindicator ROM, producing the litter that defines Quailfield. The "Business" litter contained Am. Can. Ch. Quailfield Mak'n Business ("Addy"), who was Number One All-Breed Dog in Canada in 1993 and Best of Breed at Westminster in 1993. He returned to Westminster at the age of eight and won Best of Breed and Group Fourth. He produced the top litter in 1993 and 1994, the Rusticwoods Song litter. Am. Can. Ch. Quailfield Business BIV Pleasure ("Captain"), owned by Joan Staby, is a Best in Show and specialty winner and the sire of Am. Can. Ch. Quailfield Prelude to a Kiss, Number One Sporting Dog in Argentina in 1996. Am. Can. Ch. Quailfield Risky Business is a top-winning dog in Canada, and the sister in the litter, Am. Can. Ch. Quailfield Red Hot Business ROM ("Flame"), owned by Joan Staby, has proved to be an important producer.

Flame was first bred to Hazelhill Sugar Shack, owned by Jeri Colella, and she produced the "Success" litter containing Ch. Quailfield Successful Magic, owned by Jeri; Am. Can. Ch. Quailfield Stylish Success; Am. Can. Ch. Quailfield Sure Fire Success; and Ch. Quailfield Successful Business. Bred to Ch. Tirvelda Once Upon A Time, Flame produced Chs. Quailfield Unforgettable, Moon River, and Moonglow. Quailfield True Love CD is major-pointed.

Am. Can. Ch. Quailfield Mak'n Business struts his stuff at the Westminster Kennel Club show with handler Ken Wall.

Quailfield strives for health, beauty, and overall soundness, but most importantly, they try to produce a temperament and personality that serves not only the show ring but makes a fine companion animal as well. Patti keeps about 10 to 12 dogs and breeds one or two litters a year with the help of her granddaughter Rebecca Hill Arch and her nephew, Ken Wall, who now resides in North Carolina. They have produced more than 25 champions and hope to continue the success of the Quailfield line.

Mary Olich Nie, *Glenavan*–Aptos, CA

The name Glenavan came about because Mary's mother's family came from Navan in County Meath, Ireland. In 1965, she attended her first dog show and saw her first Irish Setter. She was 12 years old and had begged her parents for a dog for six years. Her father said if she was going to get a dog, it had to be a "good dog" like an Irish Setter. She studied everything she could find on the breed, and they settled on a pet puppy, which they soon realized would never be a show dog. At the age of 16, Mary bought a bitch, linebred on Thenderin, that turned out to be Ch. Mistyglades Miss Magnificent CDX ("Maggie"), and finished her in very stiff California competition.

She was bred to Ch. Draherin County Leitrim, which was a real initiation into dog breeding for Mary. She was a senior in high school at that time, and it was a trying experience. Maggie became very ill, and only four of the nine survived, hand-fed and handraised because Maggie could not care for them. The two boys became the top-winning Ch. Glenavan Hallelulia and Ch. Glenavan Sensation. The two girls, Glenavan Magnificent Edition and Glenavan Taste O'Honey, became foundation bitches for Bynlaw and Ash-ling, respectively. Mary finished Hallelulia, who was later campaigned for a year by Mrs. Cheever Porter. Sensation was campaigned by Roy Murray and was the top Irish Setter for three years.

Maggie was bred to Ch. Webline Wizard of Macapa, and a bitch from that litter, when bred to Ch. Thenderin William Muldoon, produced Ch. Glenavan Shenandoah's Gaiety, a group winner.

Maggie was also bred to her son, Sensation, resulting in Ch. Glenavan Inspiration, who produced a nice litter for Brynlaw Irish Setters.

Deidre Morris, who owned Taste O'Honey, bred her to Ch. Draherin King's Ransom ROM. In that litter was the important sire, Ch. Ash-ling Celebration, who produced an all-champion litter for Tirvelda. Another in that litter, a bitch, was supposed to be in a show home.

Am. Can. Ch. Glenavan Inspiration winning Reserve Winners Bitch in 1975 under judge Ted Eldridge. Owned by Mary Olich Nie.

Deidre finally tracked her down. The couple who had bought her was in the midst of a terrible divorce, and "Katie" was severely neglected. She was 40 pounds of skin and bone, locked in a run in the backyard with no shelter, no water, and no food to speak of. Deidre and

Ch. LaPointe's Lady Kate Ash-ling CD VC owned by Mary Olich Nie in 1979.

Ch. Glenavan Harvest Moon, a multiple Best in Show and group winner, gives owner Mary Olich Nie a big hug.

Mary succeeded in rescuing her, and Mary took her home to nurse her back to health. When she was ready, Mary bred her to Ch. Tirvelda Hunter's Moon. The result was Ch. Glenavan Windbourne Moondance, Winners Bitch at the National Specialty in 1983; Ch. Glenavan Moonstruck; and Ch. Glenavan Harvest Moon. She was then shown and finished her championship in four months with four majors to become Ch. LaPointe's Lady Kate Ashling CD VC.

Moonstruck became the dam of many champions, and Harvest Moon ("Harvey") got his championship by going Best in Show over more than 2,500 dogs and finishing with another 5 points at the San Diego Specialty. Mary showed Harvey throughout his career to many Groups and Bests in Show. Harvey was a natural in the field and produced two field trial champions. Mary says, "I have had so many thrilling moments with my dogs over the past 34 years. However, nothing can compare with my memories of Harvey. He was and always will be the culmination of my many years of dedication to the Irish Setter breed."

Joyce Nilsen, *Thenderin*–Venice, CA

As a high school girl in Buffalo, New York, Joyce Holzman trained her first Irish Setter, Ranger's Red CD, in obedience. Before moving with her family to California in 1946, she purchased Ch. Red Ranger Pat (a son of Jordan Farm Abe), and the marvelous Ch. Kinvarra Portia ROM (Ch. Kinvarra Kermit ex Beg Pardon Rury Limerick). Portia

Ch. Thenderin Nobody Does It Better. Owned by Joyce Nilsen.

became the foundation of Thenderin Kennels, producing 12 champions. Her descendants throughout the country have had great influence on the breed.

Joyce became a professional handler and married a fellow handler, Athos Nilsen, who died in the late 1970s. Joyce has produced well over 200 champions in the years she has been breeding and showing dogs. By astutely combining her early stock and later linebreeding on her foundation, she has produced consistent winners for Thenderin and other kennels. It is impossible to list them all, but a history of a few of the great dogs and bitches gives an insight into their contribution to the Irish Setter in America.

Ch. Kinvarra Portia was bred three times. Her first litter by Ch. Ranger Red Pat produced Thenderin April Anthem, the dam of Thenderin Champagne, who became the foundation bitch for Joy and Nedra Jerome's Innisfail Kennels; Ch. Thenderin Amaranth, who when bred to Ch. Brynmount Maydorwill Brandyson, produced Ch. Thenderin Benedictine, the dam of Thenderin Wind Warrier and Thenderin Whistler, whelped in 1956, and Ch. Thenderin Endorsement, whelped in 1958; and Ch. Thenderin All Spice, who when bred to Ch. Rheola Shawn of Bail-lo produced Lucy Jane Myers' Ch. Thenderin Elixir and Joyce's Ch. Thenderin Echo of Spice.

Portia's second litter was sired by Ch. End O'Maine Luckalone and produced the great Ch. Thenderin Brian Tristan ROM, sire of 30 champions. Her third litter by Ch. Caldene Mickey Mischief, who Joyce acquired from Dr. Jay Calhoon, produced Ch. Thenderin Deeper Than Gayety and Thenderin Design By Fire.

Another very important early dog for Thenderin was the purchase of Seaforth Dark Rex ROM (Ch. Tyronne Farm Malone ex Ch. Seaford Velvet), bred by George and Barbara Brodie and whelped in 1947. He sired 20 champions and much of the quality of West Coast dogs can be traced to him. He is behind Innisfail, Webline, Varagon, Coppercountry, Whiskey Hill, and Thenderin. Rex, bred to Thenderin bitches, produced the next generation of top producers.

Among the bitches that Joyce considered her best was Ch. Thenderin Kiss. When bred to a son of Rex, Ch. Thenderin Nomad, she produced Thenderin Sunswift, who, when bred to Benedictine, produced the three prepotent sires, Wind Warrier, Whistler, and Endorsement. Kiss, when bred to her grandson, Wind Warrier, proved her worth as a brood bitch. From the first litter came Ch. Thenderin Drum Hills, whelped in 1958. He, in turn, when bred to Ch. Thenderin Mi-Spice ROM produced the "O" litter of seven champions.

Wind Warrier was never shown but was a prepotent sire. His most important offspring was Ch. Thenderin Chaparal Cayenne from his breeding to Thenderin Red Maeve (Ch. Seaforth Dark Rex ex Ch. Thenderin Echo of Spice). Cayenne was the sire of Ch. Webline Golden Jubilee, and the breeding of Cayenne to Ch. Thenderin Odyssey produced Ch. Thenderin Wind Ruler in 1963.

Wind Ruler was used predominantly on Thenderin bitches of great quality. When bred to Ch. Treasure Trove's Xmas Holly, Ch. Thenderin Winter Wind (Winner's Bitch at the first National Specialty in 1973) and Am. Can. Ch. Thenderin Woods of Autumn CD were produced. She was the dam of Ch. Thenderin William Muldoon (Ch. Thenderin Spellbinder ex Am. Can. Ch. Woods of Autumn CD). Joyce considers William Muldoon to be the best Irish Setter she ever bred. He was instrumental in the kennels of Kilgary, Kimberlin, Brookfield, and Brynlaw.

Ch. Thenderin Cherry Coke. Owned by William B. and Lois Allen.

Joyce and Athos handled all their dogs, and after his death, she continued to be active in the ring. She retired from showing upon the retirement of William Muldoon, and all Thenderin dogs after him have been handled by Charles Oldham, her longtime friend.

In recent years, Joyce has cut back on her breeding program, but some fairly recent successful combinations have all descended from her original stock. In one or two litters, she has done outcrosses. One occasion was in 1986 when she bred Thenderin Weekend Warrier to Ch. Liafail Western Venture. This could not be said to be a total outcross, however, because Western Venture was a Ch. Kilgary Dungannon son. Thenderin Timekeeper is another dog, outcrossed on the sire's sire, a son of Ch. Meadowlark's Anticipation ROM bred to Ch. Thenderin Profile. Timekeeper has sired several litters, including Ch. Thenderin Cherry Coke in 1987, owned by William B. and the late "Dilly" Allen, to whom we are indebted for the history of this kennel. He also sired Thenderin Next in Line in 1995, when bred to Ch. Thenderin No Nonsense.

The influence of Thenderin on Irish Setter history cannot be overestimated, and although Joyce seldom advertises her litters, the foundation that she laid 50 years ago lives on in the Irish of today.

Merri Norris, *Terra Cotta*–McHenry, IL

Merri has built a promising foundation on stock that descends primarily from Courtwood lines. Her foundation bitch, Ch. Sunnyhill's End of the Rainbow (Ch. Cloverleaf Follow That Dream CD ex Ch. Courtwood Bright Sunshine CD) was also her first champion.

Ch. Lili Marlene winning Best of Breed at the 1992 Westminster Kennel Club show. Owned by Merri Norris.

Rainbow was bred twice, producing three champions. One of those, Ch. Terra Cotta Melody, was Winners Bitch at the 1991 National Specialty. Her sister, Ch. Lili Marlene, was Best of Breed at Westminster in 1992. A recent litter by Ch. Seregon Foreign Diplomat ex Ch. Terra Cotta Say Good Night is now being shown.

Norbert and Sandra Novicin, *Santera*– Mt. Airy, MD

In 1970, Sandy and her former husband, Terry Newlon, purchased their first Irish Setter from David and Ruth Wilson of Wilson Farm Kennels. She was Wilson Farm Scarlet Tirvelda CD (Ch. Tirvelda Earl of Harewood ex Ch. Wilson Farm Partridge). Scarlet was bred to Ch. Ballycroy's Northern Sunset, owned by Fred and Connie Vanacore (Ch. Tirvelda Nor'wester ex Ballycroy's Rua Catlin). Santera kept two males from that litter, Am. Can. Ch. Santera Tristan Troubadour and Am. Can. Ch. Santera

Am. Can. Ch. Santera Tamberluck CD, a Best in Show winner in both the US and Canada. Owned by Sandra Novicin and Terry Newlon.

Tamberluck CD. Of the two, Tamber was the showman. He went on to go Best in Show in both the US and Canada. He was the 10th in a direct line of Best in Show winners and produced a son, Ch. Villa Dan Vallejo, that also went Best in Show.

Tristan was bred only a few times before it was discovered that he was a carrier of progressive renal atrophy (PRA). He sired five champions for Wilson Farm and Kinvarra before being retired from stud. Tamber was test-mated and found to be clear of PRA, so he was a great asset to Sandy's breeding program. She was fortunate to acquire a Tristan daughter from the Wilson's last breeding of Tristan, whom she called Wilson Farm Santera Hope. She cleared her test-mating and was thus able to be a major factor in the Santera line. Tamber and Hope are the foundation stock for their offspring.

Tamber produced 16 champions, with one litter containing 7. Erv and Ann Daniel bred the "V" litter from Tamber. He was also used on bitches from Wilson Farm, Kinvarra, Robalee, Devlin, and Wenvarra, among others.

A daughter of Tamber and Hope, Santera Hope Diamond, was bred to a grandson of Tristan and Tamber, Am. Can. Ch. Santera Bold Lightning, to produce three champions. They then bred Santera Limerick Lane Sally (Am. Can. Ch. Santera Tamberluck CD ex Wilson Farm Santera Hope) to an outcross, Ch. Ramblin' Red Kildavan,

Santera Hope Diamond, dam of many champions for Santera Kennels. Owned by Sandra and Norbert Novicin.

Am. Can. Ch. Santera Bold Lightning. Owned by Sandra and Norbert Novicin.

and kept three offspring, Santera Beau of Brooklea, Santera Splendid Aurora, and Santera Carriana. Beau is the sire of Am. Can. Ch. Santera Sterling Saber and Ch. Santera Irish Cream. Carriana is the dam of Santera Melodic Promise, who is the dam of their present young dogs.

In 1996, they introduced a Rockherin-Meadowlark combination by breeding Santera Melodic Promise to Ch. Tapestry's Royal Hue. From that litter, they kept Can. Ch. Santera Southern Sashay, who finished her Canadian championship in three shows and is pointed in the US. In 1996, they leased a bitch from Bill and Karen Kimmel (McBoscage) to breed back to Sterling Saber. McBoscage Marcella carries bloodlines of Wilson Farm that are no longer available.

During the first ten years at Santera, three or four litters were bred. Since Sandy and her husband, Norbert, have been active together in breeding and showing, they average at least one litter per year. They usually breed for themselves and look to place pups in homes where they will be beloved pets. They breed for overall soundness and have bred only dogs that have been OFA-certified and are also genetically clear of PRA. They strive to produce an Irish Setter that is healthy in all aspects. Temperament, movement, balance, and overall soundness are important. They try to produce dark mahogany coats and dark eyes.

Am. Can. Ch. Santera Sterling Saber. Owned by Sandra and Norbert Novicin.

Sandy was one of the earliest proponents of test breeding and one of the founders of the Irish Setter Genetic Registry. She is still actively involved with the DNA program for PRA and keeps the records of all test-bred, DNA, and genetically cleared dogs.

Penny Nunnally, *Scarlly*—Canton, GA

Scarlly Setters was founded in 1972, and the first dog to carry the Scarlly name was Ch. Scarlly's Sundance Rowdy. He was the first dog Penny ever showed, and he won six groups and a Best in Show, plus four Specialty Bests of Breed. Penny says, "With a beginning like that, you don't ever look back."

From 1972 through 1999, there have been a total of 265 Scarlly puppies whelped. Of that number, more than 125 have finished their championships. There are more than ten Best in Show Scarlly Setters, and Penny is into her tenth generation of direct linebreeding.

She has seven generations of ROMs on both the sire and dam's side. Penny's two foundation bitches were Ch. Rendition Irish Inspiration ROM and Ch. Rendition Razzle Dazzle ROM, and her foundation dog was from Rose Ross, Ch. Meadowlark's Masterpiece ROM (Meadowlark's Honor Guard ex Ch. Tirvelda Meadowlark's Ebbtide). The first breeding of Masterpiece to Irish Inspiration produced Ch. Scarlly's Showboat, Sassafras, and Dreamboat Annie. Ch. Scarlly's Showboat ROM was a two-time Best in Show winner and the sire of Ch. Scarlly's Show'Nuf ROM, a Best in Show and specialty winner, when bred to Razzle Dazzle.

Ch. Scarlly's Red Hot ROM, winner of 7 Bests in Show, more than 50 Group Firsts, and Best of Breed at the 1986 ISCA National Specialty. Owned by Penny Nunnally.

Penny's biggest winner and favorite of all time was Ch. Scarlly's Red Hot ROM ("Smokey") (Ch. Scarlly's Show'Nuf ROM ex Ch. Scarlly's Sweet Success ROM). He was Best of Breed at the ISCA National Specialty in 1986 and had 7 Bests in Show and more than 50 Group Firsts. His sister, Ch. Scarlly's Spitfire, co-owned with Shirlee Murray, won 6 Bests in Show and more than 30 Group Firsts.

Ch. Saxony's Evening Reflections ROM, a Red Hot son, owned by Jean Roche, was another National Specialty and Best in Show winner, when co-owned with Randy Kubacz. A Show'Nuf daughter, Ch. Scarlly's Up Front ROM, when bred to Evening Reflections, produced 15 puppies in two litters and 14 champions. Ch. Scarlly's

Four generations of ROM's from Scarlly Setters (from left to right): Ch. Scarlly's Up Front, great-granddaughter; Ch. Scarlly's My Sky, granddaughter; Ch. Scarlly's Sweet Success, daughter; and Ch. Rendition Irish Inspiration, mother.

Ch. Scarlly's Show 'Nuf ROM, a Best in Show and specialty winner. Owned by Penny Nunnally.

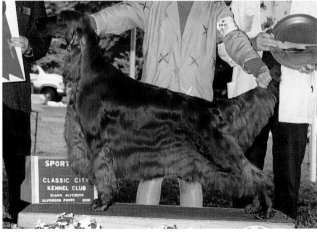

Ch. Scarlly's Gift Wrapped, winner of six Group Firsts and six specialty Bests of Breed. Owned by Penny Nunnally.

Gift Wrapped was a product of a brother/sister breeding of Up Front to Evening Relections. She won six Group Firsts and six specialty Bests of Breed. Penny feels she would have done much better, but Penny's bout with cancer distressed the bitch, and she never quite recovered the verve she had before.

In addition to the sires' tremendous influence on Scarlly and many other lines throughout the country, Penny's bitches were great producers. Ch. Scarlly's Sweet Success ROM (Ch. Meadowlark's Masterpiece ROM ex Ch. Rendition Irish Inspiration ROM) is the top-producing bitch in breed history, with 24 champion offspring. Following her, Ch. Scarlly's My Sky ROM was the dam of 19 champions. Ch. Scarlly's Up Front ROM produced 14 champions out of 15 puppies in two breedings to Evening Reflections. Ch. Scarlly's It's About Time, an Up Front and Evening Reflections daughter, was bred to her brother, Ch. Scarlly Renegade, and produced six puppies. Five are finished and two are Group First winners. Another of that breeding, Ch. Scarlly's Rampage, was the Number One Sporting Dog in Canada for two years.

Scarlly Setters was ISCA's Breeder of the Year in 1983, 1984, 1985, 1987, 1988, and 1989. This was accomplished by breeding only one litter a year. Penny is a firm believer in linebreeding and inbreeding. She has outcrossed twice in 27 years, and those outcrosses were half Scarlly breeding.

She has had especially good fortune at National Specialties. In addition to Red Hot, Ch. Scarlly's Dreamboat Annie was Best of Opposite Sex from the Veterans Class. She had two Bests of Winners—Ch. Scarlly's Road Runner, who was also Best of Breed as a Veteran, and Ch. Scarlly's Sky Rocket. A Road Runner sister, Ch Scarlly's Looney Tunes, was Winners Bitch, and the 1997 Best of Winners, owned by Ron Talmadge, Ch.

Ch. Dana Si Heartily Opulence, the first Japanese-bred Irish Setter to gain her AKC championship. Owned by Ron Talmadge.

Dana Si Heartily Opulence, is a Japanese-bred bitch directly bred from two Scarlly champions. She is also the first Japanese-bred Irish Setter to gain her AKC championship.

In 1997, Penny formed a partnership with Ron Talmadge, previously of Tokyo, Japan, and now of Portland, Oregon. Penny says she believes, "There are great new worlds to conquer and a tradition to maintain."

Jim and Glenna O'Dell, *Coolmeadow–* Fort Worth, TX

Glenna and Jim acquired their first Irish Setter in 1978, and by 1985, they became interested in dog shows. Soon after, they received their first show prospect, Ch. Sailaway's Brigantine AKC UKC CD. At the 1990 National Obedience Trial, a brace with Glenna and her two bitches placed first. In 1991, they met Jan Smith (Jadestar Kennels), and co-owned a bitch with her, Ch. Jadestar Joyride AKC UKC CD. She became the foundation for Coolmeadow Setters. Joy's first litter was sired by Ch. Tainaron Racing Silks CD, owned by Nancy Conner. The first champion from that litter is Ch. Coolmeadow Northern Spy.

Glenna and Jim credit several people for giving them help and advice. Their mentors were Sue Summers, who first introduced them to shows; Jan Creighton (Tralkillon), who taught handling classes for the Fort Worth Kennel Club and gave them so much more additional help; Jan Smith, for teaching them what dog shows are all about: "good friends and good food!" as well as giving them their start in breeding; and Nancy Conner, who has enjoyed each and every point the litter has won and has willingly shared her knowledge with and encouraged each owner of a Coolmeadow pup.

Glenn R. and Roseline G. Olsen, *Glenrose–* Wasilla, AK

The Olsens began in Irish in the 1970s with a pet that they bought through a newspaper ad. Their second Irish came a few years letter and was a rescue that was given to them. There is a great story about their dog "Kelly" and her life on the road with Glenn. He is a long-haul truck owner-operator-driver on a weekly route from Anchorage to Prudhoe Bay oil fields. Kelly went with him in his truck for eight or nine years and they had many adventures together. One of the most memorable was the time she saved Glenn from a grizzly bear. They traveled north almost every week, many times in bad weather, and had to share a sleeping bag more than once. Because of truck breakdowns, Kelly and Glenn had to be flown from Prudhoe Bay to Anchorage three or four times. The last time was in a January when the truck broke down at 60 degrees below zero. That was enough for Kelly—she never

Am. Can. Int. Ch. Glenrose Lady Rietz, a Best in Show and group winner, winning an Award of Merit at the 1998 ISCA National Specialty. Owned by Roseline and Glenn Olsen.

wanted to go again. She died in Glenn's arms at the age of 12. Some time later, the Olsens were able to trace her sketchy history possibly to Mi Jean Kennels.

After Kelly's death, they located a Mi Jean puppy and named her in remembrance of their great companion. The new Kelly, Ch. Midream's Lady Kelly ROM was a good show dog and an excellent dam, producing seven champions. In 1994, her daughter, Ch. Midream Lady Brandy, was bred to Ch. Tramore Optimus Prime, owned by Dawn Westphale. Of 14 puppies in the litter, they kept a dog and a bitch, Am. Can. Int. Ch. Glenrose Lady Rietz and Ch. Glenrose Lord Excelsior. Lady Rietz is a Best in Show and group winner and was awarded an Award of Merit at the ISCA National Specialty in 1998.

In 1998, Lady Rietz was bred to Ch. Pompei's Executive, owned by Annette and Van Pusey. Two of these puppies were retained by the Olsens and the others are in show homes throughout the country.

Glenn says, "We expect to be in this business for a long time and really love the dog show world. Hopefully, we can do our part to improve the breed. We have met many nice people and are very fortunate to know people like Annette and Van Pusey, Dawn Westphale, Colleen McDowell, Ginny Swanson, and Jean Johnson. Without their support and constructive criticism, we would not be where we are today."

Shirley Opp, *Kenshire*–Stockridge, MI
Shirley received and showed her first Irish in 1954 at the age of 14. He was an Argo Lane dog from Ch. Esquire of Maple Ridge. The family became members of the Irish Setter Club of Michigan the same year. Shirley was taught by Marge and Joe Frydrych, and she showed in obedience, conformation, field, and junior showmanship. Her first three champions were in the late 1950s and early '60s: Ch. Argo Lane's Lady Dawn of Erin CD, Ch. Argo Lane Star of Dawn, and Ch. Argo Lane Peg O'My Heart.

She married her husband Ken in 1961 and they subsequently registered their Kenshire prefix with AKC. They later owned and showed Ch. Kenshire Killarney Kinsman.

An extended hiatus from breeding and showing followed as their family grew and commanded their attention. More recently, they own and have showed Ch. Ballingarry's Jet Eire and Ch. Scarlly's Goin' to the Top. These two, and youngsters from Jet Eire bred to Ch. Killagay's Dancing the Blues CD JH, reside with Shirley. Ken passed away in 1995.

Shirley says, "The Irish have always been part of my family and there will always be several of them around."

Ch. Scarlly's Goin' to the Top. Owned by Shirley Opp of Kenshire Kennels.

Anne Perfetti, *Gallivan*–Vero Beach, FL
Anne had always wanted an Irish Setter, despite growing up with her mother's German Shepherds, and at the age of 13 she acquired a pup from Pat Gallagher that became Ch. Gala Glen Barney O'Boy (Ch. Innisfail Flashback's Design ex Gala Glen Maggie Me Love). Later, she acquired Ch. Gala Glen Moonlight & Roses (Ch. Tirvelda Meadowlark's Encore ex Ch. Gala Glen Coming Up Roses). These two provided Anne's foundation stock, from which she has bred several champions, three of which were owned by Joyce Dowling (Kenmare Kennels).

Ch. Gala Glen Moonlight & Roses, one of the foundation Irish Setters for Anne Perfetti's Gallivan Kennels.

Charlotte Prosics, *Pinray*–Lebanon, NJ

Charlotte's first Irish Setter earned a CD and was a companion to her two daughters until the dog's death at the age of 13. They were then led to Sharon Miller, from whom they acquired Willowfenn's Princess Daisy CD, the first Irish Setter to earn a CGC. Daisy was also a therapy dog, trained and handled by Charlotte's daughter, Danielle, and a star in commercials.

The second Irish to come from Sharon Miller was Ch. Willowfenn's Shasta Daisy CD JH. She was bred to Ch. Mullinahone's Post Position twice. From the first litter they kept Willowfenn's Gloriosa Daisy, and from the second they kept a boy, Pinray's Eastern Red Cedar,

who lives with Charlotte's daughter, Danielle, and her family.

Linda M. Ratkovich, *Cloverleaf*–Crete, IL

Linda's admiration for Draherin and Thenderin lines led her to the purchase of her foundation bitch from Michael Johnson (Kilgary). She became Ch. Kilgary Castle Carra (Ch. Dunholm Finn McCool ex Ch. Draherin Temara). Shortly after that, she went back to Mike and purchased a six-month-old male puppy that went on to become Best in Show and specialty winner, Ch. Kilgary Dungannon (Ch. Thenderin William Muldoon ex Ch. Charlton Auburn Tresses). Castle Carra was bred to Ch. Marverbrook Camelot (Am. Can. Bda. Ch. Shannon's Erin ex Ch. Candia Ambrosia). From this litter came Linda's first homebred champion, Cloverleaf's Stone Fox. Stone Fox bred to Dungannon produced many champions in two litters. The most notable was Ch. Cloverleaf's Ascendant, who sired many champions for kennels throughout the US. A granddaughter of Castle Carra was bred back to Ascendant and produced Ch. Cloverleaf's Millenium, a specialty and group-winning bitch. Millenium's greatest contribution was felt through her offspring. When bred to Ch. Meadowlark's Vindicator ROM (Ch. Meadowlark's Intrepid ex Meadowlark's Magical Mirage), she produced Ch. Cloverleaf's Rusty's Honor, Ch. Cloverleaf's All Puffed Up, and two top-ranked Best in Show winning bitches, Ch. Cloverleaf's Who's That Girl, owned by Annette Izydorek Pusey, and Ch. Cloverleaf's Rebecca, owned by Sandy Jones.

Linda says, "It is important to remember and thank those breeders, Mike Johnson (Kilgary), Lucy Jane Myers

Ch. Willowfenn's Shasta Daisy CD JH, posing as a new champion. Owned by Charlotte Prosics.

Ch. Kilgary Dungannon, a Best in Show and specialty winner. Owned by Linda Ratkovich.

Ch. Cloverleaf's Ascendant, sire of many champions, winning Best of Breed at the Buckhorn Valley Kennel Club. Owned by Linda Ratkovich.

(Draherin), and Joyce Nilsen (Thenderin), whose dedication, knowledge, and fortitude provided me with their gene pool to produce wonderful companions and so many top-winning show dogs. For this I am humbled and grateful to write this history and to be called a 'breeder of Irish Setters.' It's been a wonderful journey."

The Clarendon Irish sled team on summer break. Owned by Laurie Raymond and Bob Crader.

Laurie Raymond and Bob Crader, *Clarendon*– Oregon City, OR

Bob and Laurie's first Irish Setter arrived in 1975, a wonderful, unregistered companion for 12 years. In 1985, they acquired a show puppy from Leslie Russell of Avon Farms, Avon Farm Street Dancer. In those days, camping, sailing, noncompetitive hunting, and companionship were their only reasons for owning a dog. However, they began to show in field and obedience and were determined to promote their idea of the versatile Irish Setter: "A well-mannered dog that can move easily from the couch to the show ring and yet maintain that keen desire to hunt for which the Irish was originally bred."

The first Clarendon litter in 1991 was sired by Ch. Rapture's Jack of Hearts and produced three bench champions, three obedience title holders, and one field title. With very limited breeding, they have succeeded in their goal. Their Irish are an integral part of their household, so they believe in early and consistent training. The puppies have their own chores, such as picking up their dishes and stacking them in the cupboard or retrieving lost snoods and toys. From the time they are a few weeks old, puppies are introduced into the Pet Assisted Therapy Program and have had consistent human interaction. In their opinion, the Irish Setter is the perfect therapy dog, combining intelligence and aptitude

for "tricks" with genuine love and affection and some rollicking Irish humor. Other activities that Bob and Laurie enjoy with their dogs are running them on their dogsled in the winter and traveling the show circuits in their motor home the rest of the year. They try to fit in some formal field training but have little time to spend on regular field work. They feel themselves fortunate to have such healthy, happy, and intelligent Irish companions to share their lives, as well as the wonderful human friendships they have made within the dog community.

Carol Rentz, *Edenderry*–Bridgeton, MO

Carol purchased her first pet Irish in 1971 and her first show dog, Arab Irish Sunshine Patriot, who became her first champion, from Cecily Barker. In 1977, Marilyn Shaver (Summit Rise) sent her a dog that became her third champion, Summit Rise Rampart (Am. Can. Ch. Dor-Rey Esquire ex Ch. Summit Rise Sonnet of Saraval). In 1979, Ch. Courtwood Butter Cake (Ch. Candia Indeed ROM ex Ch. Courtwood Bright Siren) joined the family, followed in 1983 by Ch. Courtwood Forty Winks (Am. Can. Ch. Courtwood Summer Forecast ROM ex Charlton's To Dream of You).

Butter Cake was bred to Ch. Courtwood Marxman ROM in 1985 to produce Courtwood Amazing Grace. After breeding her again, this time to Ch. Pompei's Touch of Class, Sue took two puppies, Ch. Courtwood Grand

Ch. Edenderry Graphic Art winning Best of Breed or Variety at the Matoon Kennel Club in 1996. Owned by Carol Rentz.

Hotel and Ch. Courtwood Gracious Me. Also in that litter were Ch. Edenderry Graphic Art, Ch. Edenderry Grace Note, and Ch. Edenderry Graffiti.

Grace Note, retained by Carol, has been bred twice, first to Ch. Courtwood Heavy Rains in 1995, producing four champions, and next in 1997 to Ch. Courtwood Innkeeper, producing two champions thus far. Both of these litters were co-bred with Susan Hahnen.

Three Stoneypoint dogs also make their home with Carol, as well as a stud puppy from Duane and Jackie Drummond, from the "stone" litter (Ch. Edenderry Graphic Art ex Ch. Jamond's Cause and Effect, whelped in December 1998), Edenderry Carved in Stone.

Sharon Rice and Cynthia Mahan Kullik, *Milesian*–South Lyon, MI

Sharon's first Irish Setter was purchased in 1965 from Joanne Hurd of Apacheacre Kennels. Ch. Sharon's Sweet Molly Malone Am. Can. CDX was to become the foundation of Milesian and began the lifelong love and commitment to this breed.

Molly was bred twice, first in 1967 to Ch. Argo Lane Mike O'Rourke to produce Milesian Wisp of the Wind ROM, foundation bitch for the Kellwind Kennels of Jim and Jean Shannon. "Windy" was the dam of three field champions from her one litter.

In 1970, Molly was bred to Ch. Muckamoor Candia Audie, and with this litter the partnership with Cindy Mahan was begun and the kennel prefix Milesian was

registered. Of note in this litter were Ch. Milesian's Merrie Meighan CDX VC and Milesian's Masquerader CD.

Meighan produced three litters. In 1973, she was bred to Ch. Tirvelda Earl of Harewood, producing Ch. Milesian's Peg O'My Heart, Milesian's Royal Flush, and Milesian's Merry Maura, owned by Lynne Mehring (Shangrila). In two subsequent litters, by Ch. Tirvelda Distant Drummer in 1975 and Ch. Courtwood Spring Son in 1978, she produced several champions. One from the last litter, Milesian Spring Fantasy, was a good producer for Milesian.

Two others joined the Milesian family, Ch. Tirvelda Galway Sonnet CD and Ch. Shangrila Star Gazer, co-owned with Lynne Mehring. Star Gazer, when bred to Spring Fantasy, produced three champions.

After this litter, Sharon retired from active breeding. Cindy moved to Petosky, Michigan, married Ed Kullik, and continues the Milesian tradition with descendants of the original stock. Recent litters are sired by Ch. Courtwood Grand Hotel and Ch. Courtwood Town Hall.

Both Sharon and Cindy have been active members of the Irish Setter Club of Michigan as directors and office holders. They continue their devotion to the Irish Setter and strive to adhere to high standards. Only OFA-certified and PRA-clear stock is used. Sharon and possibly Cindy may apply to become AKC-approved judges.

Barbara J. Riegle, *Regalaire*–Okemos, MI

Barbara began her association with Irish Setters in 1972, but the name Regalaire did not come about until after their foundation bitch was purchased from the McCamon Kennel in 1979. She had met Susan McCamon (then

Ch. Regalaire Music Man ROM, Best of Breed winner at the 1991 ISCA National Specialty. Owned by Barbara J. Riegle.

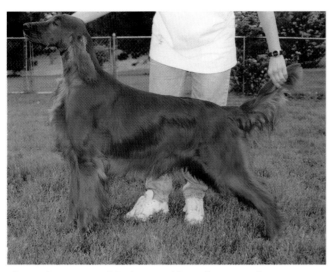

Ch. Regalaire Sweet Adelaide. Owned by Barbara J. Riegle.

Ch. Gwyndara Southern Cross taking Best of Winners at the Cudahy Kennel Club in 1996. Owned by Barbara J. Riegle.

Susan Korpan) at a National Specialty and was so impressed with her dogs, especially Am. Can. Ch. McCamon Marquis, that she was determined to start her line there. Am. Can. Ch. McCamon Northern Star was the first, followed shortly by Ch. McCamon Winter Knight. Those early years combined the kennels of Tirvelda, McCamon, and Rockherin. It was not until 1987 that the first outcross breeding took place. Regalaire Blush With Pride was bred to Ch. Meadowlark's Wyndjammer ROM, resulting in two offspring that have had significant impact on Barbara's breeding program.

Ch. Regalaire Music Man ROM won Best of Breed at the ISCA Centennial National Specialty in 1991. He is the sire of Am. Can. Ch. Regalaire McCamon Motown, Canada's Number One Irish and top Sporting Dog in 1995. Ch. Regalaire Sound of Music, a litter sister to Music Man, has also become important in their breeding program.

In 1995, a new and different line was introduced to Regalaire. A friendship blossomed between Barbara and Leeanne Jones of Gwyndara Kennels in Shepperton, Australia. Two of Barbara's bitches were bred using frozen semen from that kennel. Ch. Regalaire Sweet Adelaide and Regalaire Aussie Gentleman resulted from those breedings.

In 1996, Barbara acquired Ch. Gwyndara Southern Cross from John and Gerry Savory. "Cobber" was imported by the Savorys and has made his home at Regalaire. He has been bred to Ch. Regalaire Angel of Music, producing several promising youngsters.

The future lies in crossing the Australian-outcrossed dogs back into the original Regalaire line. Regalaire Global Diplomat and Ch. Regalaire Global Love Story are nice representatives of this strategy.

Barbara says, "The primary attribute of the Irish Setter is the magnificent beauty of the animal. There is nothing more pleasing than to see the dark mahogany color of an Irish streaking across a field or yard or strutting in the show ring. Temperament is very important with our breed. I enjoy the rollicking personality, wit, humor, and intelligence of the Irish Setter. We need to acknowledge that our Irish are first and foremost pets and companions and to focus on the genetics of the temperament we relish. Health is of utmost importance and at the top of my list of factors I look for in breeding stock. As a breeder, I prefer to select out undesirable genes or traits, even it means compromising my chance for a Best in Show winner."

Dyann S. Rivkin, *Rustic Sunset*—Nashville, TN

Rustic Sunset began on New Year's Eve, 1980, when Dyann looked into the eyes of a 10-week-old Irish puppy and fell in love. "Rusty" became the fulfillment of Dyann's lifelong dream to share her life with an Irish Setter. She named him Rustic Sunset's Promise, and with him she shared the most profound friendship of her life.

When Rusty was nearly ten, not wanting ever to be without him, she bred him to a double great-grand-daughter of Ch. Candia Indeed ROM. From the all-female litter, Dyann kept two: Rustic Sunset's Cherished One and Rustic Sunset Blaze. Blaze was bred to Tower's Down in Dixie (Ch. Sunnyhill Maverick CD ex Draherin Katie Scarlet). Of the three boys in that litter, Dyann kept a puppy that reminded her of his grandfather, Rusty. She named this puppy Rustic Sunset's Praise CGC.

Dyann says, "While I hope my puppies finish their championships, what is most important to me is that

Rusty's grandpuppies and his daughters are all champions in my heart, as was their grandfather, who with his loving heart touched my heart forever."

Bob and Pat Robinson, *Challenger*–Phoenix, AZ

Challenger Irish Setters began in 1973 with the purchase of their first show puppy, Ch. Portrait O'King's Challenge (Ch. Draherin King's Ransom ex Ch. Bryfield Portrait O'Eve) from Bob Field. A few years later, after an exhaustive search for just the right bitch, they obtained a puppy from the Courtwood Spring litter that became Ch. Courtwood Spring Breeze. Another Indeed daughter, Ch. Shawnee Prairie Challenge, was purchased as a puppy from the Farringtons. She was a litter sister to Ch. Shawnee Pipedream O'Charlton ROM. These two bitches were Challenger Setters' foundation.

The usual number of dogs residing with the Robinsons does not exceed six. Although they have bred two litters in one year on occasion, their normal schedule is to breed every two or three years, just often enough to have dogs for them to show. Pat says their pleasure is to produce competitive dogs that can be owner-handled to their titles by them and by others. They take particular pleasure in the group wins that several of ther bitches have achieved.

Over the years, their philosophy of breeding has evolved from wanting the soundest, most showy Irish Setters possible to wanting the soundest, easiest-to-live-with Irish Setters possible. "Perhaps that is a comment on our growing older," Pat says, "or perhaps it is indicative of the extreme difficulty of finishing Irish in the '70s when we began in the fancy; nonetheless, it is a point of pride that people frequently return to buy their dogs from us because they are so taken by our setters' temperaments.

"The beauty, bird sense, joie de vivre, and charm of the Irish Setter are often touted, but to my mind," she says, "it is the Irish Setter's adaptability, so often overlooked, that makes the breed truly special. Throughout its history, the Irish Setter has been a net dog, a field dog, and a personal gun dog; it has pointed, flushed, and retrieved. It has also guarded, defended, and rescued. Above all, however, these busy buffoons, these tender tornadoes, are the champions of merriment who long ago won our hearts forever to this breed."

Carolyn Roche, *Rusticwood*–Wellington, AL

Rusticwood was established in 1978 by Ann Miller-Donahue and Carolyn Thomas-Roche with the first Rusticwood litter by Ch. Courtwood Summer Forecast ROM ex Shawnee Wind N'Willow CD. This combination, known as the "Moon" litter, produced six champions. In 1982, Ch. Rusticwood Sierra Moon was bred to Ch. Thenderin William Muldoon ROM, a

Ch. Rusticwood Olympic Medalist CD ROM, sire of 50 champion get. Owned by Carolyn Roche.

breeding that produced three champions. Also in the Forecast ex Willow litter was Rusticwood Cher, who, when bred to Ch. Rebellion's Lumberjack, produced Ch. Rusticwood Olympic Medalist CD ROM. "Bo" is the sire of 50 champions, with others pointed. He was the sire of the Number One Bitch in 1994, Ch. Arista's Finest Rose. In 1986, Bo was bred to Ch. Kerry-Eire Little Rebel CD VC to produce the "Made" litter, in which five champions resulted: Rusticwoods Made in Heaven, Special Made, Made to Kiss, Made to Love, and Custom Made. Ch. Rusticwood Made in Heaven ROM was bred to Ch. Raptures Orion Rebellion (Ch. Rusticwood Olympic Medalist ROM ex Rendition Apple Blossom), which produced the "Party" litter of five champions. She was then bred to Ch. Quailfield Mak'n Business, for his first and most famous litter, the Rusticwood Song litter. There were nine champions out of ten puppies in this litter–two Best in Show and multiple group and specialty winners resulted.

Made in Heaven was then bred to Ch. Kerry-Eire Heaven Only Knows CD (Ch. Courtwood Summer Forecast ROM ex Ch. Kerry-Eire Little Rebel), co-bred with Kathy Whiteis (Sunshine Kennels). This combination

Ch. Rusticwood Made In Heaven ROM, an important dam for Carolyn Roche's Rusticwoods Kennels.

Ch. Rusticwood Love Song, a multiple Best in Show and specialty-winning bitch. Owned by Marilyn Wade.

Ch. Saxony's Southern Nights. Owned by Jean Roche of Saxony Irish Setters.

produced three champions. Her next litter by Ch. Durin's Kentucky Colonel (Ch. Meadowlark's Midnight Ryder ex Ch. Heatherwood Double Trouble) resulted in two champions. For her final litter, Carolyn arranged a breeding that she had waited 20 years for. Made in Heaven was bred to her grandson, Ch. Rendition Mercedes Benz (Ch. Rusticwood Song N'Dance Man ex Rendition Pretty Woman). There were six puppies in this litter, four of which are champions. At the time of this writing, Made in Heaven ("Joy") is the dam of 23 champions, with three more close to their titles, making her one of the top-producing bitches in breed history.

Ch. Rusticwood Love Song, owned by Marilyn Wade, was bred to Ch. Seregon Second Edition ROM before her spectacular multi-Best in Show and specialty winning career to produce Ch. Rusticwood Running Mate, a top-winning dog owned by Sheila Smith. Ch. Rusticwood Song of Hawaii is a multi-Best in Show winner, owned by Bruce and Mary Foote. Others of the Song litter have proven to be excellent show dogs and good producers, with several young litters on the ground.

Over 50 champions have been bred at Rusticwood or co-bred with others in a limited breeding program. With strong bitches as its foundation, Carolyn feels she has been very fortunate to have the depth of quality in her litters to be able to produce many champions and top winners from a small number of significant individuals.

Jean Roche, *Saxony*–Versailles, KY

Saxony Irish Setters began in the 1980s with the acquisition of a puppy bitch from Susan St. John Brown. To date, Jean has produced 13 litters. That foundation puppy became Ch. Serandida Saxony Sunflower. Bred to Ch. Marquis Midnight Special, a son of Ch. Candia Indeed

ROM, Jean retained a bitch that was to become Ch. Saxony's Midnite Forgetmenot. Sunflower was bred to Ch. Scarlly's Red Hot ROM to produce Jean's first owner-handled Best in Show winner, Ch. Saxony's Wildwood Flower. Susan was twice Best of Opposite Sex at ISCA National Specialties. Susan was bred once and produced four champions. Forgetmenot was then bred to Red Hot to produce three notable champions: Ch. Saxony's Tiger Lily, owned by Aileen Frazier; Ch. Saxony's Uptown Tangerine, a specialty winner and a good producer for Saxony; and the most important, Ch. Saxony's Evening Reflections ROM. Evening Reflections was Best of Breed at the 1994 National Specialty and was twice awarded Awards of Merit. He won a Group Second at Westminster. During his career, he was co-owned with and shown by Randy Kubacz.

Ch. Saxony's Casual Lies, a National Specialty Award of Merit winner. Owned by Jean Roche.

Tangerine was bred three times. The first litter by Ch. Scarlly's Road Runner gave her Ch. Saxony's Lacovia. The second litter by Ch. Pompei's Touch of Class produced Ch. Saxony's Southern Nights, and the last breeding to Evening Reflections gave her Ch. Saxony's Sympatico, owned by Judy Eaton.

Jean's recent combinations have been of Southern Nights to Sympatico. In the first litter, two National Specialty Awards of Merit ensued for Ch. Saxony's Casual Lies and Creme de la Creme. Jean then bred Southern Nights to Ch. Meadowlark's Irish Monarch to produce her latest litter of promising youngsters.

Jean has blended her foundation stock to outside pedigrees to strengthen quality. She feels that by going to different types of dogs, she can create the composite picture of balance, beauty, type, and flow of movement.

Rose Marie and F. Allen Ross, and Ivy Frank, *Meadowlark*–Midland, VA

Rose acquired her first Irish Setter in 1970 from Ted Eldredge, but that was not the foundation for Meadowlark. Two other bitches followed shortly thereafter. They were Tirvelda Samaria and Tirvelda Fortune Teller. From the Wilson's of Wilson Farms came Ch. Wilson Farm Royal Count. Ed and Helen Treutel sent them a full sister to Ch. Tirvelda Valentine, who was Sportmirth Pageantry. Pageantry produced three champions: Am. Can. Ch. Meadowlark's Drury Lane Am. Can. Bda. CD, owned by Curt and Nancy Conner; Ch. Meadowlark's Lance Corporal; and Ch. Meadowlark's O'Brian, owned by Velma McMullen.

Samaria was bred only once before being killed in a tragic accident. That breeding to Ch. Draherin King's Ransom ROM produced the "E" litter, containing champions Tirvelda Meadowlark Ebbtide, Tirvelda Meadowlark Elysian, Tirvelda Meadowlark Embrace, Tirvelda Ensign of Meadowlark, and Am. Can. Bda. Ch. Tirvelda Meadowlark Encore.

Rose also acquired Glen Cree Merriment ROM, who, when bred to Am. Can. Ch. Rendition Erin of Sunny Hills, contributed Meadowlark's "I" litter, Chs. Interlude, Impossible Dream, Inherit the Wind, and Indian Summer. Merrie also produced Ch. Meadowlark's Katy of Misty Morn, and when leased to Mary Ann Alston, she was bred to Am. Can. Ch. McCamon Marquis to produce Chs. Fieldstone Talk of the Town and Fieldstone Trace of Burgundy, the latter owned by Connie and Fred Vanacore.

Interlude was bred to Marquis to produce Ch. Meadowlark's Centurion, and when bred to Ch. Meadowlark's Anticipation ROM, she produced Ch. Meadowlark's Chances Are and Ch. Meadowlark Glorianna.

Ch. Meadowlark's Vindicator ROM, a top-winning show dog and Number Two sire in the history of the breed, shown here winning an Award of Merit at the 1992 Westminster Kennel Club show.

Ebbtide produced three champions by Meadowlark's Honor Guard (Ch. Tirvelda Michaelson ex Ch. Mos'n Acre Patrician): Masterpiece, who became the foundation stud for Scarlly Setters; Madrigal; and Moonlight Magic. Bred to Ch. Candia Indeed ROM, she produced Chs. Meadowlark's Anticipation, owned by Cindy Trefrey, Meadowlark's Argosy, and Meadowlark's Royal Nobleman.

Ch. Rendition Erin of Sunny Hills came to Meadowlark from Pat Haigler and produced 19 champions before his death in 1982. In addition to the Meadowlark "I" litter, Erin II produced Ch. Rendition Santana and Ch. Liafail Lovely Light. He was the grandsire of Ch. Shawnee Pipedream O'Charlton ROM.

To date, Meadowlark has produced more than 132 champions, including 7 Best in Show dogs: 5 in the US, Ch. Meadowlark's Anticipation ROM, Ch. Meadowlark's Wyndjammer ROM, Ch. Meadowlark's Vindicator ROM, Ch. Meadowlark's Top Gun, and Ch. Meadowlark's

Two fine examples from Meadowlark Kennels; Ch. Meadowlark's Masterpiece ROM (left) and Ch. Meadowlark's Antares (right). Owned by Rose Marie Ross and Ivy Frank.

Ch. Devlin Meadowlark's Illusion. Owned by Rose Marie Ross and Ivy Frank.

Meadowlark's Pop 'N Fresh. Owned by Ivy Frank.

Mischief Maker; one in Canada, Ch. Meadowlark's Muir Woods; and one in South America, Ch. Meadowlark's Rendezvous. Australian Ch. Meadowlark's Energizer, a Vindicator son, produced the first Irish Setter in 45 years to win Best in Show at the 1998 Melbourne Royal show, Australian Grand Ch. Eireannmada At Tulane.

Meadowlark has won many placements and awards at ISCA National Specialties. Vindicator was Best of Breed once and Ch. Meadowlark's Anticipation won twice, once from the Veteran's class. Those who achieved Awards of Merit are Chs. Meadowlark's Masterful, Muir Woods, Mischief Maker, Meteorite, and Vindicator. Ch. Devlin Meadowlark's Illusion was Winners Bitch and Award of Merit winner at the 1996 National Specialty, handled by Rose's dear friend, Marilyn Title.

Two recent winners that are playing a big part in Meadowlark's future are littermates Ch. Devlin Meadowlark's Illusion (bitch) and Ch. Devlin Meadowlark's Image (dog) (Ch. Meadowlark's Irish Monarch, sired by Ch. Meadowlark's Masterful ex a Wyndjammer daughter, Ch. Devlin Tara of Windsong).

Stud dogs that have made a big contribution to Meadowlark and to other kennels throughout the country and abroad are Chs. Rendition Erin of Sunny Hills ROM, Meadowlark's Honor Guard, Ch. Meadowlark's Masterpiece ROM, Ch. Meadowlark's Intrepid ROM, Ch. Meadowlark's Vindicator ROM (Number Two sire in the breed), Ch. Meadowlark's Masterful ROM, and Ch. Meadowlark's Wyndjammer ROM, the Number Three sire in the breed.

Important bitches for Meadowlark have been Glen Cree Merriment ROM, Ch. Meadowlark's Interlude ROM, Meadowlark's Magic Genie ROM, Meadowlark's Magical Mirage ROM, Meadowlark's Solitaire ROM,

Meadowlark's Forever Magic, an up-and-coming dog for Meadowlark Kennels. Owned by Rose Marie Ross and Ivy Frank.

Ch. Tirvelda Meadowlark's Ebbtide ROM, and Ch. Meadowlark's Whisperin' Breeze ROM, owned by Patti Clawson.

Rose and Ivy's current crop of bitches contains Ch. Meadowlark's Irish Bouquet (sister to Irish Monarch), Ch. Devlin Meadowlark's Etching, Ch. Meadowlark's Taylor Made, Ch. Devlin Meadowlark's Illusion, Saxony's Hide Your Heart, and Devlin Meadowlark's Forever. Also coming along are Meadowlark's Little Debbie (Ch. Saxony's Emerald Heart ex Ch. Meadowlark's Irish Bouquet), owned by Ivy, and Meadowlark's Full of Magic (Ch. Saxony's Emerald Heart ex Ch. Devlin's Meadowlark Illusion).

From Jean Roche, Rose acquired Ch. Saxony's Emerald Heart (Ch. Saxony's Sympatico ex Ch. Saxony's Southern Nights), who is becoming influential for

Meadowlark. Other up-and-coming dogs are Meadowlark's Pop'n Fresh, owned by Ivy (Ch. Saxony's Emerald Heart ex Ch. Meadowlark's Irish Bouquet) and Meadowlark's Forever Magic (Ch. Saxony's Emerald Heart ex Ch. Devlin Meadowlark's Illusion).

Ivy Frank came to live with Rose and Allen several years ago. Rose says she is all anyone would want in a friend, worker, and lover of animals. She says, "Someone would equate Ivy with winning the lotto. Both Allen and I could not imagine this kennel without her. Mention should be made of her favorite dog, Ch. Meadowlark's Antares, who passed on in 1998 and Ch. Meadowlark's Midnight Lace, who left Ivy in 1999."

Rose describes their dogs as follows: "The Meadowlark Irish Setter has a stamp of elegance. We breed for soundness, prettiness, and grace. You can always tell a Meadowlark dog by the stamp of beautiful heads, dark mascara eyes, and lots of forechest with good shoulders and upper arm. I also like good tailsets, maybe a bit high for most, and a nice let down rear with good thigh. Temperament is top on my list, remembering that though these dogs are only show dogs for a short time, they are our loving pets for a long time. I thank my dear friend Ted Eldredge of Tirvelda for that wisdom."

It is not an exaggeration to say that Meadowlark has had a vast influence on almost every kennel in the country, whether large or small. Rose has a natural breeder's eye for combinations that work, and she has never been afraid to outcross into another line if she feels that it will enhance her breeding program. Beginning with a strong foundation in Tirvelda, she incorporated Draherin stock early on and continued those two strains through Courtwood with Ch. Courtwood Marxman (Wyndjammer) and Ch. Shawnee Pipedream O'Charlton (Vindicator). Blending those strains with her Tirvelda-based bitches has encompassed every important line in the last 30 years.

Leslie Russell, *Avon Farm*–Oregon City, OR

Leslie got her first Irish when she was 13 years old, but it was not until 1981 that she began actively breeding and showing under the Avon Farm kennel name. Since that time, she has bred on average two litters a year.

Her foundation dog was Ch. Niebline Streamliner, a blend of a linebred Cherry Point bitch and Ch. Tirvelda Michaelson. From there she chose another male, Ch. Zodiac's Arista Extremist. She obtained another bitch from Niebline of Bayberry stock and bred her to both males. This resulted in her foundation bitch, Ch. Avon Farm Applause.

Applause was bred to Ch. Scarlly's Red Hot ROM to produce Chs. Avon Farm Rosalita and Glory Days, and a

dog, Avon Farm Thunder Road. She then leased a double-Michaelson granddaughter, Ch. Dunholm Margaux, from John Savory and bred her to Thunder Road to produce Chs. Dunholm Western Renewal and Avon Farm Wall Street.

Wall Street was bred to his aunt, Rosalita, to produce her next foundation bitch, Ch. Avon Farm Miss Kitty. Outcrossing Kitty to Ch. Sunnyhill Wings of the Wind produced four champions, including Ch. Avon Farm Mr.

Ch. Avon Farm Wall Street. Owned by Leslie Russell.

Debonair, a group-winning dog. A repeat gave her three girls, including Avon Farm Miss Skylight.

Linebreeding Miss Kitty to a Canadian dog, Conifer's Tawtonka (Ch. Avon Farm Colnbroook Citation ex Ch. Rockherin Atika) produced three daughters. Of these, Leslie looks to Ch. Avon Farm Miss Chevious to be her next key producer.

Attributes that Leslie considers most important are a calm, sometimes mischievious, temperament (although exuberant when it's called for), and a charming and trainable companion. She looks for a healthy, sturdy dog; an easy-keeper; a dog that looks like its gender; that has clean, smooth lines, an efficient side gait, and exemplifies the hard-to-achieve "substantial yet elegant" phrase in the

Ch. Avon Farm Mr. Debonair, a group-winning dog, winning Best of Breed in 1997. Owned by Leslie Russell.

Ch. Avon Farm Miss Chevious taking Best of Winners at the Kachina Kennel Club in 1997. Owned by Leslie Russell.

standard. She wants a moderate Irish Setter that looks as if he could run effortlessly in the field, with a dark red coat, a long, pretty head, and the sweet, soft expression essential to the breed.

Paula and Terry Sadler, *Waterford–* Watertown, MN

In 1990, the Sadlers purchased their first Irish Setter, Ch. Pin Oak Brandy Station, from Nancy and Jim Godbey. He was finished by his owners and garnered several Bests of Breed and group placements. He sired a litter in 1996 when bred to Am. Can. Ch. Orchard Farm Dream Girl. A bitch from that litter became Ch. Tealwood's Waterford Crystal.

Ch. Tealwood's Waterford Crystal. Owned by Paula and Terry Sadler of Waterford Kennels.

In 1992, they purchased Ch. Courtwood Gracious Me, who was bred in 1997 to Am. Can. Ch. Chamberlayne's Big Easy, owned by Craig Cooper. Waterford Fleur de Grace, Can. Ch. Chamberlayne's Followed Me Home, owned by Craig, and Waterford Tour de France are currently being shown. Several of the Sadler's dogs are also in competition for hunting titles because they show great bird sense.

Helen and Walt Sanderson, *McLauren–* Boca Raton, FL

The Sandersons bought their first Irish Setter in 1967 of Gala Glen breeding. Their next bitch became Am. Can. Ch. Shannon's Pamela, whom they acquired from Betty Crawford. She was bred to Ch. Dunholm Clancy of Durin, and their first homebred champion, McLauren's Starwood in Aspen, resulted. From Anne Perfetti (Gallivan) they acquired Ch. Gallivan's Hurricane and Ch. Gallivan's Simply Red CGC. Simply Red was bred to Ch. Killary's Bert Reynolds to produce McLauren's Inspiration. They also own Ch. Gallivan's Double Dee Dare, Ch. McLauren's

Ch. McLauren's Starwood in Aspen, Helen and Walt Sanderson's first homebred champion.

Pretty Woman, and two sisters by Ch. Castlebar's Command Presence ex Ch. Scarlly's Rat-A-Tat-Tat— Signature of McLauren's Place and Signature's London Place. In addition, Chantilly Glory of McLauren and McLauren's Against All Odds live with the Sandersons.

John, Geraldine, and Alistair Savory, *Dunholm–* Keswick, VA

Dunholm was established in 1963 by John and Anne Savory when they obtained their foundation bitch from Ted Eldredge, Ch. Tirvelda Bridget Susie Ann ROM. She was a Best in Show winner and the dam of 10 champions,

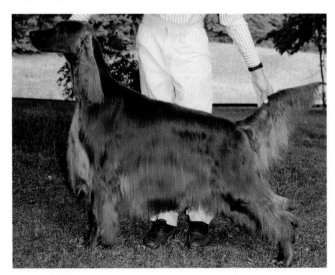

Ch. Dunholm Kildare, an influential sire for Dunholm Kennels, as well as several others. Owned by John, Geraldine, and Alistair Savory.

Dunholm Lachlan, a future Dunholm Kennel champion, winning Best of Opposite Sex and Best of Winners in 1998. Owned by John, Geraldine, and Alistair Savory.

including the Best in Show-winning Ch. Tirvelda Red Baron of Dunholm, who won Best of Breed and Group Third at Westminster in 1973.

The powerful combination of Susie Ann bred to the potent producers Ch. Tirvelda Michaelson ROM and later Ch. Shannon's Erin ROM, owned by Lucy Jane Myers, established the base for the future of Dunholm. Dunholm type was established best by breeding one of her Erin daughters, Ch. Dunholm Katrina, to Michaelson. Through this breeding emerged Ch. Dunholm Clancy of Durin, who played a key role in the Durin and Heatherwood Kennels, as well as siring a major player in Dunholm's breeding program, Ch. Rainbow Catriona of Dunholm.

The direct Dunholm line was maintained through a younger sister of Clancy, Ch. Dunholm Red Ribbons, a medium-sized, typey bitch. At about this time, John and Anne went their separate ways but maintained joint ownership of the Dunholm dogs until the time when Anne accepted a position with the AKC and had to relinquish her ownership. Dunholm continues with Geraldine and their son, Alistair, who in recent years has handled most of their dogs.

At the suggestion of Ted Eldredge, Red Ribbons was bred to Meadowlark's Honor Guard, a Michaelson son. From this breeding emerged Ch. Dunholm Margaux, who features prominently in present-day Dunholm dogs, as well as the Avon Farm dogs of Leslie Russell. Margaux, a double granddaughter of Ch. Tirvelda Michaelson, died in 1996, 34 years after her grandfather's birth, thus making her a significant link in the Dunholm heritage.

On the advice of Ted Eldredge, Ch. Rainbow Catriona of Dunholm was purchased because she was from a PRA-tested litter, a significant feature at the time as this was prior to the development of DNA testing. She was bred to Ch. Meadowlark's Anticipation ROM, and her most influential son was Ch. Dunholm Kildare. Kildare, bred to Margaux, produced the present Dunholm line. Kildare was a major influence in the McNeal's kennel, Militza. He also sired Ch. Dunholm Windsor who, in turn, sired nine champions, mainly in Australia, by Aust. Ch. Gwyndara Who's That Girl. From Trevor and Leeanne Jones, John imported Ch. Gwyndara Southern Cross. He has proved valuable to several breeders since his arrival in the US, including Avon Farm, Wingfield, and Regalaire, where he currently lives. Ch. Avon Farm Northern Dancer is a Best in Show and group winner. Ch. Dunholm Caerphilly (Kildare ex Margaux) was bred to Southern Cross and produced the current hopefuls at Dunholm, Lachlan, and Murrumbidgee. Another youngster is Wingfield Medb of Dunholm (Ch. Dunholm Windsor ex Ch. Wingfield Whimsical Remark).

John is a professor at the University of Virginia, and their kennel is situated in the foothills of the Blue Ridge Mountains. The facility reflects the influence of Tirvelda, albeit on a smaller scale. The emphasis has always been on quality rather than quantity, and only 24 litters have been raised in the past 36 years, producing 41 champions. An additional 12 Irish have been owned and finished by Dunholm. John is a licensed judge for all Setters and has judged many specialties, including the 1990 National Specialty. Alistair has judged sweepstakes occasionally, the most important being the Eastern Irish Setter Combined Specialty in 1996. John is a former director of the ISCA.

Tara Hill's Harvest Moon, an influential sire for Pamela Schaar's Quinniver Kennels.

Quinniver's Prime Suspect winning Best of Breed at six months of age at the 1998 ISCA National Specialty.

Pamela Schaar, *Quinniver*–Warrenton, VA

Pam acquired her first Irish Setter in 1969, Kilkenny's Gay Tribute (Ch. Harmony Lane's Northern Light ex Ch. Argo Lane Gay Victoria CD). When bred to Killagay's Starfel Mac, she produced Ch. Kirk's Kelly Lynn, originally sold as a pet but returned at the age of three because she preferred water and ducks to pheasant. Also in that litter was Gay Star of Erin CD.

The purchase of Tara Hill's Harvest Moon (Ch. Tirvelda Telstar ex Ch. Rockherin Rebecca) in 1975 was a wise investment for Pam. He sired the top-winning bitch, Ch. Shangrila Moonshadow, for Lynne Mehring and is behind the Godbey's Ch. Pin Oak Robert E. Lee JH and Ch. Pin Oak Vicksburg JH.

In the 1980s, two additional Rockherin bitches came to Quinniver—Rockherin Quinn and Ch. Rockherin Marlee. Quinn was outcrossed to Ch. Rossan's Raz-Ma-Taz ROM in 1988, producing three champions, including Ch. Quinniver's Intermezzo. In 1990, Marlee was bred to Intermezzo to produce Ch. Quinniver's Songbird.

In 1998, Songbird was outcrossed to Ch. Courtwood Grand Hotel, producing a litter that included the precocious Quinniver's Prime Suspect ("Emilee"), who won Best of Breed at a Specialty with more than 90 entries at the age of six months.

Pam was a professional handler during the 1970s and '80s, piloting Gordon Setters, as well as other breeds and some top Irish Setters, to impressive wins.

Quinniver has been influential in the breeding programs of Amy Maxwell (Tapestry) and Tracy McNeal (Militza).

Pam has expanded her life in dogs to include judging. She is approved for all Setters, English Cocker Spaniels, and Salukis.

Linda and Patrick Schindler, *Brandolyn*–Woodbury, MN

Linda grew up with Irish Setters. In 1970, when she got married, she already had a pet Irish. Linda started in both obedience and conformation with her first two additions. Her first champion, RoEllen Sean McGuire, was Linda's introduction to handling, and when he finished, the Schindlers were very proud.

The opportunity to own a "smashing puppy," in the words of Sue Hahnen, brought them Ch. Charlton's Moon Lover ROM. (Ch. Courtwood Summer Forecast ROM ex Can. Ch. Kinsale's Charlton). "He embodied the true spirit of the Irish, and it was an honor to have him as part

Ch. Quinniver's Intermezzo winning Best of Breed at 18 months of age. Owned by Pamela Schaar.

Ch. Charlton's Moon Lover ROM, sire of 26 champion get. Owned by Linda Schindler.

of the family," Linda says. With limited breeding, he produced 26 champions, among them Ch. Courtwood Manuscript ROM, Ch. Courtwood Marxman, and Ch. Windwood Night Hawk, a Best in Show winner.

After Moon Lover came Courtwood Winter Love, co-owned with Sue Hahnen. Sue bred her to Moon Lover, producing the Courtwood "Dark" litter.

Recently, the Schindlers have owned Ch. Courtwood Entourage (sired by Ch. Courtwood Golden Gate). He was Linda's introduction to agility, as well as a star on TV and in several print ads. His sister, Courtwood Endearment Am. Can. CDX, produced the Courtwood Easy litter, from which they own Ch. Courtwood Easy Living AX AD CGC. In 1994, she became the first

Ch. Courtwood Easy Living AX AD CGC, the first agility-titled Irish Setter in the US. Owned by Linda Schindler.

agility-titled Irish Setter in the country. She moves very well, which enables her to be a talented jumper. Linda says she taught her so much about agility that Linda is now an agility instructor.

The Schindlers' newest addition is Courtwood Rain Or Shine NA (Ch. Courtwood Heavy Rains ex Ch. Edenderry Grace Note). She is being shown in conformation and working for her advanced agility titles.

Sandra Schmidt, RN, *Piesport*– Bloomfield Hills, MI

Sandra received her first Irish Setter in 1971, and in 1977 she purchased her first show Irish, who became Ch. Crambrook's Delia CD (Ch. Aaragon's Russet Deity ex Am. Can. Ch. Starheir's Quest for Glory). "Dee" was her foundation bitch. Bred in 1984 to Ch. Kulm's Trahern Encore Edition CDX, she produced three champions— Ch. Piesport Turn the Page JH, Ch. Piesport Transit Authority JH, and Ch. Piesport A Trifle Trahern CDX JH. Offspring of these dogs carry on the Piesport line.

Taught by her father, Sandra has hunted over pointing dogs since 1966. She was introduced to field trials by friends from the Michigan Brittany clubs, and she has been an active participant in field trials since 1987. She has been a judge of both AKC and American field trials and AKC Hunting Tests, primarily Master level, since 1989. Sandra has also served as official reporter for championship events.

Although she seldom breeds, with each litter she strives to produce healthy Irish that have good breed type, that are competitive in show and field events, and that are enjoyable companions.

Ruth G. (Wyley) Scott, *Seandee*–Long Beach, CA

Ruth acquired a puppy bitch from Thenderin and Draherin lines as her first show Irish. Although she did not finish, which Ruth believes was because of Ruth's lack of experience in the ring, she was bred to Shawnee Sumac. From that litter came Ch. Seandee Comanche Tomahawk. From that promising beginning, Ruth continued with success in the show ring and in occasionally breeding their dogs. She acquired a bitch from Katherine Wheatley that became Ch. Rockherin Celebrity (Ch. Meadowlark's Vindicator ex Ch. Rockherin Sheena). The senior matron in the house, she shares Ruth's home with Patriot's Dream on Seandee, Ch. Patriot's Dazzling Dream CD, and Ch. Patriot's I've Gotta Dream CD.

Pam Seipkes and Betty J. Michael, *Windwood*– Staples, MN

Windwood Irish Setters began in the early 1970s when Betty Michael purchased her first show Irish, Can-a-ru

Four beautiful Piesport Irish Setters (from left to right); Ch. Piesport Turn the Page JH, Piesport Trillium JH, Piesport Wing River, and Ch. Piesport Transit Authority JH. Owned by Sandra Schmidt.

Midsummer Wind (Ch. Courtwood Summer Forecast ROM ex Charlton's Whisper of the Wind). She became the foundation for Windwood, producing many offspring. She was bred twice to Ch. Charlton's Moon Lover ROM, and her first litter contained Ch. Windwood's Night Hawk, a multi-Best in Show and group-winning dog, and Ch. Windwood's Mourning Dove. Night Hawk was the Number One Irish Setter for three successive years.

The second litter produced Am. Can. Ch. Windwood Firebird Jonah, who was sold in 1987 to Hollyhill Kennels in Canada, where he became Canada's Number One Irish and Number Two Sporting Dog. Another in the litter was Ch. Windwood Firebird

Ch. Windwood Phantom Skye CD JH CGC VC at eight years of age. Owned by Betty J. Michael and Pam Seipkes.

Jessica, who finished with three majors. Ch. Windwood Firebird Jacob JH became the first bench champion to earn a hunting test title.

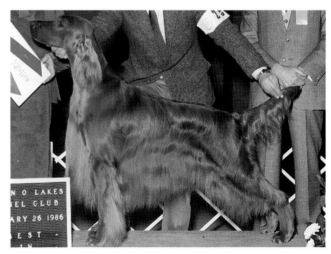

Ch. Windwood's Night Hawk, a multiple Best in Show and group winner and the Number One Irish Setter for three consecutive years. Owned by Betty J. Michael and Pam Seipkes.

119

Night Hawk was bred only seven times, one of which was to the top-winning bitch, Ch. Hallmark Courtin'N Kitchen. All in that litter finished their championships.

Ch. Windwood Mourning Dove produced two litters by Ch. Hallmark Airs Above Ground, all of which finished. Am. Can. Ch. Windwood Merry Mockenbird CD ROM became the foundation for Shadyview Kennels.

Ch. Windwood Firebird Jacob JH was bred to Ch. Windwood Thunderbird Myth to produce the foundation bitch for Casper Ziegler's Classic Kennels, Ch. Classic's Krystle Lady CD JH VC ROM.

One of the noteworthy offspring of this combination is Ch. Windwood Phantom Skye CD JH CGC VC, which Pam owns. In 1995, she was bred to Ch. Classic's Pheasants Forever JH, producing Ch.Windwood Autumn Tradition JH and Windwood Autumn Tapestry JH. The Windwood legacy continues with Pam and these two youngsters.

Kate Seymour, *Cucuhullain*–Brookfield Center, CT

Kate began her association with Irish Setters in England and continued when she arrived in the States. The first notable dog that she bred was Am. Can. Ch. Cucuhullain Chelsea Morning. Bred to Am. Can. Ch. Courtwood Summer Forecast ROM, she produced the "Diamond" litter, which also included Joanne Larsen's Ch. Cucuhullain Dr. Seuss. Can. Ch. Cucuhullain Diamond Summer died early, but before Kate lost him, he was bred to Ramblin'Red Iaslinn ROM, through the generosity of Anne Marie Kubacz. This produced the "Eternal" litter.

Am. Can. Ch. Cucuhullain Diamond Morning was the dam of Ch. Cucuhullain Good Fortune ROM, Good Morning, and Good Vibrations.

Kate's recent litter contains a National Sweepstakes winner, Ch. Cucuhullain Just So Special.

Among the attributes Kate considers important are beauty, tractability, intelligence, stamina, attitude, and energy. Irish Setters have a fine sense of fun and are totally devoted, she says. Her objective is "to breed a biddable, devoted companion of show-quality conformation that can compete against all comers and live to a ripe old age free of dysplasia, epilepsy, and other debilitating illnesses."

Marilyn and Don Shaver and Jon and Laura Root, *Summit Rise*–Bainbridge Island, WA

The Shavers' small kennel started in 1963 with the arrival of Shaver's Bonny Red Queen, followed by Killane Kate of Harmony Lane Kennels. Bred to Ch. Blayneywood Country Squire, she produced Summit Rise Sendai Doll, the dam and granddam of a number of champions.

During the '60s and '70s, Marilyn was active in club affairs in Iowa and in showing some of her young dogs. Her daughter, Laura, began to show in juniors when she was eight years old with her own dog, Summit Rise Forever Amber.

In 1977, the Shavers relocated to the Pacific Northwest, and due to other commitments, became less active in the show ring. They did co-own Ch. Summit Rise Rampart and his son, Ch. Summit Rise Banner O'Jaybrier, with Carol Rentz. They were the son and grandson of Ch. Summit Rise Sonnet of Saraval, a top-winning bitch on the West Coast.

The Shavers have retired from active showing, but their daughter Laura Root, who resides in Eagle, Idaho, is carrying on for the family. Currently, their housepets include Am. Can. Ch. Donegan's Dennis the Menace, co-owned with Cindy Lloyd, and a young bitch, Pin Oak Velvet Touch (Ch. Castlebar Country Statesman ex Ch.

Am. Can. Ch. Cucuhullain Diamond Morning winning Best of Sweepstakes at the Lower Susquehanna Irish Setter Club in 1984. Owned by Kate Seymour.

Am. Can. Ch. Donegan's Dennis the Menace winning Winners Male at the 1997 Irish Setter Club of Canada National Specialty. Owned and handled by Laura Root.

Ch. Summit Rise Rampart. Owned by Carol Rentz and Marilyn Shaver.

Ch. Shurlin's Nautical Illusion, a multiple group winner. Owned by Gloria Sheehan and JoAnna Matthisen.

Pin Oak Vicksburg JH). Marilyn hopes she will be the new foundation for Summit Rise.

Gloria Sheehan and JoAnna Matthisen, O'Sheehan–Anchorage, AK

Gloria's introduction to the breed occurred in 1964 with the purchase of her first puppy. It was in 1979 that the O'Sheehan prefix came into use with the purchase of Ch. Charlton's Tradewind. Shortly after, they purchased their foundation bitch, Ch. Charlton's Impatiens. Bred to Tradewind, Impatiens produced Chs. O'Sheehan's Tundra Express, Alaskan Freedom, and Chattanooga Chena.

Winy Arland (Charlton) offered them a puppy from Ch. Candia Indeed's last litter, a bitch that became the second important foundation for O'Sheehan. She was Charlton's Feather in the Wind. Bred to Tradewind, she produced two champions, and bred to Am. Can. Ch. Courtwood Summer Forecast ROM, two more champions resulted.

Subsequent generations produced Chs. Kelley's Lover Boy and Kelley's April Wine, both owned by JoAnna Matthisen. Their friendship led Gloria and JoAnna to become partners in O'Sheehan Irish Setters. April Wine was bred to Ch. Meadowlark's Wyndjammer ROM to produce their best-winning bitch, Ch. Shurlin's Nautical Illusion.

Nautical Illusion set the standard for O'Sheehan and, when bred to Ch. Rusticwood's Running Mate, their current winners and breeding stock resulted.

They comment, "We feel truly blessed to have shared our lives with so many wonderful and special Irish Setters. We remember those we've lost with the fondest of memories, and we're grateful for the ones who are still making us laugh today."

Karen Simmons, Nova Glen–New Lenox, IL

All of Karen's Irish Setters have their foundation in the Cloverleaf Kennel of Linda Ratkovitch. Her first was Ch. Cloverleaf's Something More, and he was followed by Chs. Cloverleaf's Now & Forever, Desert Storm, Take a Chance, and Christopher Alexander CD. Karen's new addition is Glen Rose Wish Upon a Star. Karen plans to try obedience and agility.

Barbara Simpson, Rustwood–Bakersfield, CA

Barbara's first Irish was a gift of a field-bred dog when she was 12. She and her father hunted over "Rusty" until he was well into his teens. In 1968, she decided to purchase a show-quality Irish, and in 1972, she obtained Robalee Sorcery (Ch. Innisfail Flashback's Design ex Robalee Crimson Colleen). She was followed by Robalee Jubilee of Rustwood (Ch. Innisfail Gallant Guy ex Robalee Tara of Saratoga). Jubilee competed in junior showmanship with Barbara's daughter, Rene, for five years, and she was the first of her dogs to be test-bred clear of PRA. Bred to Ch. Santera Tamberluck, she produced Ch. Robalee Rhu of Mage, also field-pointed. Barbara then acquired Draherin Enchanted Evening, who was bred to Aus. Am. Can. Ch. Tarralain Tribal Drums, producing the Rustwood Drum litter in 1989. Bred next to Sunstrand's Sunsational, she produced Am. Can. Ch. Rustwoods Even Chance, owned by Liz Fleming, and Rustwood's Encore, co-owned with Charlotte Kay (Aintree).

In 1997, Barbara purchased Kennlee Annie Oakley (Ch. Kennlee Treasure Bay ex Ch. Scarlly's Love of Kennlee). All Rustwood Irish are PRA-clear and OFA-certified before being bred.

Kennlee Annie Oakley winning Reserve Winners Bitch at the Del Monte Kennel Club in 1998. Owned by Barbara Simpson.

Charles and Frances Sloughfy, *Fyrethorn–Fleetwood, PA*

The Sloughfys have owned Irish Setters since the 1970s, but it was not until they acquired a puppy from Ernie and Joan Viola and Dana Haskell (Kinvale) that they finished their first dog. He was Ch. Kinvale Dream Chaser (Ch. Kinvale Evergreen Destiny ROM ex Ch. Meadowlark's Vanity Fair—full sister to Ch. Meadowlark's Vindicator ROM).

Seeking a mate for Dream Chaser, they were able to lease Meadowlark's Shazam from Arlene Fahmie Bower, who eventually came to stay at Fyrethorn permanently. Charlie handled her to her championship, and from the litter of these two came their homebred champion, Fyrethorn Dream Shared.

Looking carefully for the perfect mate for her, they learned that a linebreeding of uncle to niece might be the way to go. They chose Ch. Chamberlayne's Echo of Kinvale. That fortuituous match has given them Ch. Fyrethorn Constant Comment and Ch. Fyrethorn Center Court, who was Winners Dog at the 1998 National Specialty.

For the Sloughfys, part of the fun of owning a show dog is doing it yourself: grooming, handling, and especially breeding one's own puppies. Because they breed infrequently, they are careful to select mates who complement their bitches, build on their strengths, and maintain the overall balance and attitude they look for.

Fran says, "We think our growth in dogs has occurred because we went to breeders we have known for years who were willing to sell us a good dog that was thoughtfully linebred, producing puppies better than either of the parents. We have been encouraged along this

Ch. Meadowlark's Shazam, one of the foundation bitches for Fyrethorn Kennels. Owned by Charles and Frances Sloughfy.

journey by many friends/fanciers, who have made suggestions or shared ideas. We have gone to handling clinics and discussed grooming techniques. We have asked questions and more questions. Sometimes we have tried and failed...but for 22 years we have been learning. Finally, we have learned the most from Joan, Dana, and Mary Merlo, our mentors, who have shared their

Ch. Fyrethorn Center Court taking Winners Dog at the 1998 ISCA National Specialty. Owned by Charles and Frances Sloughfy.

knowledge, given us their advice, as well as their friendship. They have even occasionally offered a suggestion we did not want to hear. It is at these times that Charlie and I try to be smart enough to listen.

"Using the standard as a guide, we all strive to breed the perfect dog. For us, it is a combination of overall fit and balance, elegance that belies strength, movement that exhibits reach and drive, and a soft expression, but above all, a self-confident, happy-go-lucky personality that makes day-to-day living worthwhile."

Jan and Jack Smith, *Jadestar*–Tucson, AZ

Jadestar Irish Setters began in 1971 with the purchase of Thenderin Morello CD, bred by Leone Wixon (Coppercountry). Two years later, they obtained Whiskey Hill Windsong from Bill and Dilly Allen. Their foundation bitch, Ch. Blueprint Kachina Doll, was purchased from Dennis and Cynde Sporre in 1977.

Bred to Tapnar Ballaghaderreen, she produced the "C" litter containing three champions, including Ch. Jadestar Crystal Clear, dam of a five-champion litter that included Ch. Tapnar Cherokee Kinsman, owned by Pete Bauer.

In 1985, Ch. Tapnar Keepsake of Jadestar was acquired from Fran Behne (Tapnar). She carried on the Jadestar line, which now includes offspring sired by Ch. Tainaron Racing Silks (the "M" litter), and they have added Ch. Avon Farm Cat Ballou, co-owned with Pete Bauer. They also own Cairncross Hearts on Fire.

A recent litter is from Ch. Donegan's Done That bred to Jadestar Jasmine.

Sheila Smith, *Heatherwood*–Killen, AL

Sheila and her husband, Larry, fell in love with Irish Setters while attending their first dog show in Big Spring,

Texas, in 1971. The next year, they purchased their first, Brandy. Although not a show dog, he obtained his CDX and served as Sheila's learning dog as she practiced grooming and show handling.

Sheila's foundation bitch, Ch. Durin Kingscourt Betsy Ross ROM, whom she acquired from Carmen Hufstetler, produced many champions, some of whom became the foundation for other kennels. The stud dog that was most influential to Sheila was Ch. Seregon Second Edition ROM, owned by Marilyn Wade. He is the sire of her Best in Show-winning dog, Ch. Rusticwood Running Mate, from a breeding to Ch. Rusticwood Love Song by Carolyn Roche.

Although they maintain a small breeding program, they attempt to find the perfect blend of beauty, intelligence, temperament, and structure when selecting dogs to breed. That chemistry must work, Sheila says, because they have produced more than two dozen champions, many with obedience degrees.

Megen Olcott Spencer, *Shadyview*–Lapeer, MI

Megen started learning about Irish Setters in 1983 after breeding and showing cats for about six years. In 1987, she purchased her foundation bitch, Am. Can. Ch. Windwood Merry Mockenbird ROM ("Solean") from Pam Seipkes and Betty Michael.

Bred to Ch. Regalaire Music Man ROM, she produced the "Double" litter containing Am. Can. Jap. Ch. Shadyview's Double Time, Am. Can. Ch. Shadyview's Double Step, and Ch. Shadyview's Double Trouble. A repeat breeding produced the "Again" litter in 1991: Am. Can. Ch. Shadyview's Here Again Am. Can. CD; Am. Can. U-AgI Shadyview's Play It Again NA Can. CD, owned by

Ch. Seregon Second Edition ROM, an influential stud dog for Sheila Smith's Heatherwood Kennels. Owned by Marilyn Wade.

Ch. Rusticwood Running Mate, a Best in Show winner. Owned by Sheila Smith.

Marty Siegrist; and Am. Jap. Int. Ch. Shadyview's Just Me Again, owned by Kazuko Imai of Japan.

The next generation of Shadyview dogs is already making its mark in the US and overseas. Dutch Ch. Shadyview's Breaking Records is the Number One Irish Setter in the Netherlands.

Megen feels very fortunate in the successes she has enjoyed in Irish Setters in so short a time and with so few litters. She always strives to

Am. Can. Ch. Windwood Merry Mockenbird CD ROM, foundation bitch for Shadyview Kennels, shown here at 11 years of age. Owned by Megen Olcott Spencer.

breed sound, healthy dogs, both physically and temperamentally. She says that she does her homework, researching pedigrees and studying the dogs themselves to seek out the best combinations to achieve her goal. She says, "I hope to see a little bit of my pride and joy, Solean, in every Shadyview pup. To me, she is the quintessential Irish lady, with fire, grace, beauty, and an attitude that never quits, even at the age of 12. She's given me more than I ever hoped for. With her help I've enjoyed undreamed-of success in Irish Setters. I cannot imagine my life without her."

From the Shadyview "Again" litter, Am. Can. Ch. Shadyview's Here Again Am. Can. CD (left) and Am. Can. Ch. U-Agl Shadyview's Play It Again NA Can. CD (right).

Joan and Dick Staby, *Gleneden*–Eden, NY

Family pet Irish have graced the Stabys' home since 1965, and it was purely by chance that they became involved with the dog show scene. In 1988, at a Chamber of Commerce meeting in their town, they met Patricia Nagel and happened to ask if she knew where they could get a puppy. Pat agreed to co-own one of her next litter, which happened to be the Ch. Meadowlark Vindicator ex Ch.Kerry-Eire Coral Charm ROM litter. She picked the puppy for them, who was to become Ch. Quailfield Red Hot Business ROM ("Flame").

Dick had always wanted a male, so they went back to Patti Nagel for a littermate. Am. Can. Ch. Quailfield Business BIV Pleasure had a rough start in life, with two severe bouts of a joint disease called HOD. Because of all the attention he received during his early months, he needed a home where he would get lots of individual attention. He came on a trial basis for a weekend and never left. He went on to have a distinguished show career and retired from the ring with an Award of Merit at the 1997 National Specialty show. He has sired seven litters, five of those after he was nine years old. The first two litters contained five champions.

Flame was bred twice. The first litter was by Hazelhill Sugar Shack to produce the "Success" litter. Her second litter, in 1993, was to Ch. Tirvelda Once Upon a Time. From that litter, the Stabys kept Am. Can. Ch. Quailfield Moon River, a group-placing dog. In 1998, he finished ranked among the top ten Irish Setters.

The Stabys' newest addition is Aralyn Legend (Ch. Quailfield

Am. Can. Ch. Quailfield Moon River, a group-placing dog and one of the Top Ten Irish Setters of 1998. Owned by Joan and Dick Staby.

Business BIV Pleasure ex Ch. Kenobi Chasin' the Magic). Still a youngster, he has his major points.

Darlene Steele, *Rossan*–Naperville, IL

Rossan began with Darlene's first Irish, Colleen of Belfast CDX, a granddaughter of Ch. Blayneywood Country Squire, in 1969. Colleen became Rossan's foundation bitch and was a major factor in the success of its breeding program. At that time, Darlene was still in Junior Showmanship with Colleen and was a successful obedience competitor.

Ch. Rossan's Raz-Ma-Taz ROM, owned by Darlene Steele, pictured with Ch. Courtwood Milestone and Ch. Courtwood Golden Gate winning the Stud Dog Class in 1987.

Ch. Rossan's Afternoon Delight taking Best of Winners at nine months of age. Owned by Darlene Steele.

In 1975, Colleen was bred to Ch. Kilgary Aman. This produced six puppies and Rossan's first homebred champion, Ch. Rossan's Charlie. Charlie became a Best in Show and specialty winner, ranked Number 7 in 1978, handled by Darlene. In 1981, Colleen was bred to Ch. Kilgary Dungannon to produce Ch. Rossan's Oliver Twist CD.

In 1976, Darlene purchased a bitch with Bayberry and Tirvelda bloodlines and bred her to Ch. Rossan's Charlie. Of particular note in the resulting litter was Ch. Rossan's Afternoon Delight. She was bred to Ch. Cloverleaf's Ascendant twice, in 1980 and 1982. The second litter contained Ch. Rossan's Raz-Ma-Taz ROM ("Bogie"). He sired 29 champions, several of which were Best in Show and specialty winners. Included in his list of illustrious offspring are Ch. Courtwood Milestone, Ch. Cherry Bounce Courtwood, and Ch. Pin Oak Vicksburg JH.

Rossan's future focus lies in the recent breeding of a Bogie daughter, Ch. Pin Oak Similar Features, to the Australian import Ch. Gwyndara Southern Cross.

Ginny Swanson, *Tramore*–Evergreen, CO

Tramore began in 1972 with the purchase of a show bitch from Bob and Joan Chambers, Bo-Cham's Whisper of Tramore. Whisper was a misnomer, because she was extremely vocal, but her bloodlines were excellent, going back to Ch. Knockross O'Boy ROM and Ch. Shannon's Erin ROM.

The strength of Tramore has always been in its bitches, and Ginny now has a tail bitch line of five to seven generations bred from Whisper. One daughter, Ch. Tramore Flannery, has Ch. Shannon's Erin four times in her immediate pedigree. Her daughter, Ch. Tramore Every So Often ROM, produced 11 champions from 3 sires.

Another Whisper daughter, Ch. Tramore Couldn't Resist, was sired by Ch. Candia Indeed ROM. Her daughter, Ch. Tramore Kiandra ROM, (Ch. Tramore High Country ex Ch. Tramore Couldn't Resist) was probably Ginny's best bitch. She had beautiful balance, type, and showmanship. Most current Tramore stock descends from her.

Ch. Tramore Farpoint Curtin Call. Owned by Ginny Swanson.

Tramore is now starting to linebreed back to Kiandra. Ch. Tramore Farpoint Curtin Call, co-bred with Susan Miller, traces back to her. Her brother, Ch. Farpoint Cherokee Dreamer, is also a fine dog that Ginny hopes will play a major role in future generations. A recent puppy for which they have great expectations is Tramore Singular Sensation, by Ch. Tramore Rich 'N Famous' frozen sperm ex a daughter of Ch. Tramore Yours Truly.

More than 60 champions have come from Tramore in 25 years of breeding, averaging 1 litter a year. The majority of their puppies go to pet homes, and many go out on co-ownerships so they can be bred and shown. Ginny keeps between six and ten Irish at home in the mountains west of Denver.

Ginny believes that an Irish Setter should be balanced, have a sound front and rear, and be well angled with sufficient length to use both properly. "An Irish should not look like a well-balanced terrier," she says. "The Irish should also be sound in health, body type, and temperament. He should be able to exist 'as a dog.' Health should be a natural thing, not treated by the breeder or owner. The win should never take precedence over the health and well-being of the Irish Setter."

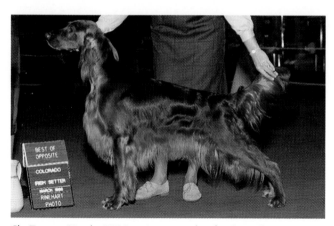

Ch. Tramore Kiandra ROM, an important dam for Ginny Swanson's Tramore Kennels.

Among the best of many male champions, Kiandra's brother, Ch. Tramore Killanon, was not well known but was an incredible dog with beautiful head, neck, and front assembly and gorgeous side movement. Ch. Tramore Never Say Never, sired by Ch. Meadowlark's Vindicator ROM, produced 19 champions. He was also a therapy dog and appeared in movies. Ch. Tramore Rich 'N Famous, sired by Vindicator's brother, Ch. Meadowlark's Equalizer, produced ten champions in four litters, including a Best in Show son. His grandson, Ch. Tramore's Yours Truly, sired by Ch. Pompei's First Class, finished at ten months in six days, without extra effort. He is turning out to be an excellent sire.

Jill Taylor, *Captiva*–Monroe, NC

Jill has been involved with Irish Setters her whole life, because her mother and father bred them, and both were professional handlers in Canada. Her first Irish came from Sue Korpan (McCamon) in 1988. Although an excellent pet, he was not show quality, so for her 21st birthday in 1992 her mother purchased a puppy bitch from Quailfield. She became Am. Can. Ch. Quailfield Stylish Success ("Windy"), a Best in Show and specialty winner and Number One Irish, Number Two Sporting Dog, and Number Ten All-Breeds in Canada in 1997.

Am. Can. Ch. Quailfield Stylish Success, a Best in Show and specialty-winning dog who was Number One Irish Setter, Number Two Sporting Dog, and Number Ten All-Breed in Canada in 1997. Owned by Jill Taylor.

A promising dog for Captiva Kennels, Captiva In Living Colour is shown here winning First Place in the 6-9 Months Sweepstakes in 1996. Owned by Jill Taylor.

From her first litter sired by Am. Can. McCamon Impresario, four finished their Canadian championships and three are finished in the US. In this litter came Am. Can. Ch. Captiva's Ride With The Wind ("Rider"). He has multiple group placements in the US and Canada in limited showing. He sired four litters while he was still less than two years of age, with several champions and pointed get resulting.

Shannonlea Aubrieta is a young bitch Jill imported from Joyce Webb in England. She has been bred to Rider twice, and Jill has kept two promising bitches, Captiva In Living Colour and Captiva Ready to Rock and Roll.

Jill also has a young litter by Rider out of Lordlarry's Spice of Life, an Impresario daughter that she hopes will carry on Rider's potential.

Windy's second litter was by Am. Mex. Ch. Sunshine's First Rate, producing Am. Can. Ch. Captiva's Wishes in the Wind, Best of Winners at the 1998 National Specialty. Her third litter by Ch. Cucucullain Good Fortune ROM looks promising.

Renee Taylor, *Kamron*–Reseda, CA

One of the stalwarts of the Irish Setter in America, Renee Taylor has spanned the generations with dogs that have made a significant impact on the breed. In the early 1960s, after a love affair of several years with Irish Setter companions, she purchased a dog that became the most titled Irish Setter in history at the time. He was Am. Mex. Can. Ch. Legend of Varagon UDT PR PU Can. CDX (Ch. Innisfail Color Scheme CD ex Ch. Innisfail Best Regards CDX). His father, Color Scheme, was owned by Ray and Valerie Gonsor of Varagon. Legend was the sire of 12 American and 17 Canadian champions, including 2 Best in Show sons, Ch. Danalee Bright Legend and Can. Ch. Julerin Image of Trofi.

Renee's first bitch was Am. Can. Mex. Ch. Enilen High Flyer CDX PC Can. CD from the Bayless' Enilen Kennels. (Madeline Bayless taught Renee about advanced obedience and tracking.) Bred to Legend, Flyer produced the first Kamron litter containing American and Canadian champions. Flyer, when bred to Ch. Webline Wizard of Macapa, gave Renee another Best in Show winner, owned by Carol Burgasser, Am. Can. Mex. Int. Bda. Ch. Kamron Dominique, a group and Best in Show winner.

Am. Can. Ch. Captiva's Ride With The Wind winning Best of Opposite Sex at the Lower Susquehanna Kennel Club in 1998. Owned by Jill Taylor.

Renee ceased to be active in breeding and showing for several years, but in 1997, she bought a puppy from Rose Ross of Meadowlark, Meadowlark's Fanfare of Kamron. She hopes this dog will become a champion and she can "get back into Setters on a bigger scale again."

Lindy Thomas, *Swashbuckler*–Lake Mathews, CA

Swashbuckler Irish Setters began in 1976 with the purchase of a puppy for Lindy's son, Jeff, which he handled in Junior Showmanship and conformation.

Some of the Swashbuckler highlights have been a litter of 20 puppies, 18 of which survived (Ch. Kerry-Eire Revolutionary ex O'Banner Victorious). Since then, many puppies later, they have achieved one ROM status bitch and presently own Am. Int. Ch. Rendition's Kiss Me I'm Irish, which they obtained from Pat Haigler. "Jake" has been the light of their lives since his arrival at Swashbuckler. He has saved Lindy's daughter twice from drowning in the pool during epileptic seizures. He is the sire or grandsire of all their present dogs, with the exception of two puppies co-owned with Barbara Miller (Windkist). These were sired by Ch. Swashbuckler Olympic Special ex Tramore Analainn's Darby. Lindy also co-owns Sweetbrier Riverdance with Candy Macaluso (Swashbuckler's All My Kisses ex Ch. OTCh. Hazelhill Shining Star UDX MH). They have hopes for another triple champion.

Win and Toni Thomas, *Tellurian*–Middleburg, FL

In 1976, Win and Toni acquired their first Irish from Norma McKendree—a pet that turned out to be Am. Can. Ch. McKendree's Thorin Oakenshield CDX. As Toni says, "For a novice handler, what a start!" Thorin became the Number 12 Irish Setter and was a multiple group winner.

In 1978, they purchased their foundation bitch, who became Ch. McKendree's Renaissance

Am. Can. Ch. McKendree's Thorin Oakenshield CDX, a multiple group winner, at ten and a half years of age. Owned by Toni and Win Thomas.

Child CDX. A series of health setbacks was discouraging for them, but in retrospect, Toni feels it made her stronger and more commited to the breed. Her first homebred champion was Ch. Tellurian's Heart Throb, but it was his sister, Sweetheart, that produced the best for them. Selectively, they moved away from pedigrees that had suspicions of seizures. Sweetheart, bred three times, produced champions in each litter. The most important for Tellurian was Ch. Tellurian's Tiger Lily. She died young, shortly after whelping a litter of six males. Three finished their championships, and one, Ch. Tellurian's Diamond Jubilee, was a multiple group and specialty winner. They then went back to Norma McKendree and purchased a puppy that became Ch. McKendree's Ruby Tuesday. Her new litter will be Tellurian's promise of the future.

Mary M. Thompson, *Rainwood*–Elkton, MD

Mary tells such a nice story of her love for the Irish that it is worth reporting in her own words: "It was the summer of 1963, and I had just finished third grade in Buffalo, New York. A new family moved into the neighborhood, and they brought with them a young Irish Setter. It was love at first sight and I literally spent my summer mornings, afternoons, and evenings sitting on their front porch with Red. They fed me lunch and gave me a dime to go to the store to buy their evening paper. I then went home, but every morning like clockwork I arrived on their doorstep at 7 am. They moved at the end of the summer, and my mother swears it was to get away from me."

Mary continued to think about Irish Setters, and in 1970, she wrote to several breeders listed in *Dog World* magazine. The only response came from Laura Cunningham of Beaverbrook Irish Setters. They corresponded for years, and in 1974, Mary purchased her first show puppy, Beaverbrook Fanfare CD (Ch. Tullamore Desperado ex Beaverbrook Country Claret). His father had sired a blind dog, and Mary felt she had to test-mate him. After waiting for two years for a blind bitch to breed to him, the results confirmed that he was a carrier. Mary says, "We have come so far with our fight with PRA. It is a tribute to our fancy that we can now do an easy blood test and eliminate the need for test-mating our breeding animals."

While in school, Mary purchased Shangrila Silhouette (Ch. Meadowlark's Masterpiece ROM ex Ch. Shangrila Moonshadow). She was shown a few times and bred to Ch. Meadowlark's Wyndjammer ROM. One of her offspring was Ch. Shangrila Wyndchime, who was to become Nancy Godbey's foundation bitch and the dam of Ch. Pin Oak Vicksburg JH.

Ch. Shangrila Wyndchime ROM, foundation bitch for Nancy Godbey's Pin Oak Kennels. Bred by Mary Thompson.

Ch. Courtwood Halls O'Ivy winning Best of Breed at the Northeastern Maryland Kennel Club in 1995. Owned by Mary Thompson.

She purchased a young male that became Ch. Drogheda Dream Weaver CD (Ch. Courtwood Golden Gate ex Ch. Charlton's Pillow Talk). He sired only one litter out of Chandar's Jessica Leah to produce the foundation bitch for Sherrie Berklin-Morgan, Ch. Chandar Symphony of Shambrio.

In 1989, she showed Ch. Courtwood Easy Street, beginning a treasured friendship with Susan Hahnen. Her favorite of Sue's bitches at the time was Ch. Courtwood Bandanna ROM. When she was bred to Ch. Courtwood Grand Hotel, Mary was given her choice of pick of the litter. There were ten bitches to choose from; a difficult task, Mary says. She came home with a puppy that became Mary's "soulmate," Ch. Courtwood Halls O'Ivy. Bred to Ch. Meadowlark's Irish Monarch, she produced the first Rainwood litter. In that litter were Ch. Courtwood Innkeeper, Ch. Rainwood Interlace, and Ch. Rainwood Impetuous, whom Mary kept.

Ch. Rainwood Impetuous winning Best of Opposite Sex at the Delaware County Kennel Club in 1997. Owned by Mary Thompson.

Mary also kept a male from the Grand Hotel ex Bandanna litter. He became Ch. Courtwood Heavy Rains, who finished easily and is siring some nice puppies from Ch. Edenderry Grace Note (co-owned by Sue Hahnen and Carol Rentz) and Ch. Summerset Special Deal (owned by Bob and Marge McKay).

Mary says, "Throughout the years, life has brought many changes, but I can honestly say that the one constant in my life has been the dogs and the strong and supportive friendships that have come from loving our breed."

Marilyn D. Title, *Marlyn*–Van Nuys, CA

Marilyn tells her own story about her start in Irish Setters: "As long as I could remember, I had always wanted an Irish Setter. In my senior year at the University of Wisconsin in 1970, I acquired my first Irish Setter, an eight-week-old puppy, Cyrano. Coming home to Southern California, it was not but a few short months that I had another puppy, Ch. Carra Lee Cinnamon Shamrock, a Webline dog that was my first show dog and whom I handled to his championship. While I attained my Masters degrees at UCLA in 1971 and Shamrock was a puppy, it did not take me long to become actively involved in the dog show world. I was teaching high school as well as working for professional handlers on weekends, and the 'dog show bug' bit me. I abandoned my teaching career and went to work for Dick and Madeline Webb of Webline Irish Setter fame on a full-time basis. It was a learning relationship that lasted professionally for eight years, and a personal friendship that will endure a lifetime. After this lengthy apprenticeship, I became an AKC-licensed professional handler, pursuing that career for about ten years."

Marilyn began her own breeding program in 1974 with her foundation bitch, Ch. Webline Moonshadow ROM, a daughter of 1976 ISCA National Specialty winner, Ch. Royal Oaks Fortune's Fella. Her first litter produced five champions, one of which, Ch. Marlyn's That's Class, was a specialty and group-winning bitch. Her last litter by Am. Can. Ch. McCamon Marquis gave her Ch. Marlyn Prelude, Best of Opposite Sex at the National Specialty in 1983, who was a group and specialty-winning bitch. Prelude's litter by Ch. Courtwood Manuscript ROM produced Chs. Marlyn Lyric ROM and Marlyn Limited Edition. Limited Edition was bred to Ch. Marlyn On Target (Ch. Courtwood Summer Forecast ROM ex Ch. Marlyn That's Class) in 1989, producing the top-winning Ch. Marlyn Intentional Foul ("Magic"). He was Number One Irish in 1994 and Number Two Irish in 1995. He established a record that stood for several years for winning the greatest number of Irish Setter specialties in

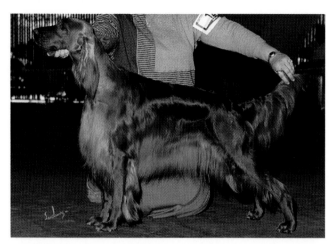

Ch. Marlyn Lyric ROM. Owned by Marilyn Title.

Ch. Marlyn Intentional Foul, a top-winning dog and Number One Irish Setter in 1994 and Number Two Irish Setter in 1995. Owned by Marilyn Title.

the history of the breed. He has produced champions both in the US and in Australia for Ankara Irish Setters.

Marilyn has produced more than 50 champions from 17 litters in the 25 years she has been breeding Irish Setters. She has been president of the Irish Setter Club of Southern California and has been a director of the ISCA since 1992.

She has judged many sweepstakes classes at specialties, including the 1991 ISCA Centennial National Specialty. She feels certain that her career in dogs will eventually lead to judging.

Joan Toy, *Toy Farm*–Mason, MI

In 1964, Joan decided to acquire an Irish Setter. She happened on the kennel of Ivor Glen, home of one of the

first dual champions in the breed, Dual Ch. Ivor Glen Mahogany Mike CDX. That day, she brought home a bitch puppy, Heather. After about 18 months of struggling to train Heather, Joan took her to obedience school, where both novice owner and rebellious dog learned a great deal. Heather had the last laugh at graduation, though. She quietly ate off the side of Joan's sweater while they were waiting for their turn. Then she proceeded to do all the exercises with nearly perfect form. Heather had several litters and lived to be 17 1/2 years old.

A real turning point for Joan came in 1969 when she drove in a blinding snowstorm to St. Louis to select a puppy sired by a son of Ch. Blayneywood Country Squire, whom Joan had rescued from a life of neglect. The puppy became Ch. Toy Farm Tilly O'Abergavenny CD. She proved to be an excellent brood bitch, producing several champions. Heartbreak occurred several years later when one of the puppies they sold developed PRA. In order to clear the line, Joan test-bred three bitches. All passed and became the foundation for subsequent Toy Farm stock.

Joan says, "Thirty-five years is a long time to have the privilege of enjoying a breed as special as the Irish Setter. Our lives have been immeasurably enriched by the many wonderful people we have met, as well as the dogs who are an integral part of our lives. I have never regretted stopping at McIvor's house and bringing home the 'red hellion.'"

Cindy Trefrey, Avon, CT

Cindy Trefrey's first show Irish was Am. Can. Ch. Barrewyne Crimson Courier in the 1970s. Her first

Ch. Meadowlark's Anticipation ROM, a top producer and winner of ten Bests in Show, one Canadian Best in Show, and many specialty and group wins, shown here winning Best of Breed at the 1984 Westminster Kennel Club show just before his retirement. Owned by Cindy Trefrey.

specialty winner was Am. Can. Bda. Ch. Kincora Blazing Banner (Ch. Tirvelda Earl of Harewood ex Wilson Farm Country Belle). He was the Number One Irish Setter in 1974.

Banner's most outstanding offspring was Ch. Rockherin Bandilane Bridget, acquired by Cindy at 13 months of age from her breeder, Joyce Diamond. Bred to Am. Can Ch. McCamon Marquis, she produced Ch. Rockherin Follow the Sun, owned by Dale Hood, and Ch. Rockherin Raffin, owned by the Wheatleys.

In 1981, Cindy acquired Ch. Meadowlark's Anticipation ROM ("Dennis") (Ch. Candia Indeed ROM ex Ch.Tirvelda Meadowlark's Ebbtide ROM) from Rose Ross. First handled by Jane Forsyth, he became the first dog in AKC history to complete his championship one day and win an All-Breed Best in Show the next. When Jane retired, Elliott Weiss took over Dennis' career and piloted him to ten Bests in Show, one Canadian Best in Show, and many specialty and group wins, including twice winning the ISCA National Specialty, first in 1983 and then in 1985 from the Veterans class. He retired from active showing in 1984, winning Group First at Westminster. He is the sire of 36 champions and appears in the pedigrees of many of today's top winners and producers. Most notable of these, Ch. Tirvelda Once Upon A Time, is a double Anticipation great-grandson.

Ch. Tirvelda Once Upon a Time and his brother, Ch. Tirvelda Time After Time (Ch. Tirvelda Trident ex Ch. Tirvelda Holly Go Lightly) were bred by Cindy and Ann Eldredge. During their careers, Once Upon a Time was co-owned by Dr. Robert Helferty. Time After Time is co-owned with Carolyn Mauritz. Once Upon a Time

("Alistair") had an illustrious career, rising to Number One Irish Setter in 1992 and 1993 and winning the National Specialty in 1993.

Cindy also owns a daughter of Ch. Tirvelda Once Upon A Time out of Ch. Rockherin Raeve—Ch. Rockherin Raeve Review, co-owned with Dr. Helferty.

Mike and Barbara Trice, *Santa Fe*–Romoland, CA

The term "Santa Fe" means the royal city of the holy faith of St. Francis, the patron saint of animals. That was the name that Mike and Barbara chose for their Irish Setters in 1982, when they bought their first pet Irish.

In 1989, they were introduced to Dick and Shirley Farrington, who sold them their first show puppy. He became Ch. Shawnee Winter Smoke CD TDI CGC ("Smokey"), their first champion and foundation stud dog. Several years later, Arista's Golden Jubilation was acquired. Bred to Winter Smoke, she produced the "Autumn" and "Country" litters.

Ch. Shawnee Winter Smoke CD TDI CGC, Barbara and Mike Trice's first champion and foundation stud dog.

In 1991, Barbara and Mike went back to their mentors Dick and Shirley and obtained Ch. Shawnee Range Bandit CGC. Bred to Jubilation, the "Darby'O" litter resulted.

Mike and Barbara began in obedience in 1994 with Smokey, who acquired his CD degree in 1996. Bandit is now working toward his first obedience title. Both Smokey and Bandit are trained therapy dogs, visiting hospitals and nursing homes. Barbara and Mike say, "Having a therapy dog is one of the most rewarding experiences a person can have. We have witnessed acute care and long-term care patients react to Smokey but to nothing else. People sitting in wheelchairs welcome him by lifting their fingers so they can feel his soft hair or touch his ears. No words

Ch. Tirvelda Once Upon A Time, Number One Irish Setter in 1992 and 1993 and National Specialty winner in 1993. Owned by Cindy Trefrey and Dr. Robert Helferty.

ever need to be spoken, because their actions or the tears in their eyes say it all.

"We have been invited not only to hospitals, but to many local schools and day care facilities so that the children can become educated about dogs and the responsibilities attached to dog ownership. It is amazing when you walk into a room full of rambunctious children, how quiet it becomes, and how they start to listen and observe."

Bandit has another career as well. He is the 4-H companion for the Trices' daughter, Kayleigh, who shows him in conformation, obedience, and agility.

Fred and Connie Vanacore, *Ballycroy–Mendham, NJ*

The first thing that Fred and Connie did when they moved into their new home in 1956 was to look for an Irish Setter puppy. Fred had always admired the breed, but Connie had never seen one. It happened that the kennel in the next town, Tercor, might be able to lead the novice couple to their puppy. The owner was the first licensed AKC professional handler, Harold Correll, who showed and occasionally bred Irish Setters. The kennel full of red dogs was overwhelming, but there were no puppies. Harold sent the couple to Westchester, New York, to the Phantom Brooks Kennel of Brooks and Dodie Emory. They returned home with their puppy, Phantom Brooks Ballycroy. Connie brought "Shannon" for Harold to see and he said, "You could show this dog. There's a show nearby in a few weeks." That show turned out to be the last great Morris & Essex show. It was such a fantastic event and such fun for the novice handler, who took a third-place ribbon, that a lifelong passion was started.

Shannon was bred once, to a Knockross bitch, and a puppy from that litter became Ch. Dureen O'Tara, the foundation for Walter Nickerson's dogs. At about the same time, Walter bought Ch. Tirvelda Rick O' Shea from Ted Eldredge. Bred to Dureen, she produced Ch. Tirvelda Beau James. As time went on, the Vanacores were occupied with raising a young family, but Connie never forgot Morris & Essex, so they looked for a bitch. A year later, they found one at the home of Ivan and Leonore Klapper of Banshee Kennels. They bought Banshee Irish Mist (Knockross O'Boy ROM ex Ch. Banshee Vogue of Antrim). Misty never finished, but when bred to Ch. Tirvelda Beau James she produced Ballycroy's Rua Catlin. In 1970, Catlin was bred to Ch. Tirvelda Nor'wester to produce Best in Show-winning Ch. Ballycroy's Northern Sunset, who sired several champions, the most notable of which were the brothers Ch. Santera Tamberluck and Ch. Santera Tristan Troubadour. Tamber became the foundation stud for Sandy Novicin's kennel.

Ch. Fieldstone Trace of Burgundy taking Best of Winners at the Trenton Kennel Club in 1982. Owned by Connie and Fred Vanacore.

Connie began her writing career, and in 1979, she purchased a bitch from Mary Ann Alston, who became Ch. Fieldstone Trace of Burgundy (Am. Can. Ch. McCamon Marquis ex Glen Cree Merriment). "Tracey" finished easily and was bred to Ch. Tioga Tegan to Kimberlin, owned by Claire Andrews. From that litter, Connie kept and co-owned Ballycroy Fieldstone Autumn with Dale Hood. Autumn, bred once to Ch. Regalaire Royal Majesty, produced Ch. Ballycroy Royal Burgundy ("Katie"). In 1994, Connie began a co-ownership with Ken Ruff of Brophy Irish Setters in hopes of producing a good field dog that was representative of what the Irish Setter could be. Ken kept a bitch from that litter by

Ballycroy Ruxton St. Clare taking Best of Winners at the Trenton Kennel Club in 1999. Owned by Connie and Fred Vanacore and Dale Hood.

Brophy's Red Storm Rising, Brophy's Ballycroy Ballina, field-pointed. "Lina's" first litter contains the newest field hopeful, Brophy's JJ of Ballycroy. Her second litter contains Brophy's Ballycroy Liberty Belle. In 1996, Katie was bred to Ch. Ballymera's Stormin' Norman to produce the "saintly" litter. Ballycroy Ruxton St. Clare, co-owned with Dale Hood, is pointed.

Connie was fortunate to follow her love of dogs into a profession. She was Features Editor of the *AKC Gazette* for almost ten years, at the same time writing a column about dogs for a local newspaper. She is the author of six books and the canine section of the *Encyclopedia Britannica*. She has been active in club affairs and is a past president of the Eastern Irish Setter Association and the ISCA, for which she is the AKC Delegate. Connie spearheaded the formation of the ISCA Health Committee, of which she is the chair and the guiding spirit for the adoption of its Principles of Integrity. She was chair of the Illustrated Standards Committee and is the author of this book. She was the recipient of the E. I. Eldredge Memorial Award. This award is especially meaningful to her because Ted Eldredge was her mentor and close friend for many years.

Connie and Fred have never maintained more than five dogs in their household. All are housepets. Their show careers are a small part of their lives, and the Vanacores realize that their dogs would rather be hunting or sharing the couch. All their dogs have been OFA-certified and DNA-cleared for PRA.

The friendships, support, and mutual interests that bind dog fanciers together have enhanced the joy of sharing their lives with the most beautiful of all dogs.

Susan E. Van Dyke, *Saliforth*—Seattle, WA

Susan's kennel was established in 1975 with a foundation bitch bred by Lorelei Windhorn and Scott Thompson. She was Am. Can. Ch. Sallynoggin Happy Ending CD (Ch. Candia Indeed ROM ex Ch. Bayberry Happy Time), a two-time group winner. She is the dam of Am. Can. Ch. Camelar the Curragh Am. Can. CD CGC, sire and grandsire of many champions. Susan also owned Can. Ch. Kinsale's Charlton, the dam of Ch. Charlton's Moon Lover ROM.

Her current dogs include Ch. Estrella My Fair Lady (Ch. Sunshine's First Rate ex Ch. Fancy Free Peg O'My Dreams, whelped in 1989), Token It Aint Necessarily So (Ch. Liafail London Pride ex Ch. U-CD Token Talk of the Town UD CGC) bred by Kay Bedeau in 1995, and Saliforth CountrygirlinParis bred by Faye Weiler in 1997 (Am. Can. Ch. Saliforth Darby Dan Can CD CGC ex Ch.Eirecrest Classy Chassis).

Susan's interests are conformation, obedience, and agility.

Ernie and Joan Viola and Dana Haskell, *Kinvale*—Huntington, NY

Ernie purchased his first Irish in 1964 from Kelly Fox. He went on to become Ch. Kilkara Firebrand CD. In 1966, he returned to Kelly and obtained Ch. Kilkara Fireflame CD. "Flame" was bred in 1969 to Ch. Tirvelda Nor'wester to produce the first Kinvale litter. Ernie and Joan were married in 1970, and at that time, Kinvale really became established. In 1971, they bred a daughter of Nor'wester and Flame to Ch. Tirvelda Middle Brother, producing Ch. Kinvale Majorette of Kendel CD ("Sandy"), co-owned with Dana Haskell. This was the beginning of a long-term friendship and partnership. Sandy was a top-winning bitch and was Best of Opposite Sex at the 1977 National Specialty, among her other wins. In 1978, she was bred to Ch. Courtwood Spring Son, and from that litter came Ch. Kinvale Royal Irish, co-owned with Mary Merlo. This, too, was the start of an enduring friendship. In 1985, Royal Irish was bred to Ch. Courtwood Manuscript ROM. Of the two in the litter, one became Ch. Kinvale Evergreen Destiny ROM ("Teddy") who became a multiple group and specialty winner, handled by Mary Merlo.

Ch. Kinvale Evergreen Destiny ROM, a multiple group and specialty winner. Owned by Joan and Ernie Viola and Dana Haskell.

In 1985, the Violas purchased Meadowlark's Mystique from Rose Ross. Bred twice to Teddy, she produced three champions in the first litter: Ch. Kinvale Call to Destiny; Ch. Kinvale Send In The Clowns, sire of ten champions; and Ch. Kinvale Captured Moment, Winners Bitch at the 1990 National Specialty and Best of Opposite Sex at the 1991 Centennial National Specialty.

Mystique's second litter contained Ch. Kinvale Black Tie Requested, co-owned with Elizabeth Goldstein; Am. Can. Ch. Kinvale Formal Attire, owned by Richard Pavlak; Ch. Kinvale RSVP to Panda Sham, owned by Doug and

Ch. Kinvale Captured Moment, Winners Bitch at the 1990 National Specialty and Best of Opposite Sex at the 1991 Centennial National Specialty. Owned by Joan and Ernie Viola and Dana Haskell.

Carol Ritchie. He is a specialty winner and the sire of champions when bred to Ch. Evergreen Return Engagement, owned by Mary Merlo. One pup in that litter, Ch. Evergreen Sweet Sensation, is now co-owned with junior handler Deirdre Dunbar.

In 1992, Teddy was bred to Ch. Chamberlayne's Think of Me. One of that litter became Am. Can. Ch. Chamberlayne's Big Easy, owned by Craig Cooper. Another brother became Ch. Chamberlayne's Echo of Kinvale ("Cooper"), owned by the Violas, Mary Merlo, and Craig Cooper. Cooper is the sire of many champions, a junior hunter, and an agility titlist.

In 1994, Think of Me was bred to Ch. Kinvale Send In The Clowns to produce Am. Can. Ch. Chamberlayne's Sassafras, a multi-group winner, owned by Craig and Mike Sicora.

Many dogs that have become significant to Evergreen, Fyrethorn, and Panda Sham kennels were derived from Kinvale, including Ch. Evergreen Poetry in Motion and Ch. Meadowlark's Vanity Fair. In 1997, Ch. Evergreen Sweet Sensation was bred to Am. Can. Ch. Evergreen Chase the Clouds JH to produce the "Dazzle" litter.

They also co-own Pin Oak Voice Be Heard and Pin Oak Medal of Valor with Nancy Godbey, Elizabeth Goldstein, and Mary Merlo. Joan is also a co-owner with Nancy Godbey and Deirdre Dunbar of Am. Can. Ch. Pin Oak Robert E. Lee.

Since 1970, there have been 14 Kinvale litters (8 for the Violas and 6 for Dana Haskell). They have stressed temperament and health before anything. With limited breeding, they strive to better the breed.

Suzanne and Charlie Walker, *Kellyglen*– Whitney Point, NY

Kellyglen had its beginnings in 1988 with the purchase of Valley View Erin's Ruby. When bred to Ch. Ballingary Phantom Jet, she produced Ch. Kellyglen's Avalon ("Jenny"), their first homebred champion. When she was bred to Ch. Devlin's North Star, one puppy resulted that became Ch. Kellyglen's Song of Avalon.

In the spring of 1992, Suzanne acquired a bitch from Shangrila Kennels that became Ch. Shangrila Sweet Alyssum. When bred to Ch. Rockherin Shangrila At Last, she produced Ch. Shangrila Molly O'Kellyglen for Lynne Mehring, Ch. Shangrila Grady O'Kellyglen for Karen Lynch, and Ch. Kellyglen's Dillon O'Ryan, retained by Suzanne. He was an elegant, typey, beautifully moving dog who finished owner-handled with a Group First from the classes. Dillon, bred to Song of Avalon, produced two bitches for Kellyglen, My Girl and Cover Girl. Also at

Ch. Chamberlayne's Echo of Kinvale, a junior hunter, agility titlist, and the sire of many champions. Owned by Joan and Ernie Viola, Mary Merlo, and Craig Cooper.

Ch. Kellyglen's Dillon O'Ryan winning Group First at the Chenango Valley Kennel Club in 1997. Owned by Suzanne and Charlie Walker.

Kellyglen is a litter by Ch. Pin Oak Robert E. Lee ex Ch. Shangrila Sweet Alyssum.

Tye and Lew Walker, *BrynMoor*—Gainesboro, TN

Two young Irish currently reside with the Walkers: Can. Ch. Ohkom Sunberry (Am. Can. Ch. Captiva's Ride With The Wind ex Ohkom Wild Strawberry) and Captiva's Dior of BrynMoor (Ch. Cucuhullain Good Fortune ROM ex Am. Can. Ch. Quailfied Stylish Success).

Under the mentorship of Jill Taylor and Linda Jacobelli, the Walkers look to a future filled with champion setters that possess the rollicking personality, solid structure, and sound movement that they feel is indicative of the breed.

Ballymera's First Encounter ROM winning Best American Bred Bitch at the 1993 ISCA National Specialty. Owned by Julianne Waters and Kim Velletri.

Ballymera's First Encounter ROM. Jewelset then co-bred a litter of Whisperin'Breeze to Ch. Quailfield Mak'n Business. Six in that litter finished their championships, which was Jewelset's "Made" litter, including Made 'N The Shade, Made It Happen, Custom Made, and Made For You. Made In the Shade bred to First Encounter produced four champions. First Encounter's second litter by Made It Happen produced three champions.

Can. Ch. Ohkom Sunberry finishing her championship in 1999. Owned by Tye and Lew Walker.

Julianne Waters and Kim Velletri, *Jewelset*—West Greenwich, RI

Jewelset Kennels began in 1973 with the purchase of their first Irish Setter from Louis Iacobucci, Celou's Tiffany McCrory. Tiffany was not a show girl, but she possessed all of the most important traits in the Irish Setter: love, loyalty, and fun. Tiffany "told" them that they had to have more setters and a home in the country.

The first show dog to come to Jewelset was Ch. Dutch Valley Sundance Kid ("Danny") from Marion Mullet of Dutch Valley Kennels in New York. That began a lifelong friendship that they still share. Danny was their first champion and group winner. Their next show dogs also carried the Dutch Valley prefix: Chs. Dutch Valley Enchantment, Mint Parfait, and Prime Contender.

Kim and Julie saw Ch. Meadowlark's Whisperin' Breeze ROM (Ch. Meadowlark's Masterful ex Meadowlark's Wyndchimes) when she was young and eventually purchased from her owner, Patty Clawson, a bitch,

Two Jewelset champions, Ch. Jewelset's Made For You (left) and Ch. Jewelset's Made 'N The Shade (right). Owned by Julianne Waters and Kim Velletri.

In 1996, their greatest achievement occurred when their bitch, Ch. Jewelset's Made For You ("Wendy") went Best in Show with Kim handling.

The future of Jewelset lies with Wendy's puppies, sired by the 1997 National Specialty Best of Opposite Sex and Best in Show winner Ch. Rusticwoods Running Mate.

They consider movement, soundness, type, and temperament to be the most important factors to be considered before producing a litter of puppies, combined with the ability to find perfect homes in which the puppies can spend the rest of their lives.

Charlotte Watson, *Stonewall*—Birmingham, AL

Stonewall came into being in 1975, after the Watsons' daughter had gone to college. Bill, Charlotte's late husband, decided he had to have another "little thing" around the house, and he had always wanted an Irish Setter. The first was Stonewall's Chivas Regal CDX. (Stonewall for a favorite Civil War hero—Chivas Regal was Bill's choice.)

While going through obedience, Charlotte became interested in the show aspect and in 1980, they acquired their first show bitch from Penny Nunnally. She became Ch. Scarlly's Show and Tell CD (Ch. Scarlly's Showboat ROM ex Ch. Rendition Razzle Dazzle ROM).

In 1982, they added Scarlly's Dream Merchant (Ch. Scarlly's Show 'Nuf ROM ex Ch. Scarlly's Dreamboat Annie). Show and Tell bred to Dream Merchant gave Charlotte her first homebred champions in 1983, Ch. Stonewall's First Edition and Ch. Stonewall's Finest Kind. A second litter by Ch. Scarlly's Red Hot ROM produced

Ch. Stonewall's Miss Liberty, owned by Bobbi Kilduff, and Ch. Stonewall's Liberty Belle ("Libby"), a group and specialty winner who won an Award of Merit at the 1990 National Specialty.

In 1988, Ch. Stonewall's Finest Kind was bred to Ch. Scarlly's Joe Montana CD to produce Ch. Stonewall's Irish Melody, owned and shown by Bobbi Kilduff. Irish Melody was bred to Ch. Rusticwoods Song N'Dance Man to produce three champions: Pal Joey, My Fair Lady, and High Kickers. My Fair Lady was bred to Ch. Rusticwoods Song of Hawaii to produce Ch. Stonewall's Highstakes Player. He is presently co-owned and shown by Charlotte's grandson, who is not above beating his grandmother in the show ring on occasion.

Charlotte says, "Dog shows opened a whole new world for my late husband and me. How grateful I am every day

Ch. Stonewall's Highstakes Player taking Best of Winners at the Atlanta Kennel Club in 1996.

Ch. Stonewall's Liberty Belle, a group and specialty winner and winner of an Award of Merit at the 1990 ISCA National Specialty. Owned by Charlotte Watson.

for it—the wonderful people we have met and the wonderful dogs who have blessed and continue to bless our lives. From generation to generation, both human and canine, the beat goes on."

Faye Weiler, *Eirecrest*—Spokane, WA

Faye has bred Irish Setters under the Eirecrest prefix since 1967. Two of her early dogs were Ch. Scarlet Bronwyn O'Wit and Ch. Malsteen Daquerie. An extended absence from the show ring and whelping box ended in 1984 when she acquired two puppies that became Ch. Rainbow Fieldstone Tiara and Ch. Redheather Marquis Diamond ("Heather"). Three litters were bred out of Heather, the first by Ch. Auburn War Eagle, one of which became Am. Can. Ch. Eirecrest Dark Jewel CD. The

Ch. Redheather Marquis Diamond taking Winners Bitch at the Sammamish Kennel Club in 1986. Owned by Faye Weiler.

second litter by Ch. Scarlly's Red Hot ROM gave Faye Ch. Eirecrest Etched in Fire CD. The third litter by Ch. Kaerdon's Broker's Tip gave her Ch. Eirecrest Classy Chassis CGC. Heather is also the granddam of Ch. Eirecrest Kaerdon's O'Deryn CDX, owned by Donna Jo Lyles and Leta Graham.

Classy Chassis was bred to Ch. Sunnyhill's Wings of the Wind and then to Ch. Saliforth Darby Dan CD. Several offspring of both of these litters are pointed.

Faye's goals as a hobby breeder are to produce Irish that are physically sound and have livable temperaments that conform to the standard for the breed.

Doreen and Lorien Weintraub, *Dorien–* Killingworth, CT

Doreen and Lorien acquired their first show Irish Setter from Jane Mahaffey of Seantalan Kennels in 1992. Lorien showed Seantalan's Risin' of the Moon CGC in juniors and Doreen showed him in conformation. A spinal injury ended his show career, but he was their "learning dog."

In 1996, they bought a bitch puppy from Charlie and Fran Sloughfy that became Ch. Fyrethorn's Cairin Cailin, owner-handled by Lorien. Currently, Cailin is training for junior hunter competition. Mother and daughter look forward to their first litter from Cailin and to continue to show, learn, and generally "have a grand time with Irish Setters."

Marlin and Linda Lee Whalen, Flint, MI

Marlin and Linda began in 1972 with a field and bench-bred Irish. As novice owners, they did not accomplish much with her, but then acquired Congre's Victoria Jean. They bred her and her offspring to some nice wins. In 1991, they acquired Lee's Granny Smith JH who turned out to be an excellent hunting dog for Marlin. Her daughter, Lee's Red Delicious JH CGC, is what Linda has been waiting for. She is big-boned, well-feathered, birdy, smart, and beautiful.

Linda says that each dog has special meaning to them, as a family member first and foremost. Anything else they accomplish is "frosting on the cake."

Frank and Katherine Wheatley, *Rockherin–* South Rockwood, MI

The Wheatley's Rockherin Kennels is one of the kennels that spans generations and has had enormous influence on the breed, primarily through their bitches. Their first Irish Setter came from Maple Ridge Kennels in 1953. Ch.

Ch. Eirecrest Classy Chassis CGC winning Best of Breed and Best of Winners at the Spokane Kennel Club in 1993. Owned by Faye Weiler.

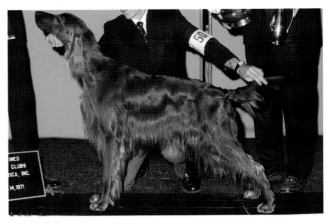

Ch. Rockherin Rebecca ROM, a top-producing bitch. Owned by Katherine and Frank Wheatley.

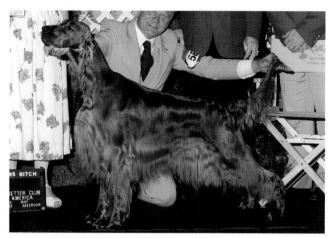

Ch. Rockherin Sheena ROM, dam of nine champion get. Owned by Katherine and Frank Wheatley.

Red Rogue of Maple Ridge was a son of Ch. Thenderin Brian Tristan ex Crosshaven Lea of Maple Ridge. Rogue produced ten champions, including two Best in Show dogs. One of his offspring was Ch. Conifer's Lance, who was top Irish in 1961 with five Bests in Show. Before his untimely death in 1963, he had sired 15 champions.

From Dr. Jay Calhoon, the Wheatleys acquired a great bitch, Ch. Caldene Ailene. She was a top-winning show dog and a great producer. When bred to Rockherin Flynn, she produced Ch. Rockherin Race, who finished undefeated in five shows, and Ch. Rockherin Rebecca, who made her mark as an important producer as the dam of Ch. Tirvelda Hunter's Moon ROM, Ch. Tirvelda Vanity Fair, Ch. Rebecca's Irish Lace, and Am. Can. Ch. McCamon Royal Burgundy, the foundation for McCamon Kennels.

A Ch. Tirvelda Hunter's Moon daughter, Rockherin Carrie, when bred to Ch. Meadowlark's Anticipation ROM, produced Ch. Rockherin Sheena ROM. Sheena was bred twice, the first time to Ch. Meadowlark's Wyndjammer ROM and then to Ch. Meadowlark's Vindicator ROM, to produce nine champions in the two litters. Many of these have become foundation stock for other kennels.

Ch. Rockherin Classie Chassis is the dam of four champions in one litter. Ch. Rockherin Neesa of Kenobi ROM, who was owned by Joe and Gerry Lee, produced seven champions in her only litter. Ch. Rockherin Dannon, also owned by the Lees, is the sire of five champions.

Their dogs and bitches have been foundation stock for Lynne Mehring's Shangrila and Pam Schaar's Quinniver Kennels, among many others.

The Wheatleys usually keep four adult dogs and never breed more than one litter a year. They feel that the most important attributes of their breeding program are the quality bitches they have consistently produced over the years.

Janice White, *Honeyrock*–Avon, NY

Honeyrock, a modest kennel in upstate New York, has seen few more than a dozen litters in more than 30 years. In 1968, Honeyrock first established the goal, "Good things come from Honeyrock."

The first Honeyrock champion was Ch. Bayberry Russet of Kinvarra in 1969. In 1971, Ch. Tirvelda Stella of Dunholm, purchased from John and Anne Savory, made history by earning 17 points in 28 days, being undefeated in the classes, and finishing with back-to-back majors.

In 1982, Ch. Honeyrock Garnet of Summerhill was Best of Breed at the ISCA National Specialty, and his litter sister, Ch. Honeyrock Galadriel, became an important producer for Jan's kennel.

A fourth-generation Honeyrock dog, Am. Can. Bda. Ch. Honeyrock West of the Moon, was an Award of Merit winner at the 1996 National Specialty Show from the Veterans class. He is the sire of numerous champion, obedience, and junior hunter-titled dogs.

Jan is now working with the seventh generation of Honeyrock dogs, all without known heritable disabilities, DNA-cleared of PRA and OFA-certified. Jan says, "The most happy note of all is that these admirable Irish Setters are more endearing for their sweet companionship than for all their achievements in the ring."

Kathy and Richard Whiteis, *Sunshine*–Temecula, CA

Dick Whiteis owned an Irish Setter as a child. His dog, Sally, always walked him to school, returned home, and in the afternoon would wait in front of the house for him to return. Naturally, when Kathy and Dick moved to

Am. Can. Mex. Ch. Kerry-Eire Heaven Only Knows CD ROM, a multiple group and specialty winner and sire of 20 champions. Owned by Kathy and Richard Whiteis.

California in 1976, they acquired their first Irish and became involved in club affairs with the Irish Setter Club of San Diego in 1979.

Since that time, Sunshine Setters has produced and shown 24 champions, with many others pointed. Although Kathy enjoys breeding and showing her bitches, it is the dogs that capture her heart. In 1981, she purchased a male puppy from Susan Griffith. He became Am. Can. Mex. Ch. Kerry-Eire Heaven Only Knows CD ROM (Ch. Courtwood Summer Forecast ROM ex Ch. Kerry-Eire Little Rebel). During his career, he was a multi-group and specialty winner, as well as the sire of 20 champions. Kathy says, "He was a once-in-a-lifetime dog and is still the heart and soul of Sunshine Setters even though I lost him in 1996 when he was 15 years of age."

The next important dog for Sunshine is Am. Mex. Ch. Sunshine's First Rate ("Chip") (Am. Can. Mex. Ch. Kerry-Eire Heaven Only Knows CD ROM ex Ch. Chandar's Laura Ashley). Chip was campaigned in the early 1990s and was always owner-handled to many specialty and group wins. He was a Best in Show winner in Mexico on the way to his title. He was an Award of Merit winner at the 1992 National Specialty. To date, he has sired 18 champions, with several more close to finishing.

The third generation is Ch. Sunshine's Remember When (Am. Mex. Ch. Sunshine's First Rate ex Meadowlark's Outrageous), co-bred with Patrice Clawson and Rose Marie Ross. He completed his championship before the age of two and is succeeding his father and grandfather in garnering specialty wins. One of his sons, Ch. Sierra Lyn Academy Award, owned by Ron and Vicki Larmour, finished his championship at 14 months.

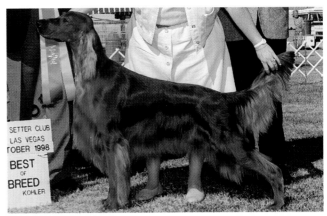

Ch. Sunshine's Remember When, a third generation champion and producer for Sunshine Setters. Owned by Kathy and Richard Whiteis.

Kathy now has high hopes for a litter that doubles up on Heaven Only Knows on both the sire and dam's side.

Phyllis and Ed Wier, *Cullan*–Fairfield, CT

The foundation for Cullan was Ch. Cucuhullain Diamond Lil, bred to Ch. Meadowlark's Wyndjammer, ROM. The first litter produced four champions, most notable of which was Cucuhullains Four Paw Drive, Winners Bitch at the 1989 National Specialty. The next Cullan litter came from Ch. Meadowlark's Vindicator ROM ex Ch. Cullan's Fortune Cookie. Four of these also became champions. Two of them, Ch. Cullan's Xmas Goose and Ch. Cullan's Take A Gander, were Winners Dog and Winners Bitch at the 1993 National Specialty.

C. B. and Alyce Williamson, *Echo*–Daytona Beach, FL

Beginning in 1973 with a dog sired by Ch. Westwind Scarlet Gay Blade, the Williamsons showed English and Irish Setters briefly. They started again in 1991 with Am. Can. Ch. Tellurian Diamond in the Ruff CD. The Echo litter by Diamond out of Ch. McKendree's Trivial Pursuit CD shows promise as Echo's foundation for the future. The Williamsons plan to produce intelligent, healthy, versatile Irish Setters that will be able to perform their original job.

Dennis and Kathie Wilson, *Willohill*–Concord, CA

Willohill began in 1975 with their first Irish Setter, bought for 75 dollars. The following year, after attending some dog shows, they decided to buy a puppy they could show. Ch. Kavaneire's Barnaby of Brask CD was a slow maturer, to say the least. He finished his championship at 8 years of age and his CD at 10, but he was their devoted companion for 13 years.

Among his many accomplishments, Am. Mex. Ch. Sunshine's First Rate was an Award of Merit winner at the 1992 ISCA National Specialty and has sired 18 champions. Owned by Kathy and Richard Whiteis.

In 1978, they purchased a puppy from Pat Haigler that was to become their foundation bitch. She became Ch. Rendition Song of Willohill ("Cricket"). She was bred twice, producing some lovely offspring that did well in conformation and obedience.

In 1989, they purchased a bitch from Carolyn Roche that became Ch. Rusticwood Willohill P. J. Party. She finished easily and has produced some nice get for Willohill. Her first litter by Ch. Kerry-Eire Heaven Only Knows CD ROM produced three puppies, one of which the Wilsons kept. Ch. Willohill Windswept finished by winning several Bests of Breed and a Group Fourth.

In 1991, another puppy arrived from Carolyn Roche that became Ch. Rusticwood Willohill Mt. Song, a male from the famous "Song" litter.

In 1993, P. J. Party was bred to Ch. Rusticwoods Running Mate, owned by Sheila Smith. She was shipped to Alabama and was stranded there due to winter storms. The Wilsons had to leave her to whelp her 13 puppies. When they were ten weeks old, eight puppies and Mom were flown to California. From that litter, several are major-pointed and one has finished. The one that the Wilsons kept is Willohill Sun Flyer.

The Wilsons also own two miniature Longhaired Dachshunds that they obtained from Mary Olich Nie.

Dennis and Kathie say, "We have made some wonderful friends through our years in Irish Setters. Our work with the Irish Setter Club of the Pacific, for which we have both served as officers, has been fun and fulfilling, and, of course, the redheads make it all possible. They are, without a doubt, the funniest, most entertaining dogs imaginable.

"They are the most beautiful and endearing creatures on Earth. Watching them run can take your breath away and make your heart skip a beat! We have been very lucky to share our home with many two- and four-legged friends during the past 22 years."

Michael and Kirsten Wilson, *Touchstone*– Lewiston, NY

Touchstone's breeding program began in 1991 when Kirsten acquired their foundation bitch, Ch. Meadowlark's Classic Touch, from Rose Ross (Ch. Meadowlark's Wyndjammer ROM ex Ch. Cloverleaf's Who's That Girl). Bred by Annette Izydorek Pusey, she combines Meadowlark, Cloverleaf, and Courtwood lines. She is a sister to Ch. Pompei's First Class and Ch. Pompei's Touch of Class.

Her first litter, the "blue" litter, was whelped in 1994 and was sired by Ch. Meadowlark's Masterful ROM. Co-bred with Rose Ross, Meadowlark acquired three of the pups, and Kirsten kept a dog and a bitch that became

Am. Can. Ch. Touchstone's Out of the Blue and Am. Can. Ch. Touchstone's My Blue Heaven. Both finished easily with specialty wins and group placements.

Classic Touch was bred in 1995 to Ch. Stoneypoint's Storm Trooper, producing the "wild" litter. Three of these are finished–Ch. Stoneypoint's Wild At Heart, owned by Jeri McClure and Dixie Demorest, Ch. Touchstone's Wild About You, and Ch. Touchstone's Wild Cherry.

In 1998, Ch. Touchstone's My Blue Heaven whelped a litter by Ch. Rusticwood's Song of Hawaii, the "heaven" litter. The dog, Vermilion's Heaven Can Wait, lives with Bruce and Mary Foote. Two bitches, Touchstone's Seventh Heaven and Touchstone's Heaven Sent, reside with the Wilsons.

Lorraine Wolk, *Glenlor*–East Hartford, CT

In 1971, Lorrie obtained her first Irish Setter from Claire Andrews, Kimberlin Gae Bonnie. She lived until the age of 13 but never finished because she was injured in a car accident.

In 1980, she obtained her foundation bitch for today's Glenlor line, Ch. Shawnee Sierra Sunstorm CD (Am. Can. Ch. Shawnee Sundance ex Am. Can. Ch. Shawnee Sierra Stormcloud). "Sunny," bred to Ch. Caitlin's Exceller, produced one champion, Ch. Glenlor's Fire n'Ice CD CGC TDI, and when bred to Ch. Meadowlark's Intrepid ROM, she produced three champions.

Lorrie liked the combination of Shawnee and Meadowlark and continued in that line, breeding Ch. Glenlor's Fire n' Ice to Ch. Dunholm Kildare. The third generation of Glenlor is a combination of Shawnee, Meadowlark, and Draherin lines from a combination of

Glenlor's Distant Star winning Best of Opposite Sex at the Holyoke Kennel Club in 1994. Owned by Lorraine Wolk.

Ch. Glenlor's Distant Star and Talcott Mtn. Shiloh, a bitch of strong Draherin lines.

Lorrie says, "My dogs have always been house dogs. I try to limit myself to five and therefore have had a very limited breeding program. Temperament has always been very important to me. I believe an Irish Setter must be of sound mind as well as body. I am very proud of the fact that the Glenlor dogs have done well as loving companions in conformation, obedience, field, and therapy work."

JoElla Young, *Glenmora*–Tampa, FL

Glenmora came about in the early 1970s with the acquisition of a Ch. Tirvelda Michaelson daughter, Peebles Ginger Gala, who spent her formative years in a hunting kennel. She was acquired at almost five years of age, so it was too late for a show career, but she made her name in the whelping box. Bred to Ch. Dunholm Clancy of Durin and Am. Can. Ch. McCamon Marquis, she produced Chs. Glenmora Michael Erin, April Morning, Sunshine of Robona, Miss Danny O'Meade, Dawn of Wildwood, and Ch. Coppertop Sunset Byrne.

A hiatus from involvement in breeding and showing in the 1980s has found JoElla back with great-grandchildren of Ginger's, co-bred with Ruth Mertsching of CAIB Irish Setters.

Jan Ziech, *Lucky Morn*–Minooka, IL

Jan Ziech purchased her first Irish Setter in 1971 as an eighth grader for a 4-H project. Sean O'Shea was far from being a show dog, but he seeded in her a deep love and appreciation for the breed.

Ch. Sir Kannonball Kilgary CD was purchased as a pup in 1977. A year later, he was joined by Am. Can. Ch. Bonne Lass of Castle Kilgary CD (Ch. Kilgary Dungannon ex Kilgary Castle Leslie), co-owned with her breeder, Virginia Bowie. She was a multiple breed winner and group-placing bitch, all owner-handled. Her first litter was by her uncle, Ch. Kilgary Dunbarry, and produced three multiple-titled dogs: Am. Can. Mex. PR. SA. Ch. of the Americas, Int. Ch. Lucky Morn Avant Garde CD CGC, Ch. Lucky Morn Ap'arition 'Kilgary CD CGC; and Am. Mex. PR. SA. Ch. of the Americas, Int. Ch. Lucky Morn Affair of the Heart CGC.

Avant Garde sired four litters and produced four champions. Affair of the Heart was bred twice. Her first litter, by Am. Can. Ch. Tapnar Cherokee Kinsman, produced four champions, including Ch. Lucky Morn Dann Eze Debonair UD CGC, co-owned with Lisa Moore, Winners Dog at the 1992 National Specialty. Her second litter by Ch. Thenderin Jazzman produced two champions, with several more pointed. All have obedience titles and have passed their Canine Good Citizen tests.

The newest star at Lucky Morn is Deep Vu Celtic Affair, (Ch. Analainn's Thyme Worthy ex Ch. Lucky Morn Thief of Hearts CDX), co-owned and bred with Lisa Moore.

Jan was president of the Western Irish Setter Club for eight years and chairs their rescue and adoption program. She serves on the Health Committee for ISCA and is the Health Convenor for the Irish Setter Club of Canada. Jan was Assistant Chair for the 1998 National Specialty in St. Louis.

Casper and Linda Ziegler, *Classic*–Grayslake, IL

The Zieglers' love for Irish Setters began in the '70s when Casper had his first Irish, "Hooker," who went everywhere with him.

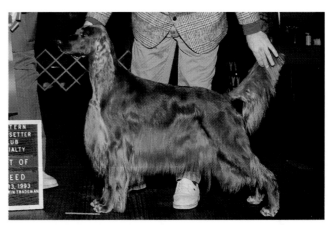

Ch. Classic Krystle Lady CD VC CGC ROM, Classic Setter's foundation bitch. Owned by Linda and Casper Ziegler.

Int. Ch. Classic Chase Manhattan VC CDX JH NA CGC at the 1998 Agility National Specialty in St. Louis, Missouri. Owned by Linda and Casper Ziegler.

Classic Setters was established in 1987 when they purchased their first show-quality Irish. She became Ch. Classic Krystle Lady CD VC CGC ROM (Maplewood My Private Eire ex Rusticwoods Sea Serenade) and was their foundation bitch. She was bred twice, first to Ch. Windwood Firebird Jacob JH to produce Ch. Int. Ch. Classics Chase Manhattan CDX NA JH VC CGC; Ch. Classics Bailey's Irish Cream JH; Ch. Windwood Kahlua Classic; and Ch. Classics Courvoisier CD TD. Her second litter by Ch. Rusticwoods Song N' Dance Man produced three puppies—Ch. Int. Ch.Classics Pheasants Forever JH, Ch. UACh. Classics Rabblerouser CD MX OAJ, and Ch. Classic Krystle's Big Chill.

The Zieglers are proud to produce quality Irish Setters that can excel in conformation, obedience, agility, and most importantly, in hunting ability.

Jay and Kellie Zirkle, *Dunbrook*–Eugene, OR

The Zirkles' interest in Irish Setters began when they saw and admired a Webline dog at a local all-breed show in 1965. Their first Irish was a male pup they brought home from Tirnanog Kennels in 1966 that became Ch. Tirnanog Charleen O'Duibhin CD ("Duffin") (Ch. Muckamoor's Marty McCuhl ex Glen Erin's Satin Sheen). Kellie credits her experiences in art and photography for developing her eye and says that "Duffin" comes close to her ideal Irish Setter. He possessed an elegant head with very dark almond eyes, long neck, tremendous topline, and that angulated shoulder with long upper arm that is missing in many of today's Irish.

Ch. Dunbrook Love Is Blue, sire of ten champion get. Owned by Kellie and Jay Zirkle.

Kellie and Jay Zirkle's first Irish Setter, Ch. Tirnanog Charleen O'Duibhin CD.

In 1966, they also purchased a bitch puppy from Ray and Val Gonsor, Varagon Crimson Classic CD. Bred to Duffin, she produced the first Dunbrook litter that included Chs. Dunbrook Debonaire, Dunbrook Dream CD, and Dunbrook Delight CD (who had 10 points). Delight, bred to Ch. Innisfail Gallant Guy (Ch. Innisfail Flashback's Design ex Thenderin Emberglo), produced Am. Can. Ch. Dunbrook Enchantment, Ch. Dunbrook Escapade, and Dunbrook Express. Enchantment went as a puppy to Pat and Carol McGarry (Windntide), and when bred to Ch. Tirvelda Hunter's Moon ROM, produced their marvelous show bitch, Ch. Windntide Sophistication.

Jay and Kellie continued to linebreed back to their original dogs. Dunbrook Express produced nine champion offspring, the most important for Dunbrook being Ch. Dunbrook Muckamoor Medley. Medley, bred to her great-grandsire, O'Duibhin, produced the Zirkle's best-known dog, Ch. Dunbrook Love Is Blue. He sired ten champions, including Ch. Dunbrook Portrait In Blue CD, OTCh. Sunshine Gatsby's Blue Love MH VC, and Ch. Windntide Hot Cross Buns.

Ann Buck (Muckamoor) used Dunbrook stock going back to O'Duibhin to continue her line, and the two kennels remained closely allied over many years.

In 1985, the Zirkles co-bred a litter with Ann Eldredge by Love Is Blue out of the lovely Ch. Tirvelda Sarsfield Cameo, who came to live with them. That litter included Ch. Dunbrook Once in a Blue Moon, Ch. Dunbrook Song Sung Blue, and Ch. Tirvelda Royal Blue. Once in a Blue

Moon, bred to his half-sister Serenade In Blue, produced Ch. Dunbrook Moonlight Madness. This dog, when bred to Ch. Windntide Cordial on the Rox, produced the group and specialty winner, Ch. Windntide Sandcastle.

Another son of Love is Blue, Ch. Dunbrook Blue Skies CD, produced Ch. Dunbrook Loves the Blues JH, owned by Marsha Henkel (Harborlights). Loves the Blues, when bred to Ch. Castlebar Command Presence, produced many titled offspring, including conformation, tracking, obedience, and agility dogs. In 1998, the Zirkles bred their Dunbrook My Girl (Ch. Dunbrook Blue Skies CD ex Ch. Dunbrook Song Sung Blue) to Marsha Henkel's Ch. Harborlight Keeps Me Dancin' TD JH. They look forward to being back in the ring.

In all, Jay and Kellie have owned and bred 24 champions, all owner-handled. From the beginning, they produced occasional litters, primarily for themselves, when time and space allowed. They are firm believers in linebreeding,

always incorporating the bloodlines of their favorite sire, O'Duibhin. Kellie feels the pedigree is an invaluable tool, but she bases her final decision on the characteristics of the proposed sire and dam and their littermates. Other than several tragic instances of gastric torsion in the early years, the Dunbrook line has been remarkably free of major health problems. The Zirkles credit their good fortune to those who have gone before.

The Zirkles have been active in various organizations since the beginning. Jay was instrumental in gaining AKC recognition for the Multnomah Irish Setter Association in the early '70s. Both have served in many capacities for that club. Kellie has been active in the Emerald Dog Obedience Club and was president of that organization in the late '80s. Jay served on the board of directors of ISCA, as director, treasurer, and then as president from 1991 to 1993. He is a recipient of the E. I. Eldredge Memorial Award.

Irish Setters Abroad

The Irish Setter, as described in the history chapter of this book, is native to the British Isles. The Irish Setter has flourished there over the years, and today it is as popular and respected for its beauty and accomplishments in the field as it is in other parts of the world. Australia has a thriving Irish Setter population, as does Canada. Because these dogs are the closest relatives to American Irish Setters, the breeders who are making an impact in their own countries as well as in the US are profiled here. We are indebted to Eve Gardner for information included in the sections on England, Ireland, and Scotland.

The Irish Setter in Britain and Ireland

It is impossible to view the Irish Setter in the last quarter of the 20th century in isolation, without having to look back at some of the characters and events that, to a very large extent, helped to shape and develop the breed in Britain and Ireland. Eileen Walker, who had started her famous Hartsbourne Kennel in the late 1920s, died in May 1970. She had been the most successful breeder of Irish Setters in Great Britain, and the last litter, which was born at about the same time that Mrs. Walker died in the US, contained yet another show champion and challenge certificate (CC) winner, making her the breeder of 32 challenge certificate winners. Her Hartsbourne prefix and the majority of the dogs were left to her friend Sybil Lennox. Sybil still keeps the famous name alive, together with her own name, Brackenfields. Sybil's kennel was started in 1946, and she is credited with having owned or bred 15 titleholders. Her latest, Sh. Ch.

Sh. Ch. Hartsbourne Snapdragon is a living legacy of the famous Hartsbourne and Brackenfields prefixes. Owned by Sybil Lennox.

Hartsbourne Snapdragon, was born in 1988, and after more than 50 years, Sybil continues to be active in the breed.

The highly influential Wendover Kennel was started by Mr. and Mrs. L. C. James only a little later than the Hartsbournes were, and Wendover stock can be found in pedigrees all over the world. Mr. L. C. James–"Jimmy" to his many friends—died in December 1981, and after Mrs. "Jay" James retired from running the kennels, their son Peter and his wife Julie took over at Wendover. Since that time, Peter has piloted two more bitches, Sh. Ch. Wendover Maid Marion and Sh. Ch. Country Girl to their titles and, more recently in 1998, Wendover Rose of the Shires won 2 CCs. This makes a total of 35 individual CC winners bred by the James family.

During the many years when the Hartsbournes and Wendovers were at the height of their power and influence and dominated the breed, it was possible to pick them out at shows without having to resort to a catalog. Their creators had carefully avoided mixing their distinctive lines and, at that time, it was possible to roughly divide Irish Setters into Hartsbournes and Wendovers and their various relations. Other breeders

Wendover Lorna represents the influential stock of the Wendover Kennels, begun by Mr. and Mrs. L. C. James and continued today by their son Peter and his wife Julie.

did not have any reservations about mixing the lines and managed to combine the two to great effect. Undoubtedly, the most successful among them was Janice Roberts, the creator of the Cornevons. Despite her untimely death at the age of 47, she bred 28 challenge certificate winners, and the last, Sh. Ch. Honeypie of Cornevon, was born in 1985. The Cornevons provided

the foundation for many highly successful breeders, not only in Britain, but all over the world.

Registrations during the last 25 years have fallen from figures in excess of 5,000 per year in the 1970s and early 1980s to a much more acceptable and healthier average of about 1,500 to 2,000 registrations per year. A very high percentage of Irish Setters seem to find their way into the show ring, and the breed often provides one of the top entries at championship shows. This is achieved without Irish Setters even appearing in the top 20 most popular breeds registered with the Kennel Club. In Britain, the Irish Setter has enjoyed enormous success in the show ring, and four have managed to win the ultimate prize, Best in Show at Crufts, in 1981, 1993, 1995, and 1999. Another was Reserve Best in Show in 1983.

Probably the single most significant and beneficial event for the breed during the last 25 years has been the development of DNA testing for Progressive Retinal Atrophy/RCD 1. In Britain, only one carrier was found among the blood samples that represented most of the known bloodlines, proving just how successful the earlier test matings had been in largely eradicating this scourge from the Irish Setter. Hopefully, the development of more

Sh. Ch. Honeypie of Cornevon was the last of 28 challenge certificate winners bred by Janice Roberts.

A tremendous influence on the breed, Sh. Ch. Kerryfair Night Fever sired 23 show champion offspring.

DNA tests in the future will help to eliminate more inherited conditions.

The other event to have had a most profound influence on the development of the breed in this country was the arrival of the great stud dog, Sh. Ch. Kerryfair Night Fever. Born in 1979, he was the product of a mixture of many of the important bloodlines already referred to and had the rare ability to pass on his many qualities to bitches of all breeding. Several of his 23 show champion children inherited the same ability and went on to produce more outstanding winners. Through his influence, the breed managed to achieve a very high standard of quality in the show ring. Night Fever's tremendous influence cannot be overestimated and will become clear in the following review of the leading kennels.

Leading Show Kennels in England

Amberwave: John and Maggie Powis
The foundation bitch Katherine of Audnam arrived in 1974. She was mated to Dunfarlyne's Peppercorn, and Sh. Ch. Amberwave Hera was born in 1978. Hera went to Night Fever and produced Sh. Ch. Amberwave Moonlight Shadow, winner of the group at Manchester in 1989. From Katherine's litter by Sh. Ch. Brinara Inula came Whispering Wind. When mated to Sh. Ch. Clonageera Tyrone, she produced Sh. Ch. Amberwave Pebbles. The highlight of her career was winning her fourth

CC at Crufts in 1997 from the Veteran class for dogs aged seven years or older. Pebbles only had one litter by Sh. Ch. Clonageera Genesis, and their daughter Lace, born in 1994, is now carrying on the line.

Balintyne: Gillian Barker-Bell
Danaway Hot Gossip CC was acquired from the Gurneys and owned in partnership with Mary Gurney. When mated to Night Fever, she produced Sh. Ch. Ma Biche of Danaway for Mary and Sh. Ch. Gold Dust of Balintyne for Gillian. The winner of 15 CCs and 8 Res. CCs, Gold Dust was mated to Free Spirit of Danaway, and Sh. Ch. Balintyne Call Me Madam and her brother Call My Tune 2 CCs 3 Res. CCs were retained. Hot Gossip's daughter, Starduster, won a CC and Res. CC before being exported to New Zealand, where she became a champion.

Ballywestow: Judy Russell
In 1956, Judy persuaded her parents to let her have an Irish Setter. Wendover Romance was bought unseen and has remained the only purchase. She won her first CC in 1961, gaining five in total. At the grand age of 11, she ran

Sh. Ch. Amberwave Pebbles won her fourth CC at Crufts in 1997 from the Veteran class. Owned by John and Maggie Powis.

Sh. Ch. Ballywestow Fleet comes from a long line of show champions of Wendover heritage. Owned by Judy Russell.

for her qualifier and became a champion. She was an excellent brood bitch and from her first litter came Ballywestow Sceptre 1 CC. However, her most successful litters were all by Sh. Ch. Wendover Vagabond, and several matings produced Sh. Chs. Wendover Ballymoss and Brulette, Ballywestow Wendover Beeswing 1 CC 3 Res. CCs, Dante, Res. CC, and Sh. Ch. Timadon Ballywestow Festoon. Judy retained Frieze, another successful brood bitch and dam of a CC winner and Sh. Chs. Kelso and Keyso, whose successful progeny won her the Romance Brood Bitch Trophy in 1980. Her litter to Sh. Ch. Twoacres Wayward Caesar contained show champion triplets Ballywestow Persimmon of Oldestone, Petite Etoile, and Pawneese. The latter was mated to Night Fever and produced Sh. Ch. Borealis, winner of the Contest of Champions in 1988. Pawneese was also mated to Sh. Ch. Sowerhill Satyr of Fearnley, and Judy retained Absurdity, who produced the show champion twins Forego and Fleet. A Frieze granddaughter, Ornament, became the dam of Sh. Ch. The Tetrarch, winner of 9 CCs 6 Res. CCs. The Ballywestows canines have always enjoyed life as house dogs.

Bardonhill: **Marita Bott**

Since its establishment in 1970, all the winning dogs from Bardonhill are descended from Moyna April at Bardonhill, born in 1978. From her first litter came Sh. Ch. Bardonhill Supergrass 11 CCs 20 Res. CCs, and Marita acquired his daughter Barleydale Ooh-La-La It's Bardonhill. Mated to Night Fever, she produced two show champions, the Reserve Group winner Bardonhill Seabreeze Over Thendara and Bardonhill Splashdown. Another sister produced a show champion, and Overboard gained his Irish show champion title. April was also mated to Night Fever, resulting in Sh. Ch. Bardonhill Kiss-A-Gram, Best of Breed, Crufts 1990, as well as the CC winner Bardonhill April Love at Brayville. Kiss-A-Gram was mated to Free Spirit of Danaway and produced Sh. Ch. Bardonhill Team Spirit at Wynjill. The current team includes a litter sister to Team Spirit,

Shenanagin Some Might Say It's Bardonhill JW. Owned by Marita Bott of Bardonhill Kennels.

Kiss-Me-Quick, dam of Winds of Future and Bardonhill Snow Joke by Sh. Ch. Shenanagin Stockbroker. Marita has also brought in Shenanagin Some Might Say It's Bardonhill JW who goes back to several Bardonhill show champions.

Barleydale: **John and Shelagh Vant**

In 1968, Twoacres Teresa was purchased. She won her title and the CC at Crufts in 1972. Difficult to get into whelp, she was mated to her brother Sh. Ch. Troilus, and the CC winner Lucetta was retained. From Teresa's second litter by Crimbledale Commanchero, Barnadine was kept and mated to Lucetta, which provided the Barleydale's basis. Twoacres Triton arrived at age four and won 2 CCs and 1 Res. CC but does not figure in the lines. Lucetta was next mated to Sh. Ch. Sowerhill Sahib and produced Mustard Seed, who was put back to Barnadine. Their daughter Mopsa had a litter by Sh. Ch. Bardonhill Supergrass and produced Sh. Ch. Barleydale Pascali, CC at Crufts in 1990. He sired Kalymnos CC and Sh. Ch. Barleydale Polgara 8 CCs 11 Res. CCs. Her daughter, Barleydale Polyantha at Harreds, has won a Res. CC. Pascali also produced Sh. Ch. Wickenberry Pretty Polly, and when mated to Ir. Ch. Wickenberry Nightingale, five littermates became Irish champions.

Bonhomie: **Bonnie Andrews**

In 1973, Bonnie bought her first Irish Setter from a puppy farm but was consistently placed at open shows. Two Sowerhill bitches arrived, but the real breakthrough came in 1983 when Sowerhill Nobleman arrived. Born of Sh.

Sh. Ch. Bonhomie Forgotten Dream is the offspring of Sh. Ch. Clonageera Forget Me Not and Sh. Ch. Clonageera Genesis. Owned by Bonnie Andrews.

Ch. Jason of Andana of Clonageera ex Fearnley Fire Ember of Sowerhill, he won 10 CCs and 5 Res. CCs. He is a special dog, and all subsequent stock is descended from him. When bred to Clonageera Holly, he sired Sh. Ch. Clonageera Forget Me Not, CC at Crufts in 1991. She was mated to Sh. Ch. Clonageera Genesis and produced Sh. Ch. Bonhomie Forgotten Dream. In 1988, Bonnie bought Marksway Marquis from Mr. and Mrs. Martin Russell. A grandson of Nobleman, he won 27 CCs and 26 Res. CCs. The winner of several groups, he also won Best in Show at Group Championship Shows and Res. BIS at General Championship Shows. Marquis won the CC and BOB from the Veteran Class at Crufts in 1997, providing Bonnie with the most emotional moment of her career in dogs.

Brayville: John and Ruth Ellis

John and Ruth acquired an Irish Setter dog in 1974. Moyna Ladybird followed and won well, but due to an injury, she was retired early. However, her daughter by Sh. Ch. Brinara Inula provided the foundation for the Brayvilles. Regal Glory 2 Res. CCs was mated to Night Fever and her litter of six puppies contained two show champions: Brayville Dynamic Delegate 9 CCs 5 Res. CCs and Demure Debutante, as well as Dynamic Diplomat 1 CC 2 Res. CCs. In 1986, Bardonhill April Love at Brayville 1 CC 2 Res.

Brayville Leading Lady JW was Top Irish Setter Puppy in 1998. Owned by John and Ruth Ellis.

CCs joined the family. By Night Fever ex Moyna April at Bardonhill, she had a litter by Delegate and produced Sh. Ch. Private Affair. Demure Debutante was mated to Sh. Ch. Bardonhill Team Spirit at Wynjill, and Fashion Leader Res. CC was retained to carry on the line. Her daughter, Leading Lady, was Top Irish Setter Puppy in 1998 and gained the new style Junior Warrant with entry into the Kennel Club Stud Book. Numbers at Branville are limited because all the dogs live indoors, and only six litters have been bred to date.

Carnbargus: Eve Gardner

In 1963, Hartsbourne Molly was acquired purely as a pet. Her half-brother followed in 1966, and all subsequent stock goes back to Sh. Ch. Carnbargus Hartsbourne O'Brady and his daughter, Red Sarah Res. CC, born in 1970. Another O'Brady daughter, Sh. Ch. Carnbargus Hartsbourne Mattie was made up, and her daughter Starlight won a CC and Res. CC. From Red Sarah came Red Silk 1 CC

Sh. Ch. Carnbargus Continuity was Top Bitch in 1998 and has won 13 CCs and 14 Res. CCs. Owned by Eve Gardner.

3 Res. CCs. Her daughter, Racing Silk 3 Res. CCs, had a litter by Glentarkie Craven-A that contained Champion Cashmere, who was trained and handled by Colin Organ. She gained her qualifier in April 1989 and also ran in two Novice Stakes. Cashmere was mated to Night Fever and produced Courage 5 Res. CCs, Top Irish Setter Puppy 1988; Caleche 4 Res. CCs; and Charisma, who was put to Sh. Ch. Shenanagin Stockbroker. Their daughter, Sh. Ch. Carnbargus Continuity, was born in 1994. Top Bitch in 1996 and again in 1998, she has won 13 CCs, including Crufts 1998, and 14 Res. CCs. From Cashmere's second litter came Cordelia, the winner of two CCs. She died tragically young, at only three years of age.

Caskeys: Bob and Christine Heron

The Heron's first dog was bought in 1965. Bred by Miss Besford of Wendover breeding and registered under that prefix, the puppy was destined to become Sh. Ch. Wendover Caskey 8 CCs and 5 Res. CCs. Caskeys Cleoni, the foundation bitch, came from a litter by Sh. Ch. Caskey ex Sh. Ch. Joanmas Lottie. Cleoni was mated to her half-brother and produced Sh. Ch. Zoe. The Herons think she was their best bitch and believe that her head was perfection. Her granddaughter, Sh. Ch. Pollyanna of Caskeys, won 8 CCs and 4 Res. CCs, which gained her the Quebec Trophy for winning the most CCs during 1979. Her daughter Babette proved to be a great brood bitch and won the Pedigree Chum Top Breeders award for Bob and Christine in 1985. She produced Sh. Chs. Caskeys Pandora and Bo Jo, as well as Pagan 3 Res. CC. The CC

From left to right; Sh. Ch. Danaway Debonair, Sh. Ch. Caspian's Intrepid, and Sh. Ch. Caspian's Night Music. Owned by Mike and Sue Oakley.

Sh. Ch. Caskeys Hummingbird is the latest titleholder from the Caskeys Kennels of Bob and Christine Heron.

winner Burgandy was, unfortunately, killed in an accident. From Babette's litter by Night Fever came Sh. Ch. Caskeys Justin, Jazzman 1 CC, and Jezamy 6 Res. CCs. Sh. Ch. Caskeys Hummingbird is the latest titleholder, and Caskeys Blarney Res. CC is winning well. Overall, dogs owned or bred by Bob and Christine have won 49 CCs.

Caspians: Mike and Sue Oakley

The first dog arrived in 1972 and two bitches, Cornevon Rainbow and Starbright, followed. Sue thought that a combination of Cornevon and Wendover lines would produce an ideal Irish Setter and concentrated on those lines. In 1983, Caspians Snowdrop was mated to Wendover Washington of Caspians and produced Coppertop Wendy of Wendover. Her daughter, Wendover Cassidy, was acquired from Peter and Julie James and mated to Night Fever, which in 1988 produced Night Music. Music's first litter by Free Spirit of Danaway contained Sh. Ch. Caspians The Music Man of Danaway and Finian's Rainbow 2 Res. CCs. From her second litter by Sh. Ch. Danaway Debonair came Sh. Ch. Caspians Intrepid 49 CCs, the current breed record holder, as well as Caspians Grace 2 CCs. A repeat mating in 1995 produced Basilio 1 CC. Music won 14 CCs and 7 Res.

CCs, a Gundog Group, and Best in Show at the Setter and Pointer Champion Show in 1992. In 1998, she gained the Irish Setter Breeders Club's Brood Bitch Trophy for the fifth time and has been *Dog World's* Top Irish Setter Brood Bitch for the last four years. Her winning offspring have enabled the Oakleys to become Top Irish Setter Breeders for the last four years.

Clonageera: Jim and Pat Rutherford

Their first bitch, Tralee of Andana, had to be returned to Joan Anderson when the Rutherfords went to live abroad. A new start was made with Bridie of Andana, but it was Bella Rosa, born in 1971, who put the Clonageeras on the map. A Gentleman daughter, she won 5 CCs, 2 Res. CCs, and a Gundog Group. Joan Anderson gave Jim Sh. Ch. Jason of Andana of Clonageera CC, winner of Crufts 1981. He has left his mark as the sire of ten show champions—a great record for a little-used dog, making

his owners Top Breeders in 1983 and 1984. A Bella Rosa daughter, Tamoretta, became the main brood bitch and when mated to Jason, produced three show champions: Clonageera Tarka, Tyrone, and Rebecca. Another Tamoretta daughter, Holly, by Westerhuys Dutch Impression, produced Sh. Ch. Clonageera Forget Me Not and Friday's Child 1 CC. Tamoretta is also the granddam of Sh. Ch. Clonageera Samantha. Bella Rosa was mated to Jason, and the result was Sh. Ch. Clonageera Megan, whom the Rutherfords consider to have been their best to date. Her son, Sh. Ch. Genesis, by Sh. Ch. Sowerhill Sahib, proved to be prepotent and is the sire of five show champions. Germaine was mated to Andana Jake and produced Sh. Ch. Clonageera Stella. She was mated to Sh. Ch. Starchelle Chicago Bear in 1995. From this litter came Sh. Ch. Flambouyant and Fenella 1 CC. This mating has been repeated twice, producing more winning youngsters. Pat and Jim have bred or owned 11 show champions.

Crimbledale: Sue and Ellen Loynd

Sue started showing Irish Setters in 1965. Her foundation bitch was the CC winner Brackenfield Fan, who was mated to Sh. Ch. Twoacres Troilus. A dog, Commanchero, was retained and became the ancestor of the subsequent winning Crimbledales, including the dual CC winner Golden Melody, who died at the age of only six. However, when her

Sh. Ch. Clonageera Stella. Owned by Jim and Pat Rutherford, who have bred or owned 11 show champions.

daughter Double Charm was mated to Gold Fever of Balintyne, she produced Sh. Ch. Crimbledale Country Gossip of Cassperosso and the CC-winning bitch, Wysiwyg. Golden Melody's brother, Sh. Ch. Crimbledale Golden Choice, also turned out to be a good producer, and his progeny includes Sh. Ch. Kerryfair Lover Boy and three other CC winners in 1998. This made him Top Irish Setter Stud Dog in the league table compiled by *Dog World*. In 1998, Sue's daughter Ellen was granted a joint interest in the Crimbledale prefix.

Sh. Ch. Crimbledale Country Gossip of Cassperosso. Owned by Sue and Ellen Loynd.

Danaway: Brian and Mary Gurney

In 1972, Wendover Colas was bought purely as a family pet. By Sh. Ch. Wendover Gentleman, he won 7 CCs, including Crufts 1977, a Gundog Group, and a Reserve Group. Although not extensively used as a sire, Colas produced three show champions. He was *Dog World's* Top Irish Setter Sire in 1984, and all subsequent Danaways are descended from him. Wendover Happy Days was brought in and her daughter, Royal Charm, had a litter to Free Spirit of Danaway. Their daughter, Danaway Hot Gossip at Balintyne 1 CC, was owned in partnership by Mary and Gillian Barker, and when mated to Night Fever, she produced Sh. Chs. Ma Biche of Danaway and Gold Dust of Balintyne. Free Spirit, by Colas ex Westerhuy's Dutch Spirit, won the *Our Dogs* Top Sire Competition for the breed in 1990. He sired five show champions, a dual CC winner, and a CC winner. His son, Sh. Ch. Caspians The Music Man of Danaway 12 CCs, won the President's Trophy and Quebec Trophy in 1995. The second Colas/Dutch Spirit mating produced Sh. Ch. Disco Dancer of Danaway. An excellent producer, she won the Irish Setter Breeders Club's Brood Bitch Trophy three times and was *Dog World's* Top Brood Bitch in 1991. Her first litter contained Sh. Ch. Danaway Baccante, and her second litter, by Night Fever, contained Sh. Ch. Danaway Debonair, the winner of 40 CCs and Best in Show at Crufts in 1993. The Gurneys rate him as their best. His sister, Danielle 2 CCs 2 Res. CCs, was unlucky and did not get made up, nor did Cornevon Dreamgirl 1 CC 7 Res. CCs. The Gurneys were *Our Dogs* Top Breeders in 1991. In 1997, Wendover Lorna was acquired, and a dog, born in March 1998 from her litter by Intrepid, Fortune Teller JW, was retained.

Delsanto: Chris Sheldon

Chris bought Fondador Martinique in 1979, and she became the foundation bitch for Delsanto. Bred by Mrs. G. G. Follows, Martinique was by Sh. Ch. Shaytell Goldfinch ex Fondador Manyana. As a mate for her second litter, Chris chose Sh. Ch. Erinade Scottish Union because "The very famous Sh. Ch. Fondador Charlene had been bred from a Fondador bitch and Scottish Union." The idea

Sh. Ch. Delsanto Roxanne won a CC at Crufts in 1996. Owned by Chris Sheldon.

worked and produced Sh. Ch. Delsanto Cassandra 5 CCs 7 Res. CCs and Best in Show at the Merseyside Gundog Club Championship Show, 1989. Cassandra had a fertility problem, but her second litter of only four puppies by Bardonhill Fido contained Sh. Ch. Delsanto Roxanne, CC at Crufts in 1996, owned by Chris, and Sh. Ch. Romarna, owned by Lynn Muir. Roxanne's first litter by Sh. Ch. Marksway Marquis contained Lucinda 1 CC 4 Res. CCs. Her litter brother Luke became a show champion in 1998.

Erinade: Viveca Vamplew

The foundation bitch Bonahaird Sierra turned out to be an excellent producer for Erinade, which was established

Sh. Ch. Ma Biche of Danaway, offspring of the legendary Sh. Ch. Kerryfair Night Fever, was born in May 1983. Owned by Brian and Mary Gurney.

Sh. Ch. Erinade Exotic, offspring of Sh. Ch. Erinade Neula of Norlan and Sh. Ch. Caspians Intrepid. Bred by Viveca Vamplew.

in 1975. From her mating to Viveca's dog Glentarkie Craven-A (Sh. Ch. Allsquare Mickey Finn ex Ch. Laurie of Allsquare) came Sh. Ch. Erinade Scottish Union. He was only used seven times at stud, but he became the sire of five show champions—all bitches. Sierra's litter by Stephenshill Justin produced Sh. Ch. Erinade Neula of Norlan, owned by Gilbert Leighton-Boyce. She was transferred back to Viveca after Gilbert's death. When mated to Night Fever, Neula produced the CC winner Norlan Sebastian of Erinade, the sire of Erinade Bewildered 2 Res. CCs. From her litter by Sh. Ch. Caspians Intrepid came Sh. Ch. Erinade Exotic, born in 1994. She is owned by Mr. and Mrs. Colin Roberts and gained her title in 1998.

Fearnley: Pat Rhodes

Brackenfield Sweep arrived at Fearnley in 1963, and two more Brackenfields followed. Flax was mated to Hartsbourne Comet, but their daughter Firefly was put to a complete outcross, Sh. Ch. Wendover Racketeer, and produced Sh. Ch. Fearnley Fireflight. The most important bitch, Sh. Ch. Fearnley Firecracker, was bought in 1965 for the princely sum of five pounds, and all the subsequent Fearnleys go back to her. In one of her two litters to Sh. Ch. Wendover Gentleman, she produced Firesprite, the dam of Sh. Ch. Fearnley Firecinders of Dallowgill. Elsa Taylor campaigned Sh. Ch. Fearnley Firegem and won the Gundog Group at Manchester in 1979 and Reserve Group at the Western England Ladies Kennel Society (WELKS) 1980. One of her sons, Sh. Ch. Fearnley Firecedar, won Best in Show at the Setter & Pointer Club Championship Show, and Platinum won a CC. Sh. Ch. Fearnley Fireflare (by Sowerhill Valentine) was made up after being returned to Pat and

Barry. The Sowerhills were to play an important role. Sowerhill Satyr of Fearnley was bought, and with 31 CCs he was the breed record holder at the time. The winner of several groups, he retired after winning Best in Show at Leicester in 1984. Fearnley breeding has provided many kennels with their foundation stock. Since Barry's untimely death in March 1996, Pat has made up the group winner Sh. Ch. Fearnley Firehurricane and has bred Sh. Ch. Ir. Sh. Ch. Fearnley Firesheen of Ranaleen.

Goldings: Gordon and Biddy Evans

The first Irish Setter puppy was bought from the Wendover Kennel in 1966. Pretty Jane, by Wendover Glade ex Wendover Katie, was mated to Sh. Ch. Wendover Vagabond, producing the first Goldings litter. Two puppies were retained, and Lord Grumpy of Goldings and Wendover Bonnie became the foundation stock for the Goldings. Bonnie was mated to Sh. Ch. Twoacres Troilus and produced the first show champion,

From left to right, Sh. Ch. Goldings Hella and her dam Sh. Ch. Goldings Heike 9 CCs 7 Res. CCs. Owned by Gordon and Biddy Evans.

A group winner from Fearnley Kennels, Sh. Ch. Fearnley Firehurricane. Owned by Pat Rhodes.

Goldings Joss Cambier, owned by Mrs. Y. Edwards. A Lord Grumpy granddaughter, Carek Holly at Goldings, was mated to Sh. Ch. Jason of Andana of Clonageera and produced Sh. Ch. Goldings Heike 9 CCs 7 Res. CCs. She was mated to Goldings Oliver, and from this litter came Sh. Ch. Goldings Hella.

Inisheer: The late Yvette Edwards, Peter and Michelle Edwards

Inisheer was established in 1965 with Atlanta of Hedgeway. In 1971, Goldings Joss Cambier joined the kennel and was made up in 1975 but was tragically killed within days of gaining his title. In 1981, Rhythm of Andana was obtained from Joan Anderson's Andana Kennel. A good winner, she proved herself an excellent brood bitch, and when mated to Joanma's Solo, she produced Sh. Ch. Inisheer Flamingo. A dog with a long career, he won a Championship Show Veteran Gundog Group at the age of 11. His litter sister Kiwi won 2 CCs and 1 Res. CC and had a litter to Fearnley Fireflyer.

Harmony 1 CC, 1 Res. CC, was retained, and when mated back to Flamingo, she produced Sh. Ch. Inisheer Falcon. Flamingo is also the sire of Sh. Ch. Laggan Macbie Lady. Since Yvette's untimely death in 1998, Peter and their daughter Michelle have continued the Inisheer Kennel.

Joanma's: Marjorie Jarosz

The first bitch of Boyne breeding was acquired in 1945. Wendover Game was bought in 1963 at the age of two and a half and won 2 CCs and 5 Res. CCs. However, his greatest success came as a highly influential stud dog. His winning progeny enabled him to become the breed's leading sire in 1967, '68, and '69. His many winners included Sh. Chs. Scotswood Barabbas, Cornevon Prince Charming and Cinderella, Joanma's Lottie, and Joanma's Kayla. Game was also the producer of dual-purpose stock including Ch. Joanma's Adriano, bred by Mrs. R. Silverman, and only narrowly missed becoming a dual champion. In 1970, Mrs. Eckersley bred Joanma's Saffron (Dutch Ch. Joanma's Don ex Wendover Chell). He was campaigned by Mrs. Jarosz and gained his title. Two of his offspring were made up: Sh. Ch. Joanma's Ranter, born in 1972 out of Sh. Ch. Joanma's Rachel, who was a granddaughter of Joanma's Wendover Yana 2 CCs; and Sh. Ch. Joanma's Scampi, born in 1973 out of Joanma's Colette. Scampi won 14 CCs and 17 Res. CCs and was Top Irish Setter in 1976.

Sh. Ch. Inisheer Falcon, pictured here with the late Yvette Edwards of Inisheer Kennels.

Joanma's Collette (left), dam of Sh. Ch. Joanma's Scampi (right). Scampi won 14 CCs and 17 Res. CCs and was top Irish Setter in 1976. Owned by Marjorie Jarosz.

Kerryfair: Sandra and Kerry Chorley

Sandra bought her foundation bitch, Cornevon Spring Melody, from Janice Roberts in 1977. She was her second Irish Setter bitch but the first one she had bought for show. Spring Melody won a Res. CC. and was mated to Sh. Ch. Sowerhill Sahib. The resulting litter was whelped on September 30, 1979, and a puppy destined to become the important Sh. Ch. Kerryfair Night Fever was retained. He won his first Res. CC in May 1981 and went on to win

Sh. Ch. Kerryfair Lover Boy was the winner of 10 CCs and a Gundog Group. Owned by Sandra and Kerry Chorley.

his 26th CC in October 1990. He became the sire of 23 show champions, 5 further winners of 2 CCs, and another 12 individual CC winners. The success of his offspring won him the Irish Setter Breeders Club Mars Stud Dog Trophy from 1983 to 1993, and he was Top Stud Dog, All Breeds, from 1987 to 1991. Sandra acquired his daughter, Glencarron Pinwinnie, and when she was mated to Sh. Ch. Clonageera Genesis (by Sh. Ch. Sowerhill Sahib), Kerryfair Prima Donna was produced. She had a litter by Sh. Ch. Crimbledale Golden Choice, and Sh. Ch. Kerryfair Lover Boy was born in 1993. The winner of 10 CCs and a Gundog Group, he died at the age of only five years. During 1998, Sandra and her daughter Kerry acquired Wendover Rose of the Shires, who has won 2 CCs to date.

Kirkavagh: Steve and Linda King

The prefix was first registered in 1974, and two Sowerhill bitches were bought. However, the foundation bitch, Sh. Ch. Fearnley Fireheather 6 CCs 4 Res. CCs, came from Pat and Barry Rhodes in 1982. Her first litter, born in 1987, was by her grandsire Sh. Ch. Sowerhill Satyr of Fearnley, and Sh. Ch. Kirkavagh Corejada was retained. A dog, Kirkavagh Fireboy of Fearnley, was returned to his breeders at five months of age and won 1 CC and 2 Res. CCs. Fireheather had two further litters, and her last, by Sh. Ch. Fearnley Firehurricane, contained Sh. Ch. Kirkavagh Musidora, the only bitch in the litter. Her daughter, Gazala, won a Res. CC in 1998. Sh. Ch. Corejada had only two litters, both by Sh. Ch. Fearnley

Sh. Ch. Kirkavagh Zabara, from Kirkavagh Kennels, won 9 CCs, 10 Res. CCs, and the group at WELKS in 1997. Owned by Steve and Linda King.

Firehurricane. Her lasting legacy to the Kirkavaghs has come through her daughter, Sh. Ch. Kirkavagh Zabara, whom Linda and Steve consider to be their best to date. Born in April 1992, Zabara won 9 CCs, 10 Res. CCs, and the group at WELKS in 1997—never an easy task for a bitch! In 1997, Zabara had her first litter by Sh. Ch. Caspians Intrepid. This mating has already produced three new style Junior Warrant winners with entry into the Stud Book, including a bitch, Khaydara, who was retained at Kirkavagh. She should help to continue the successful line.

Konakakela: Bill and Pat Harris

The first Irish Setter was purchased in 1975 when Pat and Bill lived in South Africa. A new start was made in Britain in 1986 with the first Andana bitch. Unfortunately, she was killed, and her litter sister Andana Jemimah was acquired and gained her show champion title. Her first litter, born in 1991, produced the Res. CC winner Onyx Charmer. In 1992, Jemimah was mated to Sh. Ch. Reddins Ferdinand and produced Sh. Ch. Konakakela Ziggy of Strathmead, Best of Breed at Crufts in 1994; Sh. Ch. Konakakela

Sh. Ch. Andana Jemimah is the dam of several show champions, including Sh. Ch. Konakakela Ziggy of Strathmead, Best of Breed at Crufts in 1994. Owned by Bill and Pat Harris.

Zagar by Romarne made up in 1998; and Zorro, who won his first CC in February 1999.

Kylenoe: John and Wendy Morley

The first Irish was bought in 1970, and in 1972, he was joined by Ronnetta Wild Rose of Kylenoe, who became the Morley's first show champion. She only had one litter

Sh. Ch. Laggan Uptown Girl is the latest show champion from the Laggan Kennels of Norma Wilson.

Ch. Kylenoe Crystal Spirit, owned by John and Wendy Morley, was trained and handled by Wendy to her Show Gundog Working Certificate in 1998.

but none of her offspring feature in the kennel's development. In 1979, Bucksett Bonnie of Kylenoe was purchased. By Heathcliffe Tobias ex Pepper of Brackenfield, she won a Res. CC and had three litters. From her second litter to Sh. Ch. Cornhill Pippin came Sh. Ch. Kylenoe Sun Princess, born in 1983. From Bonnie's third litter by Carnbargus Star Enterprise came Dancing Crystal. She was mated to Sh. Ch. and Ir. Sh. Ch. Autumnglow Masquerade and produced Sh. Ch. Kylenoe Crystal Spirit. She was trained and handled by Wendy and gained her Show Gundog Working Certificate in 1998, a great achievement for both of them.

Laggan: Norma Wilson

In 1978, the foundation bitch Hallglen Celandine, by Sh. Ch. Allsquare Mickey Finn, was mated to Sh. Ch. Wendover Colas and produced Sh. Ch. Laggan Bryan's Boy 9 CCs 12 Res. CCs and winner of a Gundog Group, and Starshine 1 CC. Celandine was next mated to Fetteresk Winter Legend, and the only puppy, Janek's Jem, was retained. She was mated to Night Fever and produced Sh. Ch. Laggan Macbie Lady. She was mated back to Bryan's Boy, resulting in Sh. Ch. Laggan Glen Ettrick. In 1991, it was decided to mate Macbie Lady to Sh. Ch. Inisheer Flamingo. The long journey from Scotland to Essex was

worthwhile, because the litter contained the latest show champion, Uptown Girl. Her litter sister, Southern Belle, was exported to the US where, at the time of writing, she only needs two more points to become an American champion. Norma had decided to have a litter from Uptown Girl when she was five and had two CCs. This was not an easy decision to make, but Uptown Girl's daughter Shoshoni Maiden is now carrying on the line.

Loskeran: Richard and Pat Hirons

Richard and Pat's first show champion, Sh. Ch. Clonageera Tarka went on to win the Group and Best in Show after being awarded his first CC and Best of Breed at Midland

Sh. Ch. Loskeran Oleander. Owned by Gerald and Kate Condron and bred by Richard and Pat Hirons.

Counties in 1980. His CC-winning daughter, Lorelli, was mated to Jennison Phantom twice and in 1985, she produced Sh. Loskeran Oleander, owned by Gerald and Kate Condron. In 1987, she produced Sh. Ch. Loskeran Gold Crown, owned by the Stanleys. In 1998, Loskeran Eternal Spring won a first CC at Manchester.

Moyna: Barbara Birch

The Moyna Kennels were founded with Sh. Ch. Morningstar Melanie. The highlight of her career was winning the CC at Crufts in 1969 under Mr. F. Warner-Hill. Melanie was mated to Sh. Ch. Twoacres Troilus and produced Sh. Ch. Moyna Mr. O'Hara. The mating was repeated and this time, the litter contained Sh. Ch. Moyna Michelle, who won 9 CCs, 5 Res. CCs, and a Reserve Gundog Group. Barbara was able to acquire Rickerscott Bridget Maguire by the influential sire Sh. Ch. Scotswood Barabbas. She gained her title and had the distinction of winning Best in Show at the ISAE Championship Show in 1973, at the Irish Setter Breeders Club Championship Show in 1974, and again at the Irish Setter All-England in 1977 at the age of eight. The combination of the Troilus/ Melanie lines with stock from Bridget Maguire by Moyna Jamie produced excellent bitches, providing foundations for several successful kennels.

Oakchase: Jackie Lorrimer

Jackie acquired her first Irish Setter bitch in 1975. Of Fearnley breeding, she was followed by Brackenfield Harvey and two Carnbargus bitches. However, the real breakthrough came in 1987 when Jackie bought Danaway Debonair at the age of eight weeks from the Gurneys. By Night Fever out of Sh. Ch. Disco Dancer of Danaway, he quickly gained his title and won numerous gundog groups and Best in Show awards. The winner of 40 CCs, he became the breed record holder at the time. The highlight of Debonair's career came in 1993 when he won Best in Show at Crufts. Like his sire, he turned out to be a successful stud dog and the father of Jackie's Sh. Ch. Caspians Intrepid 49 CCs, the new breed record holder for winning most CCs. He is also the winner of many groups and Best in Show awards. Intrepid was Top Gundog in 1996 and 1998 and Reserve in 1997. Two of his daughters gained their titles in 1998, helping him to win the Irish Setter Breeders Club's Mars Stud Dog Trophy.

Reddins: Jim and Priscilla Smith

The Smith's first bitch was acquired in 1972. She was of Wendover breeding and, during the 1970s, was joined by further stock bred from similar lines. Sorrel of Andana of Reddins won the kennel's first CC in 1980 and gained her

title in 1981, winning five CCs and two Res. CCs. By Scotswood Celt out of Purple Clover of Andana, she turned out to be a successful brood bitch. From her first litter by Sh. Ch. Bardonhill Supergrass came Reddins Morgan 2 Res. CCs, the sire of two show champions. In her next litter, born in May 1983 by Sh. Ch. Jason of Andana of Clonageera, she produced two show champions: Reddins Jonah and Reddins Justin of Stylersetts and Jessica 1 Res. CC, the dam of Duine 1 CC 1 Res. CC. In 1984, Sorrel was

Sh. Ch. Reddins Ferdinand won 21 CCs, 13 Res. CCs, the Gundog Group at Crufts in 1989, and further group wins at WELKS, Richmond, and the Ladies Kennel Association. He was also Best in Show at the Irish Setter Breeders Club twice. Owned by Jim and Priscilla Smith.

mated to Night Fever, and from this litter came the Waddell's Ch. and Ir. Ch. Fintan, CC at Crufts in 1988, who had gained his qualifier in Ireland, and Sh. Ch. Ferdinand 21 CCs 13 Res. CCs, Gundog Group at Crufts 1989, as well as further group wins at WELKS, Richmond, and the Ladies Kennel Association (LKA). He was Best in Show at the Irish Setter Breeders Club twice. Like his sire and dam, Ferdinand proved himself to be a successful

Sh. Ch. Reddins Myrna is the winner of 17 CCs. Owned by John Hall.

157

producer, with five show champion offspring to his name, as well as a dual CC winner and two further CC winners. The latest titleholder bred by Jim and Priscilla is Sh. Ch. Reddins Myrna. Born in 1991, she is out of the CC winner Harriet. Myrna is the winner of 17 CCs and is owned by John Hall. Her sire, Sh. Ch. Barnaby of Wesbere at Cressway, was bred by Priscilla in partnership with Sheilah Gutsell. Jim and Priscilla keep a large kennel of Irish Setters and were Pedigree Chum Top Irish Setter Breeders in 1989, '90, '92, '93, and '94.

Romarne: Lynne Muir

Long before embarking on a career as a breeder, Lynne was already well known as a handler and for piloting two bitches bred and owned by Mrs. G. G. Follows to the top. The first, Sh. Ch. Melody Minet, was born in 1968 and won her first CC at Crufts in 1971. When mated to Sh. Ch. Cornevon Lovebird, she produced a litter containing Fondador Milwalkie Res. CC and Manyana, the dam of Sh. Ch. Fondador Charlane, born in 1981. An outstanding show bitch, Charlane won 21 CCs and 15 Res. CCs between 1983 and 1989. She was Best of Breed at Crufts in 1987 and also won a Gundog Group and two Res. Gundog Groups. In 1991, Lynne acquired Delsanto Romarna, a bitch descended from Manyana. A dog, Konakakela Zagar, by Romarne, followed in 1992. Both gained their show champion titles—Romarna in 1995 and Zagar in 1998. When bred together, they produced Romarne Rheanne in 1996. To date, she is the winner of 1 CC and 8 Res. CCs.

Rua: Mary Tuite, Porschet: Colette Tuite

(Dual-purpose kennels)

Mary is determined to keep the breed's working ability alive, and Rua Affluent Shannon and Rua Damian's Dandy Avanti feature in show and field trial pedigrees. Through Dandy and through the introduction of pure field trial lines came FT Ch. Rua Connemara of Porschet. Her sister is the dam of FT Ch. Rua Marta, making Mary the breeder of two FT champions. Sirrah's sister, Syllabub, won the KC Non-Winners Stake and produced Errigal, the winner of one CC, three Res. CCs, and 50 Green Stars; and Golden Bough, winner of three Res. CCs and Green Stars. Dandy's most famous offspring was Ch. Astley's Portia of Rua, the winner of eight CCs and two Res. CCs. She was Best of Breed at Crufts in 1980 and again in 1981 when she went on to win the Gundog Group and Best in Show. She had gained her Qualifier in 1980, and her daughter Celtic Romance provided the foundation for the Porschets. Portia was mated to Night Fever and produced Mary's Flame of Tara at Rua, winner of two CCs, one Res. CC. Colette's Flame of the Forest Porschet also won two

FTCh. Rua Connemara of Porschet is an excellent example from the dual-purpose kennels of Mary Tuite (Rua Kennels) and Colette Tuite (Porschet Kennels).

CCs. She was tragically killed at the age of only 26 months. Colette acquired Rua Connemara of Porschet from her mother, and she became her first field trial champion.

Scarletti: Rita Pike

The foundation bitch, Margaretwoods Conductress, by Sh. Ch. Scotswood Barabbas ex Bridget of Castleoak, won a Res. CC. From her only litter by Sh. Ch. Cornevon Stargem came the twins, Sh. Ch. Scarletti Cockney Rebel and Sh. Ch. Hot Chocolate. Both won Res. CCs at Crufts in 1982. Another sister, Tangerine Dream, also won a Res. CC. Cockney Rebel sired Sh. Ch. Suteresett Hot Rumour and Sh. Ch. Bardonhill Supergrass, and Hot Chocolate had a litter by Sh. Ch. Zorosean Agvamarina that produced Scarletti Silver Sprint. She was mated to Bardonhill Crafty Cockney by Scarletti, full brother to Supergrass. From her "pink" litter came Lily the Pink, who was bred to Sh. Ch. Royal Archer and produced Sh. Ch. Scarletti Hill Street Blues, born in 1987. Tickled Pink won a CC and 2 Res. CCs, and Pink Panther sired Sh. Ch. Suteresett Coconut Capers and the CC winner, Artful Almond. So far, Rita has only bred nine litters.

Shandwick: Pat Butler

In her first litter, the foundation bitch Palelsa Boadicea produced Sh. Ch. Shandwick Silver Spray, born in 1980. In 1983, Boadicea was mated to Sh. Ch. Twoacres Gold Eagle, and from that litter came the two show champion bitches Shandwick Golden Spray 18 CCs 15 Res. CCs and Golden Rose, owned by Will Brown and Chris Sones.

Many of today's Sowerhill Irish Setters are the descendants of breeder Olwen Hunt's foundation bitch Norlan Tessie Belle.

Silver Spray was also mated to Gold Eagle and in 1985 produced Sh. Ch. Shandwick Starcarrier. Pat is now showing the Res. CC winner Withersdale Crystal Maze. She is out of Withersdale Livia, a Golden Rose daughter by Pat's Night Fever son, the Group winner Sh. Ch. Wickenberry Knight at Arms.

Sowerhill: Olwen Hunt

Miss Hunt owned her first Irish Setter before World War II, and her foundation bitch Norlan Tessie Belle was bred from test-mated stock. Although unshown, she proved to be an important brood bitch. From her second litter to Maydorwill Happy Lad came S. Winsford Robert 3 Res. CCs and S. Jilinda, and from her third litter to Ch. Boisdale Boggit came Sowerhill Red Mist. A high percentage of present-day Irish Setters are descended from these three dogs. In 1968, Sowerhill Red Colleen of Kitewood was acquired and won six CCs, one Res. CC, and a Gundog Group. Mated to Sh. Ch. Stephenshill Gamebird twice, she first produced Sh. Ch. Storm 18 CCs, Top Irish Setter in 1977. From the second litter came Valentine Res. CC. In 1973, Sowerhill Sarah (Gamebird ex Sowerhill Samantha) was born. She gained her title and has had a considerable impact on the breed. From her two litters to

Sh. Ch. Wendover Jeeves came Sh. Ch. Sowerhill Sahib, Sh. Ch. S. Sarong of Kingscott, and Sh. Ch. S. Satyr of Fearnley. S. Sarabelle won a Res. CC and S. Sailor of Wendover went to Sweden. Sahib has left his mark as the sire of Night Fever. The combined success of her progeny enabled Sarah to win the Brood Bitch Trophy in 1979, '81, '82, and '83. A Satyr daughter, Fearnley Fire Ember, was acquired and produced Sh. Ch. Nobleman. Three of the Best in Show-winning Irish Setters at Crufts go back to Norlan Tessie Belle.

Starchelle: Rachel Shaw

Rachel bought her first bitch in 1977 as a pet. In 1982, another bitch, Barncliffe Dutchess, arrived. Of Barnsforde/ Brackenfield/Hartsbourne lines, she was followed by a six-month-old male puppy of similar breeding, but with an outcross line. In 1985, Rachel acquired one of his daughters, and Forever Amber by Starchelle won her Junior Warrant and one Res. CC. She was mated to the outcross Sh. Ch. Clonageera Genesis and in 1990, Sh. Ch. Starchelle Chicago Bear was born. He won 13 CCs, 12 Res. CCs, and 2 groups, including Crufts in 1995 when he went on to Best in Show. He was also Best in Show at the Setter and Pointer Championship Show and three

Breed Club Championship shows. His many successes made him *Dog World's* Top Irish Setter, 1995. Chicago Bear's litter sister, Starchelle The Blue Angel, went to Chris Meldrum and also became a show champion. In 1995, the first mating between Chicago Bear and Sh. Ch. Clonageera Stella took place, and Rachel acquired Sh. Ch.Clonageera Flambouyant as Starchelle, who gained his title in February 1999. His litter sister, Fenella, has also won a CC.

Sh. Ch. Clonageera Flambouyant as Starchelle gained his title in 1999. Owned by Rachel Shaw.

Sh. Ch. Starchelle Chicago Bear, winner of 13 CCs, 12 Res. CCs, and 2 Groups, among other honors, is pictured here winning Best in Show at Crufts in 1995. Owned by Rachel Shaw.

Tatterslee: Jennie Reed

Jennie bought her first Irish Setter in 1974, followed by the foundation bitch Brackenfield Tatters in 1975. She was joined by a male puppy, Brackenfield Fagus, and when mated together later, they started the Tatterslee Kennel. Fagus also sired the first titleholder to be made up by

Sh. Ch. Tatterslee Special Effect, winner of six CCs and three Res. CCs to date. Owned by Jennie Reed.

Jennie, Sh. Ch. Coralmist Country Cotswold at Tatterslee. A Fagus/Tatters granddaughter, Topham's Trophy, the result of an outcross, was mated to Sh. Ch. Erinade Scottish Union, and a single puppy was born in 1984. Sh. Ch. Tatterslee Toute Seule gained her title at nine and a half years of age. She was mated to Rhuwind Special Edition, and Special Effect was kept. Born in 1992, he was made up in 1997. To date, he has won six CCs and three Res. CCs.

Thendara: Dee Milligan and Jeremy Bott

The Thendaras are based on three Bardonhill bitches: the litter sisters Bardonhill Bikini and Sea Breeze, by Night Fever, born in 1987; and Bardonhill Eeny Meeny of Thendara, CC at Crufts in 1992, born in 1988, by Sh. Ch. Shandwick Starcarrier. Sh. Ch. Bardonhill Sea Breeze Over Thendara 9 CCs 6 Res. CCs, won a Reserve Gundog Group and was Best in Show at two Breed Club Championship Shows. A good brood bitch, her litter to

From right to left; Thendara The Tourist, Sh. Ch. Thendara Kennedy, and Sh. Ch. Thendara Okay Yaa have been the recipients of numerous honors for breeders Dee Milligan and Jeremy Bott.

Sh. Ch. Clonageera Genesis contained Sh. Ch. Thendara Okay Yaa, Best of Breed at Crufts 1995. Popular with overseas breeders, his semen has been exported to Sweden and Australia. His three litters to the Res. CC-winning Bikini have been successful, and winners have gone all over Europe. Sh. Ch. Kennedy was retained and is the winner of 10 CCs and 6 Res. CCs, and the group wins at Bournemouth 1995 and Bath 1996. His son, The Tourist, is now helping to keep the strong male line successful.

Timadon: Geoff and Alicia Coupe

Gaelge Gariona, the foundation bitch, was born in 1962, by Ch. Brackenfield Hartsbourne Bronze ex Sh. Ch. Gaelge Gertina, a Ch. Wendover Beggar daughter. The Coupes concentrated on her Wendover lines, and Gariona was mated to Sh. Ch. Wendover Ballymoss. Bilby and Forever

Sh. Ch. Timadon Airs and Graces gained her show champion title in 1998. Owned by Geoff and Alicia Coupe.

Amber were retained. Gariona's next litter was by Sh. Ch. Wendover Gentleman (incidentally, his first). The litter contained Sh. Ch. Wendover Herald of Cuprea, who later went to Canada, and Aust. Ch. Timadon Jaunty. Forever Amber was also mated to Gentleman and produced Dorianne. She was mated to Sh. Ch. Wendover Royalist and produced the first titleholder with the Timadon prefix: Sh. Ch. Kendel. He was the sire of four show champions and a dual CC winner. In 1966, Ballywestow Festoon was acquired. She gained her title and won Best in Show at the ISAE in 1971. Mated to Gentleman, the CC winner Ballina was retained. In 1973, Tallulah of Timadon, litter sister to the important Sh. Ch. Wendover Jeeves, was obtained. When mated to Kendel, she produced Sh. Ch. Timadon Concorde. Ballina was mated to him and produced Ch. and Ir. Ch. Timadon Exclusive Edition, who gained her qualifier in 1982. Ballina was also mated to Sh. Ch. Kendel and produced Sh. Ch. Timadon Charlies Angel and Whimsical. Her daughter Brulette was the dam of Sh. Ch. Timadon Debs Delight. In 1998, his litter sister, Airs and Graces, also gained her show champion title.

Twoacres: June Coates

The first bitch was bought as a family pet but had some success in the show ring. In 1965, Musbury Melisande of Twoacres was acquired. Her first litter by Sh. Ch. Wendover Gentleman turned out to be highly successful, and Melisande still holds the record for producing the most CC winners in one litter. The "T" litter contained four show champions plus a dual CC winner. Teresa became the foundation for the Barleydales, and Traviata

Sh. Ch. Twoacres Gold Eagle, the sire of four show champions. Owned by June Coates.

did the same for the Wickenberrys. Tamburlaine won Best in Show at Windsor 1970, and Troilus was Best in Show at Belfast 1971, after having won groups at Leeds and Blackpool in 1970. Troilus was Top Irish Setter in 1971, winning a total of 21 CCs, replacing his sire as the top CC winner. Troilus turned out to be prepotent, producing six show champions as well as 14 other CC winners. His winning offspring won him the Mars Stud Dog Trophy in 1974, '75, and '76. His sister, Tosca, was mated to Sh. Ch. Timadon Kendel, and Francesca was retained. She became the first to be test-mated when the PRA scare started in the 1970s. Troilus mated with Sh. Ch. Cornevon Cinderella, and Solace of Twoacres was acquired and won a CC as a Junior. Mated to Wendover Treasurer, she produced Sh. Ch. Twoacres Gold Eagle, the sire of four show champions. Wendover Sportsgirl, by Baron of Wendover ex Wendover Lupina and born in 1978, was obtained. She won a CC and Res. CC but disliked showing. She was test-mated, and the three current bitches are descended from her. One of them, Sh. Ch. Jade, gained her title in 1998, and her son, Fergus, born in 1995, won a CC in 1998.

Wickenberry: Jean Quinn

Jean's foundation bitch, Sh. Ch. Twoacres Traviata, was born in 1968, a member of the famous "T" litter bred by June Coates. Mated to Baron of Wendover, she produced Sh. Ch. Wickenberry Baroness, the winner of 10 CCs, 11 Res. CCs, a Reserve Gundog Group, and Best in Show at the National Gundogs Championship Show in 1981. Baroness was mated to Sh. Ch. Twoacres Wayward Caesar, and from that litter came Sh. Chs. Clansman and Countess, born in 1980. In her litter by Night Fever, Baroness produced Sh. Ch. Wickenberry Knight at Arms and the dual CC winner Ir. Ch. Nightingale. Her winning children won her the Romance Brood Bitch Trophy in 1982. Countess was also mated to Night Fever, and from her litter came Sh. Ch. Nebbiolo and a dual CC winner, Nearco. The latest titleholder is Sh. Ch. Pretty Polly, born in 1986. She won her first Res. CC at Leeds in 1987 when only a few days out of the Puppy Class and her last Res. CC at Crufts in 1996 from the Veteran Class. Jean was *Our Dogs'* Top Breeder in 1986—a great achievement for her small kennel, where only an occasional litter is bred.

Wynjill: Jill Holley

In 1971, Cornevon Tranquil was bought primarily as a family pet, but Jill's parents thought that showing her would be a nice interest for their daughter. In 1972, Janice Roberts bred a litter by Sh. Ch. Cornevon Snowstorm ex Sh. Ch. Cornevon Violet, and Jill went to see the puppies every week. Eventually, she chose Woodsprite, who became Jill's first CC winner at Leeds in 1974, where she also won Best of Breed under Joe Braddon. She went on to win seven CCs and six Res. CCs. On Janice Roberts' advice, Tranquil was mated to Margaretwoods Caretaker of Scotswood, and Wynjill Red Robin was retained. He won his first CC in 1975 and gained five more in 1978, as well as Best of Breed at Crufts in 1979. He remains Jill's favorite Irish Setter. Two litter

Wynjill Angel Delight JW gained the new Junior Warrant in 1998. Owned by Jill Holley.

sisters were also successful, winning a CC and Res. CCs. In 1975, Robin and Woodsprite were mated and produced Sh. Ch. Wynjill Country Fragrance. At that time, Jill owned four Irish Setters—three of them show champions. In 1990, Bardonhill Team Spirit at Wynjill was obtained. By Free Spirit of Danaway, he gained his title and is proving himself a successful sire. A bitch, Angel Delight, gained the new Junior Warrant in 1998. Danaway Country was also acquired and is winning well.

Scotland

Bonahaird: Mary Bowman

Mary bought her first Irish Setter in 1969. Normar Cheree came from mostly Raycroft and Wendover lines and was mated to Sh Ch. Cornevon Lovebird twice. A bitch from the second mating, Bonahaird Sierra, became the successful foundation bitch for Viveca Vamplew's Erinade Kennel. In 1981, Mary bought Cornevon African Violet. She was mated to Sierra's son, Sh. Ch. Erinade Scot-

Sh. Ch. Bonahaird White Diamonds has won 5 CCs and 2 Res. CCs to date. Owned by Mary Bowman.

tish Union, and a daughter, Sh. Ch. Snowboots, gained her title. Another bitch, Truffetti of Erinade, joined the Bonahairds in 1982 and produced two Res. CC winners in two litters. In 1989, Snowboots was mated to Bardonhill French Fry at Helecam and produced an Irish Sh. Ch. Mary's Bonahaird After Eight. She went to Sh. Ch. Shenanagin Stockbroker, and Sh. Ch. White Diamonds, 5 CCs, 2 Res. CCs to date, resulted. In 1998, she was mated back to her grandsire and a bitch, Snow in Summer, was retained to continue the line.

Clachnahar: Sheila Buist and Andrew Wyllie

The kennel was started in 1981 with a litter brother and sister, bred from Cornevon lines. When the bitch produced a litter to a dog of Wendover breeding, two bitch puppies, including Clachnahar Petit Bebe, were retained. Strathmead Blue Moon arrived in 1989 and became a show champion in 1994. Petit Bebe was mated to Blue Moon, and their daughter Sh. Ch. Clachnahar Cocoa arrived in 1993. To date, she has won six CCs and was awarded one of her

Sh. Ch. Clachnahar Cocoa has won six CCs and was awarded one of her three Res. CCs at Crufts in 1997. Owned by Sheila Buist and Andrew Wyllie.

three Res. CCs at Crufts in 1997. Another Blue Moon daughter, Jonola Southern Blue at Clachnahar, has achieved the new style Junior Warrant.

Dunnygask: Ailsa Harvey

Ailsa bought her first Irish Setter as a pet but decided to improve her stock. The real turning point came when Ailsa acquired Westerhuy's Dutch Spirit, by Sh. Ch. Cornevon Lovebird ex Sh. Ch. Cornevon Westerhuy's Cloggy. Her two litters by Sh. Ch. Wendover Colas were of considerable importance, and all the subsequent Dunnygasks go back to that combination. Sh. Ch. Dunnygask Spirit of Spring was retained from the first mating. Her litter to Fearnley Bucks Fizz produced Dunnygask Vital Spark CC, Best of Breed at Crufts in

Sh. Ch. Dunnygask Allegra (left) and Dunnygask Aristotle (right), both out of Sh. Ch. Dunnygask New Dawn. Owned by Ailsa Harvey.

Sh. Ch. Shenanagin Stockbroker is the winner of 16 CCs, a Group, and a Reserve Group. He was Top Irish Setter Puppy in 1992 and Top Irish Setter in 1994. Owned by Alister and Catherine Watt.

1992 and sire of a CC winner. His sister Tutti Frutti was mated to Sh. Ch. Shenanagin Stockbroker and produced Sh. Ch. Dunnygask Verbena, owned by David and Sandra Christian. Tutti Frutti's litter by Sh. Ch. Caspians Intrepid contained Gladiator 2 Res. CCs. Spirit of Spring was mated to Night Fever, and Dunnygask Red Grouse gained his title for Debbie Fryer. His sister Skylark was mated back to Free Spirit and produced Sh. Ch. Dunnygask New Dawn. Her son Aristotle won his first CC in 1998, and her daughter Allegra, by Sh. Ch. Reddins Ferdinand, gained her title in 1998. This makes Ailsa the breeder of six show champions.

Shenanagin: Alister and Catherine Watt

Alister's first Cornevon died tragically, and Sh. Ch. Cornevon Lovebird 15 CCs 10 Res. CCs was acquired. He was Top Irish Setter in 1974 and won the CC at Crufts that same year. He was Best in Show at the Setter & Pointer Club Champion Show and at the ISAE in 1975. He also won Res. CCs at Crufts in 1976 and 1977. He sired four titleholders and a further five CC winners, making him the breed's Top Stud Dog in 1977 and 1978 and runner-up twice. A Lovebird granddaughter, Dunnygask Enchanting Spirit Res. CC, became the foundation bitch and was mated to Sh. Ch. Bardonhill Supergrass. Shilling was retained and mated to Wendover Raffles, by Night Fever. This combination produced Sh. Ch. Sugar and Spice. She was mated to Sh. Ch. Bardonhill Team Spirit at Wynjill, and from this litter came Sh. Ch. Shenanagin Stockbroker 16 CCs, a Group and Reserve Group Winner. Stockbroker was Top Irish Setter Puppy 1992 and Top Irish Setter 1994. Three of his daughters have gained their titles. His daughter, Fetteresk Take That to Shenanagin 2 Res. CCs, was acquired, and her daughter Shenanagin That's It to Karidell, born in 1996, has won

two CCs and one Res. CC. Only eight litters have been bred so far.

The Republic of Ireland

In their native land, Irish Setters are popular as working dogs, show dogs, and pets. Annually, approximately 400 are registered with the Irish Kennel Club Ltd., and there are 21 all-breed championship shows, 2 gundog group championship shows, 1 Irish breeds championship show, and a championship show for the breed. There are also several open and limited shows every year. The Irish Red Setter Club is more than 100 years old and mainly oriented toward field trials. However, the show committee organizes the annual championship show.

In order to win the title of champion, a dog must win 40 Green Star points, including four "Majors" of at least 5 points each. The number of points available at any show depends on the number of dogs actually present at the show, but some shows carry a guaranteed Major, regardless of the number of dogs exhibited. The Green Star Index is adjusted annually by the Irish Kennel Club and depends on the number of dogs exhibited during the previous year. Dog and bitch awards do not always carry the same number of points, but the Best of Breed winner will receive the same number as the Opposite Sex winner if the latter has won a higher number. To become a champion, a field trial "qualifier" is required. It is only since 1990 that the title of "show champion" has come into existence, but just as many dogs are running for their "qualifiers" as ever. Most of the successful show stock has been imported from the UK and, due to the relative ease of access, British stud dogs have been used to good effect. Irish dogs have made their presence felt at British shows and have often returned home with top honors. The following is a list of some of the most influential Irish kennels.

Ardbraccan: Trudy Walsh

Ch. Ardbraccan Aristocrat proved himself a dog of all-around excellence. He was Irish Setter of the Year in 1978, 1979, 1980, 1981, and 1985, and topped this by becoming Show Dog of the Year, All Breeds, in 1979-1980. Many times Best in Show at all-breed and club championship shows, he won more than 50 Green Stars and a Reserve CC. A first prize winner at obedience, he was also an excellent gundog. Mainly of Wendover breeding, he produced Chs. Ardbraccan Celtic Charm and Everglade. Celtic Charm was Irish Setter of the Year in 1993, and Everglade is the sire of Icelandic Ch. Ardbraccan Famous Grouse. The group winner Brandy Beau would have been a show champion had the award been recognized in his time.

Among other honors, Ir. Ch. Ardbraccan Aristocrat was Irish Setter of the Year five times and Show Dog of the Year, All Breeds, in 1979-1980. Owned by Trudy Walsh.

Dunswood: Jean and Martyn Turner

Ir. Ch. Wickenberry Nightingale, born in 1982 by Night Fever ex Sh. Ch. Wickenberry Baroness, won 20 Green Stars with 145 points, 2 CCs, and 3 Res. CCs, but was unlucky not to have gained her UK title as well. She was Best in Show at an all-breeds championship show and Reserve Best in Show at two UK breed club championship shows. She was also a finalist at the Top Irish Show Dog of the Year Competition in 1987. Nightingale gained her qualifier at the Wicklow and

Wexford Field Trial in October 1986. A highly successful brood bitch, in her first litter by Sh. Ch. Barleydale Pascali she produced five Irish champions. Birdsong was retained, and the other four gained their titles under different ownerships. From her second litter by Ir. Ch. Dunswood Little Owl (Sh. Ch. Twoacres Gold Eagle ex Wendover Maeve) came yet another Irish Champion, Night Owl, as well as the Res. CC winner Ir. Sh. Ch. Dunswood Florence. This makes Nightingale the dam of six Irish champions and one Irish show champion, an outstanding brood bitch record. Florence's daughter Ir. Sh. Ch. Dunswood Dochas was made up in 1998, and the Turners hope to run her for her field trial qualifier soon.

Ir. Ch. Dunswood Birdsong, one champion from the first litter of Ir. Ch. Wickenberry Nightingale, a Night Fever daughter. Owned by Jean and Martyn Turner.

Ir. Ch. Dunswood Night Owl from Ir. Ch. Wickenberry Nightingale's second litter. Owned by Jean and Martyn Turner.

Loughantarve: Mae and Rodney Trenwith

Ch. and Ir. Ch. Timadon Exclusive Edition put the Loughantarves on the map on both sides of the Irish Sea. She won Best in Show at the Irish Red Setter Club Championship Show twice and Best in Show at the Irish Breeds Society Championship Show. She gained her qualifier at the Wexford Gundog Club Trial in 1982. In Britain, she won seven CCs and five Res. CCs and was Best of Breed at Crufts in 1985 and 1986. Mated to Sh. Ch. Corriecas Fagan, she produced Ir. Ch. Loughantarve Fagan, winner of two Best in Shows at all-breed championship shows. His sister, Ir. Ch. Kerry Lynn, had won one CC and one Res. CC when illness ended her show career. Her sister, Sally, also gained her Irish Champion title. When mated to Sh. Ch. Sowerhill Satyr of Fearnley, Exclusive Edition produced Ir. Sh. Ch. Kerry Erin Res. CC.

Pairk-Na-Glos: Kate Bride

(Dual-purpose kennel)

Kate acquired her first bitch in 1962. In 1965, Lady of Greenfield was mated to Cilldara Shannon, by Ch. and Ir. Ch. Cilldara Robinhood. They produced Shanliss Rose, a championship show and field trial winner. In time, Rose was mated to another championship show and field trial winner, and from one of her daughters came French Ch. Pairk-na-Glos Gabha. Another daughter from Rose was mated to Bagatelle Argot and produced Ir. FT Ch. Pairk-na-Glos Ros, winner of the Field Trial Class at Crufts and numerous Firsts at championship shows. A second bitch, Achill, was also mated to Argot, and Pairk-na-Glos Colm also became a French champion. Both Gabha and Colm were trained and handled by Kate in Ireland, where they won at field trials and championship shows. Kate also handled both of them in competition in France.

Ranaleen: Brian Grace

Brian campaigned Ir. Ch. Dunswood Thunderbird to his title and qualifier. His Ir. Sh. Ch. Reddins Declan won a CC and Best of Breed. He acquired Fearnley Firesheen of Ranaleen in 1996 and won two Res. CCs with her in 1997. Firesheen was Best in Show at the Irish Red Setter Club Championship Show and became an Ir. Sh. Champion when aged only 20 months. During 1998, she won two CCs and in January 1999, after winning her third CC, she also gained her show champion title in the UK.

Northern Ireland

Rohanmor: Cathy Loughlin

A frequent visitor to mainland UK and to shows south of the border, Cathy has made up Ir. Sh. Ch. Bardonhill Overboard. He also won four Res. CCs and was Northern Ireland's Show Dog of the Year in 1989 and Gundog

Sh. Ch. Ir. Ch. Fearnley Firesheen of Ranaleen, winner of three CCs and two Res. CCs. She was also Best in Show at the Irish Red Setter Club Championship Show and became an Irish Show Champion at only 20 months of age. Owned by Brian Grace.

Ir. Sh. Ch. Rohanmor the Real McCoy. Owned by Cathy Loughlin of Belfast, Ireland.

of the Year in 1992. Bonahaird Black Magic also became an Ir. Sh. Champion, as did her son by Overboard, Ir. Sh. Ch. Rohanmor the Real McCoy.

Australia

There is little documentation of Irish Setters in Australia until the late 1800s. Champion Garry (imported from the UK) won a first at the Royal Melbourne Show in 1899, and a number of dogs from well-known British kennels were imported at about that time. These included familiar English names such as Hartsbourne and Wendover. By the 1960s, the breed had become popular

"Down Under," to the point where it suffered the consequences of overpopulation. By the late 1980s, however, the glut of pet Irish Setters had leveled off. The eastern portion of the country has a larger population today than other areas, and competition is much stiffer in the show ring. The most significant development in the breed in the 1990s has been the introduction of American bloodlines, either through imported dogs or imported frozen semen. This trend will probably continue as quarantine regulations are reduced. English bloodlines have also been imported into Australia, giving breeders a wider selection of breeding stock from which to choose.

To gain the title of Australian champion, dogs must win a total of 100 challenge points under at least 4 different judges. Points are awarded on the basis of 5 points for the challenge and 1 point for each dog of the breed being exhibited that day, to a maximum of 25 points. A group win earns 25 points, but the challenge points cannot be added to the group points. If no other dog or bitch is exhibited, a minimum of six points is gained. Judges have the right to refuse a challenge. (This information comes from Eve Gardner's book *Irish Setters Today,* Howell Book House, New York, NY, 1998.)

Here is a look at some of the Irish Setter breeders making their mark in Australia today:

Ardglen: Jim and Jo Gossage, Cessnock, New South Wales

Aust. Ch. Meadowlark's Energizer, a littermate of Aust. Ch. Meadowlark's Elysian, is a Best in Show winner and prepotent sire for Ardglen. Owned by Jim and Jo Gossage.

Jim's involvement with Irish Setters began in 1971 when he purchased and finished his first Irish Setter bitch. He then purchased a bitch from Norma Hamilton's Quailmoor Kennels. She was bred to an English import, Aust. Ch. Timadon Jaunty, owned by Greg Browne. This litter gave him Ch. Ardglen Kilkenny and Ch. Ardglen Gentle Kate, both specialty winners. In 1984, Jim was given a puppy, Quailmoor Cinzano, who went on to win five Royal challenges, many specialty wins, and multiple all-breed Bests in Show.

In 1992, two Meadowlark dogs arrived,

Aust. Ch. Meadowlark's Elysian was imported from the US to enhance the breeding lines of Jim and Jo Gossage's Ardglen Kennels.

Aust. Ch. Ardglen All Spice, sired by Ch. Eireannmada Act of Defiance ex Ch. Meadowlark's Elysian, is a specialty and Best in Show-winning bitch.

littermates sired by Ch. Meadowlark's Vindicator ex Meadowlark's Solitaire. The bitch, Ch. Meadowlark's Elysian, won many groups, and Ch. Meadowlark's Energizer was a Best in Show winner. He is best known, however, for his prepotency as a sire. He has produced most of the top-winning Irish in the country, including Grand Ch. Eireannmada At Tulane and Ch. Eireannmada Sequoia. He also sired the Gossage's Ch. Quailmoor Natasha, a multiple group and Best in Show winner. Ch. Meadowlark's Elysian was bred to Ch. Eireannmada Act of Defiance to produce Ardglen All Spice, a specialty and

Best in Show-winning bitch, and Ch. Ardglen All Style, a specialty and Best in Show-winning dog.

Eireannmada: Greg Browne, Diggers Rest, Victoria

Greg's prefix was registered in 1968. However, Aust. Ch. Ballina of Irishflame, imported from South Africa in 1973, provided the important foundation for the kennel and introduced Kinvarra, Tirvelda, and Bayberry bloodlines to Australia. Her breeding with existing Australian stock based on Hartsbourne and Wendover lines produced Aust. Ch. Eireannmada Arizona, one of the most successful sires of the '70s. His son, the multiple Best in Specialty and All-Breed Best in Show winner, Aust. and NZ Ch. Eireannmada Montana, continued the tradition,

Aust. Ch. Eireannmada At Harvard—just one champion representative from Greg Browne's Eireannmada Kennels.

Aust. NZ Ch. Eireannmada Montana, a multiple Best in Specialty and all-breed Best in Show winner. Owned by Greg Browne.

Jack Flash, Aust. Am. Ch. Quailmoor Jamaican Rum, and Aust. Ch. Brookfire Anzac Blue.

The bloodlines of Aust. Ch. Meadowlark's Energizer (imported from the US), owned by Jo and Jim Gossage, has provided this kennel with the opportunity to consolidate previously introduced American bloodlines. Energizer has sired a host of champions for Eireannmada, including Grand Ch. Eireannmada At Tulane, Aust. Ch. Eireannmada At Harvard, Aust. Ch. Eireannmada Times Square, Aust. Ch. Eireannmada Liberty, Aust. and NZ Ch. Eireannmada Sequoia, and Aust. Ch. Eireannmada Santa Monica.

producing many of the top winners in Australia and New Zealand throughout the '80s. Other notable sires for Greg were Aust. Ch. Timadon Jaunty (imported from the UK), NZ Ch. Redstone Oakley, Aust. and NZ Ch. Ballymoss O'Dougal, and NZ Ch. Ballymoss O'Carrig, all imported from New Zealand. Eireannmada dogs have sired well over 100 champions, and their bloodlines can be found in the pedigrees of most of the successful kennels in the country.

In 1982, Charlton's Marigold (heavily linebred on Ch. Candia Indeed ROM) was imported from the US to consolidate the lines previously introduced by Ballina Irishflame. Marigold was bred to Montana to produce Wells Fargo, the sire of a string of champions and Royal Challenge winners, including Aust. Ch. Eireannmada Dodge City, Aust. and Indian Ch. Pendoric Parade, Aust. Ch. Pendoric Izy For Real, Aust. Ch. Quailmoor Jumpn

Aust. Ch. Eireannmada Pastina. Owned by Greg Browne.

Ch. Eireannmada At Tulane, owned by Carrie Paine, Best in Show at the Melbourne Royal in 1998, is sired by Ch. Meadowlark's Energizer ex Eireannmada Irish Whimsey, who combines English Cornevon and Wendover lines in her pedigree.

Aust. Ch. Eireannmada Liberty. Owned by Greg Browne.

Outstanding bitches at Eireannmada include Aust. Ch. Eireannmada Hi Jinx, NZ Ch. Eireannmada Heirloom, Aust. Ch. Eireannmada Zeralda, Aust. Ch. Eireannmada Ecstacy, Aust. Ch. Eireannmada Pastina, Aust. Ch. Eireannmada Matilda, Aust. and NZ Ch. Eireannmada Sequoia, Aust. Ch. Eireannmada Liberty, and Aust. Ch. Eireannmada Requiem.

The return to Australia of Aust. Ch. Marigold Maximum Delight in whelp to Am. Ch. Sunshine's First Rate provided Greg with the exciting young male Eireannmada Ode to Autumn. The use of frozen semen from America and England has also benefitted the lines. English Sh. Ch. Thendara Okay Yaa has sired Aust. Ch. Eireannmada Top Class, Aust. Ch. Eireannmada Top Gun, and the brood bitch Eireannmada Top Drawer. Am. Ch. Sunnyhills Wings of the Wind has sired Indian Ch. Eireannmada Manhattan and one of Greg's most valued brood bitches, Eireannmada Salina.

Eireannmada dogs have been sought in countries in Asia and Europe, including India and Malaysia. Aust. Ch. Eireannmada Mustafa, the sire of Aust. Ch. Marigold Maximum Delight, is now in the Netherlands with Piet and Marga Roks.

Greg restricts his show activities to Royal and Specialty shows but derives pleasure from the success of others who own and show Eireannmada dogs. He was awarded life membership by the Irish Setter Club of Victoria.

Gwyndara: Leeanne and Trevor Jones, Shepparton, New South Wales

The Jones began sharing their lives with Irish Setters in 1974, and Ch. Taraglen Juturna, their foundation bitch, was purchased in 1979. Tara and her nephew, Ch. Taraglen Plantagenet, and his son, Ch. Kelibri Carbon Copy, were the cornerstones of their kennel. Tara produced only one litter of six, sired by Carbon Copy, which included Ch. Gwyndara Georgie Girl and Ch. Gwyndara

Play It Again CD. Georgie bred back to her grandsire, Plantagenet, and produced four champions: Chs. Gwyndara Who's That Girl, The Girl Is Mine, The Bitch Is Back, and Open To Offers.

Open To Offers is the sire of the only frozen semen litter in the US. A bitch from this breeding, Am. Ch. Regalaire Sweet Adelaide, is owned by Barbara Riegle. Ch. Gwyndara The Bitch Is Back is the dam of Am. Ch. Gwyndara Southern Cross, imported by Dr. John Savory to America and now living at Regalaire.

Ch. Gwyndara Who's That Girl is the dam of 13 Australian champions and one American champion. Her first litter by her grandsire, Carbon Copy, produced five champions, and her next two litters were by frozen semen from Am. Ch. Dunholm Windsor, owned by John Savory. Her most illustrious progeny are the littermates Ch. Gwyndara Montpelier, Grand Ch. Gwyndara Go It Alone,

Aust. Ch. Gwyndara You Wear It Well (above) and Aust. Ch. Gwyndara Montpelier (below), both Best in Show winners, are littermates out of Ch. Gwyndaras Who's That Girl. Owned by Leeanne and Trevor Jones.

Ch. Gwyndara You Wear It Well, and Ch. Gwyndara Total Eclipse. All four are Best in Show winners.

The Hearns are proud of their 24 Australian, 2 American, and 1 Singaporean champions. Their breeding program has been rewarding, and they are pleased to still see Plantagenet's influence on their Irish. The use of their lines in the US has been interesting and exciting, and they treasure the friendships they have formed on both sides of the Pacific.

Aust. Ch. Gwyndara The Bitch Is Back is the dam of Am. Ch. Gwyndara Southern Cross, imported by Dr. John Savory to America and now living at Regalaire Kennels. Owned by Leeane and Trevor Jones.

Aust. Ch. Pendoric Izy for Real. Owned by Leigh and Anne-Marie Hearn.

Martinridge: Peter and Bernie Martin, Adelaide, South Australia

Martinridge was registered as a prefix in 1985. Their foundation bitches were Ch. Idylewins Alexis and Ch. Eireannmada Matilda, both by Aust. and NZ Ch. Eireannmada Montana.

Alexis produced Ch. Martinridge Balarney, a specialty winner and dam of two champions. Matilda produced four champions: Chs. Martinridge Carousel, Charisma, Eireannmada Times Square, and Eireannmada Liberty. Grand Ch. Marigold By The Way joined their kennel in 1988, becoming a Best in Show winner and the sire of four champions. In all, Martinridge has produced seven champions and titled four outside-bred Irish to their titles. They have consistently won all around Australia and are the top Irish Setter kennel in South Australia.

Pendoric: Leigh and Anne-Marie Hearn, North Warrandyte, Victoria

The Hearns started in Irish in 1972 with the acquisition of a puppy bitch of UK Raycroft lines. They showed fairly consistently and successfully until 1981, when they were given their foundation bitch, Ch. Taraglen Opus One. She was a combination of Parr Leyn and Tatlow lines. Bred to Aust. and NZ Ch. Eireannmada Montana, she produced Chs. Pendoric Pulsar, Purdy, and Palladin. They then bred Ch. Taraglen Flair to Aust. and NZ Ch. Ballymoss O'Dougal (a dog of Wendover breeding).

Pendoric Prim N Proper was bred to Ch. Eireannmada Wells Fargo (a Montana son out of an American import, Charlton's Marigold). Two very typey brothers came from this mating, Ch. Pendoric Izy for Real and Ch. Pendoric Parade.

At the same time, the Hearns produced another bitch from a mating of Aust. and NZ Ch. Ballymoss O'Dougal to Ch. Pendoric Purdy. This was the start of another prefix, "Marigold" in combination with Greg Browne, as a tribute to Charlton's Marigold, who was tragically lost in a house fire with her second litter at foot. Marigold Aphrodite was bred to Quailmoor Defiance to produce Aust. and NZ Ch. Marigold Mad About Men and her brother Aust. Ch. Marigold By The Way. Many champions ensued, with puppies going to the US, New Zealand, India, and throughout Australia.

In 1992, the Hearns imported from the US frozen semen from Ch. Meadowlark's Fire N'Rain. The bitch they bred, Eireannmada Red Echo, produced Grand Ch. Pendoric Fire N'Ice and her brother Ch. Pendoric Pandemonium. Both these littermates have been very successful in the show ring, garnering many specialty and Best in Show wins. Marigold Elusive

Charlton's Marigold, an import from the US, was tragically lost in a house fire with her second litter at foot. Although she produced just one surviving litter, she was one of the most influential American imports to Australia. Owned by Leigh and Anne-Marie Hearn.

Quest was also bred to Fire N'Rain with frozen semen, producing Aust. Ch. Pendoric Annie Laurie.

From fewer than 20 litters, the Hearns have produced more than 20 Australian champions, some of whom are also champions overseas. Their objective is to produce Irish Setters of outstanding type, quality, and soundness by using the top-producing Australian, American, and English bloodlines.

Aust. NZ. Ch. Ballymoss O'Dougal, a Best in Show and specialty winner and influential sire.

Quailmoor: Norma and Graham Hamilton, Moss Vale, New South Wales

Graham and Norma Hamilton established Quailmoor Kennels in the 1960s with Ch. Parr Leyn Symphone. She was sired by Ch. Parr Leyn Perry O'Shea out of English import Wendover Jeannie.

Symphone had a successful show career, winning all-breed and specialty Bests in Show. Her last litter produced Best in Show winners Chs. Quailmoor Royal Gem, Royal Rogue, and Royal Leason. Gem was the dam of the famous Ch. Quailmoor Outrageous. She won 13

Aust. Ch. Quailmoor Indian Summer, shown here with owner Norma Hamilton at the presentation of Number One All-Breeds in 1992, holds the breed record with 29 Bests in Show.

Bests in Show, including the Brisbane Royal in 1980 over approximately 5,000 entries.

Two additional acquisitions added to the foundation of Quailmoor; Ch. Parr Leyn Sonata O'Erin and Ch. Taraglen All Aglow. These bitches also had very successful show careers and were great producers.

An All Aglow son, Ch. Quailmoor Faustas, was bred to Greg Browne's imported Ballina of Irishflame to produce Ch. Eireannmada Arizona, one of the most influential sires in the breed. A litter brother to Faustas, Quailmoor Fireball was bred to Ch. Parr Leyn Sonata O'Erin to produce Chs. Quailmoor Premonition, Periwinkle, Pepper, and Prelude. Periwinkle was bred to Outrageous to produce Ch. Quailmoor Zee, who in turn produced Ch. Quailmoor Kiss Me Kate.

A Prelude daughter, Ch. Quailmoor's Aria, was bred to the US import, Ch. Seregon Second Coming, to produce Ch. Quailmoor Georgia Brown. Georgia won 20 Bests in Show and although her daughter, Ch. Quailmoor Indian Summer, surpassed her show record, Norma considers Georgia to have been her best bitch. Summer was Number One All-Breeds in Australia in 1992 and holds the breed record with 29 Bests in Show.

Aust. Ch. Quailmoor Georgia Brown, shown here with some of her grandchildren, won 20 Bests in Show. Owned by Norma and Graham Hamilton.

Georgia's second litter by Ch. Meadowlark's Energizer produced four Best in Show winners: Chs. Quailmoor Ninoska, Natasha, Notorious, and Night Lark.

Night Lark was sent to Finland, where she was twice Best in Show at the Helsinki International over about 7,000 dogs each time. At the World Show in 1998, she won her World Winner title as well as Best in Show for dam and progeny for all breeds.

Ch. Quailmoor Indian Summer also produced well. From her first litter came Chs. Quailmoor Jerry Hall, Jumpn Jack Flash, and Jamaican Rum. Both Jack and Rum are Best in Show winners. Jamaican Rum was sent to Finland where he was Best in Show at the Helsinki International twice. No kennel has ever won this show four times. In 1999, Ch. Chic Choix Abington, a son of Jamaican Rum and Night Lark, won Best in Show there. Jamaican Rum is now in the US with Caren McWeeny (McDerry Irish Setters).

Indian Summer's last litter includes Chs. Quailmoor Calvin Klein and Carla Zampati, who was Best of Breed at the Sydney Royal show in 1998.

Rosslare: Peter Frost, Melbourne, Victoria

Peter's association with Irish Setters began in 1972 with the purchase of a puppy as a family pet. Encouraged to show, he won a ribbon his first time in the ring. That pet became the group-winning Ch. Carndonach Cavalier. In 1975, he purchased his foundation bitch, Quailmoor Inelda. With a very limited breeding program of only six litters, he has owned and shown Ch. Rosslare Best Regards, Ch. Rosslare Man About Town, Ch. Rosslare Scarlett O'Hara, and Ch. Rosslare Touch of Paradise, all of whom were group winners.

In 1993, he bred the first Irish Setter frozen semen litter in the state when Ch. Scarlett O'Hara was mated to Am. Ch. Castlebar's Command Presence. The resulting litter produced the multi-group-winning and runner-up Best in Show and specialty winner, Ch. Rosslare From a Distance. His latest dog is an import from the US kennel of Jean Roche. He is Saxony's

Aust. Ch. Rosslare Scarlett O'Hara, dam of the first frozen semen litter in the state of Victoria, which produced Ch. Rosslare From a Distance. Owned by Peter Frost.

Aust. Ch. Rosslare Man About Town, a group winner. Owned by Peter Frost.

Evening Tide (Ch. Meadowlark's Irish Monardi ex Ch. Saxony's Southern Nights).

Peter has held many offices in the Irish Setter Club of Victoria, of which he was made a life member in 1998. He is currently president of the National Irish Setter Breed Council of Australia. He is a licensed judge for all sporting and terrier breeds and has judged throughout Australia and overseas, including the 1998 ISCA National Specialty.

Taraglen: Keith McCarthy, Melbourne, Victoria

Taraglen was established in 1967 with Ch. Mavang Amber Glow, followed by Ch. Greglynn Giselle. Amber produced 11 champions, including Best in Show winners Troilus, Achilles, Aurora, Elektra, Excalibur, and Toccata. Toccata was the outstanding Irish of her time, winning the Melbourne Royal at 20 months of age. She dominated the breed in Victoria from 1972 until her retirement in 1977.

Giselle's first litter produced Ch. Taraglen Timandra, a Best in Show winner. A son, Ch. Taraglen Tannhauser, sired 15 champions, including several Best in Show winners.

Aust. Ch. Taraglen Spellbinder, an outstanding representative of the Taraglen Kennels of Keith McCarthy.

Tullane: Carrie Paine, Radcliffe, New South Wales

Carrie's first Irish Setter, Aust. Ch. Showdream Septimus CDX, was purchased in 1975 and became a Best in Show and an obedience trial winner. He was bred from a combination of Colclough and Carrbridge lines.

In 1986, Carrie acquired from Greg Browne Aust. Ch. Eireannmada Act O'Defiance CD CDX UD ET TD (Quailmoor Defiance ex Aust. Ch. Eireannmada Pastina). He won multiple Bests in Show and Best in Obedience Trials. He also

Aust. Ch. Eireannmada Act O'Defiance CD CDX UD ET TD, the most titled Irish Setter in Australia, won multiple Bests in Show and Best in Obedience Trials. He also won a title for endurance and tracking. Owned by Carrie Paine and bred by Greg Browne.

won a title for endurance (20-kilometer run in two hours) and tracking, both of which he performed with true Irish Setter enthusiasm.

In 1993, Greg Browne bred another truly outstanding individual. He was Aust. Grand Ch. Eireannmada At Tulane (Aust. Ch. Meadowlark Energizer, imported

In 1980, two important litters were born. From the first came Ch. Taraglen Plantagenet, owned by Leeanne and Trevor Jones, and Ch. Taraglen Tamsin, a top-winning bitch. The second litter produced Ch. Taraglen Toccason, Top Irish Setter Dog for 4 years and the sire of 26 champions, including the outstanding Ch. Taraglen Spellbinder.

A puppy by the American import Ch. Seregon Second Coming ex Ch. Taraglen Entrechat was acquired. He was Ch. Shelomith Renaissance. He had an outstanding career: four-time top Irish Setter in Australia in the National Dog point score; winner of 22 Bests in Show; and the sire of 2 great winners, Ch. Taraglen Maria, the dam of Spellbinder, and Spectre De La Rose. Renaissance also sired Ch. Taraglen Xtravaganza.

To date, the kennel has produced 109 champions and since 1989, Taraglen Irish Setters have won the Victoria specialty 8 times. Several quality youngsters are currently emerging at Taraglen.

Aust. Ch. Taraglen Xtravaganza was sired by the accomplished show dog, Ch. Shelomith Renaissance. Owned by Keith McCarthy.

Aust. Ch. Eireannmada At Tulane won four Royal Best in Group Awards, as well as Best in Show at the Melbourne Royal in 1998. He was Number One Irish Setter in 1997 and 1998, and Number Two Gundog and Number Nine All-Breeds in 1998. Owned by Carrie Paine and bred by Greg Browne.

from the US, ex Eireannmada Irish Whimsey). This dog won four Royal Best in Group Awards, including three times at Melbourne Royal, and in 1998 was the first Irish Setter in 45 years to win Best in Show at the Melbourne Royal. He was Number One Irish Setter in 1997 and 1998, Number Two Gundog, and Number Nine all-breeds.

In 1995, Carrie obtained a puppy bitch from Jim Gossage (Ch. Eireannmada Act O'Defiance ex Aust. Ch. Meadowlark's Elysian, imported from the US). She became specialty and all-breed Best in Show winner Aust. Ch. Ardglen All Spice. She was bred to Aust. Grand Ch. Martinridge Kiss O Fire (Aust. Ch. Martinridge Flaminbeauty ex Eireannmada Shamira) in 1996 to produce multiple Best in Show winner Aust. Ch. Tullane Fiery Thyme and group winner Aust. Ch. Tullane Cinnamon Kiss. Also in 1995, Carrie obtained a puppy bitch from Norma Hamilton (Eireannmada At Tulane ex Aust. Ch. Quailmoor Indian Summer), which became the 1998 Sydney Royal Best of Breed winner Aust. Ch. Quailmoor Carla Zampati. Bred to Aust. Ch. Eireannmada At Harvard (Aust. Ch. Meadowlark Energizer ex Eireannmada Irish Whimsey), she produced the 1998 Irish Setter Association's Bitch of the Year, Aust. Ch. Tullane Thesis By Design.

Canada

The population of Irish Setters in Canada in no way approximates that of the US. Even in the 1970s, when population rose at the same rate as that of the US, the numbers were quite low. In 1998, there were 38 litters, with 240 puppies registered. Throughout the '90s, there continued to be considerable influence of American dogs on Canadian breeding stock.

Several dogs, both a combination of US and all-Canadian bloodlines, made their mark in Canada during the 1970s and 1980s. Can. Am. Ch. McCamon Marquis, owned by Susan Korpan (McCamon), and his mother, Can. Am. Ch. McCamon Royal Burgundy, also owned by Sue, were important as show winners and producers of Can. Am. Ch. O'Irish Dangerman, Ch. Wyndfield's Olav Olympia, Can. Am. Ch. Dunholm Finn McCool, Ch. Renegade of Lenair, Can. Am. Ch. Rebecca's Irish Lace. Can. Am. Ch. McCamon's Impresario (Am. Ch. Kimberlin Killea O'Top O ex Can. Am. Ch. McCamon's Grande Dame, Marquis' sister) was Number One Irish Setter for three years and Number One All Breeds in 1987. He was owned by Dave Carey and shown throughout his career by Mr. Carey's son, William Alexander.

Other dogs of importance in Canada during that time were Ch. Beaverbrook Canadiana (Ch. Candia Indeed ex Beaverbrook Country Charlett), owned by Jack and Gloria

Langelier; Ch. Breen (Ch. Kilaine Prince ex Rojan's Lady Arnel), owned by James McCaffery; Ch. Bertragh Boy's Baron of Red Coat (Heatherstone Muldoon ex Gay Dutchess of Bertragh Boy), top Sporting Dog in 1979, shown by Brian Taylor; Ch. Kilaine Blaze of Shanibyle (Ch. Bronze Blaze of Tamarisk ex Shanibyle Royal Holly); and Ch. Draherin Bachelor Boy, owned by Anne Threlkeld, top Irish Setter and top Sporting Dog for several years during the 1970s.

Winners in the 1990s were Can. Am. Ch. Quailfield's Mak'n Business (Ch. Meadowlark's Vindicator ex Ch. Kerry-Eire Coral Charm); Can. Am. Ch. Quailfield Stylish Success (a grandaughter of Vindicator and Coral Charm); Can. Am. Ch. Meadowlark's Muir Woods (Vindicator ex Meadowlark's Solitaire); and Can. Am. Ch. Orchard Farm Dream Girl (Am. Ch. Meadowlark's Masterful ex Ch. Orchard Farm Kayla). It is interesting to note that all of these are American-bred dogs.

Here are profiles of some of the breeders who are currently making their mark in Canada:

Allegro Farm: Arlene Skene, Langley, BC

Arlene had always wanted an Irish Setter but had to wait until she was on her own to purchase her first dog. Although he finished his championship at a young age, he developed spinal problems early in life and was in considerable pain. From that experience, Arlene developed her breeding philosophy: to breed not only for beauty and soundness but also for health and temperament. She wanted dogs that were easy to train and a joy to live with. Her experience in breeding and showing horses and her university genetics training stood her in good stead in establishing her breeding program.

She was drawn to the Meadowlark dogs that she had seen and was able to purchase a bitch that became Am. Can. Ch. Meadowlark's Allegro (Ch. Meadowlark's Vindicator ex Meadowlark's Wyndsong). When she was about 18 months old, another bitch joined the household: Am. Can. Ch. Meadowlark's Inspiration (Ch. Meadowlark's Intrepid ex Meadowlark's Magical Mirage), a full sister to Ch. Meadowlark's Vindicator. Both of these bitches produced healthy, companionable, and typey puppies.

The foundation sire for Allegro Farm is Am. Can. Ch. Meadowlark's Muir Woods, a Best in Show winner that possesses style, type, health, and exceptional temperament. He won an Award of Merit at the 1991 ISCA National Specialty and was Number Two Irish Setter in Canada and Number Eight Sporting Dog in the US in 1993. He has proven to be an excellent sire, with many champions to his record. His daughter out of Am. Can. Ch. Meadowlark's Inspiration, Am. Can. Ch. Allegro Farm

Dance 'Til Dawn, won the 1995 Irish Setter Club of Canada National Specialty.

Arlene guaranteed the health of her dogs and used a combination of linebreeding and outcrossing to produce what she hoped will be the very best both in the show ring and on the couch. She was active in clubs in both the US and Canada, doing rescue and as an officer and committee person. Fanciers on both sides of the border mourned her untimley passing in 1999.

Carannagh: Anne Perkins, Osgoode, Ontario

Anne's interests are in obedience, agility, and the field, although she does plan to breed a litter from her foundation bitch, Fairline Kiersey. She has owned Irish Setters for more than 20 years, and her senior citizen, Maronova's Kavannaugh Jiggs CD CGC, attained his Canadian CD at the age of 10 years, 8 months. Her bitch, Kiersey, is competing in agility, which she loves.

Maranova's Kavannaugh Jiggs CD CGC is shown attaining his Canadian CD at the age of 10 years, 8 months. Owned by Anne Perkins.

Marjorie Davis, Cornwall, Ontario

Marjorie became interested in obedience with her Irish Setter, Can. Ch. Can. OTCh. Fianna's Lady Meegan CDX, after being very impressed by Onesquethaw Tracie Devlin working in utility with owner Mary Diesem. The two have been friends since that day. Margie, inspired by Mary, has accomplished much with her own Irish Setters in the obedience ring. Meegan and her grandson Major achieved two AKC Utility legs, but Meegan's age made it impossible for her to continue, and Major died early of Cushings' Disease. Major was the sire of Can. Ch. Can. OTCh. U-UD Merrileas Sweet Mignonette UDX Bda. UD Mex. UD. Marjorie says, "I was advised to place her when young, but I loved her and persevered. We just love each other, an old team working together...in my eyes she is a great girlie."

Fallowfield: Joan S. Colbourn, Nepean, Ontario

The first Irish Setter came into the household when Joan was very young. She was very successful as a field dog, and at home in Toronto, the dog and Joan became inseparable. Joan showed The Duchess of Wildair to her championship. After Joan's marriage to Ken Colbourn in 1954, their Christmas gift was an Irish Setter puppy from Wildair. A few years later, their foundation bitch, Ch. Shillalegh Maeve CD was acquired. Fallowfield Kennels was registered with the Canadian Kennel Club (CKC) in 1961.

Throughout the years, the prime focus of Fallowfield dogs has been intelligence coupled with type and structure. An excellent example of this goal was Ch. Fallowfield Adonis CD, a multi-specialty winner.

Can. Ch. Fallowfield Adonis CD, a multiple specialty winner, in a painting by Dorothy Oxborough. Owned by Joan S. Colbourn.

After heavy involvement with the organization and running of dog shows and educational programs for owners and breeders, knowledge about breeding and handling Irish Setters was accumulating at Fallowfield. Extended sojourns overseas forced a reduction in their dog activities, and on their return to Canada, the Colbourns started a new line based on Wendover breeding. Ch. My William of Wendover CD became their first representative. All breedings from this point on were with PRA-clear, test-bred dogs. Ch. Fallowfield Electra CD was the first PRA-clear, test-bred Irish Setter bitch in Canada.

Fallowfield continues on a restricted scale today because of Joan's judging schedule both in the US and Canada and her position as administrator of the Human Animal Bond Association of Canada. Over the last 35 years, Fallowfield dogs have served as foundation stock for some of the inest lines in North America, with correct structure, type, and superior intelligence.

Highfeather, Reg.: Wendy Edgecombe, Newfoundland

Wendy's interest in Irish Setters goes back to her late teens, when she acquired her first dog, Benjy, in 1979. She soon found out that he was not show quality, so in 1980 she acquired Copperlane's Lord Shane

Can. Ch. Tirvelda Country Cavalier. Owned by Wendy Edgecombe.

(Can. Bda. Ch. Bertragh-boy Baron of Redcoat ex Can. Ch. Copperlane's April Lady CD), who was sired by the Number One Irish Setter and Number One Sporting Dog in 1979. Unfortunately, he died of bloat at 17 months of age.

Her first champion was Can. Ch. Padraics Bit O'Heather (Am. Can. Ch. Charlton's a Friend Indeed ex Can. Ch. Tirvelda Tweed of Gabhantyr). She also owned Can. Ch. Tirvelda Country Cavalier

Can. Ch. Highfeather Country Child, a homebred champion at Highfeather, Reg. Owned by Wendy Edgecombe.

(Wilson Farm Country Boy ex Am. Ch. Tirvelda After Dark), and Can. Ch. Tirvelda Tour de Force (Am. Ch. McCamon Winter Knight ex Am. Ch. Tirvelda After Dark.) Tour de Force was a multiple group winner.

There have been three homebred champions in residence at Highfeather, Reg. They are Can. Chs. Highfeather Country Child, Highfeather Trademark, and Highfeather Flirtation, littermates whelped in 1984 out of her first champion, Heather.

A new face at Highfeather is Russell's Roxy Roller (Am. Can. Ch. Allegro Farm Quinn ex Am. Can. Ch. Cairncross Forerunner), a young, lovely bitch that will be shown upon maturity.

Highfeather was registered with the CKC in 1983 and is a small hobby kennel with major emphasis on showing and breeding occasional litters. Health issues are always a primary concern. Wendy has been a member of the Canadian Kennel Club since 1979 and the ISCA since 1984.

Kulana: Valerie and Heidi Gervais, Cobble Hill, BC

Valerie's first Irish was purchased in 1970. He became Am. Can. Ch. O'Leprechaun Bangor Boy, purchased from Lorne and Avis Mackie. Through the Mackies, they contacted Lucy Jane Myers, and from her they purchased

Litter sisters Am. Can. Ch. Kulana Kallme Kylie CD CGC (left) and Am. Can. Ch. Kulana Klassic Kian CD (right) have proved to be outstanding bitches that are still in the winners' circle at the age of 12. Owned by Valerie and Heidi Gervais.

Am. Can. Ch. Lyn Erin Midnight Blue, bred by Linda and Ernie Acquavella of New York, has been an important foundation dog for Valerie and Heidi Gervais' Kulana Kennels.

Maronova: Ronald and Marianne Buck, Victoria, BC

In 1986, Ron and Marianne acquired their foundation bitch, Oxfords Pride of Padraics (Ch. Scarlly's Irish Super Star ex Ch. Tirvelda Tweed of Gabhantyr). Although "Scootie" hated the show ring, she turned out to be a great producer. She was bred to Can. Ch. Sardonyx Northern Lights CD, and her first litter was born in 1988. Can. Ch. Maronova's Autumn Melody, owned by Bob Gibson of Hilloch Kennels, finished her championship before the age of two. Her two sons, Can. Ch. Hilloch's Rebel With A Cause and Can. Ch. Hilloch's Patrick, finished their titles in 1993.

For her second litter, Scootie was bred to Huronridge Jessie's Johnny Reb in 1990. From this litter, they kept a bitch that became Can. Ch. Maronova's Tiffany Blaze.

In 1992, the Bucks acquired Can. Ch. Confettis Casanova (Can. Ch. Devlin Farfadet de Confettis ex Can. Ch. Confettis Alizarine Fragrance) from Helene Viaud. Tiffany was bred to Casanova in 1994 and produced Maronova N Hilloch's Easterlea, owned by the Hillochs. Easterlea was bred twice to Can. Ch. Hilloch's Rebel With A Cause. The Bucks took Hilloch's Bailey O Maronova, and they co-own Can. Ch. Hilloch's Callahan of Maronova with Anne Perkins. A recent addition is Forest Glen's Finale at Maronova (Can. Ch. Forest Glen's Irish Tenor ex Forest Glen's Tiffany Lights), born in 1998.

Because Ron's profession necessitates frequent moves, the Bucks have engaged in a limited breeding program. Nonetheless, Maronova puppies are placed with great

their foundation bitch, Can. Ch. Draherin Will O' The Wisp. The mating of these two began the line of Kulana Setters that continues today.

Over the past 30 years, Lucy Jane has guided them and introduced them to many dogs of her breeding. In 1984, she sent them an outstanding bitch, Am. Can. Ch. Lyn Erin Memory, bred by Linda and Ernie Acquavella in New York. Linda then sent her brother, Am. Can. Ch. Lyn Erin Midnight Blue to Valerie. These two dogs brought Valerie and Heidi to their current standing. In the late '80s, Blue was ranked in the top three Irish in Canada for two years and has left his mark on his progeny, the most famous of which is AKC Dual Ch. Cordon Bleu Bright Star JH, owned by Wendy Czarnecki of Petaluma, California.

Lyn Erin Memory was bred to Ch. Meadowlark's Wyndjammer and in her first litter produced two outstanding bitches that are still in the winners' circle at the age of 12, Am. Can. Ch. Kulana Kallme Kylie CD CGC and Am. Can. Ch. Kulana Klassic Kian CD. Kylie was bred to Am. Can. Ch. Mi Jean's Court Jester and produced another multiple group-placing bitch, Am. Can. Ch. Kulana Mystique. Mystique bred to Midnight Blue produced Am. Can. Ch. Kulana Qismet's Rhuzara CD TD Am. TD CGC and Ch. Kulana Que Sera Sera, owned by Lucy Jane Myers. Kylie's second litter produced Ch. Kulana Start Somethin'. The Gervaises also own Am. Can. Ch. Edenrock Red Ribbons of Tara, a bitch acquired from Dee Swan.

Kulana Irish Setters is a small breeding kennel producing one or two litters a year and concentrating on healthy, happy dogs.

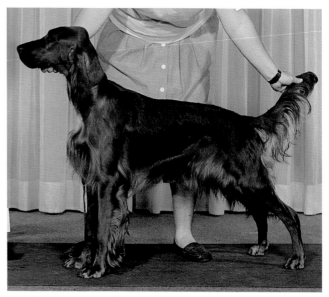

Can. Ch. Maronova's Tiffany Blaze. Owned by Ronald and Marianne Buck.

care, and the Bucks have kept in touch with all of the owners. They believe that an all-around Irish Setter best represents the breed and encourage all their clients to enjoy a wide variety of activities with their dogs.

McCamon: Susan McCamon, Vancouver, BC

Sue McCamon, known during her most active years with Irish Setters as Sue Korpan, started in Irish Setters in Saskatoon with two Irish from the Ardee Kennels of Harry Dean. Although of pet quality, they were excellent hunting dogs. The third addition was a Shannon's Erin daughter that finished her Canadian championship. She was Can. Ch. Pacesetter Morgan McCamon. In 1971, realizing that they would not attain their goal of producing show-quality Irish unless they started with the best pedigrees they could find, the Korpans took a 4,000-mile journey to find the right bitch. On the advice of Ted Eldredge of Tirvelda Farms, they ended up at the kennels of Beurmann and Elizabeth Brewbaker and bought from them a daughter of Ch. Tirvelda Michaelson ex Ch. Rockherin Rebecca. She became Am. Can. Ch. McCamon's Royal Burgundy ROM. She was a magnifi-

Am. Can. Ch. McCamon Marquis was top Irish Setter in the US in 1977 and 1979. He was owner-handled to the top spot in Canada in 1981. Owned by Susan McCamon and Lillian Gough.

cent bitch, a top winner, Number One Irish Setter in Canada, and dam of 23 Canadian and 7 American champions. One of the most successful combinations was the mating of Burgundy to Ch. Tirvelda Telstar ROM, a breeding that was repeated three times. From the first litter came the most influential show dogs and producers, including Am. Can. Ch. McCamon Marquis and his ister, Am. Can. Ch. McCamon Grand Dame. Marquis was top Irish Setter in the US in 1977 and 1979, co-owned with Lillian Gough and shown by George Alston. He was owner-handled to the top spot in Canada in 1981. Although Sue is no longer showing and breeding Irish Setters, these two dogs, plus others produced from these lines, have had a major influence on the breed on both sides of the border.

Orchard Farm, Reg.: Mary Klinck, Cottam, Ontario

In 1938, Mary's parents Harold and Edith Klinck attended a large show in Detroit, Michigan, to select a breed of dog for the family. They fell in love with the Irish Setters belonging to Jack Spear of Tyronne Farm Kennels. From him they purchased their foundation bitch, Tyronne Farm O'Shea. They produced several champions, the most notable being Can. Am. Ch. Lucky of Orchard Farm and his son, Can. Am. Ch. Danny of Orchard Farm.

Mary's father passed away in 1965, and Mary decided that with her mother's help, she would continue the kennel. In 1971, they purchased a puppy from Beurmann and Elizabeth Brewbaker. This puppy turned out to be Can. Am. Ch. Rebecca's Irish Lace "Lacey" (Am. Ch. Tirvelda Michaelson ex Am. Ch. Rockherin Rebecca). All of the Orchard Farm dogs of today can be traced directly to Lacey.

Shortly after purchasing Lacey, Mary was fortunate to meet Frank and Katherine Wheatley of Rockherin. She has always admired their Irish Setters, especially their bitches. She has sought their advice on choosing stud dogs and grading puppies, and she has learned a great deal from them.

Lacey was bred to Am. Ch. Bayberry Tobago to produce Can. Am. Ch. Orchard Farm Catch the Wind, Can. Am. Ch. Orchard Farm Shamaranne,

Can. Am. Ch. Rebecca's Irish Lace, an important foundation bitch for Mary Klinck's Orchard Farm Kennels.

These Orchard Farm littermates have all had exceptional careers in the show ring (left to right): Can. Am. Ch. Orchard Farm Saranda, owned by Nancy Haupt; Can. Am. Ch. Orchard Farm Fax, owned by Carol Kravets; and Can. Am. Ch. Orchard Farm Devon, owned by Mary Klinck.

and Can. Ch. Orchard Farm Sundance. Shamaranne was bred to Can. Am. Ch. McCamon Marquis to produce Can. Am. Ch. Orchard Farm Julianne. A stud service puppy from Can. Am. Ch. Orchard Farm Catch the Wind bred to Jan O'Flanagan's O'Flanagan's Daring-Do was one of Mary's favorite show dogs. She was Can. Am. Ch. O'Flanagan's Writ'n on the Wind. She was a breed winner and group-placing bitch that loved every minute of being a show dog.

Julianne was bred to Am. Ch. Rockherin Royal Ragen and produced four champions: Can. Am. Ch. Freelance, Kayla, and Close Encounter (co-owned with Gary Newman); and Can. Ch. Orchard Farm Hayley. Kayla was a Best in Show bitch, producing only one litter of five sired by Am. Ch. Meadowlark's Masterful. Of those, two finished: Am. Ch. Orchard Farm Canadian Dream and Can. Am. Ch. Orchard Farm Dream Girl, who is the foundation bitch of the Tealwood kennels of Dave Carey and Michelle Ross.

Mary's best producer to date is Can. Am. Ch. Orchard Farm Close Encounter. Her first litter, sired by Am. Ch. Meadowlark's Vindicator, contained Am. Can. Ch. Orchard Farm Valiant; Am. Ch. Orchard Farm Kelsey (sire

Can. Am. Ch. Orchard Farm Allycia was a Best in Show and specialty-winning bitch, as well as Number Three Irish Setter in the US in 1993. Owned by Mary Klinck and Gary Newman.

179

Can. Am. Ch. O'Flanagan's Writ'n On The Wind, one of Mary Klinck's favorite show dogs, was a breed winner and group-placing bitch that loved being in the ring.

Palarset: Pam and Larry Legault, Langley, BC

Striving for versatile, healthy companions with fun temperaments, the Legaults have had Irish Setters since 1975. Their dog, Ch. Challenge Heirloom O'Palar CD TT FD, was the first Irish Setter to tour with the Canadian Superdogs flyball and agility drill teams from 1985 until 1990.

Can. Am. Ch. Tramore Phaedra O'Palar is the foundation bitch for Palarset Kennels.

Am. Can. Ch. Tramore Phaedra O'Palar is the foundation bitch for Palarset. Her son, Am. Can. Ch. Palarset Sultan's Red Storm CDX CGC, was third in conformation and second in obedience in Canada in 1998. The Legaults compete in all aspects of the sport and contribute to their local club's efforts to educate the public about the lovely attributes of the Irish Setter.

of the Godbey's Am. Can. Ch. Pin Oak's Robert E Lee); Can. Ch. Orchard Farm Vanna Redd, owned by Louis King; and Can. Am. Ch. Orchard Farm Allycia, co-owned with Gary Newman. Allycia was a Best in Show and specialty-winning bitch. In 1993, she was Number Three Irish Setter in the US, handled by Dennis Laturie.

The second litter from Close Encounter was sired by Am. Ch. Meadowlark's Wyndjammer and co-bred with Jean Ryan of Killybeg's Kennel in London, Ontario. That litter contained Can. Am. Ch. Orchard Farm Fax, owned by Carol Kravets; Can. Am. Ch. Orchard Farm Saranda, owned by Nancy Haupt from Ohio; Can. Am. Ch. Orchard Farm Devon; Can. Ch. Killybeg's Winjammer's Barley, owned by Jean Ryan; and Killybeg's Killarney Gede CDX, also owned by Jean Ryan.

Fax is a multiple breed and group-placing dog and the sire of several Canadian and American champions. Nancy Haupt's Saranda is also a group and specialty winner and was among the Top Ten Irish Setters in the US in 1994 and 1995.

Mary's future hopefuls are in two litters out of Can. Am. Ch. Orchard Farm Devon. Her first was sired by Can. Am. Ch. Tealwood Principal Shareholder CD. It contains Can. Am. Ch. Orchard Farm Dream Catcher, Orchard Farm Only Zoey, and Orchard Farm Cherrywood Legacy, owned by Peg Wismann. Devon's second litter, sired by Can. Am. Ch. Quailfield's Mak'n Business, are still puppies at this writing, including Orchard Farm Mak'n Magic, Orchard Farm Mak'n Memories, and Orchard Farm Roses Are Red, owned by Carol Kravets.

Ch. Challenge Heirloom O'Palar CD TT FD was the first Irish Setter to tour with the Canadian Superdogs flyball and agility drill teams. Owned by Pam and Larry Legault of Palarset Kennels.

Redmeath: Shirley Culpin, Chilliwack, BC

Shirley has been breeding and exhibiting under the Redmeath prefix in British Columbia since 1973. Her foundation stock was a blend of the old Draherin, O'Leprechaun, and Tirvelda lines. Her goal of breeding for beauty, brains, and versatility has paid off, because many Redmeath dogs have completed championship, obedience, and field titles.

Two of Redmeath's recent winners were Am. Can. Ch. Redmeath Keepsake FD. "Bryn" was the first Best in Show Irish Setter to earn a field title in Canada, which he accomplished at the age of five after being retired from the show ring. Also well known in the Pacific Northwest is Am. Can. Ch. Redmeath Morning Light, a specialty winner on both sides of the border. Currently, Can. Ch. Redmeath Promises to Keep (Ch. Redmeath Keepsake FD ex Ch. Redmeath Morning Light) is working toward her American championship. Her sister, Can. Ch. Redmeath Keepin' the Beat, owned by Rose and Fred Wilson and Reagan O'Hagan of Darkisle Kennels, is a multiple group winner in Canada and has started her American championship quest.

Can. Ch. Redmeath Promises to Keep is currently working toward her American championship. Owned by Shirley Culpin.

Am. Can. Ch. Redmeath Keepsake FD was the first Best in Show Irish Setter to earn a field title in Canada. Owned by Shirley Culpin.

While Shirley is pleased with the accomplishments of her dogs over the years, she is most proud of the fact that all of the dogs owned by Redmeath have been breeder/owner trained and handled to all of their successes in conformation, field, and obedience.

Shirley lives with her husband, Michael Goldman, who has bred top-winning Dalmatians under the Volanta prefix for 30 years, on a small acreage in the mountains in Chilliwack, British Columbia. Because of judging commitments, they are both cutting back on breeding and showing but are still seen periodically in the ring or at field events.

Silverstone, Reg.: Constance O'Brien, Mountain, Ontario

Silverstone has been registered since 1996, even though Connie has had a lifetime of involvement with Irish Setters. There was an Irish Setter in her home when she was born and all during her youth. She competed as a junior in both conformation and obedience.

Her marriage to an Army officer delayed active breeding of Irish Setters until his retirement, but competition and the accumulation of knowledge about the breed were constant throughout her life. She considers herself fortunate to have met a number of great dogs during their tours in England, such as Wendover Gentleman and Wendover Satyr. She visited Wendover, Cornevon, and Marrona Kennels and learned much from their breeding programs.

Silverstone really started with the acquisition of a son of Can. Am. Ch. McCamon's Impresario in 1989. Can. Am. Ch.Confettis Automne Fragrance CD FD was their foundation dog. Silverstone's foundation bitches are an Impresario granddaughter, Can. Am. Ch. Confettis Damoiselle Shelby, and an Impresario daughter, Can. Am. Ch. Captiva Heart's Desire FDJ.

Connie is a member of the Irish Setter Club of Ontario and is an active participant in Irish Setter Rescue with the Irish Setter Club of Canada and the ISCA. She is an all-breed professional handler with a preference for Irish

Can. Am. Ch. Confettis Automne Fragrance CD FD was the foundation dog for the Silverstone Kennels of Constance O'Brien.

Setters. She has bred Irish Setters of which she is proud for their accomplishments in the show ring and in the field.

Tealwood: Dave Carey and Michelle Ross, Moffat, Ontario

Tealwood, formerly Sunrise and Muckross Irish, has been showing and breeding Irish Setters since the early 1970s. Dave's first competitive dog was Ch. Wynfield's Olav Olympia, which he bought from his eighth owner. Although he had never been shown, after two years and some grooming and training, Olav finished his championship in four shows. He became a multiple Best in Show dog and Number One Irish Setter in 1974 and 1975, as well as Number Two Sporting Dog and Number Ten All-Breed at eight years of age. Olav passed his winning ways and strong movement to his sons, Ch. Muckross Heir Apparent and Sunrise Devilment. Olav was bred by Rose Ironson and her daughter, Joyce Snyder of Wynfield Kennels. He was sired by Casey O'Leary ex Sunny Irish Rose, dogs tracing back to Tirvelda and Starheir lines.

In the early 1980s, Dave's son, Will Alexander, began to show dogs professionally. He received a call from Sue McCamon asking him to show a dog to his Canadian championship. The dog was to be finished in Canada and then sent to Florida to be shown and possibly sold there. Will asked his father to buy the dog before he left, and Dave obliged. The dog became Can. Am. Ch. McCamon's Impresario, Canada's Top Dog in 1987 and Number One

Irish for four years. He was also a notable sire, with grandsons and granddaughters winning in the show ring. A grandson of Impresario, Jill Taylor's Can. Am. Ch. Captiva's Ride With the Wind, was Number One Irish Setter in Canada in 1998 .

After a short break from breeding and showing, Dave purchased a bitch from Mary Klinck of Orchard Farm. Ch. Orchard Farm Dream Girl became the foundation of Tealwood kennels, because Will had taken the Muckross name with him. Dream Girl finished in three shows, winning the Canadian National Specialty over the Number One Irish for that year, who was being shown by Will. She was bred to Can. Am. Ch. Quailfield Mak'n Business, producing a number of good show dogs. Among them are Am. Can. Ch. Tealwood's Principal Shareholder CD and Can. Am. Ch. Tealwood's Nine to Five ("Annie"). Annie is well respected in the show ring and on the flyball circuit. She is a flyball champion. She has a strong attitude and love for the show ring, which she has passed on to her progeny. Annie was bred to Am. Can. Ch. Pin Oaks Robert E Lee JH in 1996. From this litter they have a number of champions, but one in particular has turned heads— "Dutch," Can. Am. Ch. Tealwood's Dutch Rose. In Dave's opinion, he is the epitome of Irish Setters. His sister, Can. Ch. Tealwood's Dressed for Success won both her majors at large specialties. Another brother, Can. Am. Ch. Tealwood's Despite All Odds Am. NA, although also a good show dog, is working at his agility titles. He will most likely go into the field.

The Standard
for the
Irish Setter

Every breed recognized by the American Kennel Club is guided by an official standard of perfection for that breed. The standards are developed over time by individuals interested in that breed who wish to protect the look, temperament, and function of the breed as it was developed. The written standards may be compared to blueprints for the breed. Many breed clubs have developed materials that amplify what the written standards say. These can be used as tools to teach people more about the breeds and how to look at them in the show ring or in the field. The standards are approved by members of the Parent Clubs for each breed and are then accepted by the American Kennel Club and put into written form. The clubs own the standards for each breed, but the American Kennel Club can use them to teach aspiring judges or as a basis for dispensing information about a particular breed.

On the pages that follow is the complete illustrated standard for the Irish Setter. Both the written standard and its explanation with complementary drawings are shown in detail. No word or picture, however, can replace the experience of seeing Irish Setters in person, as anyone who has ever admired one can attest.

The Irish Setter is one of the handsomest of all breeds with its glorious coat, extroverted personality, and elegant bearing. It is little wonder that it draws admiring glances wherever it goes.

Looking at the complete dog, one should be immediately struck by several important things. First, it should look like an Irish Setter. It should possess those qualities of head, expression, stature, coat, and gait that stamp it at once as possessing true Irish Setter type.

The dog should be in balance. Whether moving or standing still, all parts should fit together to form a graceful whole. No part of the dog's anatomy, whether head, neck, length of back, or height, should stand out in jarring fashion from the rest. The temptation to exaggerate one aspect of a dog, under the impression that more is better, has caused serious problems in many breeds. Nature tries to preserve basic balance, despite the mischief that breeders sometimes do. For instance, one cannot get a short neck and a long body without throwing the whole dog out of balance.

The head of the Irish Setter is distinctive. The expression should be intelligent and kind, with eyes that are dark and soulful. The skull should have length and be equal from occiput to stop and from stop to tip of nose. It should not be broad and short. The ears are long and low-set, lying close to the head. The combination of equal and level planes and expression make the Irish Setter one of the most appealing of all breeds.

The burnished coat may vary in individual dogs from chestnut red to dark mahogany and should be flat with sufficient feathering on the chest, body, legs, feet, tail, and tips of ears. A healthy coat shines and feels silky to the touch. It should not be coarse, harsh, or dry.

The neck blends into smooth, well-angulated shoulders. The back is of moderate length and has well-sprung but not barrel-shaped ribs. The back slopes gently from withers to tail. The set of the tail should be almost level with the back and carried straight out or with a gentle, upward curve. The feet should be small, the hind legs well bent at the stifle joint. Angulation in the rear should correspond to angulation at the shoulders. Exaggeration

This is the correct Irish Setter—balanced and elegant, yet substantial in build. All parts fit smoothly into one another, and the angulations in the front and rear are approximately the same.

of the hindquarters coupled with straight shoulders and upper arms does not allow the dog to move with a graceful gait. When standing, the dog will appear out of balance.

One should almost see the temperament of the Irish Setter. He should give the impression of friendliness and intelligence. He should never cringe or appear wild, vicious, wary, or aloof. The outgoing personality should be evident to anyone who meets him. The standard is specific about calling for a "rollicking" temperament. This is not to say that the Irish Setter should be out-of-control or hyperactive. True Irish Setter temperament calls for a dog that is sensitive and responsive, yet ready for a game of catch or a day's hunting in the field.

Physically and mentally, the Irish Setter should be in balance. Let's take a look at the individual parts and how they fit into the complete picture of the dog, standing and moving.

Official American Kennel Club Standard for the Irish Setter

Sporting Group

General Appearance

The Irish Setter is an active, aristocratic bird dog, rich red in color, substantial yet elegant in build. Standing over two feet tall at the shoulder, the dog has a straight, fine, glossy coat, longer on ears, chest, tail and back of legs. Afield, the Irish Setter is a swift-moving hunter; at home, a sweet natured, trainable companion.

At their best, the lines of the Irish Setter so satisfy in overall balance that artists have termed it the most beautiful of all dogs. The correct specimen always exhibits balance, whether standing or in motion. Each part of the dog flows and fits smoothly into its neighboring parts without calling attention to itself.

Size, Proportion, Substance

There is no disqualification as to size. The make and fit of all parts and their overall balance in the animal are rated more important. 27 inches at the withers and a show weight of about 70 pounds is considered ideal for the dog; the bitch 25 inches, 60 pounds. Variance beyond an inch up or down is to be discouraged. *Proportion*—Measuring from the breastbone to rear of thigh and from the top of the withers to the ground, the Irish Setter is slightly longer than it is tall. *Substance*—All legs sturdy with plenty of bone. Structure in the male reflects masculinity without coarseness. Bitches appear feminine without being slight of bone.

This dog is underdone and weedy. Note the extreme tuck-up and lack of substance in body and leg bones.

This dog is overdone—somewhat coarse and cloddy without elegance.

This dog is too short in back or too long on leg.

This dog is too long in back or too short on leg. Often, a dog that is long in back will not have a firm topline.

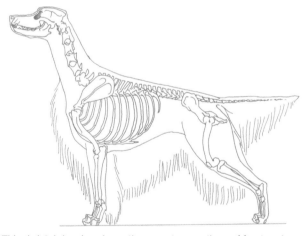

This skeletal drawing shows the correct proportions of front and rear, length to height. In the standard, overall balance is rated more important than size alone. However, because the Irish Setter was bred for endurance, dogs measuring more than an inch over or under the ideal height are not correct.

187

Head

Long and lean, its length at least double the width between the ears. Beauty of head is emphasized by delicate chiseling along the muzzle, around and below the eyes, and along the cheeks. *Expression* soft, yet alert. *Eyes* somewhat almond shaped, of medium size, placed rather well apart, neither deep set nor bulging. Color, dark to medium brown. *Ears* set well back and low, not above

This dog's eyes are set too wide, and they are round, giving a startled expression.

This dog's eyes are slanted, which is incorrect. He also has high-set, short ears.

This shows small, triangular eyes, which are incorrect. The ear set is correct.

This shows a dog that is apple-headed or domey, with too much prominent skull from the eyes to the occiput (rear of skull).

This dog (left) and bitch (right) show the ideal Irish Setter heads. Note the correct planes, chiseling, ear set, and large nose. The bitch is somewhat more refined.

level of eye. Leather thin, hanging in a neat fold close to the head, and nearly long enough to reach the nose. The *skull* is oval when viewed from above or front; very slightly domed when viewed in profile. The brow is raised, showing a distinct stop midway between the tip of the nose and the well-defined occiput (rear point of skull). Thus the nearly level line from occiput to brow is set a little above, and parallel to, the straight and equal line from eye to nose. *Muzzle* moderately deep, jaws of nearly equal length, the underline of the jaws being almost parallel with the top line of the muzzle. *Nose* black or chocolate; nostrils wide. Upper lips fairly square but not pendulous. The *teeth* meet in a scissors bite in which the upper incisors fit closely over the lower, or they may meet evenly.

This front view shows the correct soft expression and proper shape and placement of the eyes.

This head lacks stop and also drops off in backskull.

This dog has a snipy muzzle.

This dog's head is too heavy. Although in proportion, it is too short and deep, with too much flew.

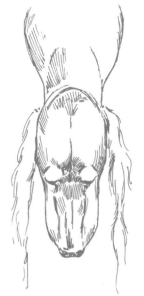

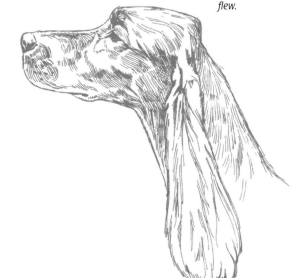

The proper configuration of the head when viewed from above (left) and in profile (right). Note that there are no protruding skull bones on the side of the head. Also note the parallel planes and the equal distance from nose to stop and stop to occiput.

Neck, Topline, Body

Neck moderately long, strong but not thick, and slightly arched; free from throatiness and fitting smoothly into the shoulders. *Topline* of body from withers to tail should be firm and incline slightly downward without sharp drop at the croup. The *tail* is set on nearly level with the croup as a natural extension of the topline, strong at root, tapering to a fine point, nearly long enough to reach the hock. Carriage straight or curving slightly upward, nearly level with the back. *Body* sufficiently long to permit a straight and free stride. *Chest* deep, reaching approximately to the elbows with moderate forechest, extending beyond the point where the shoulder joins the upper arm. Chest is of moderate width so that it does not interfere with forward motion and extends rearwards to well sprung ribs. *Loins* firm, muscular and of moderate length.

This dog has an exaggerated topline, sometimes referred to as a "ski slope" topline.

This shows a dropped croup.

This dog has a stovepipe neck in which the neck fits into the shoulders at a steep angle, giving an unpleasant, choppy outline.

This dog's tail is set on too low and carried too high, giving a choppy appearance to the outline.

190

This dog's chest is too shallow, and he has an exaggerated tuck-up.

This dog has a steep shoulder blade and a short, straight upper arm. Both are incorrect.

This dog is out at the elbows and has a paddling forward stride.

This dog has a correct front, showing moderate width of chest and a straight and true forward stride.

191

Forequarters

Shoulder blades long, wide, sloping well back, fairly close together at the withers. Upper arm and shoulder blades are approximately the same length, and are joined at sufficient angle to bring the elbows rearward along the brisket in line with the top of the withers. The elbows moving freely, incline neither in nor out. *Forelegs* straight and sinewy. Strong, nearly straight pastern. *Feet* rather small, very firm, toes arched and close.

This dog has a correct shoulder and upper arm assembly. A correct foot is shown at bottom left along with an incorrect foot (down on the pastern) on the right.

Hindquarters

Hindquarters should be wide and powerful with broad, well developed thighs. Hind legs long and muscular from hip to hock; short and perpendicular from hock to ground; well angulated at stifle and hock joints, which, like the elbows, incline neither in nor out. Feet as in front. Angulation of the forequarters and hindquarters should be balanced.

This rear lacks substance through the thigh. It is straight in stifle with inadequate angulation.

This dog is overangulated. The second thigh is too long. This dog is also unbalanced in the front and rear as well as sickle-hocked.

Coat

Short and fine on head and forelegs. On all other parts of moderate length and flat. Feathering long and silky on ears; on back of forelegs and thighs long and fine, with a pleasing fringe of hair on belly and brisket extending onto the chest. Fringe on tail moderately long and tapering. All coat and feathering as straight and free as possible from curl or wave. The Irish Setter is trimmed for the show ring to emphasize the lean head and clean neck.

The top third of the ears and the throat nearly to the breastbone are trimmed. Excess feathering is removed to show the natural outline of the foot. All trimming is done to preserve the natural appearance of the dog.

Color

Mahogany or rich chestnut red with no black. A small amount of white on chest, throat or toes, or a narrow centered streak on skull is not to be penalized.

This shows the correct length and lay of the coat. This dog is trimmed, but no clipper or scissor marks are apparent. Acceptable natural variations in coloring include a dark body coat with light feathering and lighter coloring on the tops of the ears and on the skull.

Gait

At the trot the gait is big, very lively, graceful and efficient. At an extended trot the head reaches slightly forward, keeping the dog in balance. The forelegs reach well ahead as if to pull in the ground without giving the appearance of a hackney gait. The hindquarters drive smoothly and with great power. Seen from front or rear, the forelegs, as well as the hind legs below the hock joint, move perpendicularly to the ground, with some tendency towards a single track as speed increases. Structural characteristics which interfere with a straight, true stride are to be penalized.

This dog is cowhocked.

This dog is bowlegged and toeing in.

This dog is out at the elbows and has a paddling forward stride.

These dogs are gaiting correctly.

This dog has no front reach or rear drive.

This dog is hackneying in front and overreaching from the rear.

This dog, seen from the side, is moving correctly. The front and rear angulations are approximately the same.

Temperament is difficult to evaluate in the show ring, but judges know that the correct Irish Setter is, above all, an outgoing, happy-go-lucky character and a loving companion at home.

Temperament

The Irish Setter has a rollicking personality. Shyness, hostility or timidity are uncharacteristic of the breed. An outgoing, stable temperament is the essence of the Irish Setter.

Approved August 14, 1990
Effective September 30, 1990

The
Irish Setter Club
of America, Inc.

The Irish Setter Club of America, Inc. (ISCA), is one of the oldest breed clubs in America. It was formed in 1891, only a few years after the AKC was organized in 1884. All national clubs representing individual breeds are called parent clubs and are considered by the AKC and by all fanciers of that breed to be the guardian and protector of the breeds they represent. It is the task of the parent club to hold specialty shows and obedience and field trials, showcasing the best that the breed can offer. It provides educational materials, such as booklets, videos, and periodicals to existing and prospective members. The ISCA publishes an annual Breeders' Directory, in which those who meet stated criteria are listed. It also funds an active Health Committee, which donates money to research into diseases that affect the Irish Setter. It also publishes a magazine, *Memo to Members*, six times per year, and every five years it publishes a *Pictorial*, an elaborate book of photos and pedigrees of current and past Irish Setters submitted by their owners.

As a parent club, the ISCA provides information and help to local Irish Setter clubs throughout the country. It approves local club events, such as specialty shows and field trials, and its board of directors is drawn from four regions of the US. The ISCA is the spirit, guiding light, and fulcrum of the breeder under whose aegis all local Irish Setter clubs function.

The organizing meeting of the ISCA was held in New York City in February 1891 with 21 dedicated Irish Setter fanciers benched together at the Westminster Kennel Club show. The charter members at that meeting were H. B. Anderson, Glen View, NJ; E. M. Beale,

Lewisburg, PA; E. B. Bishop, Coffeyville, PA; J. B. Blossom, Morrisania, NY; William H. Child, Philadelphia, PA; B. L. Clements, New York, NY; Louis Contoit, West Farms, NY; Dr. G. G. Davis, Philadelphia, PA; William Dunphy, Peekskill, NY; Michael Flynn, Jr., Bristol, RI; Dr. William Jarvis, Claremont, NH; George T. Leach, High Point, NC; J. J. Mannioers, Pittsburgh, PA; Frank H. Perry, Des Moines, IA; Dr. N. Rowe, Chicago, IL; Boyd D. Rothrock, Williamsport, PA; John J. Scanlon, Fall River, MA; Charles T. Thompson, Philadelphia, PA; and Max Wenzel, Hoboken, NJ (who judged Irish Setters that year at Westminster).

William H. Child was chosen as the first president of the ISCA. He later became the third president of the AKC. Dr. N. Rowe, editor of *American Field*, was elected vice president, and later became the ISCA's second president. Dr. Gwilym G. Davis was secretary-treasurer and later served for 23 years as president of the ISCA. An ardent supporter of Irish Setter affairs for three decades, Dr. Davis owned the Currer Kennels.

The Executive Committee members were Max Wenzel (a judge and founder of Fisher's Island Field Trial Club), Charles T. Thompson (Rockwood Kennels), and F. L. Cheney (Nota Kennels), from the east. The west, which extended only to Kansas, was represented by E. B. Bishop and Frank Perry. The majority of the original members were from the east, a few reaching to North Carolina and west to Kansas and Iowa.

At the time, the Irish Setter in both Great Britain and America was used primarily as a hunting dog. One of the first ventures of the ISCA was to hold a field trial at High Point, North Carolina, on November 23, 1891. There were

24 starters in two stakes. The club donated cash prizes of $350. With its success, additional trials were run in 1892, '93, and '95. Interest in field trials waned until they were revived by the ISCA in 1907-1908, when they were held at Barber Junction, NC. This was largely due to the influence of Dr. Davis, who was a strong supporter of field dogs and field trials.

One of the first official acts of the ISCA was to adopt a "standard of points of judging the Irish Setter." This standard had been in effect since 1886 and was patterned after one used by the Irish Red Setter Club of Dublin, Ireland. Preservation of certain bloodlines, prolonged purity of strains, types that were successful in field and show, popularity, and sales value were the elements for a standard, or blueprint, of type for a particular breed, especially at a time when breeds were undergoing great changes.

The early standard emphasized breed characteristics such as a long, lean head, well-defined occipital protuberance, and a deep chest, among other things. It was quite satisfactory over a long period, undergoing only slight revisions in 1895, 1908, and 1919. This standard established arbitrary ratings for 11 parts of the ideal Irish Setter: *Head:* 10; *Hind legs:* 10; *Eyes:* 5; *Tail:* 8; *Ears:* 5; *Coat and feathering:* 8; *Neck:* 5; *Color:* 8 *Body:* 15; *Size, style, and general appearance:* 14; *Shoulders, feet, and forelegs:* 12; *Total:* 100.

The standard withstood the test of time. It was revised in 1960 to give a more complete description of the Irish Setter and to eliminate the point system of scoring. It was further clarified in 1990, and an illustrated standard was drawn up shortly thereafter. A full description of the standard appears in a separate chapter in this book.

During the 1920s, the ISCA conducted a campaign to promote the breed and encourage breeders to improve their stock by offering generous prizes at bench shows and field trials. By 1926, the ISCA was flourishing, with more than 200 members, and was the most active and progressive specialty organization in the dog fancy. It still maintains that reputation more than 100 years later.

The decade prior to the Great Depression was a productive growth period for the dog world. In January 1926, AKC made a constructive attempt at better communication among the breeds by offering member clubs a column in the *AKC Gazette* for their news items. The ISCA's first breed correspondent was William Cary Duncan, a professional writer who worked in this capacity until 1945. Mr. Duncan was a director of the AKC, ninth president of the ISCA, its delegate, and a well-known judge. He also edited the *Irish Setter Club's News*, the forerunner of the present *Memo to Members*. The latter was begun in 1945 by the 14th president, John

C. Neff. The *News* was a four- to eight-page newsletter, prepared after each executive session to inform members of the club's activities. It contained items about show events and dog accomplishments.

The *Memo* expanded under a series of editors, in addition to Duncan and Neff, to include several presidents, among them Ivan Klapper, Louis Iacobucci, and Connie Vanacore. Shirley Boyer, Valerie Buehler, and Joyce Mumford were instrumental in upgrading the quality and increasing the number of pages and advertising in the publication. A subscription to the *Memo* is included as part of the membership of the ISCA and has been a great attraction, helping to bring membership to approximately 1,800, including many international members.

The ISCA conducted its first Combined Specialty and Field Day in Albany, New York, on August 26, 1927. The second event was held at the Milson Kennels in Harrison, New York, on October 6, 1928. The third and fourth Specialty shows followed in succession on the estate of Miss Elizabeth Stillman, Cornwall, New York, and the fifth was held in conjunction with the Storm King Kennel Club All-Breed show. Then came six specialties associated with the spectacular Morris & Essex shows in Madison, New Jersey (1932-1937), followed by eight specialties held in conjunction with the Westchester Kennel Club (1938-1946). The great show dog, Ch. Milson O'Boy, an Irish Setter handled by Harry Hartnett, won Best in Show at Morris & Essex in May 1935.

Local clubs have played an important part in the growth of Irish Setter fanciers over the years. The first local club was the Irish Setter Club of New England, chartered on November 14, 1928. Next came the Irish Setter Club of Southern California, formed in late 1931 or early 1932. The Western Irish Setter Club came next in 1935, and the Eastern Irish Setter Association was formed in January 1936.

When the AKC revised its field trial rules in 1931, the ISCA, cognizant of the hunting potential of the Irish Setter, offered attractive prizes to stimulate interest in field trials.

The first championship points under the new rules were awarded to Ch. Elcova's Admiration, and the first AKC Field Champion was Elcova McTybe. In 1938, to perpetuate this great start, the club offered the Elcho prize of $500 to be awarded to the first Irish Setter winning ten points in field competition with Pointers and Setters. In order to emphasize dual purpose, the dog must also have won at least five regular classes at dog shows with at least four competitors in each class. The concept of the Irish Setter that can do it all has been encouraged throughout the years through various programs. Among the most successful was one established by president Edward Treutel in 1978, called the Versatility Program. In order to qualify for a Versatility Certificate, a dog must have had to qualify in conformation, field, and obedience. A further modification was instituted in 1982 with the VCX (Versatility Excellent) program for which the qualifications are more rigid. Since the AKC instituted its Hunting Dog program in the early 1990s, many Irish Setter fanciers have entered their dogs in that field endeavor to earn Junior, Senior, or Master Hunter titles.

The ISCA honors its dual dogs at its annual awards ceremony by awarding special prizes in those categories.

The importance of Sweepstakes and Futurity programs is noted in a booklet published by the ISCA in 1946: "To encourage the production of excellent stock." The first Irish Setter Futurity was held by the Eastern Irish Setter Association on June 11, 1938. Futurities were held through the next decades until they ceased to draw sufficient interest. They were replaced by Sweepstakes classes at most local specialty shows, and these have been a popular and enduring activity for breeders and owners to showcase their young stock. Veteran Sweepstakes have become an integral part of the National Specialty beginning in 1991, and most local clubs have added this feature to their specialties. These classes are for dogs and bitches eight years and older and gives new exhibitors and spectators an opportunity to see the senior Irish Setter citizens that provided the breeding stock for the new generations. Futurities are still held, however, in conjunction with the National Field Trial each year.

A collection of E. I. Eldredge Award winners in 1998 (left to right): Ken Ruff, Anne Savory-Bolus, Marion Pahy, "Doc" Helferty, Joyce Mumford, Connie Vanacore, Jay Zirkle, and Paula McAteer.

The first regional field trial, hosted jointly by the Western Irish Setter Club and the Irish Setter Club of Milwaukee, was held on October 24, 1965, and was followed by other regionals, leading to the establishment of the National Field Trial Championship in 1979. From a two-day trial, the National Field Trial has grown to a week-long event, with stakes for puppies, derby dogs, older dogs, and the national and national amateur championships. Versatility tests and AKC hunting tests are included in the events, as well as a directors' dance, an auction, and hospitality provided by individual clubs throughout the week.

The first independent National Specialty show was held in August 1973, at Valley Forge Military Academy, Wayne, Pennsylvania. Since that historic occasion, National Specialties have rotated around the four regions of the country, growing more elaborate in production and importance. From two days at the beginning, the National Specialties have grown to a week of activities, ranging from seminars, local sightseeing tours, hospitality, the annual ISCA meeting, the annual awards banquet, and whatever other enticements the local host clubs arrange.

In recent years, other activities have played an important role in the ISCA activites. In 1982, a health committee was established, headed by Connie Vanacore. This committee raises money for research and has funded large amounts to PRA and bloat research. There is an ongoing study of the genetic basis of idiopathic epilepsy in the breed.

A Register of Merit program was established in 1990 to honor the top producers of all time, living and dead. A dog must have produced 20 champions and a bitch must have produced 7 champions. A field dog must have produced five field champions, and a field bitch must have produced three field champions.

Upon the death of one of the great breeders and gentlemen in the breed, AKC Delegate and AKC Board member Ted Eldredge, a memorial was offered by George and Mary Ann Alston, Irish Setter supporters and retired professional handlers of some of the great dogs of recent times. The ISCA accepted the award to be given at the annual awards banquet each year. The award is presented to the person who "best exemplifies those attributes most closely associated with Ted Eldredge. These are good sportsmanship, compassion, kindness, integrity, courtesy, and devotion to the welfare of the breed." The award is called the E. I. Eldredge Memorial Award.

Throughout its long history, the ISCA has been the guiding spirit for Irish Setter affairs. The objectives of the parent club are pronounced in the Constitution:

Recipients of the E.I. Eldredge Memorial Award

1985	Anne Savory-Bolus
1986	Constance B. Vanacore
1987	Clayton R. Webb
1988	Emily Schweitzer
1989	Marion J. Pahy
1990	Joyce Mumford
1991	Dr. Robert Helferty
1992	Not given
1993	Mrs. Paula S. McAteer
1994	Anne Marie Kubacz
1995	Kenneth Ruff
1996	Claire Andrews
1997	Jay R. Zirkle
1998	Not given
1999	Betty Crawford

AKC Delegates

The ISCA has had few delegates representing them at the AKC throughout its long history. Among them are an AKC president, William Cary Duncan, an executive vice president, John C. Neff, and an AKC board member, E. I. Eldredge.

G. H. Thompson	1896-1910
Walter Creuzbaur	1910-1922
William Cary Duncan	1925-1945
John C. Neff	1945-1965
Joseph P. Knight	1965-1968
E. Irving Eldredge	1968-1985
Bernard Baron	1985-1987
Dr. Robert Helferty	1988-1998
Constance Vanacore	1999-

"To encourage and promote the breeding of pure-bred Irish Setters and to do all possible to bring their natural qualities to perfection, to encourage the organization of independent Irish Setter Specialty clubs, to promote, amend, and define a standard of the breed, to do all in its power to protect and advance the interest of the breed, to encourage sportsmanlike competiton at all events, and to conduct Sanction Matches and Specialty shows, Field Trials, and Obedience Trials under the rules of the AKC."

Past Presidents of the Irish Setter Club of America, Inc.

1891-1892	Wm. H. Childs
1893-1894	W. L. Washington
1895-1918	Dr. G. G. Davis
1919-1920	Joseph Wall
1921-1922	Dr. C. A. Gale
1923-1927	Dr. J. D. DeRonde
1928-1929	Walter Arnold
1930	Mrs. E. A. Sturdee
1931-1933	Wm. Cary Duncan
1934-1935	Walter Ellis
1936-1937	Joseph A. Cuneo
1938	Walter Ellis
1939	Dr. G. S. Currier
1940-1946	John C. Neff
1947-1949	Joseph P. Knight, Jr.
1950-1952	Lee M. Schoen
1953-1960	Lester Gatchell
1961-1969	Ivan Klapper
1970-1975	Louis Iacobucci
1976-1978	Edward Treutel
1979-1981	Virginia Hardin
1982-1984	Bernard Baron
1985-1987	Dr. Robert Helferty
1988-1990	Mrs. Constance Vanacore
1991-1993	Jay R. Zirkle
1994-1996	Edward P. Meyer
1997-1999	Mrs. Shirley A. Farrington
2000	Sam Houston McDonald

Irish Setter Club of America
National Specialties

1st National Specialty—Valley Forge Military Academy, Wayne, PA—August 10–11, 1973

Best of Breed—Ch. Mos'n Acre Wilson Farm Harmony

Best of Opposite Sex—Ch. McKay's Red Baron

Winners Dog—Fleetwood Farms Grand Marshall

Winners Bitch—Thenderin Winter Wind

2nd National Specialty—Waterford Oaks Recreation Area, Pontiac, MI—June 14–15, 1974

Best of Breed—Ch. Thenderin William Muldoon

Best of Opposite Sex—Ch. Bayberry Sonnet

Winners Dog—Renegade of Lenair

Winners Bitch—McCamon's Royal Burgundy

3rd National Specialty—The Lovett School, Atlanta, GA—June 20–21, 1975

Best of Breed—Ch. Herihunda's Jennifer O'Shannon

Best of Opposite Sex—Ch. Apacheacre's De-Ka-Mik

Winners Dog—Rendition Santana

Winners Bitch—Thenderin Guarantee

4th National Specialty—Randolph Park, Tucson, AZ—April 30–May 1, 1976

Best of Breed—Ch. Royal Oaks Fortune's Fella

Best of Opposite Sex—Am.Can.Ch. Rendition Chantilly Lace

Winners Dog—Candy K's How Sweet It Is

Winners Bitch—Draherin My Fair Lady

5th National Specialty—Dulles Marriott Hotel, Washington, DC—May 20–21, 1977

Best of Breed—Ch. McCamon Marquis

Best of Opposite Sex—Ch. Kinvale Majorette of Kendall

Winners Dog—O'Gradyi's Most Happy Fella

Winners Bitch—Charnel's Ruffian

6th National Specialty—Holiday Inn, Elyria, OH—Sept. 29–30, 1978

Best of Breed—Am. Can. Ch. Tirvelda Sprig Of Gabhantyr

Best of Opposite Sex—Am. Can. Ch. Shawnee Sundance

Winners Dog—Can. Ch. Donoval's Crimson Crown

Winners Bitch—Windntide Sophistication

7th National Specialty—W. W. McAllister Park, San Antonio, TX—May 11–12, 1979

Best of Breed—Ch. McCamon Marquis

Best of Opposite Sex—Ch. McCamon Anastasia

Winners Dog—Red Shadows Magic Brew

Winners Bitch—Meadowlark's Chances Are

8th National Specialty—Orange County Fairgrounds, Costa Mesa, CA—June 27–28, 1980

Best of Breed—Ch. Shawnee Pipedream O'Charlton

Best of Opposite Sex—Ch. Windntide Sophistication

Winners Dog—Glenavan Harvest Moon

Winners Bitch—iafail Lovely Light

9th National Specialty—Radisson Ferncroft Hotel, Danvers, MA—June 12–13, 1981

Best of Breed—Ch. Shawnee Pipedream O'Charlton

Best of Opposite Sex—Ch. Charlton's Oriental Jade

Winners Dog—Palomar's Skyrocket Corcaigh

Winners Bitch—Meadowlark's Glorianna

ISCA National Specialties

10th National Specialty—Kentucky Fair and Exposition Center, Louisville, KY—June 18–19, 1982
Best of Breed—Ch. Honeyrock Garnet of Summerhill
Best of Opposite Sex—Ch. Liafail Lovely Light
Winners Dog—Costa Brava's Diplomat
Winners Bitch—Shangrila Moon Shadow

11th National Specialty—Thunderbird Resort Hotel, Jacksonville, FL—June 17–18, 1983
Best of Breed—Ch. Meadowlark's Anticipation
Best of Opposite Sex—Ch. Marlyn Prelude
Winners Dog—Scarlly's Road Runner
Winners Bitch—Glenavan Windbowne Moondance

12th National Specialty—Loretto Heights College, Denver, CO—June 15–16, 1984
Best of Breed—Ch. Herihunda's Joint Venture
Best of Opposite Sex—Ch. Courtwood Bright Idea
Winners Dog—Somersets Royal Woodsman
Winners Bitch—Corcaigh's Fly-N-Solo

13th National Specialty—Holiday Inn, Mechanicsburg, PA—June 21–22, 1985
Best of Breed—Ch. Meadowlark's Anticipation
Best of Opposite Sex—Ch. Stoneypoint's Ruff Stuff
Winners Dog—Scarlly's Sky Rocket
Winners Bitch—Scarlly's Looney Tunes

14th National Specialty—Buder Park, St. Louis, MO—June 13–14, 1986
Best of Breed—Ch. Scarlly's Red Hot
Best of Opposite Sex—Ch. Russett Hill Sassafras
Winners Dog—Tapnar Cherokee Kinsman
Winners Bitch—Evergreen Promises Promises

15th National Specialty—Landmark Hotel, Metairie, LA—June 19–20, 1987
Best of Breed—Ch. Ramblin' Red Kildavan
Best of Opposite Sex—Ch. Scarlly's Dreamboat Annie
Winners Dog—Caitlin's Celebration
Winners Bitch—Rockherin Sheena

16th National Specialty—Marina Park, San Leandro, CA—June 17–18, 1988
Best of Breed—Ch. Meadowlark's Vindicator
Best of Opposite Sex—Ch. Saxony's Wildwood Flower
Winners Dog—Kimberlin Killian
Winners Bitch—Windntide Hot Cross Buns

17th National Specialty—Fort Adams State Park, Newport, RI—June 16–17, 1989
Best of Breed—Ch. Scarlly's Road Runner
Best of Opposite Sex—Ch. Saxony's Wildwood Flower
Winners Dog—Cucuhullain Eternal Prince
Winners Bitch—Cucuhullain Four Paw Drive

18th National Specialty—LeBaron Hotel, Dallas, TX—June 15–16, 1990
Best of Breed—Ch. Courtwood Silver Chalice
Best of Opposite Sex—Ch. Cloverleaf's Rebecca
Winners Dog—O'Kerries State Trooper
Winners Bitch—Kinvale Captured Moment

ISCA National Specialties

19th National Specialty—Sugar Loaf Resort, Cedar, MI—June 17–22, 1991

Best of Breed—Ch. Regalaire Music Man
Best of Opposite Sex—Ch. Kinvale Captured Moment

Winners Dog—Meadowlark's Fire 'N Rain
Winners Bitch—Terra Cotta's Melody

Awards of Merit:
Ch. Arista's Finest Rose
Ch. Cloverleaf's Rebecca
Ch. Evergreen Return Engagement
Ch. Powderhorn's Call to Glory
Ch. Lili Marlene

Ch. Meadowlark's Muir Woods
Ch. Cucuhullain Eternal Encore
Ch. Saxony's Evening Reflections
Ch. Copperleigh's Ryan O' Balcaire
Ch. Meadowlark's Mischief Maker

20th National Specialty—Lewisville Park, Battle Ground, WA—June 25–27, 1992

Best of Breed—Ch. Scarlly's Main Switch
Best of Opposite Sex—Ch. Powderhorn Call To Glory

Winners Dog—Lucky Morn Dann Eze Debonair
Winners Bitch—Kimberlin Of Thee I Sing

Awards of Merit:
Ch. Rusticwood Olympic Medalist
Ch. Sunshine's First Rate
Ch. Mariah Showbiz
Ch. Sunnyhill Corpus Christi

Ch. Kulana Klassic Kian
Ch. Quailfield's Mak'n Business
Ch. Bromwich's Triple Crown

21st National Specialty—Friar Tuck Inn, Catskill, NY—June 23–26, 1993

Best of Breed—Ch. Tirvelda Once Upon A Time
Best of Opposite Sex—Ch. Quailfield's McCalls

Winners Dog—Cullans Take A Gander
Winners Bitch—Cullans Christmas Goose

Awards of Merit:
Ch. Saxony's Evening Reflections
Ch. Estrella Candlestick
Ch. Sunnyhill Wings of the Wind
Ch. Trendsetter's Steppin' Out

Ch. Quailfield's Mak'n Business
Ch. Cloverleaf's Who's That Girl
Ch. McCamon Impresario
Ch. Cucuhullain Eternal Encore

22nd National Specialty—Parke Hotel, Canton, OH—June 22–25, 1994

Best of Breed—Ch. Saxony's Evening Reflections
Best of Opposite Sex—Ch. Meadowlark's Captured Dream

Winners Dog—Cardinal Talk Show
Winners Bitch—Scenario Irish Mist

Awards of Merit:
Ch. Castlebar Command Presence
Ch. Pin Oak Robert E. Lee
Ch. Seantalan Tirvelda Tradition
Ch. Meadowlark's Meteorite
Ch. Ramblin' Red Phaegan

Ch. Heatherae Heartbeat of America
Ch. Rusticwoods Love Song
Ch. Cullan's Xmas Goose
Ch. Dreamtime April Magic
Ch. Trendsetter's Steppin' Out

23rd National Specialty—Reaves Arena, Perry, GA—June 21–24, 1995

Best of Breed—Ch. Pin Oak Vicksburg
Best of Opposite Sex—Ch. Marlyn Intentional Foul

Winners Dog—Chamberlayne Echo of Kinvale
Winners Bitch—Red Barn Valley View Velvet

Awards of Merit:
Ch. Jamond's Bostonian
Ch. Fyrethorn Dream Shared
Ch. Pin Oak Robert E. Lee
Ch. Rusticwood's Song of Hawaii
Ch. Stoneypoints Make My Day

Ch. Rusticwood's Love Song
Ch. Seregon Holiday at Tainaron
Ch. McDerry's Lil' Miss Understood
Ch. Cloverleaf's Who's That Girl
Ballingary I'm Now 'N Later

ISCA National Specialties

24th National Specialty—Cashman Field Center, Las Vegas, NV—June 20–22, 1996

Best of Breed—Ch. Ballymera's Stormin' Norman
Best of Opposite Sex—Ch. McDerry's Lil Miss Understood

Winners Dog—Ballymera's Ridin' The Wind
Winners Bitch—Devlin Meadowlark's Illusion

Awards of Merit:
Ch. Saxony's Sympatico
Ch. Rusticwood's Son of Hawaii
Claddagh Preferred Stock
Ch. Honeyrock West of the Moon

Ch. Analainn Cat Dancing
Ch. MiJean's Every Now and Then
Devlin Meadowlark's Illusion
Ch. Red Barn Molly Pitcher, JH

25th National Specialty—The Holiday Inn at the Crossings, Warwick, RI—June 18–21, 1997

Best of Breed—Ch. Ramblin' Red Fortune Teller
Best of Opposite Sex—Ch. Rusticwood Running Mate

Winners Dog—Kimberlin Out of the Blue
Winners Bitch—Dana Si Heartily Opulence

Awards of Merit:
Saxony's Casual Lies
Ch. Quailfield Business B1V Pleasure
Ch. Rusticwood's Song of Hawaii
Ch. Avon Farm Mr. Debonair
Ch. Ballymera's Stormin' Norman
Ch. Scarlly's Gift of Love
Ch. Evergreen Chase The Clouds CGC

Ch. Chamberlaynes Sassafrass
Ch. Seantalan Tirvelda Tradition
Kimberlin Out of the Blue
Ch. Castlebar Garden Party
Ch. Pompei's The American Way
Ch. Rusticwood's Song N' Dance Man

26th National Specialty—Purina Farms, Gray Summit, MO—June 17–20, 1998

Best of Breed—Ch. Quailfield Mak'N Business
Best of Opposite Sex—Ch. Ramblin' Red Fortune Teller

Winners Dog—Fyrethorn Center Court
Winners Bitch—Captiva's Wishes In The Wind

Awards of Merit:
Ch. Rusticwood Running Mate
Ch. Scarlly's Gift Wrapped
Ch. Ballymera's Ridin' The Wind
Ch. Avon Farm Mr. Debonair
Ch. Jamond's Call The Play
Ch. Kennlee Treasure Bay
Ch. Glenrose Lady Rietz

Ch. Evergreen Chase The Clouds JH
Ch. Pompei's The American Way
Kennlee Duenotunderestimate
Ch. Saxony's Creme De La Creme
Ch. Rusticwood's Song of Hawaii
Ch. Cairncross Petite Syrah
Ch. McDerry's Lil' Miss Understood

27th National Specialty—Greater Jacksonville Fairgrounds, Jacksonville, FL—June 24–26, 1999

Best of Breed—Ch. Ramblin' Red Fortune Teller
Best of Opposite Sex—Ch. Devlin's R.D. Reilly JH

Winners Dog—McKendree's Gameroom Cowboy
Winners Bitch—Quinniver's Agatha Christie

Awards of Merit:
Ch. Sandcastle Knight Eternal
Ch. Evergreen Chase The Clouds JH
Ch. Morrigan's Red Skye At Night
Ch. Kintyre's Debutante
Ch. Castlebar's Ruxton Olympia

Ch. Chamberlayne's Sassafrass
Ch. Shadowmere's Penny Saved
Ch. Chamberlayne Echo of Kinvale
Ch. Avon Farm Mr. Debonair

ISCA Register of Merit (as of 5/20/2000)

Dogs

Ch. Blaneywood Country Squire
Ch. Cairncross Second Wind
Ch. Camelar Joker of Charlton
Ch. Candia Indeed
Ch. Charlton's Moon Lover
Ch. Courtwood Manuscript
Am. Can. Ch. Courtwood Summer Forecast
Ch. Draherin County Leitrim
Ch. Draherin Irish Regardless
Am. Can. Mex. Ch. Draherin King's Ransom
Am. Can. Ch. Esquire of Maple Ridge
Ch. Higgin's Red Coat
Ch. Innisfail Color Scheme
FC AFC Ivor Glen Ruben
Ch. Kerry-Eire Heaven Only Knows
Ch. Kinvale Evergreen Destiny
Ch. Kinvarra Kermit
Ch. Kleiglight of Aaragon

Knockcross O'Boy
Dual Ch. Mahogany Titian Jingo
Am. Can. Ch. McCamon Marquis
Ch. McKendree's Bold Venture
Ch. Meadowlark's Anticipation
Ch. Meadowlark's Intrepid
Ch. Meadowlark's Masterful
Ch. Meadowlark's Masterpiece
Ch. Meadowlark's Vindicator
Ch. Meadowlark's Wyndjammer
Ch. Meadowlark's Irish Monarch
Am. Can. Ch. Michael Bryan Duke of Sussex
Ch. O'Kerrie's Armagh
Ch. Pompei's First Class
Am. Can. Ch. Quailfield's Mak'n Business
Am. Can. Ch. Red Star of Hollywood Hills CDX
Ch. Regalaire Music Man
Ch. Rendition Erin of Sunny Hills
Ch. Rozzan's RazMaTaz

Ch. Rusticwood's Olympic Medalist
Ch. Saxony's Evening Reflections
Ch. Scarlly's Red Hot
Ch. Scarlly's Show Boat
Ch. Scarlly's Show 'Nuf
Ch. Seaforth's Dark Rex
Am. Can./BDA Ch. Shannon's Erin
FCh. Shawn of Kaymar
Ch. Shawnee Pipedream of Ch.arlton
Ch. Starheir's Aaron Ardee
Ch. Sunshine's First Rate
Ch. Thenderin Brian Tristan
Ch. Thenderin William Muldoon
Ch. Tirvelda Distant Drummer
Ch. Tirvelda Earl of Harewood
Ch. Tirvelda Hunter's Moon
Ch. Tirvelda Michaelson
Ch. Tyronne Farm Malone II
Ch. Weblyn Mystic Mark

ISCA Register of Merit (as of 5/20/2000)

Bitches

Ch. Arab Irish Jayne Mansfield
Ch. Balcaire Paprika
Ch. Ballymera's Best Yet
Ballymera's First Encounter
Beaverbrook Canadiana
Ch. Beaverbrook Shayne Serenade
FC AFC Blue Angel's Cherry Pie
Ch. Boxley Holly Ann
Brophy's Ragtime Lass
Cameo Cute Crissy
Ch. Celou's Tracy MacRory
Ch. Charlton's Indeed I Do
Ch. Charnel's Sailway Moonsong
Charnels Scarlet Huntress
Ch. Charnels Spendrift CDX
Ch. Classic's Krystle Lady VC CD CGC
Ch. Cloverleaf's Millenium
Ch. Cloverleaf's Who's That Girl
Ch. Corry Hill's Kelly O'Reilly
Ch. Courtwood Bandanna
Ch. Courtwood Bright Ruby
Am. Can. Ch. Devlin's Windsong of Tara Am. Can. CD
Ch. Draherin Annie Laurie
Ch. Draherin Echo of Elixir
Ch. Draherin Echo's Hope
Am. Can. Ch. Draherin Vanity Fair
Ch. Durin Kingscourt Betsy Ross
Ch. Erinfyr Brianna CD
Glen Cree Merriment
Ch. Glenmora April Morning CD
Am. Can. Ch. Hallmark Courtin 'N Kitchen
Ch. Hartsbourne Sallyann of Tirvelda
Am. Can. Ch. Heatherwood's All Systems Go
Ch. Hotze's Red Rose

Dual AFC Karrycourt's Rose O'Cidermill
Ch. Kennlee Sunny Days
Ch. Kerry-Eire Coral Charm
Ch. Kerry-Eire Little Rebel CD
Ch. Kinvarra Bootsie
Ch. Kinvarra Portia
Ch. Knockcross Ruby
FC AFC Kopper Key Boni of Brownhaven
Ch. Legacy Summer Surprise
Ch. Marlyn Lyric
Ch. McCamon Royal Burgundy
Meadowlark's Magic Genie
Meadowlark's Magical Mirage
Meadowlark's Solitaire
Ch. Meadowlark's Whisperin' Breeze
Ch. MiDream's Lady Kelly
Milesian Wisp of the Wind
Mount Forest Tailspin
Ch. Mount Forest Wait N' See
Norab's Tribute to Red
Am. Can. Ch. Onesquethaw Mourna Fleming
Palomar's Joy of Chandar
Am. Can. Pr. Ch. Powderhorn Glory Road (Ch. of the Americas—1985)
Dual Ch. Red Arrow Showgirl UDT
Ch. Red Barn Revolutionary Star
Red San of Charles
Ch. Redwhiskey Royal Victory
Am. Can. Ch. Rendition's Indian Summer
Ch. Rendition Irish Inspiration
Ch. Rendition Razzle Dazzle
Ch. Rendition Wild Poppy
Ch. Rockherin Neesa of Kenobi
Ch. Rockherin Shana of Shangrila
Am. Can. Ch. Rossel Bridie Rose

Ch. Rusticwood's Made In Heaven
Ch. Ruxton's Mollie O'Day
Sage Hill Neich O'Day
Ch. Scarlly's My Sky
Ch. Scarlly's Sweet Success
Ch. Scarlly's Up Front
Ch. Seekay's Berry Gay Rhu CD
Ch. Shamrock Heather
Ch. Shangrila Scarlet O'Hara
Ch. Shangrila Wyndchime
Am. Can. Ch. Shannon Kelly O'Green
Ch. Shawnee Indian Breeze CD
Ch. Shawnee Indian Sonnet
Ch. Shawnee Indian Summer
Ch. Shawnee Night Lace
FC AFC Sunny of Ivor Glen
Swashbuckler's Zinfandel
Ch. Thenderin Elixir
Ch. Thenderin Mispice
Ch. Tirvelda Bayberry Sundown
Am. Can. Ch. Tirvelda Bridget Susie Ann
Ch. Tirvelda Cathy O'Rinn
Ch. Tirvelda Meadowlark's Ebbtide
Ch. Tirvelda Nutbrown Sherry
Ch. Tirvelda Queen Mab
Ch. Tirvelda Sarabande
Ch. Tramore Every So Often
Ch. Tramore Kiandra
Trophy's Torch of Apache Acres
Tyronne Clementine Kelly
Ch. Tyronne Farm Gloribee
Am. Bda. Ch. Villa-Dan Stacy Shine Brite
Ch. Webline Moonshadow
Ch. Wilson Farm Country Charm
Ch. Windwood Merry Mockenbird CD

Irish Setters in the Field

The first Irish Setter to win a scheduled field trial, according to available literature, was Queen, owned by Charles V. Kaeding, a San Francisco sporting goods dealer. It was a match race with four starters at 50 dollars per entry, held in Marin County, California, in 1870.

Another purely local event was run October 8, 1874, a few miles from Memphis, by the Tennessee State Sportsmen's Association in the Free-for-All Stake, with an entry of ten gun dogs. H. C. Pritchett's black setter, "Knight," placed first, and J. H. Drew's red-and-white setter placed fourth.

The second Memphis trial the following year was a battle between the native bird dogs and the blue-blooded imports from Europe. Imported English Setters won all three places in the Puppy Stake, but the native red-and-white setter Tom (sired by Joe-Buck, Sr.) owned by George W. Campbell, Spring Hill, Tennessee, won the Free-For-All Champion Stake with five starters. Tom was a rugged dog with plenty of pace, range, and class. Campbell, who handled him, was a big fellow with a voice to fit his size. As he walked through a cornfield, he would fill his pockets with ears of corn. When Tom came tearing by, George would yell and fire an ear at him. Then Tom, a hardheaded rascal, would turn on more speed and get as far away as possible. He was the first Irish Setter to win a Championship Stake and was said to be an excellent shooting dog and bevy finder. Colonel Hughes of Texas paid 300 dollars for him, a very good price in those days.

At the fourth annual Tennessee trials held on General Harding's Belle Meade Estate near Nashville, the famous English Setter, Gladstone, won the Puppy Stake, and the native red setter, Joe, Jr., owned by M. C. Campbell, won the Champion Stake with 20 starters. The battle between the bluebloods and the natives was reopened in 1878 at the fifth and last Tennessee Association trials, when Joe, Jr. and Adam's Drake tied for first place in the Champion Stake.

The culmination of the feud was probably the two-day match race on quail at Florence, Alabama, in December 1879, when Joe, Jr. defeated the renowned Gladstone by a score of 61 to 52 points. Joe was a fast dog with a wonderful nose and great bird sense. Bigger than average, he traveled with a long-stretching, wolf-like gait. He was red with a little bit of white and was registered as an Irish Setter. His sire was the noted Irish Setter Ch. Elcho and his dam was the native crossbred Buck, Jr., one of the Campbell strain.

During the next decade, Ch. Elcho's progeny (Berkley, Raleigh, Jessie, Leigh Doane, Yoube, and Bruce) were prominent in the trials of the Fisher's Island, Eastern, and Philadelphia clubs. The significant thing about this period was that the Irish Setter owners ran their bench dogs in the field trials and also used them as shooting dogs.

The inaugural trials of the ISCA were held at High Point, North Carolina, on November 23, 1891. There were four annual Carolina trials at which the dogs of George E. Gray, Dr. Gwilym G. Davis, and E. B. Bishop predominated. Gray was a professional trainer of field dogs. Davis was long the president of ISCA, and Bishop was proprietor of the Glenmore Kennels in Kansas.

In general, the picture for the first 20 years of the 20th century was not encouraging. According to the records, there were only 18 Irish Setter field trial placements in open stakes during that period. Five of these were obtained by the Law strain of dogs of F. A. Johnson of Detroit, who made a sincere effort to further the cause of the red setter afield.

It was also during this period that the Fremont, Nebraska, fancier Otto Pohl assembled his Donegal Kennels of Irish Setters with a similar purpose in mind. When he died in 1919, he was making good progress toward achieving the goal of a pure Irish Setter that could compete successfully in the field. He had acquired stock from the Law strain, from the West Coast, and from England's Rheola Kennels. Among the best, reportedly, was small, dark-mahogany Rheola Pedro.

A prefix to gain considerable notoriety about this time was Smada, which when spelled backwards referred to breeder Dr. L. C. Adams, one of the early presidents of the Dayton Pointer Club. This sportsman, who had owned Irish Setters for 30 years, obtained the Donegal dogs after Pohl died. He raised a few litters from them, one of which contained Donegal Morty Oge II (Donegal's Morty Oge ex Donegal's Noreen). Morty II sired two champions, but his real claim to fame lay in being the sire of the famous little field trial winner, Smada Byrd.

J. Horace Lytle of Dayton, dog writer and field trial judge, obtained Byrd as a puppy, trained her, handled her in trials, and cherished her until her death in 1935. Much of her success afield might be attributed to the bond of affection and mutual understanding that existed between the little setter and her master. Lytle described her in his biography, *Breaking a Bird Dog* (1924).

Some excellent field stock of the day came from Ireland. A popular import was Tipperary Eamon, brought over by G. O. Smith in 1920. In three years, he sired 47 litters, which included four field trial winners.

At the time, every part of the country had its field trial advocates. In California, Irish Setters were represented for a number of years by the Valley View prefix of Dr. J. C. Negley of Los Angeles. His initial stock came from Dr. R. H. Washburn of Colorado, who raised ten litters from one pair of setters, his own Major Clanderrick and Patsy Jane Law. Negley obtained Valley View Peggy from one of these matings and bred her to Duke Clanderrrick, thereby making a double cross to imported Ch. Rheola Clanderrick. Valley View Jiggs resulted, the prolific sire of more than 200 registered dogs from 46 bitches. Perhaps the greatest of his offspring was Ch. Valley View Pat, a bench champion as well as a field trial winner.

About 1932, the new field trial rules of the AKC went into effect. To acquire the title of field champion, a setter had to obtain a total of ten points by winning first place in approved field trials, the number of points per stake

being based on the number of starters in the stake. Under the American Field rules, the winner of a designated championship stake was referred to as a field trial champion, but if the dog's performance was not considered of championship caliber, the title was withheld by the judges.

This turn of events more or less classified the Irish Setter field trial dogs into those that placed in restricted breed trials and those that won in open competition against Pointers, English Setters, and other breeds. Very few Irish Setters competed in the major circuit trials, but there was a marked increase in the number of entries in Irish Setter Stakes at all-breed trials and special club events. About this time, the Western Pointer and Setter Club, Jersey Irish Setter Club, Irish Setter Club of Southern California, Irish Setter Club of New England, and others held field trials.

The ISCA, which renewed its field trial program in 1927, had an impressive list of first-place winners in the All-Age Stakes of the pre-war years.

AKC Title Abbreviations

| Field Champion | FC |
| Amateur Field Champion | AFC |

National Championship titles are for specific years of winning those events, so dogs can become multiple champions.

National Field Champion	NFC
National Amateur Field Champion	NAFC
Multiple National Champions	2xNFC (e.g.)

Hunt Test Titles

Junior Hunter	JH
Senior Hunter	SH
Master Hunter	MH

Field Trialers in the Past

FC Elcova McTybe

FC Elcova McTybe (Ch. Elcova's Terence McSwiney ex Modoc Bedelia), the first Irish Setter field champion under the new AKC rules, sired seven field trial winners.

Sulhamstead

The Sulhamstead Kennels of Mrs. Florence Nagle of England, which bred so many splendid field trial setters from 1925 to 1965, were represented in American trials of the pre-war period by Sulhamstead Beppo D'Or and Sulhamstead Trace D'Or, both imported by Ernest D. Levering. In 1976, Mrs. Nagle moved to Maryland. Unfortunately, no dogs came with her.

Joffre Rookwood

S. L. Taylor, Mount Sterling, Kentucky, owned a prepotent sire of good field stock called Joffre Rookwood (Appreciation Joffre ex Walters' Fay), an honest bird dog, big-going, with brains and bird sense. He would rapidly cover a 40-acre field and snap decisively into a stylish point upon locating quail. Joffre was solid red, compact in build, and about 24 inches at the shoulder. Although he was never entered in field trials, he was the sire of eight field trial winners. His progeny must have numbered in the hundreds, for most American-bred shooting dogs of the '50s had him as an ancestor. Later on, Mr. Taylor sold numerous puppies sired by Joffre's great-grandson, Rookwood's Field Master, and out of Trace D'Or's Belle, a daughter of Sulhamstead Trace D'Or.

AKC FC Askew's Carolina Lady

In the early '50s, a group of sportsmen was organized under the banner of the National Red Setter Field Trial Club. Club members held semiannual field trials for the red dog alternately in Delaware and Ohio, the first event on April 13, 1952. The first National Red Setter Open Shooting Dog Championship Stake, run on October 17, 1953, was won by Askew's Carolina Lady (Kentucky Bill ex Poker Faced Alice), though the title was withheld. Despite this, Carolina Lady gave many fine performances in her long career and later was awarded the title of AKC Field Champion. She won at least 28 stakes, defeating more than 300 dogs. She was also a great-producing dam of 15 field trial winners and the granddam of many more. She had six litters by Ike Kendrick, Ike Jack Kendrick, Willow Winds Duke, and Willow Winds Hobo. Lady, a key bitch in the Willow Winds breeding program of Ned LeGrande (a founder of the National Red Setter Club), was bred by Earl Bond, Albert Lea, Minnesota, from a mating that was repeated six times. She descended from Rookwood and Midwestern kennels. In 1972, AKC FC Askew's Carolina Lady was elected to the Field Trial Hall of Fame, sponsored by the American Field. She was the first Irish Setter and the only one to date to be selected.

The most noted of her sons was FC Ike Jack Kendrick. "Happy Jack" was a perfectly trained, plucky little shooting dog that possessed great heart and a most appealing personality. Afield, he was conscientious and thorough, exhibiting unusual endurance and stamina. Like his dam, he pointed and backed with high style. He was a small, compact, dark-red setter, strong in loin and hard

as nails. At least 30 bitches were mated to Jack, some of which had several litters sired by him. The progeny out of FC Askew's Carolina Lady, Lady's Colleen, and Willow Winds Kate seemed to be especially successful at trials. Several of Jack's sons carried on as producing sires, including Bruns Red Ike, Draherin Lord Kendrick, and Cherry Point Nickjack, who was Lady's last son.

Besides Lady and Jack, Ned LeGrande owned Willow Winds Smada and Citation Lass of Ardee as foundation stock at his kennels in Douglassville, Pennsylvania. About 1955, he imported Sulhamstead Norse D'Or ("Shane") from Mrs. Nagle and found afterward that some of the same Sulhamstead blood appeared in the background of FC Askew's Carolina Lady. In the 13 years following 1952, LeGrande setters and their progeny placed in more than 500 recognized field trials, conducted by both the National Red Setter Club and the AKC. Ned passed away in 1999 at the age of 88.

Norse D'Or was a top contender and also a potent stud. He sired as many as 21 field trial winners, including four from the Valli Hi kennels of David and Jane Hasinger of Philadelphia. Another of his sons was Schnet's Little Red, owned by Lt. Col. Edward L. Schnettler of St. Cloud, Minnesota. Ed Schnettler owned field trial Irish Setters since the 1930s, and the Schnet prefix appears in the names of many well-known dogs.

Edgar W. McIvor: "Mr. Field Trial"

The first dual champion made up under AKC rules was Tyrone's Mahogany Mike CDX, bred and owned by "Mr. Field Trial," Edgar W. McIvor of Blanchard, Michigan. Ed McIvor's association with the field spanned 35 years. He started with bench stock in addition to Mahogany Mike, but decided early on to try to develop a dog with high style and class, breeding from the original bloodline descended from Mike. His interpretation of "style" was a dog that hunts with a happy, eager spirit, covering ground with a minimum of handling, locking up on birds with a high head and tail on point. One of the first to finish, combining all the attributes Ed sought, was FC Ivor Glen Duffy O'Mike, a grandson of the original dog. He then purchased Ivor Glen Jim Dandy from Canada, whose greatest contribution to the line was intensity and high style on point. He also purchased Cannon's Irish Duke, a great-grandson of Mahogany Mike, a powerful, big-running dog.

In the early 1970s, Rod and Kelly Martin became associated with Ed and co-owned and co-bred several top-winning field dogs with him. The first, and one of the most influential, was FC AFC Sunny of Ivor Glen. She proved to be an outstanding winner and producer for both Ed and the Martins. Among her most notable get were

FC Runnymeade's Ivor Glen Rowdy. Owned by Kevin Culver.

FC AFC Devilera of Ivor Glen; FC Ivor Glen Dinah, owned by Mike; FC Ivor Glen Ruben, owned by Ken Ruff; and Ivor Glen Duke Too, owned by Curtis Martin. The Martins also owned FC Ivor Glen Delphinium with Ed. Another dog to come from Ivor Glen was FC Ivor Glen Rowdy, owned by Kevin Culver. Ed passed away in 1984.

Ch. Red Arrow Show Girl UDT

Another famous dual champion of the 1960s was Ch. Red Arrow Show Girl UDT, who won top titles in field, obedience, and bench, plus a Mexican obedience degree. Owned by Lawrence and Eleanor Heist of Fontana, California, she placed in 20 field trial stakes and was the dam of eight bench champions. Two of these were sired by Dual Ch. Tyrone's Mahogany Mike, and the other six were in a litter sired by Am. Can. Ch. Esquire of Maple Ridge.

O'Lannon Kennels

Another dual champion came from the O'Lannon Kennels of Dale and Irene Walker. He was Dual Ch. Titian Duke CD. He, in turn, produced Dual Ch. Mahogany's Titian Jingo when bred to FC Mahogany Friction CDX in 1955. Dual Ch. Mahogany's Titian Jingo ROM produced seven field champions, a first in AKC records. He started in the field in May of 1965 and finished his field championship in May of 1966. He was also entered in 14 bench shows and won a total of 36 points.

Many other famous dogs were produced by the O'Lannon Kennels, finishing both in the field and in conformation. Jingo's son, FC Mahogany's Red Baron of

Pauncefoot Kopper Key pointing a quail in 1980. Owned by Patricia and Stephen Salt.

Erin, when bred to Red-San of Charles, produced FC Blue Angel's Cherry Pie, owned by Tony Baron of Norab Kennels.

Tony and Sue Baron

Tony and Sue Baron of Wadsworth, Illinois, began in Irish in 1965 with a bitch puppy of Charles River breeding. She was Red-San of Charles. Bred to Dual Ch. Mahogany's Titian Jingo, she produced three field champions: Norab Duke, Kahlua's Red Baron, and Shamrock Sue O'Shannon. Cherry Pie was the Baron's star field performer, but on a trip south they saw a bitch with great potential, whom they bought on a co-ownership with Diane Camp of Atlanta, Georgia. In 1975, she became Dual Ch. Cynthia of Woodland Brook.

Ardee Kennels

Another famous kennel that spanned 30 years was the Ardee Kennels of Harry Dean of Saskatoon, Canada. He owned or bred more than 25 Canadian Irish Setter champions, and in 1967, Ron Surdam of Laramie, Wyoming, brought the Ardee Kennels south of the border. Two influential dogs to arrive were FC AFC Lord Mike of Ardee and FC Lady Claire of Ardee II. The most outstanding was Lord Mike, who earned 40 field trial wins. He produced two field champions and numerous winners.

Kopper Key Kennels

Other field trial participants in the 1970s were Faunt and Helen Ekey of Spencerport, New York. They owned eight field trial winners at their Kopper Key Kennels. Dennis and Georgia Brown of Brownhaven Kennels, Canyon Lake, Texas, started their program with 2x NAFC FC AFC Kopper Key Boni of Brownhaven, who won her championship in 1981. They continue their interest in field trialing today in partnership with Ray Dohse, a professional handler from Georgia who breeds under the Eshod prefix. Jim Haupt's Basham Kennels in Ohio is another successful training ground for field trialers.

Elizabeth "Jill" Ross

One of the most beloved field trialers of the 20 years spanning the 1970s through the early '90s was Elizabeth Ross, who was one of a pair of twins born in 1920. Their mother announced their birth by saying, "Jack and Jill have arrived." The nickname stuck, and Elizabeth was known for the rest of her life as Jill. The large family spent summers and weekends at a log cabin in the Black Hills where they learned to ride, always accompanied by their Irish Setter, Brian. Jill's father was a mining engineer, and through him Jill met a Princeton geologist, Reuben Ross, Jr., whom she married during World War II.

As a war bride, she worked as a tool planner in Chicago, and at the end of the war, when Reuben returned from duty in the Army Air Corps, they continued their education. In 1952, they moved to Denver. After Jill's childhood companion setter died, Reuben's Irish Setter, Mr. Dooley, joined the household. Jill began to become interested in field trials in the 1960s, and she eventually bought Siobhan O'Shillelagh ("Shauny") (Bo-Cham's Rusty Red Irish ex Kinvarra Ember Glow, a daughter of Ch. Kinvarra Flicker) who became her first field dog. In 1968, the Rosses took a geological and sightseeing trip to

Jill Ross as a young girl with her first Irish Setter companion, Brian.

the UK and left Shauny with Shirley Polson for training. She showed so much potential that Jill entered her in a field trial, where Shauny won a Derby ribbon. That was the beginning of Jill's passion for field trialing.

Shauny's career was inauspicious, but when bred to one of Irene Walker's dual champions, she produced Bridget O'Shillelagh. Next bred to one of Ron Surdam's Ardee dogs, Shauny produced Cairnad O'Shillelagh, who was the dam of FC AFC Dubhagan O'Shillelagh ("Dugan") when bred to County Clare's Hogan. Dugan won two national championships and was the love of Jill's life. Through him, Jill achieved her dream to prove that purebred Irish Setters could compete with the best of any hunting breed. In fact, when hunting pheasant with Reuben, Dugan proved to be an impeccable bird dog. He was a solid-red, upstanding dog of good stature and intensity on point. It was expected that this legacy would continue after Jill's death through Scallawag O'Shillelagh, daughter of Leigh Given's Irish Rover O'Shillelagh and Dennis Hidalgo's Lucky Lady. However, it was not Irish Rover but her littermate Red Devil Deagh O'Shillelagh that won the National Amateur Field Trial Championship in 1996 and the National Field Trial Championship in 1998.

Jill's work and leadership in promoting Field Trial Irish Setters is well known. She spent hours helping conformation and obedience trainers start their dogs in the field and was instrumental in beginning the versatility program. She served on many field committees and was a director of the ISCA and show chairman for the National Specialty in 1984.

Although seriously ill with lung cancer, she insisted in taking part in the National Field Championships in Booneville, Arkansas, in 1992. None of the members of the Irish Setter Club of Colorado will forget Jill coming to the club's first all-breed match in January 1993 before her death in August of that year. Tributes to Jill poured in to Reuben, and he created a special memorial trophy to be awarded to the futurity winner at the National Field Trial each year.

Separation of Field and Bench Stock

For many years, since the inception of the National Red Setter Club in the 1950s, concern was raised among Irish Setter fanciers about the separation of field and bench stock. The two strains became more and more divergent, and with the practice of reciprocal registration between the AKC and the American Field Stud Book it was difficult to control. In 1975, the ISCA, through its delegate, Ted Eldredge, was able to persuade the AKC to rescind its policy of reciprocal registrations. Henceforth, in order for a dog registered with the American Field to

achieve AKC registration privileges, the owner would have to prove his pedigree independently. This policy enables AKC and Irish Setter breeders to have better assurance about the integrity of their breeding stock.

Field Trialers Today

Irish Setter field trial enthusiasts of today span several generations and can trace their breeding stock to many of the field trial greats of the past. Many are seriously commited to breeding and trialing dogs in the manner of the early trialers, in which the Irish Setter could go from field to conformation without losing the style and the looks that are distinctive to the breed. Profiled here are a few of the field trialers currently running their dogs in competition.

James Sr. and Beverly Basham, Nova, OH

Jim and Bev purchased their first Irish Setter in 1968 as a family pet. Basham's Tipparary Red CD was pointed on the bench, but an accident that broke his leg ended his show career. Jim enjoyed hunting and became involved in training dogs for field work. In 1972, they purchased a farm in Nova, Ohio. He worked at a steel mill at night and came home and started training dogs during the day. He trained and handled mostly Irish Setters for several years, never running in the Amateur stakes. His first two field champions were FC Dawn the XIV and FC Shaughn's

FC AFC Karrycourt's Wild West Hero. Owned by Jeannie Wagner and trained by James Basham, Sr.

Shannon. Numerous other Irish Setter field champions followed. Among the most notable was Dual Ch. Shane's Irish High Noon, which he co-owned with Jim Haupt, who showed him in conformation. Next came FC Cidermill's Bridget of Aaragon, owned by George and Georgia Ann Clark, followed by FC Dylan's Trinity Ware, owned by William Dixon, and FC Ivor Glen Rose, owned by Ed McIvor. Jim did the initial gun dog training for Dual AFC Karrycourt's Rose O'Cidermill ROM, owned by Jeannie Wagner and George Clark. He also helped Jeannie train and finish FC AFC Karrycourt's Wild West Hero. FC AFC Karrycourt's Toby of Tobie Lee, owned by Terry Harbach, was also trained by Jim, as well as Susan Borocz's FC AFC Karrycourt's Prairie Fire and AFC High Winds Big Stock.

In the late 1970s and '80s, when Irish Setter popularity plummeted, Jim expanded his training to include all pointing breeds. Jim is retired from the steel mill but still trains the bird dogs he loves every day.

Kevin Culver, *Runnymeade*–Waldorf, MD

The name Runnymeade was taken from Kevin's father, who owned a racehorse farm in Virginia. It means "place of many waters." Kevin's love for the Irish Setter goes back to the 1940s, when he would accompany his dad as he hunted over his Irish Setter, "Terry."

Kevin and his wife, Jean, who breeds and shows Skye Terriers, started in 1971 with Runnymeade's Murphy (Basham's Tipperary Red CD ex Ch. Oakhill Carmine's Treasure). Their plan was for Jean to show Murphy and for Kevin to run her in field trials. In 1973, Murphy won first place in a gun dog stake at a local trial, and that started Kevin's interest. Their first few Irish Setters had show and field stock from Kinvarra, Wildhaven, Killagay, and Ivor Glen. His first field champion was FC Runnymeade's Ivor Glen Rowdy in 1981. Since then, Kevin has continued with Ivor Glen lines, including Karrycourt (Jeannie Wagner) and Brophy (Ken Ruff). His current field champion is Runnymeade's Genie O'Brophy, who finished her title in 1999.

Wendy, Matt, and Tracy Czarnecki, *Bright Star*–Petaluma, CA

Wendy's goal in her 25 years of owning Irish Setters has been to own a dual champion. Her successes in attaining this ambition on the bench are described in the conformation chapter of this book. This portion of the Bright Star story concerns itself with Dual Ch. AFC Cordon Bleu Bright Star JH ("Tempe"). Tempe was sired by Am. Can. Ch. Lyn Erin Midnight Blue out of Am. Can. Ch. Scarlet Victory Bright Star AM. Can. CD JH VC. ("Nike") and was in a litter of 12, whelped in 1993. Tempe

FC Runnymeade's Genie O'Brophy. Owned by Kevin Culver of Runnymeade Kennels.

finished on the bench at the age of 26 months and finished her field championship with two major wins and her amateur field championship with another two majors. Wendy characterizes Tempe this way: "She is very intelligent and confident. Her desire for birds is extreme. She completed her Junior Hunter title at the age of 12 months and 1 week, earning a perfect score for her last qualifying leg. Her range is not extreme, but she is always snappy and hard-working."

Wendy and Matt are now working with Tempe's litter brother, "Seamus," Am. Can. Ch. Rhythm N'Blues Bright Star JH. After finishing his championship in 1997, he is working toward becoming Bright Star's second dual champion.

Smokey and Herb Hiles, *Lu–Chorpan*–Seaford, DE

Herb and Smokey obtained their first Irish Setter in the mid-1960s for companionship and occasional hunting. He was purchased from a breeder in Virginia that combined Midwest hunting Irish Setter bloodlines with those bred by a priest from Ireland who lived in

Baltimore. He was registered as Lu-Chorpan Clancy of Titian CD. Clancy earned his Companion Dog degree at the age of 11 and lived on for 14 years. He sired a dynasty that continues to the present.

FC Lu-Chorpan Huntress Molly as a ten-month-old puppy. Owned by Smokey and Herb Hiles.

The Hiles' first field trial campaigner was Lu-Chorpan's Ferdinand CD VC NAVDA Prize 1 ("Fred"). Although he never achieved his field championship, Fred made a believer out of several field trialers for his pointing and scenting ability.

Their first AKC field trial champion in the mid-Atlantic region was FC Veda Mae. The Hiles had purchased her and her sister from J. B. and Pam Owen of Tennessee because they were bred on County Clare lines. She finished in 1975. The next two field champions from Lu-Chorpan occurred in the 1980s. They were FC Lu-Chorpan Huntress Molly and FC AFC Lu-Chorpan's Trudy CD VC.

Paul Long, one of the premier bird dog trainers in the East, taught Smokey how to train her own dogs. She trained and handled her dogs until she was stricken with Lyme disease in the mid-'80s, which caused her to curtail much of the Lu-Chorpan activities.

She did train and finish a bitch in the '90s, bred from Lu-Chorpan lines, which she co-owned with the breeder, AFC New Order Hope JH CD VC.

Lu-Chorpan has also been active in the obedience ring, having taken 13 Irish Setters and two Welsh Springer Spaniels to their Companion Dog titles. They advocate the ISCA's Versatility Program, and ten of their dogs have versatility titles. They have also taken numerous Irish Setters to their Junior and Senior Hunter titles.

FC Veda Mae winning the Open Gun Dog Stake in 1975, with owners Herb Hiles (left) and Smokey Hiles (right), trainer and handler Jim Jackson (middle), and judges Fritz Moorehouse and Dennis DeSabato (standing).

The Hiles breed Irish Setters to be companions that have the ability to be great hunting buddies. All breeding stock has been proven in the field either through the AKC or American Field programs, the North American Versatile Hunting Dog Association (NAVHDA), or the National Birdhunter's Association programs.

Catherine Ochs, Durham, CT

Catherine's first dog to be trained in the field is Tainaron's Celtic Piper JH CGC. She also owns McDerry's Lady of the Moor, whom she hopes to train in the field as well.

Marion Pahy with Faith Farm Spunky Sue, receiving her first qualifying score in the Senior Hunt Test at the National Field Trial in Booneville, Arkansas.

Paulette Peckol, Easthampton, MA

Paulette's Am. Can. Ch. Devlin's Red Devil Reilly JH is passionate about hunting. Paulette began training him in the spring of 1998, and she is now working him toward his Senior Hunter title.

Tainaron's Celtic Piper JH CGC. Owned by Catherine Ochs.

Marion Pahy, *Faith Farm*—San Antonio, TX

Dan and Marion Pahy began with bench dogs that Dan enjoyed taking afield. They were bred from McGovern lines combined with FC Sulhamstead Norse D'Or. Dan acquired Faith Farm Lehigh Little Bit but passed away before he was able to finish her field titles. Marion continued in the field and trialed Little Bit to her field championship. Marion continues her activities in the field with Faith Farm Cinnamon Toast JH, a rescue Irish that became the first Junior Hunter in Texas. Marion is involved with the Irish Setter Club of San Antonio and its rescue efforts. She was an officer of the ISCA and a recipient of the E. I. Eldredge Memorial Award.

Am. Can. Ch. Devlin's Red Devil Reilly JH. Owned by Paulette Peckol.

FC AFC Damika's Wild Wisk Kay CD JH VC CGC, foundation bitch for Jean and Kevin Plummer's Redwing Kennels.

Jean and Kevin Plummer, *Redwing*—Dunbar, KY

FC AFC Damika's Wild Wisk Kay CD JH VC CGC ("April") was the Plummers' foundation bitch. She was a great hunting dog, easy to train, and loved to retrieve on land or in water. April is the first and only Irish Setter in Maryland to earn both AKC field titles. She has been on television and in print ads. She was an approved therapy dog for the elderly, children, and mentally ill. April was bred twice, once to Redwing Celtic Knight, and once to FC AFC Karrycourt Wild West Hero (owned by Jeannie Wagner). Most of these offspring are in training for the field and have earned their Canine Good Citizen awards. Kevin has judged AKC and American Field trials since 1993. Both are active in the Maryland Association of Field Trial Clubs and the Three Rivers Sportsman Club. Jean is also first Vice President of the Irish Red and White Setter Club of America.

Ken and Linda Ruff, *Brophy*—Sycamore, IL

Brophy's Irish Setters began in 1972 with the purchase of dogs bred by Tony Baron of Norab Kennels and a dog from Ed McIvor of Ivor Glen Kennels. In 1974, the Ruffs moved to the country with their four boys and three Irish Setters.

An early cross between the two lines became the basis for their foundation stock. The Ivor Glen background has played the dominant role in their breeding program. Ken has always maintained that intelligence and natural pointing instinct were the two most significant traits in a field breeding program. Over the years, they have only bred dogs that have shown a strong hunting instinct, good trainability, and the loving and jovial personality that makes them Irish Setters. Ken feels breeders need to produce Irish Setters that hunters are proud to take afield and that also are capable of being maintained as housepets.

NFC 2x NAFC FC AFC Ivor Glen Ruben ROM was their main foundation dog. Ruben was bred seven times and produced seven field champions, as well as four offspring that won seven national championships between them. He was a prepotent male that the Ruffs based their breeding program on, linebreeding to him for several generations.

NFC NAFC FC AFC Brophy's Mahogany Fielder is a son of Ruben that they used to continue the Ruben line. He was a solid producer whose offspring included NFC FC AFC Brophy's Pumpernickel, a bitch that defeated the most AKC dogs in a single year in all-breed competition.

Brophy's Red Storm Rising, a male owned by Bob Geddeis of Rockport, Illinois, was a prepotent male that moved the line forward. He unfortunately died at a young age but left several significant offspring. NAFC AFC FC Brophy's Center Fielder, owned by Ray and Jackie Marshall of Stillwater, Minnesota, is a full brother to Red Storm Rising. He is having a major impact on the breed, producing excellent stock for the future.

NFC FC AFC Hazelwood's Speedy Gonzales ROM, owned by Robin Baker and Marion Pahy, is the most consistent-producing female in Irish Setter history. She has produced three field champions to date and has several more that have the potential to make her the all-time best-producing field dam. She is a granddaughter of Ruben out of a litter produced by Georgia Brown, who was a grandaughter to her 2x NAFC FC AFC Kopper Key Boni of Brownhaven.

In the interest of promoting the dual dog, Ken bred Red Storm Rising to Connie Vanacore's Ch. Ballycroy Royal Burgundy. They retained a bitch from that litter, field-pointed Brophy's Ballycroy Ballina. Ballina was bred to Clancy of Brophy's, and from that litter of promising pups they retained Brophy's JJ of Ballycroy, who at this writing is just starting her field training with Ken. A subsequent litter of Ballina to Brophy's Absolute Power (NAFC AFC Brophy's Center Fielder ex NFC AC AFC

NFC FC AFC Brophy's Center Fielder is a becoming a top producer and a major influence on the breed. Owned by Ray and Jackie Marshall.

NFC NAFC FC AFC Brophy's Mahogany Fielder. Owned by Ken and Linda Ruff.

Brophy's JJ of Ballycroy at three months of age. Owned by Ken Ruff and Connie Vanacore.

Brophy's Midwest Express) has given them Brophy's Ballcroy Liberty Belle.

Ken is a vice president of the ISCA and is a recipient of the E. I. Eldredge Memorial Award.

Stephen and Patricia Salt, *Pauncefoot Kennels—Berea, KY*

Pauncefoot Kennels began in 1965 in the English Midlands with a bitch of Wendover bloodlines. Work took the Salt family to Jamaica in 1969, and the Irish Setters went along with them. Showing in conformation, they had Jamaica's first Irish Setter show champion. They also bred a male that became the second champion.

In 1973, work necessitated another move, this time to Canada. Since their dogs were past show-ring age, Pat and Steve imported a bitch from England of Marrona-Wendover stock. Marrona Mystic Star of Pauncefoot not only gained her championship but became Canada's first Irish Setter to achieve the Field Dog title, equivalent to the AKC's Senior Hunter title.

Pat and Steve aimed to produce dual-quality stock but recognized that it would take several litters per year, as well as a lot of luck, to achieve this goal. Since the Salts preferred to breed infrequently, devoting a lot of individual time to each puppy, they decided to concentrate on improving the reputation of the Irish Setter in the field. Their current breeding program is based on FC AFC Kopper Key Ms. Nellie, a descendant of Carlysle Emerald Jewel, whom they acquired from the late Faunt Ekey. Nellie

was bred only once. Her grandchildren include AFC Pauncefoot Pageant and Pauncefoot Perennial. Both of these dogs have placed in the National Field Trials.

The Salts plan to continue breeding on a limited basis, using their current bloodlines based on Emerald Jewel, the Brophy lines of Ken Ruff, and the Damika lines of the late Diane Maas. This mixture has produced stylish bird-finding dogs of attractive build and size that are chestnut or mahogany in color. Puppies are reared in their home with lots of TLC. They are evaluated for temperament and bird instinct.

In keeping with their first love of showing, the Salts also have a young show-bred bitch that is both "birdy" and a great-great-grandaughter of Can. Ch. Marrona Mystic Star. Over the years, the Salts have finished homebred dogs in show, obedience, and field, but the working Irish Setter today has pride of place.

Jeannie and Michael Wagner, *Karrycourt—Wellington, OH*

The Wagner's first Irish Setter was purchased in December of 1972, and on the recommendation of a neighbor, they took the three-month-old puppy to obedience classes. Although he was meant to be Mike's dog, he bonded to Jeannie. She took him through training to the surprise of the instructor, who told her the dog couldn't be trained. He went on to become Rory Hayes McClaffey CDX VC. The Wagners bought another Irish Setter, McClaffey's Velvet Meggin CD VC, who was Mike's personal hunting dog and also acquired some field trial placements.

Pauncefoot Perennial on point at the 1996 National Amateur Championship. Owned by Patricia and Stephen Salt.

Pauncefoot Pageant. Owned by Patricia and Stephen Salt.

Three of Jeannie and Michael Wagner's Karrycourt champions (from left to right): FC AFC Karrycourt's Prairie Fire; FC AFC Karrycourt's Toby of Toby Lee; and Dual Ch. AFC Karrycourt's Rose O'Cidermill ROM.

In 1973, they became more heavily involved in all aspects of the sport, joining the Irish Setter Club of Ohio and the Ohio Red Setter Club. One day, Mike came home from a garage sale with a two-year-old Irish Setter bitch. He had rescued her from life in a crate. She became FC AFC Shannon's Bonnibelle Sherrie CD VC. She was bred four times, most notably to Dual Ch. Shane's Irish High Noon. From that breeding came Karrycourt's Royal Flush. Although an excellent bird dog, her range of field was too short to win enough points for her field championship, but she was the only get out of Irish High Noon to be bred. She was bred to Ch. Wynquest Troop Commander, but her most outstanding litter was by FC AFC Cidermill's Gonna Fly Now, owned by George and Georgia Ann Clark. From this litter came Dual AFC Ch. Karrycourt's Rose O'Cidermill ROM, whom the Wagners co-owned with the Clarks. She earned all her field points in all-breed competition and was often the only Irish Setter entered in the trial. She was owner-handled to all three titles. Her initial gun dog training was by Jim Basham, Jr., and it was under his tutelage that Jeannie finished Rose's training and that of the dogs that followed her. Rose was bred first to NFC NAFC FC AFC Brophy's Mahogany Fielder. Only

three male puppies resulted, one of which became FC AFC Karrycourt's Toby of Tobi Lee, owned by Terry Harbach. Her other litter by Karrycourt's Teddy Bear CD VC, who was lost to cancer before completing his field title, produced FC AFC Karrycourt's Prairie Fire, owned by Susan Borocz and Jeannie, and AFC Karrycourt's Bonnie Belle. These three earned Rose her ROM.

Over the years, the Wagners have infused their bloodlines with both field and show stock. Those original dogs were from Knockross, Shannon, Fleetwood Farms, Wilson Farm, and O'Flannagan. They added Ivor Glen, Brophy, Damika, Blue Time, Aeris, and Saturday Night dogs. Their most recent winner, FC AFC Karrycourt's Wild West Hero, is a combination of show and field lines.

Jeannie has been active in 4-H for 25 years and was president and director of the Irish Setter Club of Ohio, field secretary for the ISCA's National Field Trial, and chairperson of its Dual Dog Committee, as well as holding many other positions. She is a freelance writer for various dog publications.

The Wagners plan to continue their commitment to the dual Irish Setter by breeding good-looking, trainable bird dogs.

Dual Ch. Shane's Irish High Noon won his dual championship in 1979. Bred by James Haupt and owned by James Haupt and James Basham, Sr.

Dual Ch. Karrycourt's Rose O'Cidermill ROM won her dual championship in 1987. Bred by Jeannie Wagner and Joan Poole and owned by Jeannie Wagner and George Clark.

Dual Ch. AFC Cordon Bleu Bright Star JH won her dual championship in 1996. Bred and owned by W. R., Matthew, and Tracy Czarnecki.

Dual Champion Irish Setters

Since 1979, five Irish—one dog and four bitches—have added their names to the honor roll of dual champion Irish Setters, all of whom have had impressive accomplishments. It is interesting to note that many of the dual champions have attained numerous additional titles or accomplishments. These five modern-day duals are no exception. When you talk to the owners of duals, you will find that their road to fame was not an easy one. Often they received little or no moral support in one of the disciplines. Duals have been labeled as mediocre—which is not quite fair when one considers what the Irish Setter is supposed to be. A dual is not going to be the big-winning extreme special or field trial winner because they are balanced between the two. Often they will be better in one discipline than the other, but they are generally not going to be Best in Show winners or National Champions. We need those extreme dogs to use in our breeding programs to produce dogs of dual stature. The implementation of the Versatility Program and the AKC Hunter Tests has given many more people the opportunity to explore the field side of their dog and the chance to prove their dog's hunting ability without the high cost of campaigning on the horseback field trial circuit. Many owners, after they realize how much their dogs enjoy working in the field and see how much fun they have, often become field trial competitors.

In October 1979, Dual Ch. Can Ch. Killagay's Image of Tara Am. Can. CD VCX (Ch. Robilee Endeavor ex Fld Ch. Killagays Bit O'Dellarobia) became the 13th dual champion. "Cricket" was bred and owned by Connie and Glen Christie. She was trained and handled in the field by Jake Huizenga. Cricket earned puppy and derby points, with her final field championship points being a major win at a Gordon Setter trial. Patty Harris handled her to those last points because Jake was ill. She did not start her show career until after she finished her field championship. She was six years old and went on to complete both an American and Canadian championship and an American and Canadian CD. She was the first Irish Setter to earn the VCX title. Cricket also placed at the first ISCA National Championship. She was 13 years old when she died of an autoimmune deficiency. She was bred to Am. Can. Ch. Rust of Fur's Howdy Dowdy, brother of Dual Ch. Rust of Fur Blue Thyme Babe CD VCX.

Duals had a banner year in 1979. In December 1979, Dual Ch. Shane's Irish High Noon (Am. Can. Ch. Major O'Shannon ex Ch. Kerrymac Kelly CD), owned by Jim Haupt and Jim Basham, completed his title. "Luke," bred by Jim Haupt, was 13 months old when he started his field training. Jim Haupt and Jim Basham had been friends for years, and when Luke came along he seemed to be the dog they had been looking for. They formed an alliance: Jim Basham did all of Luke's field training and Jim Haupt showed him on the bench. He was campaigned on the bench during the field trial off-season. He earned his first derby placement in September 1977 and finished his field championship on October 13, 1979, by winning a four-point gun dog major at the Irish Setter Club of Michigan. He defeated 157 dogs on the way to his field championship. At the end of the trial season, he went back on the bench, and with his coat in working-dog condition, he finished his bench championship by winning two three-point majors and a four-point major. Luke was only three-and-a-half years old when he completed both championships. Judge James Darroch, in his critique of the September 1979 ISCO Open Gun Dog Stake, had this to say: "This dog put all together from the breakaway to the finish, good control throughout, always ranging ahead, excellent hunting pattern, hit the right objectives, finished strong and topped it off with a bird find with real style." Luke was only bred twice—once to FC Dawn XIV, owned by Jim Basham, and then to Shannon's Bonnibelle Sherrie CD, owned by Mike and Jeannie Wagner. It will never be known if he would have had an impact on the breed, because after these two litters, an undetected infection rendered him sterile. All the pups except for Karrycourt's Royal Flush went to hunting homes and were not bred. Karrycourt's Royal Flush was owned by Jeannie Wagner and Joan Poole and was bred twice, most notably to FC AFC Cidermills Gonna Fly Now, producing Dual Ch. Karrycourt's Rose O'Cidermill ROM.

In 1981, Dual Ch. Rust of Fur Blue Thyme Babe CD VCX (Rust of Fur Royal Flush ex Rendition Gingerly Spiced) finished her title. "Jamie" was five years old. She was bred by Don and Patty Harris and owned by Robin and Bill Johnston. Robin says that Jamie was a show dog, field dog, producer, companion, and best friend. She always gave her best. She was bred to Ch. Glenavan Harvest Moon and produced FC Blue Thyme Lemonade. "Lemmie" was bred to Ch. Tainaron Masterstroke and produced Ch. Blue Thyme Drummer Boy, who is dual pointed.

It would be six years before the next dual champion. Dual Ch. AFC Karrycourt's Rose O'Cidermill ROM (FC AFC Cidermill's Gonna Fly Now ex Karrycourt's Royal Flush) finished her dual championship in March 1987. She was bred by Jeannie Wagner and Joan Poole and was owned by Jeannie Wagner and George Clark. Rose was granddaughter of Dual Ch. Shane's Irish High Noon, and

Dual Champion Irish Setters

As of December 1998, 17 Irish Setters have obtained the title of Dual Champion:

Date	April 1956		Date	Oct. 1966
Name	Dual Ch. Tyrone's Mahogany Mike CDX		Name	Dual Ch. Mahogany's Titian Jingo ROM
B/D	D		B/D	D
Parents	Lord Tyrone Trent ex Mc Ivor's Kathleen		Parents	Dual Ch. Titian Duke CD ex Mahogany's Miss Fireball
Br/O	Br/O Ed and Roberta Mc Ivor		Br/O	Br/O Irene Walker

Date	March 1958		Date	1970
Name	Dual Ch. Red Arrow Show Girl UDT ROM		Name	Dual Ch. Merry Kerry Quite Contrary CD
B/D	B		B/D	D
Parents	Ch. Hollywood Hills O'Shaughnessy ex Marted Annie Rooney		Parents	Bold Traveler of Varagon ex Erin of Edinburgh
Br/O	Br/O Lawrence and Eleanor Heist		Br/O	Br—Cheryl Yates O—M. J. and K. J. Gerdis and D. L. McGinnis

Date	April 1963		Date	April 1972
Name	Dual Ch. Titian Duke CD		Name	Dual Ch. Duffin Miss Duffy CD
B/D	D		B/D	B
Parents	Mahogany Tim II ex King Size Scarlet Lady		Parents	Merry Dell's Gay Gremlin ex Verbu Miss Duffy
Br/O	Br—Irene Walker O—Michael and Phillip Eberhardt		Br/O	Br—Mr. & Mrs. Davil L. Nygren O—Emily Schweitzer

Date	Oct. 1964		Date	Oct. 1973
Name	Dual Ch. County Corks's Red Knight UD		Name	Dual Ch. Donnington Crackerjack
B/D	D		B/D	D
Parents	Greenhill's County Cork Count ex Greenhill's Countess Colleen		Parents	Red Arrow Gold Feathers ex Webline Kavala of Donnington CD
Br/O	Br/O Buck and Laverne Stines		Br/O	Br—Kenneth and Ann Robie O—Barbara Turner

Date	Sept. 1966	
Name	Dual Ch. Molly Coddled Misty CD	
B/D	B	
Parents	Ch. Runwild Finnagain ex Molly Coddled Mayhem	
Br/O	Br/O Robert and Dorothy Frisch	

B = Bitch, D = Dog
Br = Breeder, O = Owner

Dual Champion Irish Setters

As of December 1998, 17 Irish Setters have obtained the title of Dual Champion:

Date	Nov. 1975
Name	Dual Ch. AFC Cynthia Of Woodland Brook
B/D	B
Parents	Ch. Harmony Lane's Red Oak ex Camp's Penelope of Pace
Br/O	Br—Mr & Mrs H.E. Camp Jr. O—Diane Camp and Anthony Baron

Date	1976
Name	Dual Ch. Saraval Jadestar
B/D	D
Parents	Ch. Tirvelda Rustic Duke ex Ch. Dunholm Saraval Sue Eireann
Br/O	Br—L. B. and J. A. Ramon O—V. Mangis, L. B. Ramon and J. Delucca

Date	1978
Name	Dual Ch. Audra Sage Of Emerald Hills
B/D	D
Parents	Ch. Danalee Bright Legend ex Ch. Sarsfield Golden Sherry
Br/O	Br—Audra M. Bietz O—Lynni Robson

Date	Oct. 1979
Name	Dual Ch. Can. Ch. Killagay's Image Of Tara Am. Can. CD VCX
B/D	B
Parents	Ch. Robilee Endeavor ex FC Killagay's Bit of O'Dellarobia
Br/O	Br/O Connie and Glen Christie

Date	Dec. 1979
Name	Dual Ch. Shane's Irish High Noon
B/D	D
Parents	Am. Can. Ch. Major O'Shannon ex Ch. Kerrymac Kelly CD
Br/O	Br—James Haupt O—James Haupt and James Basham, Sr.

Date	1981
Name	Dual Ch. Rust Of Fur Blue Thyme Babe CD VCX
B/D	B
Parents	Rust of Fur Royal Flush ex Rendition Gingerly Spiced
Br/O	Br—Don and Patty Harris O—Robin and Bill Johnston

Date	March 1987
Name	Dual Ch. AFC Karrycourt's Rose O'Cidermill ROM
B/D	B
Parents	FC AFC Cidermill's Gonna Fly Now ex Karrycourt's Royal Flush
Br/O	Br—Jeannie Wagner and Joan Poole O—Jeannie Wagner and George Clark

Date	April 1996
Name	Dual Ch. AFC Cordon Bleu Bright Star JH
B/D	B
Parents	Am. Can. Ch. Lyn Erin Midnight Blue ex Am. Can. Ch. Scarlet Victory Bright Star CD JH VC
Br/O	Br/O W. R. Czarnecki, Matthew F. and Tracy Czarnecki

B = Bitch, D = Dog, Br = Breeder, O = Owner

like her grandfather, she was campaigned on the bench and in the field at the same time. She earned her first bench championship points in August 1983 by going Best of Winners for a major under judge Arlene Thompson. She also garnered a Best of Breed and a major under judge Virginia Harding. She finished under judge Charles Ruppert. Rose was owner-handled to all three of her titles. Her initial gun dog trainer was James Basham, Sr., and it was under his guidance that her fieldwork continued with her owner Jeannie Wagner. Rose finished her amateur championship in March 1996, and it was another year before she finished her dual at the ISCO trial. Rose was running in field trials during the time that the Irish Setter plummeted in popularity. That, along with a recession, caused people to travel less, and most clubs had resorted to opening all stakes at their trials to all pointing breeds. Rose earned all her points from senior stakes and all of them in all-breed competition. She defeated 383 dogs in her field career. She was named Associated Bird Dog Clubs of Ohio's 1986 Ohio Dog of The Year Amateur Gun Dog Runner-Up and 1985 and 1986 Ohio Dog of the Year Winner Open Gun Dog of the Year. She also placed fourth in the National Amateur Championship in 1985. Though she never earned an obedience title, Rose often served as a demo dog in classes conducted by her owner. She also served as a therapy dog and visited numerous nursing homes. Rose was bred twice—the first time to NFC NAFC FC AFC Brophy's Mahogany Fielder. This litter produced three males, one of which became FC AFC Karrycourt's Toby of Tobie Lee JH, owned by Terry Harbach. Her second litter was by Karrycourt's Teddy Bear CD VC, who died of cancer at age five just three single points shy of his amateur field championship. This litter produced FC Karrycourt's Prairie Fire, owned by Susan Borocz, and AFC Karrycourt's Bonnibell JH, owned by Jeannie Wagner. These three dogs earned her the ISCA Register of Merit for producing field champions. Rose passed away at the age of 14. At ten years old, she was still spry enough to snatch a three-point major gun dog win, retiring in style.

The newest dual champion is Dual Ch. AFC Cordon Bleu Bright Star JH (Am. Can. Ch. Lyn Erin Midnight Blue ex Am. Can. Ch. Scarlet Victory Bright Star CD JH VC). She was bred and owned by Wendy, Matthew, and Tracy Czarnecki. "Tempe" was whelped on February 19, 1993. She is the product of five generations of Bright Star breeding. She was handled in the ring exclusively by Tracy and Wendy Czarnecki and handled to her JH in junior field trial stakes by Wendy and Matt Czarnecki. She was trained for gun dog stakes and handled to her open field championship by Randy Mackey. Matt handled her to her amateur field championship. Tempe was Best in Sweeps at the ISC Central California Specialty Show under breeder-judge Linda Acquavella in August 1994. She finished in the ring with back-to-back specialty Winners Bitch wins from the Bred by Exhibitor classes under breeder judges. Her first points were under judge Pat Robinson at the ISC Sacramento Specialty in April 1995, and she finished under judge Joyce Mumford at the ISC Southern California Specialty in June 1995. All of Tempe's bench points came from either the Puppy or Bred by Exhibitor classes. She was ISCA First-Place Puppy in the Derby of 1994, and she placed third in Open Derby at the ISCA National Trial in 1995. She finished her Junior Hunter title at 12 months of age with scores of all 10s. She finished her field championship with an open gun dog major in April 1996 at the ISCA trial hosted by ISC Central California and finished her amateur field championship in November 1996 at ISC Central California. Tempe is still currently running in trials and adding to her win record.

In June 1989, the ISCA established a Register of Merit for top-producing sire and dams, with sires needing 20 champions and dams 7 champions. In 1992, the ROM was adjusted to establish separate criteria for top field trial sire and dams. Field sires must have five field trial champions, and field dams must have three field trial champions. Three dual champions have currently earned a ROM: Dual Ch. Mahogany Titian Jingo ROM, Dual Ch. Red Arrow Show Girl UDT ROM, and Dual Ch. AFC Karrycourt's Rose O'Cidermill ROM.

Irish Setter National Championships

The forerunner to the National Field Trial was held in 1973 in Lenexa, Kansas, with the first official National Field Trial being held in 1974 at Ft. Ord, California. Both of these field trials had excellent participation in a multitude of events. In 1975, at the trial in Medford, NJ, the club began holding a classic as a prelude to a national championship. The first winner of the Open Gun Dog Classic was FC AFC Blue Angel's Cherry Pie, owned by Ray Dohse and Tony Baron. In 1976, the National Field Trial was held in Wisconsin and then Illinois for the Classic and Futurity Program. The winner was FC Popper, owned and handled by Faunt Ekey. Delmar Smith's home grounds in Oklahoma hosted the trial the following year. An open classic, along with an amateur classic, were won by Anne Marie Kubacz's phenomenal young male, FC AFC Ramblin' Red Banshee.

In 1978, the ISCA's first club championships were awarded at the National Field Trial, held in Colorado. The winner of the open championship was FC Leprechaun Riley O'Donnel, owned by Leon Mudgett. The winner of the amateur championship was FC Sage of Johnny Red, owned by Jim Fike. The original classics, along with this

The ISCA first National Gun Dog Championship.

club championship, were held as two-series events, with a 30-minute qualifier and a 30-minute second series.

After successfully completing these events, the AKC Board of Directors approved the club to hold a National Championship and a National Amateur Championship event annually. The field trial committee decided that the format should be changed for the championships. Thus, in the fall of 1979, the club held a 45-minute, single-series National Championship and a 35-minute, single-series National Amateur Championship. It was the club's intent to hold the championships on native birds so that the national champion showed his ability and manners on wild birds. The stage was set for the first championship to be held at Rend Lake, Illinois. The first winner of the National Championship was FC AFC Ramblin' Red Banshee, owned by Anne Marie and Randy Kubacz and handled by Anne Marie. The winner of the National Amateur Championship was FC Ivor Glen Dinah, owned by Mike Jones and handled by Ken Ruff.

This was a very successful event, with a large representation from all over the country and many attendees from the AKC and ISCA Board of Directors. Following this event, a field trial advisory committee was formed, with Jill Ross as chairman and representatives from each region participating, to oversee and manage the future National Championship trials. It was decided at this time to keep the National in the central part of the US in hopes of attracting as large a national participation as possible. The venue in 1980 was to be the grounds at Lake Murray State Park in Oklahoma and was to alternate between there and Rend Lake.

At this point in time, there was a division among the field trialers around the country. Many were not happy with the championship no longer rotating around the country, and others didn't like the idea of a single series with extended times of the braces (the amateur championship was increased to 45 minutes). Some were upset with the interpretation of the rules that allowed collaring after the shot—and some just weren't happy! The championship fell on hard times, with a greatly decreased entry at the 1980 event in Lake Murray, Oklahoma, but the diehards still were there. Folks like Anne Marie and Randy Kubacz, Dennis and Georgia Brown, Ray Dohse, Richard and Jayne Scurlock, Jim Fike, Jill and Rube Ross, and Ken and Linda Ruff weren't about to let the event flounder, and they committed themselves to supporting the championship program. The 1980 championship might have been short on entries, but

The ISCA Second National Field Trial

Open Puppy Stake placements.

Second Place—Mack with President and J. B. Owens.

Third Place—Ramblin Red Avelle with President and Anne Marie Kubacz.

Fourth Place—Dearg's Titian Patrick with President and R. Pollich.

Among many other accomplishments, 2XNFC NAFC FC AFC Ivor Glen Ruben ROM was the winner of the 1981 National Field Trial Championship. Owned by Linda and Ken Ruff.

included Marie Kubacz's great performer, NFC FC AFC Ramblin' Red Banshee. The National Amateur Championship saw seasoned veteran FC Sage of Johnny Red win with a spectacular limb find. The advisory -committee decided to hold the national at Rend Lake for the next three years. This was due in part to the poor entry but mainly because of the poor bird population at Lake Murray, with no improvement in sight.

In 1981, there was a slight increase in overall participation at Rend Lake. This year's winner of the National Championship was FC Ivor Glen Ruben, owned by Ken and Linda Ruff and handled by Ken. This fine young product of Ed McIvor's breeding program was destined to leave his mark on the breed. Ruben became the foundation male for Ken and Linda Ruff's breeding program. The National Amateur Championship was won by FC AFC Kopper Key Boni of Brownhaven, owned by Dennis and Georgia Brown and handled by Georgia. This fine female was a consistent performer and producer of some of the stars of the future.

In 1982, the Nationals returned to Rend Lake. This year, the National Championship was won by Jill Ross's great male FC AFC Dubhagan O'Shillelagh; a past winner of the ISCA Futurity. Jill would continue to win many times with this fine male and made him one of the all-time winningest Irish Setters in AKC competition. The National Amateur Championship was again won by

NAFC FC AFC Kopper Key Boni of Brownhaven, owned by Dennis and Georgia Brown and handled by Georgia. Boni just loved being at Rend Lake and won the event after a second series was needed due to a lack of bird work in the regular running.

The 1983 trial was once again at Rend Lake, with an ever-increasing level of participation but a huge decrease in the bird population. In the National Championship, the title was withheld, which means that no first place was awarded because the judges felt that none of the performances merited the title of National Champion. In the National Amateur Championship, the winner was NFC FC AFC Ivor Glen Ruben, owned by Ken and Linda Ruff and handled by Ken. The judges had to run a second series for bird work to award the title.

In 1984, the advisory committee decided to alternate grounds again, and the championships were back at Lake Murray, Oklahoma. That year's winner of the National Championship was FC Ricane Strawberis 'N Cream, owned by Richard and Jane Scurlock and handled by

Winner of the 1984 National Amateur Championship, FC AFC Dubhagan O'Shillelagh with owner and handler Jill Ross.

Richard. This young female was bred by the Scurlocks, which made it even more exciting for them. The National Amateur Championship was won by NFC FC AFC Dubhagan O'Shillelagh, owned and handled by Jill Ross—another stellar performance for Jill's shining star.

In 1985, the Nationals were in Rend Lake with the promise of a better bird population. While it wasn't great, there was a significant improvement in the number of birds. There was also an abundance of rain! It started on the first afternoon of the trial and things went downhill from there. The clubhouse looked like a laundry, with gloves and coats hanging up to dry. Attendees bought the local stores out of hair dryers to dry out gloves, and the mud was deep by the end of the week. A Springfield, Illinois, newspaper reporter spent some time at the event and couldn't believe the great attitude of everyone, despite the terrible weather. One of the judges, Mary Karbiner, joked for years afterward that she wouldn't judge in the rain ever again. It was a mess, but spirits were high the entire time and it proved to be a very memorable national. The winner of the National Championship was FC AFC Brophy's Cuna Mara, owned by Ken and Linda Ruff and handled by Ken. This was the first of Ruben's offspring to win the National. In the National Amateur Championship, the "old man" himself, Ken Ruff's NFC NAFC FC AFC Ivor Glen Ruben ROM, came back one more time at nine years of age to become the first Irish Setter to win a third National AKC Championship title.

The 1986 trial was held at Lake Murray with an ever-increasing entry and birds supposedly on the upswing.

NFC FC AFC Brophy's Cuna Mara, winner of the 1985 National Field Championship. Owned by Ken Ruff.

FC AFC Brophy's Ruby, winner of the 1986 National Field Championship. Owned by Ken and Linda Ruff.

Still, the National Championship required a full second series with birds released along the course in order to place the winners. At the end of the second series, FC AFC Brophy's Ruby, owned by Ken and Linda Ruff and handled by Ken, emerged as the winner. She was a Ruben daughter out of Dennis and Georgia Brown's Kopper Key Boni of Brownhaven, who Ken had leased for this litter. The National Amateur Championship was won by FC Brophy's Tigger Too, owned and handled by Robin Baker. Tigger was also a Ruben/Boni offspring that Robin had made a past Futurity winner.

The 1987 trial returned to Rend Lake without the flooding and with a few more birds. This was the first year that we held the Open Championship as a one-hour event, with the Amateur remaining at 45 minutes. Our dogs were building up stamina, both through better breeding and new training techniques. The winner of the National Championship was FC Cedar Creek's Mollaroo, owned by Ed and Kathy Liermann and handled by Ed at his first AKC Irish Setter National. The National Amateur Championship was won by NFC FC AFC Brophy's Ruby, owned by Ken and Linda Ruff and handled by Ken. This was the second championship for the Ruben/ Boni daughter. At this point, the Field Trial Advisory Committee decided it was time for a change, because the grounds at Lake Murray did not have a large enough bird population to hold a quality event. New grounds were opening up in Booneville, Arkansas, that had excellent facilities and were being managed strictly as field trial grounds—almost 4,000 acres for 3 one-hour courses. Plans were made to try them in 1988, with a return to Rend Lake every other year.

The 1988 event brought the trial to Booneville, and what a treat—beautiful grounds with a very well-managed bird program that blended wild birds with a strong covey release program in late summer. There was a huge barn, kennels, outside corrals, RV hookups, and a building with kitchen facilities. While the town lacked some of the amenities of the other facilities, the grounds more than made up for it. The National Championship and the National Amateur Championship were both won by FC AFC Brophy's Mahogany Fielder, owned by Ken Ruff and Gregg Schjoth and handled by Ken. This was another son of Ruben that was steadily leaving his mark on the breed.

In 1989, the trial returned to Rend Lake for the last time. While it was a very good event, the birds were dwindling, so after this National, a permanent move was made to Booneville, Arkansas. The winner of the National Championship was FC AFC Hazelwood's Speedy Gonzales, owned by Robin Baker and Marion Pahy and handled by Robin, a second national win for Robin. "Reba" was a second-generation Ruben/Boni granddaughter, bred by Georgia Brown. The National Amateur title was withheld that year.

In 1990, a five-year commitment to the State of Arkansas secured the use of the Booneville grounds, which were called the Blue Mountain Wildlife Demonstration Area and later renamed the Perry Mikkles Field Trial Grounds. The winner of the National Championship was Tobasco's Tomahawk, a fine young performer bred, owned, and handled by Bob Dupuis. Unfortunately, this dog met an untimely death within a year. The winner of the National Amateur Championship was FC AFC Brophy's Center Fielder, "Kirby," owned and handled by Ray Marshall. Kirby is a Ruben grandson out of Saturday Night Eddie J bred to Brophy's Ragtime Lass, ("Megan"). This Eddie J/Megan breeding has since had a

NFC FC AFC Brophy's Pumpernickel, winner of the 1994 National Field Trial Championship. Owned by Chad and Ken Ruff.

NFC FC AFC Brophy's Margarita, winner of the 1997 National Field Championship. Owned by Jenny, Phil, and Ken Ruff.

very significant impact on the future of the Irish Setter in the field.

In 1991, NFC NAFC FC AFC Brophy's Ruby, owned by Ken and Linda Ruff and handled by Ken, repeated as National Champion. This three-time National Championship winner was nine years old, the same age that her father, Ruben, was when he won his third. The National Amateur Champion was FC AFC Hazelwood's Rex-a-Roni, owned and handled by Robin Baker, her third winner at the nationals. This male was another out of the Eddie J/Megan breeding that was building a reputation.

A new star emerged in 1992 in FC AFC Darth Raider O'Reily, owned and handled by Mike Geving. This fine young male won both the National and National Amateur Championships, with stellar performances in both events. He was the product of Dennis Hildalgo's breeding program.

In 1993, the National Champion repeated, with NFC NAFC FC AFC Darth Raider O'Reily winning the big one. The National Amateur Championship was won by FC AFC Colo's Gunner, owned and handled by Jack Haines. This fine dog was a littermate to Darth Raider out of Dennis Hildalgo's breeding program.

The year 1994 was a time for change. Ken and Linda Ruff missed their first National while Linda nursed Ken back to health. Bob Ruff took the reins for his dad and piloted FC AFC Brophy's Pumpernickel, owned by Ken and Chad Ruff, to the National Championship. This was quite a win for Bob, with friends keeping Ken posted via cellular phone. At this trial, the National Amateur Championship was changed to a one-hour event, and the

long-term plans of the 1980 Field Advisory Committee were attained. Today's Irish Setter has shown a marked increase in stamina across all the entrants at the one-hour level. The National Amateur was won by FC Kriss Kross, owned and handled by Stan Zdanzewicz, and out of his breeding program.

In 1995, we had a down year for birds at Booneville due to a drought, but there were still enough to get the job done. The winner of the National Championship was FC Joey Zan Sett, owned and handled by Glenn Sicotte, a dog out of the Zdanzewicz program. The National Amateur Championship was won by FC AFC Brophy's Midwest Express, owned by Ken and Linda Ruff and handled by Ken. This fine young female was out of Brophy's Red Storm Rising, another male out of the Eddie J /Megan nick that died at a young age. He was owned by Bob Geddeis, and even though he died young, he made his mark by producing several very good dogs. He also was himself a Futurity winner and Field Sire of the Year for several years.

There was another increase in entries, again in 1996, numbering in the high 20s for both championships. The winner of the National Championship was NAFC FC AFC Brophy's Midwest Express, owned by Ken and Linda Ruff and handled by Ken. The winner of the National Amateur Championship was FC AFC Red Devil Deaugh, owned by Sue and Charlie Williams and handled by Dennis Hildalgo. This fine male is the product of Dennis Hildalgo's very successful breeding program.

There were 30 or more entries in both championships in 1997 and the quality to match. The winner of the National Championship was FC AFC Brophy's Margarita, owned by Phil, Jenny, and Ken Ruff and handled by Ken. This female was another offspring of the Eddie J/Megan breeding, the third National winner of the litter. The winner of the National Amateur Championship was FC AFC Hazelwood's Betsy of Brophy, owned by Ken Ruff and Robin Baker and handled by Robin Baker. Betsy is a daughter of Robin's past winner, NFC FC AFC Hazelwood's Speedy Gonzales, bred to Ken's NFC NAFC FC AFC Brophy's Mahogany Fielder.

Finally, 1998 was the largest National yet, with the number of entries well into the middle 30s. The winner of the National Championship was NAFC FC AFC Red Devil Deaugh MH, owned by Sue and Charlie Williams and handled by Tim Hildalgo. The National Amateur Championship was won by FC AFC Celtics Sunshine Girl, owned and handled by Rick Didyoung at his first AKC Irish Setter National. This very nice young female is out of Paul Ober's successful breeding program.

The 1999 National Championship was won by Pebo, bred and owned by Stan Zdanzewicz. The National

Ametaur Championship was taken by Brophy's Sandhill Spirit, "Willa"(NAFC FC AFC Brophy's Center Fielder ex NAFC FC AFC Hazelwood's Betsy of Brophy) bred by Ken Ruff and Robin Baker and owned by Jacquelyn Marshall. This was an especially sweet victory for Jackie, who was compelled to spend the week in the clubhouse due to a hip injury.

The history of the ISCA National Championships was contributed by Ken Ruff.

Statistical Review of the National Program

In compiling the history of the National Field Trial Program, some interesting facts make themselves apparent. When the Red Setter program was initiated in the early 1950s, certain purebred Irish Setters became the foundation stock for most of the different breeding programs. When looking at the results of our AKC National Field Trials, you will find that 137 of the 141 dogs that have placed in the National Championships can trace their ancestry to at least 2 or 3 of the following Irish Setters: FC Askew's Carolina Lady, FC Sulhamstead Norse D'Or, and Ike Jack Kendrick.

Upon further evaluation of Ed McIvor's breeding program during the '50s, '60s, and '70s, there was an obvious plan to develop a specific type of bird dog. In the breeding to get to NFC 2x NAFC FC AFC Ivor Glen Ruben ROM, he used the above three foundation dogs, plus DC Tyrone's Mahogany Mike CDX and DC Mahogany Titian Jingo, ROM.

He worked with a blend of the best he could find in the field and coupled that with the dual champions that developed into a line of good-looking Irish Setters that could compete successfully with any breed in the field. These dogs exhibited great athletic ability with exceptional hunting instincts.

Ken and Linda Ruff used Ruben as their foundation male for the Brophy dogs. They coupled their line in the following ways:

• They bred to Tony Baron's Norab dogs, which had a very strong relationship to Irene Walker's Dual dog line. He crossed that with the Shawn of Kaymar dogs that had a strong Saturday Night influence.

• They leased 2xNAFC Kopper Key Boni of Brownhaven to breed to Ruben, who had a strong relationship to the same three foundation Irish Setters.

• They bred Ruben to a bitch they leased, FC AFC Mandie's Folie, who had a strong Ivor Glen background that was out of a sister of Ruben.

• Ken and Ray Marshall bought back Brophy's Ragtime Lass ("Megan") a Brophy bitch from Arizona, and bred her to Saturday Night Eddie J.

Ruben was only bred seven times, and of those breedings, only four play a significant role in today's Irish Setters. It should be noted that of the 97 dogs that placed at the Irish Setter National starting in 1985, 67 of these are either a Ruben offspring, grandchild, or great-grandchild. This works out to 69 percent of all dogs placed since his first son won. In the Futurity program, since it restarted in 1983, 41 of the 49 placed dogs, or 84 percent, are related to Ruben within two generations. Ruben's contribution through the breeding program started by Ed McIvor is extremely significant to today's Irish Setter.

Field Notes

Judges

Over the years, we have been very fortunate to be able to retain some of the greatest names in field trial history to judge our trials:

John Rex Gates	Lee Sienkowski Sr.
George Evans	Dr. Stan Haag
Bill West	Bonnie Evans
Delmar Smith	Lynn Hadlock
John Criswell	Ed Husser
Keith Severin	Tom Swertfeger
Bob Weisz	Mary Karbiner
Bob Ice	Jim Batson
David Taylor	Dennis Spada
Kevin Wade	Mike Walsh

Each of these judges has taken the time to tell us what a truly wonderful event we put on. The Irish Setter Club National Field Trial is a showplace for fine dogs and sportsmanship. We have a very family-oriented, fun-loving group that is dedicated to the improvement of our Irish in the field. Every member is dedicated to leaving future generations with a healthy gene pool. It is obvious from the improvement in stamina, pointing instinct, and style on point and while running, as well as trainability, that the AKC National Field Trial Program has played a major part in the rebirth of the Irish Setter in the field.

Obedience
and
Agility

Obedience has always been a part of Irish Setter history. Anyone who has tried to teach a rambunctious puppy manners has already begun the process of obedience training. Many puppy owners decide they cannot do it properly on their own, so they seek an obedience school, a club that teaches obedience to its members, or even a private trainer to come to the house. All of these formal sessions teach the owner how to teach their dogs the lessons that will make them into manageable animals that are a joy to live with. Field-trained setters are also taught basic obedience. They must stop on command (the field trialer's term is "Whoa!") and must hold a point. Some dogs do this instinctively, but the majority need some formal training. To be a successful hunting companion, the dog must learn to retrieve and release the bird. A field trial dog learns to leave the birds alone and point until the owner flushes and releases the dog. These functional lessons are mimicked in the formal world of obedience. The difference is that in obedience, the goal is perfect form and timing in order to present a dog that is totally under control and instantly attentive to his handler's commands. There is little forgiveness for minor infractions of style in the obedience ring.

The rigors of formal obedience have proved to be stumbling blocks for some enthusiasts who desire to go beyond basic obedience with their dogs. The Irish Setter's exuberant nature rebels against the sometimes-rigid confines of the obedience ring. Irish Setter owners who go for the challenge must have patience, a knowledge of their dogs, and a sense of humor. The Irish Setter rarely makes the same mistake twice, but the deviltry in his eye

will tell you that he has another trick to pull—almost never in training, but always in the ring. Spectators at the obedience rings love to watch the Irish. They usually put on a great show, even though it may not be exactly what the judge is looking for. There is nothing lovelier, however, than a happily working Irish going through the exercises, proud of himself and delighted that his owner seems to be so happy!

Obedience training and performance builds a special bond between owner and dog that carries through the dog's whole life. Obedience competition builds friendships that endure. Most exhibitors are helpful and kind to one another. They are happy to share their training tips and newest theories, much as show exhibitors do.

Because obedience dogs are willing to please, many go on to the noble task of becoming therapy dogs. Basic obedience is a requisite, but beyond that, the dog must have the gentle, understanding, sensitive nature that allows him to behave well for adults and children who will respond lovingly to these beautiful and patient Irish Setters. Visiting hospitals and nursing homes is one of the ways that therapy dogs play an important role in helping the ill or disabled find something to smile about.

For those Irish Setter owners who find formal obedience training and competition too confining, other related sports have emerged, the most popular of these being agility. Agility is the fastest-growing segment of performance events for the AKC, and there are also other agility organizations that put on trials and award degrees for various levels of performance.

Agility participants must have basic obedience training, but beyond that, the exercises that they do are unique to the sport. Dogs love agility, and the owners take delight in encouraging their dogs to perform to their maximum potential. It is a team effort between dog and handler once the dog has learned the routines.

In this section, we highlight those stars of obedience and agility that have shown the world that the Irish Setter is not only a beautiful dog, but an accomplished one as well.

Obedience Trial Champions

To earn an Obedience Trial Championship, a dog must first earn the CD, CDX, and UD obedience titles. As a finished UD dog, he continues to compete in Open B and Utility B classes, earning:

A) Three first-place ribbons at licensed AKC Obedience Trials under three different judges. At least one first place must be in Utility B with a minimum of three dogs competing, and at least one must be in an Open B class with at least six competing. The third first place may be from either of the above two classes.

B) 100 OTCh. points. Points are awarded for first and second placements in Open B and Utility B at all-breed or specialty trials. The number of points awarded depends on the number of dogs competing in the class and the placement. Fewer dogs are needed for the same number of points in Utility B than in Open B. The chart of OTCh. points is printed in the trial catalog and is the same for all states except Alaska, Hawaii, and Puerto Rico.

UDX Irish Setters

The AKC initiated the Utility Dog Excellent title on January 1, 1994. The title is awarded to dogs that, after earning the utility degree, continue competing in Open B and Utility B. Ten legs must be earned. A leg is defined as a qualifying score in both Open B and Utility B awarded at the same trial. To date, 14 Irish Setters have earned the UDX title:

Ch. OTCh. Hazelhill Shining Star UDX MH VC	Tom and Candy Macaluso
Valley View Flambeau UDX	Dr. Rienhardt Ross
Ch. Killagay's Mr. Nash B Good UDX	Diana Behrend
Rebellion's Sawmill Sally UDX	Elisabeth and Donn Fisher
OTCh. U-OCh. Willowfenn Abington Square UDX	Evelyn and Daniel Kearon
Ch. OTCh. Bentree's Tickle My Fancy UDX	Ann and Charles Alves
Can. Ch. Can. OTCh U-U Merrilea's Sweet Mignonette	
UDX Bda. UD Mex. UD	Marjorie Davis
Ch. U-CD Bentree's King Colin UDX	Monica Wilson
Cranberra's Steel Magnolia UDX	Kris Hahn
Can. OTCh. Shangrila Thomas of Kismet UDX	Paul and Sarah Martini
Bramblebush Dakota O'Malley UDX	Patty Beddows
U-CDX Setter Woods Gentleman Bo UDX Can. CDX TDI CGC TT	Arlene and Peter Pilcer
Ch. OTCh. U-UD Bentree Token's Iceman Cometh UDX	Kay and Bill Bedeau
U-CDX Token's Unsinkable Molly B UDX TD	Kay Bedeau

Irish Setter
Obedience Trial Champions

Note: A Canadian Obedience Trial Championship is earned by completing the Canadian Utility Dog title. It is not the equivalent of an American Kennel Club Obedience Trial Championship.
Since its inception July 1, 1977, the following Irish Setters have been awarded the AKC Obedience Trial Championship (OTCh.):

OTCh. Liffey Claire Kenna	Charles Hornbach	1978
OTCh. Scarlet Miss O'Shaunecy	Patrick J. Higgins	1978
OTCh. Kathy's Ben	Timothy and Kathy Heckaman	
OTCh. Red Irish Sun	Brian Trapp	1979
OTCh. Blue Mink	Karen Bishop	1979
Can. Ch. Am. Can. OTCh. Marand's Kiss Me Kate Am. Can. TDX	Marsha Henkel	
OTCh. Shenandoah Frost	Janice DeMello	
OTCh. Duggan Michael Anthony	Frank Gangemella	
OTCh. Shamrox Shenanigans	Janice DeMello	
OTCh. Atkinson's Rum and Coke VC	Gina Hemphill and Ray Atkinson	1985
OTCh. Red Arrow's Tyrone	Karen and Ron Cole	1985
OTCh. Ringo Starr II	Chris Tomanovich	1986
OTCh. Rave On Katy	Betsy Sessler	1987
OTCh. Sunshine Gatsby's Blue Love MH VC	Fred and Flori Page	1988
OTCh. Fleetwood Farm Belle Star	Sandy Rowen	1991
OTCh. Mirkwood's The Red Terror	Bonnie Henry	1992
Ch. OTCh. Bluewin's Fancy O'Shaughnessy JH VC	Kay and Bill Bedeau	1992
Ch. OTCh. Hazelhill Shining Star UDX MH VCX	Tom and Candy Macaluso	1993
Ch. OTCh. Bentree's Tickle My Fancy UDX	Ann and Charles Alves	1997
OTCh. U-OCh. Willowfenn's Abington Square UDX	Evelyn and Daniel Kearon	1998
Ch. OTCh. U-UD Bentree Token's Iceman Cometh UDX	Kay and Bill Bedeau	1999

ISCA National Specialty Winners

In 1973, the ISCA held its first independent National Specialty Show and Obedience Trial in Valley Forge, Pennsylvania. Highest Scoring Dogs in Trial and Highest Combined Scoring Dogs are listed below.

ISCA National—High in Trial Winners

1973	Tagalong Toly Shauleen	Thomas and Billie Jensen
1974	Ch. Red Cedar Prince Michael UD	Bill and Lynne Mehring
1975	Carriepatch's Redcoate Casey UD	David and Marilyn Coate
1976	Wilson Farm Country Magnolia	Scott Willsey and M. Matheny
1977	Brandy's Cherry Delight	Lissa N. Wall
1978	Greenwood Gypsy Gaiety	Joan Herbon
1979	Scarlet O'Hara Glenacre	Stephen and Lynette Freeman
1980	Bywood's Merry Anne UD	Ray Gates
1981	Can. OTCh. Red Feather Mystique UD	Judy Zieve (Bonfiglio)
1982	Miller's Rusty Red River CD	Thomas and Connie Miller
1983	Taramagh's Autumn Harvest UD	Diane Robbins
1984	OTCh. Rave on Katy UD	Betsy Sessler
1985	Fleetwood Farms Crimson Faith	Sharon Rezaback (Miller)
1986	OTCh. Can. OTCh Ringo Starr II	Christine Tomanovich
1987	OTCh. Rave on Katy UD	Betsy Sessler
1988	OTCh. Sunshine Gatsby's Blue Love MH VC	Fred and Flori Page
1989	OTCh. Bluewin's Fancy O'Shaughnessy JH VC	Kay and Bill Bedeau
1990	Ch. OTCh. Bluewin's Fancy O'Shaughnessy JH VC	Kay and Bill Bedeau
1991	Ch. OTCh. Bluewin's Fancy O'Shaughnessy JH VC	Kay and Bill Bedeau
1992	OTCh. Sunshine Gatsby's Blue Love MH VC	Bill and Flori Page
1993	Ch. OTCh. Bluewin's Fancy O'Shaughnessy JH VC	Kay and Bill Bedeau
1994	OTCh. Hazelhill Shining Star UDX MH VCX	Tom and Candy Macaluso
1995	Shadyview Touchstone CDX	Dan and Ann Graham
1996	Hazelhill Escapade UD JH	Tom and Candy Macaluso
1997	Ch. Halsey's Young Man's Fancy UD SH NA CGC VC	Nina Johnson
1998	U-CD Rate Exchange Genesis Am. Can. CD	Sarah Kumpula
1999	Can. OTCh. U-CDX Genesis Precious Gem UD S-CDX	Dorothy Kumpula

ISCA National—High Combined Winners

1973	not awarded	
1974	Ch. Red Cedar Prince Michael UD	Bill and Lynne Mehring
1975	not awarded	
1976	Aldebaran Scarlett O'Hara UD Can. CD	Michael and Margaret Malik
1977	Tirvelda Tudor Minstrel UD	Mrs. Robert H. Gibbon
1978	Ginger's Glory Colleen CDX	Joyce Gelser Napieralski
1979	Carriepatch's Redcoate Casey	David and Marilyn Coate
1980	not awarded	
1981	Can. OTCh. Red Feather Mystique UD	Judy Zieve (Bonfiglio)
1982	Ch. Can Ch. Radar O'Riley UD	Carolyn (Chipper) Klicman
1983	Taramagh's Autumn Harvest UD	Diane Robbins
1984	OTCh. Rave on Katy UD	Betsy Sessler
1985	not awarded	
1986	Daniel's Sweet Molly Malone	Daniel and Evelyn Kearon
1987	not awarded	
1988	OTCh. Atkinson's Rum and Coke VC	Gina Hemphill and Ray Atkinson
1989	Willowfenn's Christopher St. UD	Daniel and Evelyn Kearon
1990	Ch. OTCh. Bluewin's Fancy O'Shaughnessy JH VC	Kay and Bill Bedeau
1991	Lady Shamrock of Erin UD	Pam Wink
1992	OTCh. Sunshine Gatsby's Blue Love MH VC	Bill and Flori Page
1993	Ch. OTCh. Bluewin's Fancy O'Shaughnessy JH VC	Kay and Bill Bedeau
1994	not awarded	
1995	Token's Into the Woods UD	Patti Normandin
1996	not awarded	
1997	OTCh. U-OCh Willowfenn's Abington Square UDX	Daniel and Evelyn Kearon
1998	not awarded	
1999	U-CDX Setter Wood's Gentleman Bo UDX Can. CDX	Arlene and Peter Pilcer

Names in Obedience and Agility

Profiled here are some of the active participants in obedience and agility today. It would be remiss, however, not to mention two of the stars of yesteryear. Miss Emily Schweitzer of Verbu Irish Setters trained and handled her dogs in conformation, field, and obedience. Her Ch. Verbu Missy Oogh CDX set the benchmark for Irish Setters to follow in years to come. In California, the Red Arrow dogs of Lawrence and Eleanor Heist were excellent conformation, obedience, and field dogs. The lead dog in the film *Big Red* was Am. Mex. Ch. Red Arrow Scraps Am. Mex. UD, who was also trained for tracking. The most titled of the Heists' dogs was Dual Ch. Red Arrow Show Girl UDT Mex. PC. Today, the reigning multi-titled star of conformation, obedience, and field is Ch. OTCh. Ch. Hazelhill Shining Star UDX MH VCX, whose story is told in this chapter.

Ann Alves, *Fallon*—Belleville, IL

Ann started in Irish Setters with a pet Irish in obedience. Her ten-year-old Brandy's Pal Maggie CD earned her title in 1992. Arab Irish Sweet Molly Brown CDX followed in 1993.

Ann contacted Kay Bedeau (Token) to obtain her next Irish, which she hoped would excel in obedience and conformation. The puppy that Kay picked for her became Ch. OTCh. Bentree's Tickle My Fancy UDX. She completed her obedience title in 1997 and her bench title in 1998. She was bred to Ch. Cucuhullain Good Fortune ROM, and Ann hopes that Fancy's puppies will follow in their mother's pawprints.

Ch. OTCh. Bentree's Tickle My Fancy UDX completed her obedience title in 1997 and her bench title in 1998. Owned by Ann Alves.

Gail Beauchemin, *Kelarn*—Attleboro, MA

Gail entered her first obedience trial in 1965 with Murphy's Irish CDX Can. CD. In 1969, she purchased her first bitch, Shamrock's Sheilah McGuire UD, followed by a field bitch, Scarlett Princess of Erin UD.

Sheilah was bred to Ch. Kimberlin Constancy, from which litter she kept two puppies, both of which attained their CDX titles. One of the daughters, Kelarn's Kellah Kelearney CDX, was bred to Can. Ch. Tamarack Kerrigain Knight, from which Gail kept Kelarn's Leah of Tamarack CD.

After a hiatus of several years, Gail obtained a puppy that became Am. Can. SKC. Ch. Honeyrock Bold Krystl Kelarn U-CDX Am. Can. CDX JH TT SKC-CD CGC.

When Krystl retired, Gail purchased U-CD Seanpat-Kelarn-If-I-Could-Dream Am. Can. ASCA CD from Pat Lyons. She also purchased an Irish import, U-CD Lurgavon Kate Kearney Am. Can. ASCA CD.

Am. Can. SKC U-CDX Honeyrock Bold Krystl Kelarn Am. Can. CDX JH TT CGC SKC-CD. Owned by Gail Beauchemin.

Karen and Bill Bedeau, *Token*—Hot Springs, SD

Kay and Bill's first Irish Setters were pets for their three children, who showed them in obedience and tracking as part of their 4-H experience. In 1985, they purchased their first show prospect, who became Ch. OTCh. Bluwin's Fancy O'Shaughnessy UD JH VC ("Sean"). Over the years, Kay has put numerous tracking and advanced obedience titles on her dogs. In addition to Sean, the Bedeaus' dogs include Ch. U-UD Token's Talk of the Town UD, U-CDX Token's Unsinkable Molly B UDT, and Ch. OTCh. U-CDX Bentree Token's Iceman Cometh UD.

All of Kay and Bill's dogs are house dogs. Puppies are raised in the kitchen, each with daily individual play/socialization time.

Sean is heavily linebred on Charlton lines, and wanting to continue in that direction, the Bedeaus leased Ch. Fancy Free Peg O'My Dreams CD from Jeanette Holmes. Bred to Ch. Sunshine's First Rate, she produced Talk of the Town and Molly B.

Talk of the Town has been bred twice, resulting in four champions from litters by Ch. Liafail London Pride and Ch. OTCh. U-CDX Bentree Token Iceman Cometh UDX, including Ch. Token's Whiffenpoof Song and Ch. Token's Down Town Brown.

Molly B was bred to Ch. Charlton's Irish Derby, resulting in three champions.

Kay and Bill moved to 100 acres of the Black Hills near Hot Springs, South Dakota, in 1994. With an indoor training facility, Kay trains their Irish Setters and teaches competition obedience year round. She occasionally gives obedience seminars. Kay is a director of the ISCA.

U-CDX Token's Unsinkable Molly B UDT winning High in Trial at the Irish Setter Club of Colorado in 1997. Owned by Karen and Bill Bedeau.

The 1992 ISCA National Obedience Trial First Place Team (from left to right): Ch. OTCh. Bluewin's Fancy O'Shaughnessy UD JH VC with Kay Bedeau; OTCh. Sunshine Gatsby's Blue Love UD MH VC with Fred Page; OTCh. Fleetwood Farms Belle Star UD with Sandy Rowan; and Ch. OTCh. Hazelhill Shining Star UDX MH VCX with Tom Macaluso.

Patty Beddows, Jupiter, FL

Patty's first obedience dog became BrambleBush Dakota O'Malley UDX CGC (Ch. BrambleBush Heart's Desire ex BrambleBush Peregrine Falcon), purchased from Charlene Kickbush and Tom Greer. Patty and Dakota enrolled in obedience classes, which resulted in her UDX degree. She is now in training to be a therapy dog.

Patty's other Irish arrived as a rescue dog in 1996, after having been dropped in a night box in Daytona with a note, "Needs an active home." That analysis proved to be correct, but Patty's husband, Tom, wanted the dog, and so he came and stayed. Patty got his CD and CGC, and he is now Justin The Nick of Time, currently in training for agility and open obedience.

BrambleBush Dakota O'Malley UDX, Patty Beddows' first obedience dog, on a perfect finish.

Diana Behrend, *TindDia*—Milan, IL

Sagittarius Sam entered Diana's life in 1969. She was her constant trail-riding companion and confidante all through her school years and was even there for Diana's wedding. Diana and Sam had 16 years together.

After Sam was gone, Diana purchased a puppy that became Fleetwood Farm's Lacey O'Love UD. When the puppy began obedience at nine weeks of age, the instructor told Diana to put her puppy to sleep and get a Shetland Sheepdog. Eventually, though, she and Lacey defeated the instructor's Sheltie.

Two rescue Irish came along about the same time. One was a natural, and at the age of 10, Lucas O'Lucky earned his CD title. Her other rescue, Kelly O'Lee CD, taught Diana how to smile in the face of adversity. Despite multiple health problems, Kelly always had a "light heart."

In 1989, Diana purchased a puppy from Connie Christie of Killagay. He became Ch. U-Ch. U-AGI U-CDX Killagay's Mr. Nash B'Good UDX CGC TT. Diana's goals for Nash were to give him opportunities and to have fun along the way. Sometimes, Nash has more fun than Diana. At the age of 10, he is still learning new things.

Diana feels blessed to have had Irish Setters in her life. Her mentor, who has passed on a wealth of knowledge through books and stories, has been Connie Christie, and Diana's only litter carries the Killagay name. Diana does not consider herself a breeder but a promoter of the Irish Setter who tries to help and educate newcomers.

UKC AKC Ch. U-AGI U-CDX Killagay's Mr. Nash B'Good UDX CGC TT at the 1998 AKC Agility National Specialty. Owned by Diana Behrend.

242

Joy Benton, *Bentree*—Kingsland, TX

In the late 1960s, while living in Hawaii, the Bentons decided to buy a family dog. A neighbor had an Irish Setter that would wait patiently on the front porch for his owners, and his beauty and obedience convinced them that this was the breed for them. They had to wait for 18 months for a litter to be born, and with the realization that their puppy needed training, they enrolled in obedience school. The breeder also encouraged them to attend matches and shows, and on the islands, this was a wonderful introduction for the novice.

After returning to the mainland, they eventually settled in Texas. They have always had Irish as housepets and most of Joy's dogs have been trained through Utility titles. Ch. U-CDX O'Flynn's Heather of Joy CDX is Joy's "once in a lifetime" dog. During her years of competition, she won two High in Trials on the same day and earned many scores of 199.

In 1989, Joy met Kay Bedeau (Token), with her Ch. OTCh. Bluewins Fancy O'Shaughnessy JH VC, and in 1991, Heather was bred to Sean to produce the only litter for both sire and dam. The resulting five puppies became: Bentree Carolina Chickadee CDX; Ch. Bentree Gabriel Semper Fi CDX CGC RTD Ch U-CD; Bentree's King Colin UDX; Ch. OTCh. U-CDX Bentree Token's Iceman Cometh UD; and Ch. OTCh. Bentree's Tickle My Fancy UDX.

Karen Gregory Bishop, Garland, TX

Karen's first Irish and first obedience dog was OTCh. Blue Mink in the 1970s. She trained the puppy herself while she was still in school. After Blue Mink died, Karen purchased Draherin Evening Moonlight CDX ("Kerry") in 1985 from Lucy Jane Myers. At the same time, Karen and Kerry were introduced to agility. Kerry loved it, and she was a natural. Her specialty was the weave poles, and she flew through them. She was one of the first Irish to compete in the sport, and although she never achieved her titles because of physical problems, she was a crowd pleaser.

When Kerry retired, Karen acquired Ch. Kennlee Make No Mistake CD JH VC, co-owned with Shirlee Murray, her first dog to have a title at both ends.

Karen and her husband, Jon, do field work, conformation, and tracking in addition to obedience and agility. Karen also teaches competitive obedience at her Top Dog training school. They now live with six Irish Setters and two Golden Retrievers.

Ch. U-CDX O'Flynn's Heather of Joy CDX placing First in Obedience at the 1989 ISCA National Specialty. Owned by Joy Benton.

OTCh. Blue Mink winning High in Trial in 1979. Owned by Karen Gregory Bishop.

Shirley, Hugh, and Erin Callahan, Toledo, OH

In 1983, the Callahans obtained their first Irish Setter, Seamus, who, unfortunately, was lost to cancer at the age of three. Shirley and Hugh then decided to get a conformation dog for their daughter, Erin, to show. Ch. Scarlly's Top O'The Morning came home in 1987. In 1992, Ch. Pompei's American Classic CDX was added. Erin showed him to specialty and group wins, while Shirley began his obedience career.

In 1993, Ch. Kenshire's Captured Lupracan CD arrived. He finished both his championship and his CD easily and is now training for open and utility. American Classic's son, Shadyview's Erin's Time, is also part of the Callahan family.

Ch. U-CDX Trendsetters Clearly Barney CDX CGC, Esther Dolder's first obedience Irish Setter.

Ch. Pompei's American Classic CDX, a group and specialty winner, taking the high jump. Owned by Erin and Shirley Callahan.

Gaye Cocoman, Bedford Heights, OH

Lunn's I Love Lucy TDI is Gaye's therapy dog. She passed the required tests when she was only 18 months old in 1994, and Lucy and Gaye have been regular visitors at Fairview Hospital in the Cleveland area ever since.

Esther J. Dolder, Taylors, SC

Ch. U-CDX Trend Setters Clearly Barney CDX CGC was Esther's introduction to the world of purebred dogs. His breeder, Kathleen Landon, showed him to his championship, and Esther started him in obedience when he was four years old.

Ch. Glenarrif's Remembrant TDI is the first dog Esther handled in the breed ring, and at the age of four, he passed his test to become a therapy dog. Esther also plans to work him in the field toward his hunting title. Esther describes him as "kind, gentle, playful, forgiving, and patient...just as an Irish should be."

Jo Ferguson, Anchorage, AK

Jo's first obedience Irish was Copperas Red Token UDT, who kept Jo and her young son safe from moose and bear on many a hike and cross-country ski jaunt. Almost all of

Three of Jo Ferguson's obedience titleists (from left to right): Killarney's Midnight Sun UDT; Mi Jean's Fyreweed Classic UD; and Copperas Red Token UDT.

Jo's knowledge of utility training came from a book. Next came Killarney's Midnight Sun UDT ("Daisy"). Token and "Daisy" made a terrific skijoring team, pulling Jo down snowy trails. The final arrival was Mi Jean's Fyreweed Classic UD. She was part of the first-place team in obedience at the National Specialty in 1989.

Elisabeth and Don Fisher, Milpitas, CA

Elisabeth was born in Germany. Classical music and photography were her passions. Upon moving to the US, she attended community college in San Diego to study the arts—specifically sculpture—receiving several awards from the San Diego Art University for her welded sculptures. She also attended San Jose State University to continue her education in the arts.

Their first Irish Setter, Jenny, didn't need training, but the next, Rebellion's Sawmill Sally UDX (Ch. Rebellion's Bachelor Button ex Ch. Rebellion's Cream Puff) definitely did. Starting Sally in obedience proved to be fun for both Elisabeth and Sally, and in 1996, she achieved her UDX title. Elisabeth's new girl is Starlin's Moonbeam CD (Ch. Mariah Showstopper CD JH ex Ch. Ramblin' Red Reflection), purchased from Dr. Gary and Iben Brown.

Elisabeth writes, "When not training, my Irish Girls provide sunshine, rain, and occasional thunder, but most of all laughter, in my life. What happened to the artist? She is still there, but the dogs have taken over...for now."

Rebellion's Sawmill Sally UDX flies over the solid jump. Owned by Elisabeth and Don Fisher.

Cathy Flynn, Lakewood, OH

Cathy's first Irish was acquired as a companion for her husband in 1976. Cathy trained him for obedience and he became O'Flynn's Errol Flynn CDX. She then purchased

Donoval's I Love a Parade CDX and after attaining her title, she was bred to Am. Can. Ch. Sheridan's Radar O'Riley UD. A puppy from that litter became Ch. U-CDX O'Flynn's Heather of Joy CDX, owned by Joy Benton. When Joy bred Heather to Kay Bedeau's Sean, Cathy jumped at the opportunity to acquire a puppy, who became Bentree Carolina Chickadee CDX. She is an honest, willing, and funny little bitch that is catching on to the agility routines faster than her owner.

Training is more important to Cathy than competition, but the essence of her relationship with her dogs has been built during daily runs. All of her Irish Setters have taken a turn being Cathy's running buddies as well as her

Bentree Carolina Chickadee CDX. Owned by Cathy Flynn.

frequent hiking, walking, backpacking, and camping companions. Cathy says her dogs have never declined an opportunity to go out and "do something," and that's the part she likes best about them.

Anita and Tom Gage, *Firle Oak*–Fortuna, CA

Ch. Thenderin Schivis Regal UD, Thenderin Lasting Edition UD, Thenderin Gentle On My Mind UD, and

Thenderin Sportsman CD were all obtained from the late Ann Savin Dunn. They started the Firle Oak tradition of combining conformation and obedience. The Gages continue to breed and show their own dogs to dual titles, including Ch. Okelyn Bolero UD, a Sportsman daughter, and Ch. Firle Oak Lady Cayenne CDX and Ch. Firle Oak Lord Chutney CD, both Bolero offspring. In their limited breeding program, they have produced 19 champions. They encourage new owners to train their dogs in obedience for maximum enjoyment.

Frank Gangemella, Florissant, MO

OTCh. Duggan Michael Anthony was one of the first Irish Setters to complete the requirements for an obedience trial championship. Frank writes, "Duggan was a wonderful dog as well as a great showman."

Ray Gates, Santa Barbara, CA

Sean Baby UD was a unique Irish Setter and a famous one in his day. He lived from 1968 until 1979, after Ray and his family rescued him from a life of neglect. He was a totally disobedient habitual runaway when Ray's son found him. The original owners didn't want to keep driving hundreds of miles to bring him home, so he joined the Gates family. Ray began training him for self-preservation, and he did so well in obedience classes that Ray entered him in a trial. At their first show, Sean was awarded highest-scoring dog. From that beginning, Sean set new records for Irish Setters in obedience in more than 100 trials.

Sean was featured in magazines and newspapers, but Ray, an obedience judge, writes, "None of his articles mention his greatest achievement, and that is the love and devotion he gave to us. There is no way I can begin to relate the bond that I had with my friend. I didn't use clickers, food, trick collars, or any other gimmicks. Just pure love."

Ray, also had another fine obedience dog in the 1980s, Bywoods Merry Anne UD ("Meg"). She was from Red Arrow lines, and Ray picked her because some Irish Setter fanciers thought that Sean Baby might have come from that family.

Dan Graham, Mount Morris, MI

Dan started training Irish Setters in 1967 with the family's first dog, Aaragon's Titian Huntress CDX. Her son, Good Time Charley UD, was his first High in Trial dog. He was Dan's teacher because of his inventive personality. From him, Dan learned patience and the importance of making your dog "a partner, not a puppet." Apacheacre T.C. Luci UD whizzed through her titles, permitting Dan to put Charley's training to good use.

Ch. Shadyview Touchtone CDX Can. CD CGC winning High in Trial at the 1995 ISCA National Specialty. Owned by Dan Graham.

Bywood's Merry Ann UD. Owned by Ray Gates.

At the 1995 National Specialty, his dog, Ch. Shadyview Touchtone Am. Can. CD was High in Trial.

Dan has trained many different breeds through his boarding and training kennels, but the Irish Setters and their wonderful personalities have always been his favorites. He has put 21 obedience titles on Irish Setters with numerous High in Trials.

In addition to dog training, Dan has become interested in dressage, which is basically obedience training and physical development of the horse. His Arabian stallion reminds him of an Irish Setter—very intelligent, fun-loving, mischievous, competitive, and loyal unto death.

Pat Hair, Roswell, GA

Pat became involved with Irish Setters in the 1970s after watching the Disney movie, *Big Red*. She trained both her new Irish and a Poodle at the same time. Her top-winning Ch. Cameo Carbon Copy UD (Ch. Donoval's Crimson Crown ex Cameo Cute Crissy CDX), bred by Leslie Leland, was born in 1982 and lived for almost 16 years. She was the first and perhaps only multiple High in Trial and group-placing Irish Setter in breed history.

Pat also owns Ch. Scarlly's Tug O'War AX CGC (Ch. Scarlly's Main Switch ex Ch. Scarlly's Direct Hit). He is Pat's introduction to agility, and like Carbon before him, has been featured on television and in print advertising.

Ch. Scarlly's Tug O'War AX CGC is an accomplished agility dog and has been featured in television and print advertising. Owned by Pat Hair.

Kris Hahn, Mokena, IL

Kris has owned Irish Setters for 25 years and became involved in obedience about 10 years ago when she bought a puppy from Elizabeth Fleming (Sunstrand Kennels). Liz encouraged her to compete with her first obedience dog, Sunstrand's Mr. Beau Jangles CDX. She now is trialing with Cranberra's Steel Magnolia UDX. Her latest arrival is a rescue dog, Bud, that she hopes to take to an obedience trial championship.

Elyse Hansberry, Commerce City, CO

Elyse's journey with Irish Setters began in 1969 when she purchased a puppy with the money she saved by not smoking. His name was Shamrock's O'Leary, a Saturday Night Ed son. O'Leary earned his CD in three shows and Elyse was hooked, figuring she'd traded one addiction for another. Since then her dogs have earned 11 CDs, 6 CDXs, 1 UD, 4 breed championships, and 3 VCs.

Ch. Tramore Never Say Never CDX TDI (Ch. Meadowlark's Vindicator ex Ch. Tramore Hurrah) was bred and co-owned by Ginny Swanson. "Conor" was Elyse's "once in a lifetime" dog. He finished his

Ch. Tramore Never Say Never CDX TDI is a group winner, sire of 18 champions, and a registered therapy dog. Owned by Elyse Hansberry.

championship easily, was a group winner, sired 18 champions, and earned his CDX in 1993. He was a registered therapy dog, visiting a local rehabilitation hospital.

In 1988, Elyse co-owned a puppy that became Ch. Estrella Sand Dollar UD CGC TDI, bred by Paul Holmes. She finished her championship but shone in obedience. She is now retired but occasionally is shown in Open B or Veteran Sweepstakes.

Jan Hasart, Marshfield, WI

Echowood Accent UD earned many High in Trial awards during her career in obedience. She was also a personal hunting dog and a therapy dog. Jan owns six German

Shorthaired Pointers but is always on the lookout for another special Irish Setter.

Marty and Linda Haspel, Seneca, MD

Marty and Linda purchased their first Irish Setter as a companion to their young son 27 years ago. Subsequently, they became interested in obedience with Ch. Ruibin's Padraig O'Peg UD. Marty is an obedience judge, and he feels that obedience "gives the dog-handler team the opportunity to compete against a personal best, and everyone can win."

Kathy Heckaman, Massilion, OH

Kathy had dreamed of owning a purebred dog since she was a little girl, and after marriage and family, she acquired an Irish Setter puppy that became OTCh. Kathy's Ben Can. CDX. In 1979, Ben became the third Irish Setter to achieve an obedience championship.

In 1979, OTCh. Kathy's Ben Can. CDX became the third Irish Setter in breed history to earn an obedience championship. Owned by Kathy Heckaman.

Gina and Ray Atkinson Hemphill, *Shine–On*–Tracy, CA

OTCh. Atkinson's Rum and Coke VC was Gina and Ray's first dog. They knew little about choosing a dog but knew they wanted an Irish Setter. The pet they picked became the first obedience trial champion to earn a VC. She was the producer of two champions with obedience titles. Coke also ran on a scent hurdle team for many years and was a personal hunting dog.

They then bought Ch. Brian of Tarnywood CDX. Bred to Coke, they produced Ch. Shine-On Red Ryder UD and Ch. Shine-On McDuff CD.

Two additional dogs are currently in competition at Shine-On. They are Ch. Rapture's Dirty Dancing CD and Souvenir's Perfect Timing, now being shown and preparing for obedience.

Marsha Henkel, *Harborlight*—Gig Harbor, WA

Marsha has owned Irish Setters for 30 years and competes in all areas of the sport. Her first Irish was Marand's Dusty Rose Am. Can. CDX. She was followed by Am. Can. OTCh. Can. Ch. Marands Kiss Me Kate

OTCh. Atkinson's Rum and Coke VC was the first Irish Setter obedience trial champion to earn his Versatility Certificate. Owned by Gina Hemphill and Ray Atkinson.

Am. Can. Ch. Can. OTCh. Marand's Kiss Me Kate Am. Can. TDX, a multiple High in Trial winner and to date the only Irish Setter to have earned a TDX. Owned by Marsha Henkel.

An all-champion family (from left to right): Am. Can. Ch. Harborlight Promises to Keep JH MX AXJ OAC OGC EJC, owned by Bev Wallace; the mother of the bunch, Ch. Dunbrook Loves the Blues JH; Am. Can. Ch. Harborlight For Keeps TD JH OA NAC NJC; and lying in front, Ch. Harborlight Keeps Me Dancin' TD JH.

Am. Can. TDX. She was a multiple High in Trial winner and to date is the only Irish to have earned a TDX. Marsha's current family includes Ch. Dunbrook Loves the Blues JH and her all-champion litter by Ch. Castlebar Command Presence, including Ch. Harborlight Keeps Me Dancin' TD JH, Am. Can. Ch. Harborlight For Keeps TD JH OA NAC NJC, and Am. Can. Ch. Harborlight Promises to Keep JH MX AXJ OAC OGC EJC, owned by Bev Wallace.

Bonnie Henry, *Mirkwood*—Spokane, WA

Bonnie's first obedience dog was Deacon UD, whom she trained in the 1980s. Her next Irish was OTCh. Mirkwood's The Red Terror, who became an obedience champion in 1992. Bonnie's current Irish are Mirkwood's Bedevil'D O'Deryn Am. Can. CDX and U-CD Mirkwood's O'Deryn Shadowman Am. Can. CD. Bonnie teaches obedience classes for the Spokane Training Club.

OTCh. Mirkwood's The Red Terror winning High in Trial in 1992. Owned by Bonnie Henry.

249

Patrick Higgins, Louisville, KY

Pat has owned three Irish Setters, the most notable of which was OTCh. Scarlett Miss O'Shaunecy. She was one of the first obedience trial champions, finishing her title in 1978. Pat says, "Owning an Irish is always an adventure. They are often a little stubborn, but you always know who they own." Pat judged obedience at the 1993 National Specialty and is a licensed judge of all AKC obedience classes.

In 1978, OTCh. Scarlett Miss O'Shaunecy became one of the first Irish Setter obedience trial champions. Owned by Patrick Higgins.

Charles Hornback, Riverside, CA

The first Irish Setter obedience trial champion came from a pet shop. When Charles went to buy a pair of shoes at the mall, he came home with "Kenna" instead. She excelled in obedience as a puppy and eventually became OTCh. Liffey Claire Kenna. She was campaigned in obedience for about five years during the 1970s.

Patti Hunsicker, Keatchie, LA

Patti has owned Irish Setters for more than 20 years, purchasing her first dog in 1974. When she met professional handler and Irish Setter breeder Shirlee Murray, Patti became interested in conformation. She has purchased and co-owned several Irish with Shirlee. Shirlee shows the dogs in the show ring, and Patti shows them in obedience. In 1994, she purchased Ch. Kennlee Silver Dollar Speshal CD CGC TDI from Shirley. She also owns Ch. Kennlee Treasure Bay with Shirlee. He was an Award of Merit winner at the 1998 National Specialty.

Lyn Jensen, Silver Spring, MD

Lyn's Irish Setter Tagolong Toly Shauleen CDX was the Highest Scoring Dog in Trial at the first ISCA National Specialty in 1973.

Tagolong Toly Shauleen CDX was the Highest Scoring Dog in Trial at the first ISCA National Specialty in 1973. Owned by Billie Lyn and Thomas Jensen.

Nina Johnson, Houston, TX

Nina has participated in the sport since 1972. She has trained six Irish to one UD, three CDX, and two CD titles. Ch. U-CD Halsey's Young Man's Fancy CDX SH VC was High in Trial at the National Specialty in 1997. Nina tries to promote obedience by encouraging all dog owners to train their dogs. She also works her dogs in the field.

Ch. U-CD Halsey's Young Man's Fancy CDX SH VC winning High in Trial at the 1997 ISCA National Specialty. Owned by Nina Johnson.

Daniel and Evelyn Kearon, Branchville, NJ

The Kearons' involvement with Irish Setters began in 1981 when they adopted Daniel's Sweet Molly Malone UD from a local shelter. Molly won a ribbon in obedience class, which was the beginning of the couple's quest for obedience titles. Molly was followed by Bridget (Can.

A rare photo of the famous dog trainer, Bill Koehler, with Apple, owned by Bob Lyons, and OTCh. Liffey Claire Kenna, owned by Charles Hornback.

OTCh. Willowfenn's Christopher St. UD), who earned his UD in just seven-and-a-half months from his start in obedience. Bobby (Am. Can. SKC Ch. U-CD Hallmark Art O Dressage, Am. Can. SKC CD), a High in Trial winner and sire of champions, junior hunters, and obedience title holders, came next, followed by his son, Myles (OTCh.U-CDX Willowfenn's Abington Square UDX).

The three dogs have had a career in television and print ads in addition to their performances in the ring. Molly, Bridget, and Myles were high combined scorers at the National Specialties in 1986, 1989, and 1997. Myles was High in Trial at the National Specialty in 1997. Currently, Myles is training in agility, and the newest, Emmet (Willowfenn's Breezy Point) is training in agility and obedience.

Carolyn Klicman, Talmadge, OH

For Carolyn, nicknamed Chipper, several family dogs were part of the Klicman household. Her success in obedience began with the purchase of a puppy that became Ch. Sheridan's Radar O'Riley UD. Radar was High Combined at the 1982 National Specialty, at the same time competing in the breed ring. He is the sire of several notable obedience dogs, including Ch. U-CDX O'Flynn's Heather of Joy CDX, owned by Joy Benton. Chipper passed away in January 1998.

Dorothy Kumpula, Memphis, MI

Dorothy acquired her first Irish Setter, Murphy (Can. OTCh. U-UD Sir Murphy of Walker UD JH VC TT), in 1980. With that good experience, she looked for another Irish after Murphy completed his utility degree. From Linda Lenehan (Ballingarry Irish Setters), she purchased a bitch that already had a CD degree. She became Can. OTCh. U-UD Ballingarry Genesis UD TT CGC ("Jenny").

As Dorothy's daughter, Sarah, was growing up, she would do hand signals with Murphy and Jenny. Jenny became Sarah's special dog from the time she was 8 years old. When Sarah was 11, a Jenny grandaughter became available, Can. CD Rate Exchange Genesis CD TT CGC ("Token"), and was purchased for her. The second show at which 13-and-a-half-year-old Sarah competed with Token was the 1998 National Specialty, at which the pair won High in Trial. They are now working in Open and Utility.

Jo-Anne Larsen, Hoosick Falls, NY

In 1972, Jo-Anne bought her first Irish Setter. Nine months later, she acquired her first competitive dog, which became Ch. Marabu's Crackling Rose CD. She took "Rosie" through obedience training to her CD degree and then bred her to Ch. Tirvelda Hunter's Moon. Her goal was to have a utility-degree Irish, and through a succession of Rosie's offspring, she continued to work in obedience as time allowed.

In 1992, Jo-Anne purchased a puppy from Kate Seymour that became Ch. Cucuhullain Dr. Seuss CDX ("Doc"). He was the dog that defined the sport for her. Doc's enthusiasm in the ring, causing Jo-Anne to hang on to the lead for dear life on many occasions, was a source of great ringside amusement. Unfortunately, he injured

Can. OTCh. U-UD Ballingarry Genesis UD TT CGC. Owned by Dorothy and Sarah Kumpula.

Ch. Cucuhullain In Flight CDX. Owned by Jo-Anne Larson.

himself before he was able to acquire his UD, but his last-born son, Ch. Cucuhullain In Flight CDX has exceeded his dad in the fun-to-train category as they work toward their UD.

Jo-Anne says that each of her dogs has taken her places that she has never been before. Doc's great-grandson, owned by the Drummonds, Jamond's Go the Distance, is working in the field as well as in the show and obedience rings.

She says, "In our journey it is not just the dogs that have inspired me, but people as well. First, Evelyn Kavanaugh, who introduced me to positive motivation before it became vogue. Later, Sharon Rogner, who owned Doc's daughter, Ch. Fieldstone Doneghael Debut, urged us to be as competitive as we could and introduced me to Nancy Opie, who raised the bar for us. Janice DeMello was instrumental in teaching us about attention training, and more recently, Kay Bedeau has been our guru. Kay has always been just a phone call away to help keep us on track on our quest for that lifetime goal, a UD."

Tom and Candy Macaluso, *Sweetbrier*— Huntington Beach, CA

Tom and Candy's first Irish Setter was Tradition Dear Abby, purchased in 1981. At six months of age, Abby started in obedience. When Tom saw Irish Setters in utility, he decided that this was what he wanted to do. He took Abby to a utility degree. Following Abby was Rendition Sandcastle UD JH, who provided Tom with his first experience in the field.

Their greatest success has been with Ch. OTCh. Hazelhill Shining Star UDX MH VCX (Ch. Summerset Double Trouble ex Ch. Hazelhill Sweetcakes) bred by Jeri Colella. Star was the first Irish to earn the UDX title and the second Champion/Obedience Trial Champion bitch. Tom began field work with Star right after she finished her OTCh. in 1993 at the age of three and a half. In 1999, Star achieved her Master Hunter and VCX titles, again making breed history.

Ch. OTCh. U-CD Hazelhill Shining Star UDX MH VCX has made breed history by becoming the first Irish Setter to earn the Utility Dog Excellent, Master Hunter, and Versatility Certificate Excellent titles. Owned by Tom and Candy Macaluso.

Star has been bred twice, first to Ch. Rendition Mercedes Benz and then to Swashbuckler's All My Kisses. Star's daughter Sweetbrier Suzi Stardust CD SH, by Mercedes Benz, is Tom's newest Irish Setter competing in obedience, conformation, and field. The Macalusos also own Hazelhill Escapade UD JH (Ch. Quailfield Mak'n Business ex Ch. Hazelhill Sweetcakes), co-bred with Jeri Colella. She is currently working toward her obedience championship.

Mike and Peggy Malik, Oceanside, CA

Aldebaran Scarlett O'Hara UD Can. CD was the High Combined winner at the 1976 National Specialty and winner of numerous High in Trials—not bad for a bitch that was initially trained in obedience because she was a runaway.

Can. OTCh. Shangrila Thomas of Kismet UDX was ranked Number One in Obedience in Canada in 1997. Owned by Paul Martini.

Paul Martini, Howell, MI

Paul's first Irish was acquired in 1977, and after taking that dog to obedience trials, he became a fan of the sport. His current winner is Can. OTCh. Shangrila Thomas of Kismet UDX, who ranked Number One in Canada in obedience in 1997 and Number Six in the United States during his career.

Tom and Connie Miller, Greenville, OH

Tom and Connie bought their first Irish Setter in 1979, and after Tom took over Rusty's education, he became Miller's Rusty Red River UD. He was High in Trial at the

1982 National Specialty. Tom and Connie frequently took Rusty to entertain audiences in the park, showing people that Irish Setters are really trainable dogs. Rusty also did his part by visiting nursing homes as a member of a pet therapy program.

Tom passed away in 1984, and Connie has continued with two new Irish, Modder Rhu of Kelsey Corner and Morgan.

Patti Normandin, Houston, TX

Patti became involved in obedience in 1970 when Normandin's Mai Tai, her first Irish Setter, won first place at obedience school graduation. She has since put obedience titles on several additional Irish. In 1989, she purchased U-CDX Token's Into the Woods UD ("Nissa") from Kay and Bill Bedeau. Nissa had a successful obedience career, including High Combined at the 1995 National Specialty. She is also an eager and sensitive therapy dog. In 1995, Patti added Gypsy (Ch. Token's Let

Not only does U-CDX Token's Into the Woods UD RTD have a successful obedience career, she is a wonderful therapy dog. Owned by Patti Normandin.

Me Entertain You) to the household. Gypsy was Patti's first venture into the conformation ring, and she handled Gypsy to her championship.

Patti serves as instructor and training director for the All-Breed Competition Training Club. She has been a

temperament evaluator for therapy dogs, has taught her own obedience classes, and has received several community citations for her work with dogs and for sportsmanship.

Fred and Flori Page, Huntington Beach, CA

Flori had an Irish Setter when she was a child, and shortly after she and Fred married, she insisted on having another. Kaylor's Marguerite Sue UD ("Maggie") was the result of that request and began a lifelong interest in obedience. When Fred and Flori lost Maggie at the age of 14, they purchased Daisy, who became OTCh. Sunshine Gatsby's Blue Love MH VC (Ch. Dunbrook Love Is Blue ex Ch. Sunshine's Desert Moonlight), from Dick and Kathy Whiteis. She completed her obedience championship at the age of three years and three months, eventually accumulating 543 championship points, the most lifetime points of any Irish Setter to date. She won or placed in many competitions in addition to AKC-licensed trials, and in those she had six perfect 200 scores. She was High in Trial at the 1988 National Specialty and High in Trial and High Combined at the 1992 National Specialty.

Daisy was the first obedience champion to earn a Senior Hunter title and until 1999 was the only Irish Setter obedience champion to earn a Master Hunter title.

Daisy is Fred's hiking and fishing buddy. She likes fishing almost as much as hunting. She is Fred's true friend and almost constant companion.

Helen Phillips, Arvada, CO

Helen's obedience career began with Rhodesian Ridgebacks, but through her friend Joann Berry of Bangor Irish Setters, she became involved with the breed when she agreed to take one of Joann's dogs through obedience. She then acquired Bangor Quintessa O'Hara UDT, followed by Redflair Daphne Dabbles, who was more of a clown than a serious competitor. She eventually moved out of Irish Setters and now has Border Collies and sheep.

Arlene and Peter Pilcer, *Setter Woods–* Chatham, VA

In 1971, the Pilcers acquired their first two Irish, and in 1988, they were persuaded to take their fifth Irish, Molly, to class. Molly became U-CDX Setter Woods Hello Molly Am. Can. CDX CGC TDI TT. In 1990, Arlene saw an ad for puppies by Am. Can. Ch. Tirvelda Instant Replay UD. Because she admired this dog, she acquired Bo, who became U-CDX Setter Woods Gentleman Bo UDX Can. CDX TDI CGC TT. Bo has earned many obedience awards, including nine High in Trials. He is a therapy dog and is active with the elderly and 4-H children. At

U-CDX Setter Woods Gentleman Bo UDX Can. CDX JH VC TDI CGC TT has won multiple obedience awards, including nine High in Trials. Owned by Arlene and Peter Pilcer.

Sandy Rowan, Anchorage, AK

Sandy always wanted an Irish Setter and was finally able to purchase her first from a pet store. He was a great companion and after he died, she purchased a puppy from Fleetwood Farms that became OTCh. Fleetwood Farms Belle Star.

In 1991, the year Belle Star completed her championship, she was ranked Number One Irish in obedience. This was no mean feat, considering the size and infrequency of shows and the distances one has to travel in Alaska to compete.

OTCh. Fleetwood Farms Belle Star, Number One Irish Setter in Obedience in 1991. Owned by Sandy Rowan.

Betsy Sessler, Dallas, TX

One of Betsy's fondest memories is of the warm response she got from so many ISCA members after her "final performance" at the National Specialty in New Orleans. Betsy says, "From a sport whose mission is to identify

the age of eight, he recently completed his UDX title. In 1997, he sired a litter of 14 out of Tainaron Setter Woods Abbey CD CGC TT.

Peter and Arlene teach classes in obedience, agility, breed handling, and more at their training facility.

Tim and Diane Robbins, Gulf Breeze, FL

All Diane ever wanted was a reasonably well-behaved Irish Setter, so she went to class with her puppy, "Harvey." By 1982, Taramagh Autumn Harvest was top Irish with his Utility Degree, and in 1983 he was High in Trial at the National Specialty. He was Diane's special dog and constant companion.

Christine Tomanovich Riutta, Redford, MI

Christine's first Irish, Am. Can. OTCh. Ringo Starr II, was whelped in 1979. He was the first dog she had trained, and he went on to win his obedience championship and High in Trial at the 1986 National Specialty. She also co-owned Am. Can. Ch. Toy Farm Callahan Am. Can. CD with breeder Joan Toy.

Dr. Reinhardt Ross, Bellingham, WA

Valley View Flambeau UDX completed her title in 1995, making Flambeau the second Irish Setter to win this degree. She also earned five agility titles before this became a formal AKC sport. Dr. Ross died shortly after finishing Flambeau's UDX, and Flambeau, at 14, lives with Mrs. Dotti Ross.

Valley View Flambeau CDX, a multiple agility title winner, conquers the A-frame with ease. Owned by Dr. Reinhardt and Dotti Ross.

and produce the highest quality animals, it was touching to see everyone rally behind a dog from the wrong side of the tracks, dumped at an animal shelter not once but twice, unwanted, 'too large for the yard,' shy, afraid of men, and probably abused." Obedience training gave "Katy" the confidence to overcome her past, and Betsy chose to continue to work toward an obedience championship not only because she loved the sport and the people, but to prove something with a breed that is always fighting an image problem. Along the way Katy and Betsy developed a deep dog/human relationship. She wasn't the flashiest dog in the world, but her low-set little tail wagged as she worked, and her eight High in Trials, including two at the Nationals in 1984 and 1987, speak volumes for the potential of secondhand dogs and for the importance that ISCA places on its rescue program. Katy became OTCh. Rave on Katy, and Betsy writes, "To all those involved in rescue, keep up the good work. I'll call on you when my heart is ready for another."

Marilyn Shroyer, *Terracotta*–Bellflower, CA

In 1981, Marilyn saw Irish Setters in a park near her home and knew right away that she had to have one. Shinfayne's Holiday Luv CDX became part of Marilyn's family and her introduction to obedience. Following this first experience came Holiday Luv's daughters, Terracotta Red Velvet CDX, Shawnee Northern Terracotta CDX, and his

A trio of Terracotta Irish Setters (from left to right): U-CD Shawnee Northern Terracotta CDX CGC; Terracotta Stylesetter; and Terracotta Silverado CDX CGC. Owned by Marilyn Shroyer.

U-CDX Suttle's Darby Delight CD TT CGC JH VC (left) and Ch. Dunholm Eagle Kachina CD TT (right) show off their skills. Owned by Lara and Marc Suttle.

son, Terracotta Silverado CDX. All were involved with conformation, scent hurdle races, and team competition. Silverado and his sister Kayla remain with Marilyn, who hopes to start anew one day with another generation of redheads.

Lara and Marc Suttle, *Subtle*–Waxhaw, NC

Lara acquired her first Irish Setter in 1971, but it was not until another decade had passed that Irish became part of the family. Ch. Dunholm Eagle Kachina TT CD, co-owned with Cheryl Withington Stephens, was the first real show dog to arrive. He wasn't entered in obedience trials until the age of nine. By contrast, U-CDX Suttle's Darby Delight TT CGC CD JH VC finished her first title at the age of 11 months. Her desire to hunt was evident, and soon she had Marc and Lara committed to hunting and the ISCA VC/VCX program.

The Suttles now have Dunholm Subtle Panache and Dunholm Subtle Inferno, which they plan to train for obedience and field.

Brian Trapp, Glendale, AZ

OTCh. Red Irish Sun was born in 1974, and Brian started his first obedience class when "Sunny" was about a year old. He finished his championship in 1979 and lived until 1987.

Lynn Vaughn, Forest Lake, MN

All of Lynn's dogs are bred by and co-owned with Sue Hahnen (Courtwood). The first was Courtwood Endearment Am. Can. CDX CGC (Ch. Courtwood Golden Gate ex Ch. Courtwood English Cheers). Endearment bred

to Ch. Courtwood Bogtrotter produced the first Irish Setter to earn an agility title, Ch. Courtwood Easy Living AX AD CGC, owned by Linda and Patrick Schindler. Lynn also owns Ch. Courtwood Barcelona, Am Can. CD (Ch. Ballingarry Phantom Jet ex Ch. Courtwood Silver Slippers).

Mary Walker, Cicero, NY

Rusty UD was Mary Walker's first obedience Irish Setter in 1978. He earned his utility title in 1986. Her second Irish, Northwinds Thunder Orion Am. Can. CD, is working toward his advanced degrees.

Bev Wallace, *Bonnybrook*–Bothell, WA

Bev has been competing in conformation, obedience, tracking, field, and agility since 1972, when she purchased her first Irish Setter, Talrona Athena CDX. In 1977, Bev acquired Ch. Windntide Symphony UDT from Pat and Carol McGarry, and in 1984, another bitch from the McGarrys arrived, Windntide Love on the Rox CDX. This bitch was bred to Ch. Tainaron Masterstroke in 1988 to produce Bev's only litter, from which she kept two males, Ch. Bonnybrook Ringmaster and Am. Can. Ch. Bonnybrook Spotlight Am. Can. CDX JH VC.

Bev's most recent addition is Am. Can. Ch. Harborlight Promises to Keep JH MX AXJ EAC EJC OGC, bred by Marsha Henkel from a litter of three, all of which are champions and junior hunters.

Am. Can. Ch. Bonnybrook Spotlight Am. Can. CDX JH VC. Owned by Bev Wallace.

OTCh. Red Irish Sun finished his championship in 1979. Owned by Brian Trapp.

Courtwood Endearment Am. Can. CDX CGC. Owned by Lynn Vaughn and Sue Hahnen.

Bev considers herself a pet owner who enjoys showing. Because all of her dogs are house dogs, she keeps no more than four at one time, usually fewer. All of her dogs have been owner-trained and handled to all their titles. She cherishes the friendships made along the way and the fond memories of the process.

Monica and George Wilson, Canton, OH

In 1975, when Monica lived in an apartment with her first Irish Setter, Brandy, obedience training was mandatory to make her into a good housepet. The pair found competition interesting, and Brandy achieved her UD degree. Since then, other Irish Setters have found their way to the Wilsons, all of which have earned obedience degrees. In 1992, Monica purchased a puppy from Joy Benton that became Ch. Bentree's King Colin UDX (Ch. OTCh. Bluwin's Fancy O'Shaughnessy UD JH VC Ch. U-CDX ex O' Flynn's Heather of Joy CDX). In 1995, she obtained Ch. Token's Royal Ascot (Ch. Charlton's Irish Derby U-CD ex Token's Unsinkable Molly B UDT) from Bill and Kay Bedeau. Monica finished his championship and is beginning his obedience career.

During this time, George decided to try his hand at obedience with another of their Irish. Under his tutelage, Bishop's Checkmate earned his CDX CGC TDI.

Pam Wink, Des Plaines, IL

The highlight of Lady Shamrock of Erin UD's eight-year obedience career was her award of High Combined in Open and Utility at the 1991 National Specialty. Pam's current competitor is Classic Proud Clarion CDX. She also worked with Am. Int. Ch. Classic Chase Manhattan CDX JH NA VC CGC, whom his owner, Casper Ziegler asked her to train. Chase earned his CDX in one show cluster under Pam's guidance.

Lady Shamrock of Erin UD winning High Combined in Open and Utility at the 1991 ISCA National Specialty. Owned by Pam Wink.

Mike and Joanne Wright, Raleigh, NC

Mike and Joanne acquired their first Irish Setter shortly after they were married, and from that beginning they added Shannon Black Nose CDX and subsequently a full brother from a later breeding, Patrick Black Nose CDX. Both Shannon and Patrick are still actively competing for their advanced titles.

Judy Zieve (Bonfiglio), Dearborn, MI

Even though she came from a newspaper ad, wasn't show quality, and had no special pedigree, Can. OTCh. Red

Ch. Token's Royal Ascot as a new champion taking Best of Winners in 1997. Owned by Monica Wilson.

Am. Can. Ch. Can. OTCh. Shangrila Getting To Know You UD. Owned by Lynne Mehring and Judy Zieve.

Feather Mystique UD was Judy's "soul mate." Judy says, "She was my constant companion and friend as well as a good obedience dog. Showing was just another thing we did together." Judy's most thrilling moment was when Feather won High in Trial and High Combined at the 1981 National Specialty.

Another of Judy's dogs was Am. Can. Ch. Can. OTCh. Shangrila Getting to Know You UD, whom she co-owned with breeder Lynne Mehring (Ch. Shangrila Stargazer ex Milesian's Merry Maura). "Brett" was Shangrila's first champion and utility dog, and he won several High in Trial awards and placed in Sporting Groups in the US and Canada.

Agility

Agility is the fastest-growing sport in the realm of purebred dogs. Before the AKC made agility part of its formal events program, there were other groups that had formalized this activity. The numbers of degrees that an agility dog can win are almost mind-boggling, and in the interest of clarity, we have listed at the end of this chapter those titles and the organizations that offer them so the reader will have some idea of what the alphabet soup of letters indicates.

Most competitors in agility have engaged in other aspects of the dog sport as well. Those people and dogs that have placed special emphasis on agility are included in this section, even though their profiles indicate participation in conformation, field, or obedience. As this chapter reflects, the companionship of dogs and owners is of paramount importance in any successful endeavor. Working with dogs creates a closeness between dog and owner that can only be achieved through understanding and a loving relationship. Those owners whose interests reflect multiple categories may be found in other sections of this book.

Ron and Margie Beebe, *Oakshadow*—Canton, OH

Ron and Margie Beebe spent three years observing dog events before deciding to purchase their foundation bitch, Ch. Jamond's Olympic Dream Am. Can. CD OA NAJ, from Duane and Jackie Drummond. The following year, they purchased another, also from the Drummonds, that became Am. Can. Ch. Jamond's Caught In The Act JH

Ch. Jamond's Olympic Dream Am. Can. CD OA NAJ, foundation bitch for Ron and Margie Beebe's Oakshadow Kennels, at the 1998 AKC Agility National Specialty.

NA NAJ. They are now training both of these dogs for advanced degrees.

Charles Devenny, Hialeah, FL

Charles and his Irish, Satinwood's Autumn Dancer CD NA CGC 2/3OA ("Cinnamon") (Ch. Scarlly's Main

Satinwood Autumn Dancer CD NA CGC 2/3OA sails through the tire jump. Owned by Charles Devenny.

U-AGII Sunnyhill's Les Saintes MX NAC NGC is the first Irish Setter to earn an AKC Master Agility Excellent title. Owned by Sue Hansen.

Arista's Grand Irish Creme CD CGC negotiates the weave poles. Owned by Catherine Dever.

Switch ex Laggan American Beauty) have been working by word of mouth and with video clips to get more Irish Setter fanciers interested in agility in Florida. At this time, Cinnamon is the only Irish in that state to compete, so all of his wins have been in competition with other breeds.

Catherine Dever, El Cajon, CA

Catherine obtained her first Irish Setter in 1971. She trained "Chrystal" to a CDX, but then took a long hiatus from competing. After almost 20 years, she acquired Arista's Grand Irish Creme CD CGC. "Bailey" is currently competing in Novice Agility and also in conformation.

Sue Hansen, Milwaukee, WI

Sue has the distinction of owning the first Irish Setter to earn an AKC Master Agility Excellent title. She is U-AGII Sunnyhill's Les Saintes MX NAC NGC.

Meadowlark's Star Burst AX AXJ at the 1998 AKC Agility National Specialty. Owned by Kim Holmes.

Kim Holmes, Toledo, OH

Kim Holmes' Meadowlark's Star Burst ("Poppy"), not yet three years old, has her Agility Excellent (AX) and Agility Excellent Jumpers (AXJ) titles. Major-pointed and working in obedience, Poppy will be aiming for her agility championship.

Kris Kamholz, Crystal Lake, IL

Ch. U-ACh. Classic Rabblerouser CD MX OAJ is the second Irish Setter in breed history to earn a Master Agility title and the first champion and first bitch to finish an MX.

Sue Mertens, *Heartsong*–Carlsbad, CA

In 1991, Sue purchased her foundation bitch from Paulette Kovac and Susan Trotter (Rapture). She became Ch. Rapture's Ring of Fire CDX JH VC MX AXJ FM CGC TT TDI. Sue and Fire began playing and training the moment they met, with Fire exhibiting an intense desire to retrieve. As a young puppy, she was introduced to obedience, agility, conformation, and therapy dog work. In her role as a therapy dog, she has visited hospitals and nursing homes. During one memorable visit, Fire's attention prompted a woman to speak who had not spoken in two years.

Fire is also adept at flyball, an event sponsored by the North American Flyball Association. Fire earned her Junior Hunter title in 1996 and is training for her Senior and Master levels. She was bred to Ch. Meadowlark's Quartermaster in 1996, producing eight puppies, including one champion, with others pointed, three Junior Hunters, and one agility titleist. One of Fire's daughters, Casey, has completed several agility titles at the age of two.

Ch. U-ACh. Classic Rabblerouser CD MX OAJ is the second Irish Setter to earn a Master Agility title and the first champion bitch to finish a Master Agility Excellent title. Owned by Kris Kamholz.

Ch. Rapture's Ring of Fire CDX JH MX AXJ VC FM CGC TT TDI excels in her role as a therapy dog. Owned by Sue Mertens.

U-CD U-ACHX Pog Mo Dearg Deireadh of Madison Am. Can. ASCA CD TD OA NAJ OAC OCG AD CGC TDI, the first Irish Setter to earn titles in all four of the US agility organizations. Owned by Anne Schilling.

U-AGI Grainuaile Ghost Rider NA CGC TT. Owned by Karol Southerland and Claudia Grzych.

Alda Morris, Bay Village, OH

Alda and Karen Morris own two champion and agility dogs, Can. Ch Lunn's Bartholomew NA CGC TDI and Ch. Lunn's MacMillan Hellfire Am. Can. CD NA CGC TDI AAT. Both of these dogs are registered therapy dogs that also give demonstrations to show how well behaved these special animals have to be.

Anne and Tom Adams Schilling, Sun Prairie, WI

Anne's Irish, "Bozo," is the first Irish Setter to be titled by all four of the US agility organizations. She is U-CD U-ACHX Pog Mo Dearg Deireadh of Madison Am. Can. ASCA CD TD OA NAJ OAC OGC AD CGC TDI. In addition to her agility, obedience, and tracking titles, Bozo does therapy work and participates in flyball and scent hurdle demonstrations. She also enjoys swimming, field work, and just running in the woods. Anne says, "I have to thank Bozo for filling a void in my life that I didn't even know existed. Her joy in simply living has made my life happier in every way. Having her as my constant companion makes me one of the luckiest people in the world."

Karol K. Southerland, St. Clair Shores, MI

Karol has owned Irish Setters since 1979 and has achieved titles in conformation, field, obedience, and agility. She currently co-owns, with Claudia Grzych, U-AgI Grainuaile Ghost Rider NA CGC TT. Rider's favorite activity is agility, and Karol is working with him toward his advanced degrees.

Obedience and Agility Titles

Note: Abbreviations of titles generally follow the dog's name, with one exception: all United Kennel Club titles precede the dog's name. Abbreviations of championships generally precede the dog's name, with several exceptions: the NADAC, USDAA, AAC, and ASCA Agility Championships, which follow the dog's name.

Obedience Titles

The American Kennel Club (AKC):

CD	Companion Dog
CDX	Companion Dog Excellent
UD	Utility Dog
UDX	Utility Dog Excellent
TD	Tracking Dog
TDX	Tracking Dog Excellent
VST	Variable Surface Tracker

*UDT = UD + TD, UDTX = UD + TDX

Championships:

OTCh.	Obedience Trial Champion
CT	Champion Tracker

Canadian Kennel Club (CKC)

Can. CD	Companion Dog
Can. CDX	Companion Dog Excellent
Can. UD	Utility Dog
Can. TD	Tracking Dog
Can. TDX	Tracking Dog Excellent

Championship:

Can. OTCh.	Obedience Trial Champion

Note: The Can. OTCh., unlike the AKC and UKC obedience championships, is automatically conferred on any dog earning the Can. UD

United Kennel Club (UKC)

U-CD	Companion Dog
U-CDX	Companion Dog Excellent
U-UD	Utility Dog Championship:
U-OCH	Obedience Trial Champion

Kennel Club of Mexico

PC (or Mex. CD)	Perro Companero
PCE (or Mex. CDX)	Perro Companero Excelente
PU (or Mex. UD)	Perro Utilidad

Bermuda Kennel Club

Bda. CD	Companion Dog
Bda. CDX	Companion Dog Excellent
Bda. UD	Utility Dog

States Kennel Club (SKC)

SKC-CD	Companion Dog
SKC-CDX	Companion Dog Excellent
SKC-UD	Utility Dog
SKC-TD	Tracking Dog

Australian Shepherd Club of America (ASCA)

ASCA titles may be earned by breeds other than Australian Shepherds.

ASCA CD	Companion Dog
ASCA CDX	Companion Dog Excellent
ASCA UD	Utility Dog
ASCA T	Tracking

Championship:

ASCA OTCh.	Obedience Trial Champion

Agility Titles

AKC (American Kennel Club)

NA	Novice Agility
NAJ	Novice Agility Jumper
OA	Open Agility
OAJ	Open Agility Jumper
AX	Agility Excellent
AXJ	Agility Excellent Jumper
MX	Master Agility Excellent
MXJ	Master Agility Excellent Jumper Championship:
MACh.	Master Agility Champion

UKC (United Kennel Club)

U-AgI	Agility I
U-AgII	Agility II
U-ACH	Agility Champion
U-ACHX	Agility Champion Excellent
NAC	Novice Agility Certificate
O-NAC	Outstanding Novice Agility Certificate
S-NAC	Superior Novice Agility Certificate
NGC	Novice Gamblers Certificate
O-NGC	Outstanding Novice Gamblers Certificate
S-NGC	Superior Novice Gamblers Certificate

NADAC (North American Dog Agility Council)

NADAC offers 3 titling paths: Standard, Veteran (dog over 7 years of age), and Junior Handler (handler under 18 years of age).

NJC Novice Jumpers Certificate

O-NJC	Outstanding Novice Jumpers Certificate
S-NJC	Superior Novice Jumpers Certificate
OAC	Open Agility Certificate
O-OAC	Outstanding Open Agility Certificate
S-OAC	Superior Open Agility Certificate
OGC	Open Gamblers Certificate
O-OGC	Outstanding Open Gamblers Certificate
S-OGC	Superior Open Gamblers Certificate

OJC Open Jumpers Certificate

O-OJC	Outstanding Open Jumpers Certificate
S-OJC	Superior Open Jumpers Certificate
EAC	Elite Agility Certificate
O-EAC	Outstanding Elite Agility Certificate
S-EAC	Superior Elite Agility Certificate
EGC	Elite Gamblers Certificate
O-EGC	Outstanding Elite Gamblers Certificate
S-EGC	Superior Elite Gamblers Certificate

EJC Elite Jumpers Certificate

O-EJC	Outstanding Elite Jumpers Certificate
S-EJC	Superior Elite Jumpers Certificate
NATCH	NADAC Agility Trial Champion
O-NATCH	Outstanding NADAC Agility Trial Champion
S-NATCH	Superior NADAC Agility Trial Champion

Veteran Titles

AC-V	Veterans Novice Agility Certificate
O-NAC-V	Veterans Outstanding Novice Agility Certificate
S-NAC-V	Veterans Superior Novice Agility Certificate
NGC-V	Veterans Novice Gamblers Certificate
O-NGC-V	Veterans Outstanding Novice Gamblers Certificate
S-NGC-V	Veterans Superior Novice Gamblers Certificate
NJC-V	Veterans Novice Jumpers Certificate
O-NJC-V	Veterans Outstanding Novice Jumpers Certificate
S-NJC-V	Veterans Superior Novice Jumpers Certificate
OAC-V	Veterans Open Agility Certificate
O-OAC-V	Veterans Outstanding Open Agility Certificate
S-OAC-V	Veterans Superior Open Agility Certificate
OGC-V	Veterans Open Gamblers Certificate
O-OGC-V	Veterans Outstanding Open Gamblers Certificate
S-OGC-V	Veterans Superior Open Gamblers Certificate
OJC-V	Veterans Open Jumpers Certificate
O-OJC-V	Veterans Outstanding Open Jumpers Certificate
S-OJC-V	Veterans Superior Open Jumpers Certificate
EAC-V	Veterans Elite Agility Certificate
O-EAC-V	Veterans Outstanding Elite Agility Certificate
S-EAC-V	Veterans Superior Elite Agility Certificate
EGC-V	Veterans Elite Gamblers Certificate
O-EGC-V	Veterans Outstanding Elite Gamblers Certificate
S-EGC-V	Veterans Superior Elite Gamblers Certificate
EJC-V	Veterans Elite Jumpers Certificate
O-EJC-V	Veterans Outstanding Elite Jumpers Certificate
S-EJC-V	Veterans Superior Elite Jumpers Certificate
NATCH-V	Veterans NADAC Agility Trial Champion
O-NATCH-V	Veterans Outstanding NADAC Agility Trial Champion
S-NATCH-V	Veterans Superior NADAC Agility Trial Champion

Agility Titles

Junior Handler Titles (No Gamblers)

NAC-J	Junior Handler Novice Agility Certificate
O-NAC-J	Junior Handler Outstanding Novice Agility Certificate
S-NAC-J	Junior Handler Superior Novice Agility Certificate
NJC-J	Junior Handler Novice Jumpers Certificate
O-NJC-J	Junior Handler Outstanding Novice Jumpers Certificate
S-NJC-J	Junior Handler Superior Novice Jumpers Certificate
OAC-J	Junior Handler Open Agility Certificate
O-OAC-J	Junior Handler Outstanding Open Agility Certificate
S-OAC-J	Junior Handler Superior Open Agility Certificate
OJC-J	Junior Handler Open Jumpers Certificate
O-OJC-J	Junior Handler Outstanding Open Jumpers Certificate
S-OJC-J	Junior Handler Superior Open Jumpers Certificate
EAC-J	Junior Handler Elite Agility Certificate
O-EAC-J	Junior Handler Outstanding Elite Agility Certificate
S-EAC-J	Junior Handler Superior Elite Agility Certificate
EJC-J	Junior Handler Elite Jumpers Certificate
O-EJC-J	Junior Handler Outstanding Elite Jumpers Certificate
S-EJC-J	Junior Handler Superior Elite Jumpers Certificate

Note: There is no NATCH-J as they do not do Gamblers

USDAA (United States Dog Agility Association)

AD	Agility Dog
AAD	Advanced Agility Dog
MAD	Masters Agility Dog
RM	Pairs Relay Master
SM	Snookers Master
GM	Gamblers Master
JM	Jumpers Master
ADCH	Agility Dog Champion

Note: USDAA also has a "Performance" division for dogs of any age that the owners wish to jump lower. It replaces their Veterans program.

AAC (Agility Association of Canada)

AD-C	Agility Dog of Canada
AAD-C	Advanced Agility Dog of Canada
MAD-C	Masters Agility Dog of Canada
RM-C	Pairs Relay Master of Canada
SM-C	Snookers Master of Canada
GM-C	Gamblers Master of Canada
JM-C	Jumpers Master of Canada
ADCH-C	Agility Dog Champion of Canada

Note: AAC also has a "Performance" division, similar to the USDAA's.

ASCA (Australian Shepherd Club of America)

Like NADAC, ASCA has three titling paths; standard, veterans, and junior handlers.

Standard

RS-N	Regular Standard Novice
O-RS-N	Outsanding Regular Standard Novice
S-RS-N	Superior Regular Standard Novice
GS-N	Gamblers Standard Novice
O-GS-N	Outstanding Gamblers Standard Novice
S-GS-N	Superior Gamblers Standard Novice
JS-N	Jumpers Standard Novice
O-JS-N	Outstanding Jumpers Standard Novice
S-JS-N	Superior Jumpers Standard Novice
RS-O	Regular Standard Open
O-RS-O	Outstanding Regular Standard Open
S-RS-O	Superior Regular Standard Open
GS-O	Gamblers Standard Open
O-GS-O	Outstanding Gamblers Standard Open
S-GS-O	Superior Gamblers Standard Open
JS-O	Jumpers Standard Open
O-JS-O	Outstanding Jumpers Standard Open
S-JS-O	Superior Jumpers Standard Open
RS-E	Regular Standard Elite
O-RS-E	Outstanding Regular Standard Elite
S-RS-E	Superior Regular Standard Elite
GS-E	Gamblers Standard Elite
O-GS-E	Outstanding Gamblers Standard Elite
S-GS-E	Superior Gamblers Standard Elite
JS-E	Jumpers Standard Elite
O-JS-E	Outstanding Jumpers Standard Elite
S-JS-E	Superior Jumpers Standard Elite
ATCH	ASCA Agility Trial Champion
O-ATCH	Outstanding ASCA Agility Trial Champion
S-ATCH	Superior ASCA Agility Trial Champion

Agility Titles

Veterans

RV-N	Regular Veterans Novice
O-RV-N	Outstanding Regular Veterans Novice
S-RV-N	Superior Regular Veterans Novice
GV-N	Gamblers Veterans Novice
O-GV-N	Outstanding Gamblers Veterans Novice
S-GV-N	Superior Gamblers Veterans Novice
JV-N	Jumpers Veterans Novice
O-JV-N	Outstanding Jumpers Veterans Novice
S-JV-N	Superior Jumpers Veterans Novice
RV-O	Regular Veterans Open
O-RV-O	Outstanding Regular Veterans Open
S-RV-O	Superior Regular Veterans Open
GV-O	Gamblers Veterans Open
O-GV-O	Outstanding Gamblers Veterans Open
S-GV-O	Superior Gamblers Veterans Open
JV-O	Jumpers Veterans Open
O-JV-O	Outstanding Jumpers Veterans Open
S-JV-O	Superior Jumpers Veterans Open
RV-E	Regular Veterans Elite
O-RV-E	Outstanding Regular Veterans Elite
S-RV-E	Superior Regular Veterans Elite
GV-E	Gamblers Veterans Elite
O-GV-E	Outstanding Gamblers Veterans Elite
S-GV-E	Superior Gamblers Veterans Elite
JV-E	Jumpers Veterans Elite
O-JV-E	Outstanding Jumpers Veterans Elite
S-JV-E	Superior Jumpers Veterans Elite
VATCH	ASCA Veterans Agility Trial Champion
O-VATCH	Outstanding ASCA Veterans Agility Trial Champion
S-VATCH	Superior ASCA Veterans Agility Trial Champion

Junior Handlers (No Gamblers)

RJ-N	Regular Junior Novice
O-RJ-N	Outstanding Regular Junior Novice
S-RJ-N	Superior Regular Junior Novice
JJ-N	Jumpers Junior Novice
O-JJ-N	Outstanding Jumpers Junior Novice
S-JJ-N	Superior Jumpers Junior Novice
RJ-O	Regular Junior Open
O-RJ-O	Outstanding Regular Junior Open
S-RJ-O	Superior Regular Junior Open
JJ-O	Jumpers Junior Open
O-JJ-O	Outstanding Jumpers Junior Open
S-JJ-O	Superior Jumpers Junior Open
RJ-E	Regular Junior Elite
O-RJ-E	Outstanding Regular Junior Elite
S-RJ-E	Superior Regular Junior Elite
JJ-E	Jumpers Junior Elite
O-JJ-E	Outstanding Jumpers Junior Elite
S-JJ-E	Superior Jumpers Junior Elite

Flyball Titles

North American Flyball Association (NAFA)
(Covers US and Canada)

FD	Flyball Dog—20 pts.
FDX	Flyball Dog Excellent—100 pts.
FDCH	Flyball Dog Champion—500 pts.
FM	Flyball Master—5,000 pts.
FMX	Flyball Master Excellent—15,000 pts.
ONYX	20,000 pts.—named after the founder's dog
FDGCH	30,000 pts.—Grand Champion

Some of these titles were developed as the sport evolved—all points are earned as a team based on team times—so as the sport developed and people got faster dogs, the last three titles came about. Flyball is a very popular sport. There are teams that have a variety of breeds and race for fun. There are also the very competitive teams like Touch 'n' Go of Las Vegas, with all Border Collies and a *fast* Jack Russell or two to lower jumps. The Las Vegas team has two women who train team dogs five days a week—swimming, running, ball work, etc. Tournaments are big now, and teams are seeded in divisions based on current times—it is very sophisticated. In Michigan, they have tournaments with 3 judges and 80 teams.

Miscellaneous

TT	Temperament Tested by the American Temperament Testing Society (ATTS)
CGC	Canine Good Citizen—Offered by AKC

What Puppy Buyers Should Know

Because you are reading this book, it is safe to assume that you would like to own an Irish Setter. Before you start looking for a reputable breeder, you must honestly evaluate whether an Irish Setter is the dog for you. Here are some fundamental questions that you must answer for yourself before embarking on a quest for an Irish Setter: Do you have the space to accommodate an exuberant dog that may grow to 80 pounds and has a tail that swishes everything off the coffee table? Do you have the patience to train this animal from the time you bring him home until he matures at two or three years of age? Do you have the requisite exercise facilities or someone in the family who will maintain an exercise regimen faithfully? Do you have the temperament and sense of humor to enjoy an Irish Setter? Are you committed to a lifetime of care and responsibility for this animal? Are you prepared to include your dog as a true member of the family?

If you can honestly answer yes to all of these questions, then perhaps an Irish Setter is the dog for you.

There are some things to consider when you go to buy your puppy. The breeder, whether she is someone who owns one bitch and breeds an occasional litter or someone who runs a large kennel with several litters a year, must run a responsible operation. The place, whether family room or kennel, must be clean, and the puppies well maintained and contented. You should be able to see the mother or receive a convincing explanation as to why the mother is not with the puppies. Most breeders should have the dam on the premises with the puppies, although occasionally the puppies were born elsewhere. This is acceptable, unless the puppies were bought commercially for resale. You may see the sire, but most often the sire is not present, because breeders often go far to find the perfect mate for their bitch.

At three weeks of age, these adorable littermates by Chs. Red Barn Ranger Walker ex Red Barn Erin Mavoureen are much too young to go to their new homes.

The breeder of your chosen puppy must run a responsible operation, whether it is large or small. You should be able to meet the puppy's mother and other family members. Pictured are five generations of Scarlly Setters with breeder Penny Nunnally.

You should see a copy of the pedigree of the puppies, plus pictures of the sire, if he is elsewhere. You should be given proof that the puppies can be registered with the AKC.

As a prospective buyer, you are entitled to an honest evaluation of the litter. Ethical breeders produce puppies that they hope will improve the breed. They may be breeding for certain characteristics that they hope to achieve. Some may be looking for the ideal show champion, and others may be breeding for the best field potential. Still others may look to combine all the attributes of show, field, and obedience. They may be interested in producing the best pets with stable temperaments and adequate looks. Whatever the goals are for the breeders, they should honestly convey them to you.

Here are a few caveats: Do not accept the word of the breeder who guarantees you a champion when the litter is eight weeks old. Even though the puppies may look wonderful at that age, too many variables are possible for an honest breeder to sell puppies on that basis. Do not be pressured into buying a puppy if you have any doubts about the condition of the litter, the dam, or the breeder. Look around. Once you find a line that you like, you may have to wait for a puppy. Don't take the first puppy that you see unless all the conditions are right.

Almost every litter contains dogs of varying quality. Depending upon the lineage, some may turn out to be showstoppers, while others have minor faults that in no way prevent them from being excellent pets. A puppy from one of these litters is a very good bet, because you are pretty well assured that the breeder has done his or her best to produce top quality in looks, temperament, and health.

If you are in an area in which dog shows are held or in which a local Irish Setter Club is active, take the time to go to a show and see the puppies and older dogs. Meet the breeders and exhibitors and get a feel for what is available in your area. Take your time. Remember that this puppy will be part of your family for a long time, so you want to make the best choice possible.

Don't be surprised if the breeder asks as many questions about you as you do about the puppies. In fact, be happy that the breeder is concerned about where his or her puppy is going. Responsible breeders put an enormous amount of time, energy, emotion, and money into a litter. They want to make sure that the puppies are going to appropriate homes where they will be happy and well cared for their entire lives.

Breeders who sell pet puppies that they do not consider of top breeding quality may require a spay or neuter agreement from the buyers. They may also sell a puppy with limited registration papers, which would preclude any offspring of that puppy from being registered with the AKC. Most people who buy a pet are happy to have it altered, and this has no bearing on whether the puppy will be a good pet.

What to Expect from the Breeder

Once you have selected a puppy from a litter you have chosen, the breeder should provide the following:

1. You should receive the AKC registration form, which is the application enabling you to register your puppy with the AKC. Sometimes breeders prefer to register all their puppies with kennel names beforehand, and this is acceptable, just as long as it is done promptly and the necessary transfer papers are timely and in order. It is against AKC regulations and policy for a breeder to charge for the registration application, and it is unethical to charge for a pedigree.

2. You should receive the pedigree at the same time you purchase the puppy or earlier. You should not have

Responsible breeders put an enormous amount of time, energy, emotion, and money into a litter. This healthy puppy, Pauncefoot Perchance T Dream shown at seven weeks of age, was bred by Mr. and Mrs. Stephen Salt.

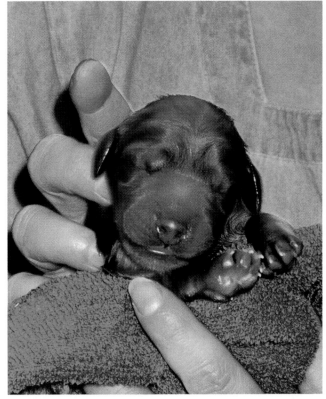

Ethical breeders will ensure that both parents are clear of any genetic problems in order to produce the best puppies possible. Pictured at just four minutes old, Red Sky Soloist is owned and bred by Linda L. Beck.

to wait for this. It is part of the breeder's responsibility to keep her paperwork current.

3. You should receive a list of vaccinations that the puppy has received and the name of the veterinarian who has given them. Some breeders vaccinate their own puppies, but you should receive a document stating when the vaccinations were given and which pharmaceuticals were used. In addition, you should receive a document stating when and if the puppies were wormed and which medications were given. If the puppies were examined by a veterinarian, there should be a certificate of health provided by the examining doctor.

4. Several genetic problems may occur in the Irish Setter breed. Ethical breeders address these problems up front and will provide proof that the parents have received health clearances for those genetic diseases for which there are scientific tests. In addition, the ISCA annually publishes a Breeders' Directory. Breeders who are listed must sign a Principles of Integrity statement in order to be entered.

5. The breeder should recommend that you take the puppy to a veterinarian of your choice within a specific time. Usually, 48 hours from the time of purchase is considered reasonable. If, at that time, the puppy is found to be ill or to have some visible defect, the breeder should be willing to take the puppy back and issue a refund.

6. You should receive a guarantee in writing that the puppy is healthy and free of known defects at the time of purchase.

7. The breeder should state in writing that she will take the puppy back if the buyer is unable to keep him, or that she will do her utmost to place the puppy in another home within a reasonable time.

What the Breeder Expects from You

Just as you have reasonable expectations as a buyer when you go to purchase a puppy, the breeder, who has put so much heart and soul into this litter, has the right to expect certain things from you:

1. If the breeder has suggested that you follow a certain regimen in raising the puppy, you should abide by those suggestions concerning feeding, grooming, and exercise to the utmost of your ability. It is always advisable to consult with your veterinarian about this.

When you adopt an Irish Setter, your family should be prepared to care for the dog for his entire lifetime.

2. The breeder has the right to expect you to keep the puppy clean and healthy.

3. If you agreed to have the puppy altered, you are obligated to do so within a reasonable time. Six to nine months is usually considered the norm.

4. The breeder has the right to expect that you have represented yourselves and your family honestly regarding your ability to care for this animal.

5. The breeder has the right to expect that you will come back for advice if you have a problem you cannot solve. Most breeders are willing and happy to help you if there are things you do not know.

6. If you have signed a breeding contract that governs how and when a bitch or dog will be bred, you are bound to abide by that contract. It is important to a breeder that puppies they produce are, in turn, bred to improve the line. It is for this reason that many breeders sell puppies, particularly bitch puppies, with strings attached. You should know what the conditions are, and the breeder should explain them to you thoroughly before any contract of purchase is signed.

Co-Ownerships

Many breeders like to co-own their show stock so that they can have a voice in the show career and breeding potential of that dog. There are many kinds of co-ownerships, and the responsible breeder will explain the details to you before you buy your puppy. There are also many pitfalls to co-ownerships, so the buyer needs to understand thoroughly what is involved. Co-ownerships are a little like marriage. You and the other owner(s) must like each other and know each other very well before engaging in any complicated arrangements. Co-ownerships work best when the details are thoroughly understood and all parties have the same expectations.

If you, as a puppy buyer, have doubts about co-ownerships, but you really want to buy from a particular breeder, a limited-time agreement sometimes works best. That way both of you can evaluate one another to see if this "marriage" will work. Such a contract would continue through the first litter or until the dog is mature and shows his worth as a show dog. You can then decide whether to terminate the contract or continue with it if both parties are satisfied.

Breeding contracts involve knowing who pays the stud fees and who pays for the care of the bitch. Who gets the stud fees, if a male is involved? Which puppies from a litter is the breeder entitled to receive as part of the co-ownership contract? Will the breeding contract extend for more than the first litter, and if so, for how long?

In addition to breeding rights, co-ownerships can often involve the show career of an animal. It is important to know what the expectations of the breeders might be if the dog turns out to be show quality. Financial responsibilities are an important part of a show contract. Who pays for what? Some expenses include entry fees, handling fees (if a professional handler is involved), advertising fees, and many other expenditures involved in showing a dog to his championship or beyond.

The same type of co-ownerships can occur with dogs bred for field trialing. It is essential to know up front what costs the breeder expects the buyer to pay. Training and handling a dog in the field can be a very expensive hobby.

Whatever arrangements are made, they should be clearly spelled out in writing before the puppy is bought. Doing this may not avoid all co-ownership problems, but they can certainly be minimized if both parties enter into a written agreement in good faith.

Where to Find Your Irish Setter

Deciding where to look for an Irish Setter can be quite a challenge. Irish Setters have become relatively rare in many parts of the country, and you may have to search long and hard to find one. Any dedicated owner and breeder will tell you they are worth the wait. A good place to start with is at the AKC. You can either call for information or you can access their Web site at www.akc.org and go from there to a link to the ISCA. The ISCA has its own Web site, irishsetterclub.org, which contains lots of useful information. Both methods will put you in touch with officers of the club or regional directors who can advise you about where to look for a puppy.

If you are interested in finding an older dog in need of a good home, most local Irish Setter clubs have rescue services, and the ISCA also has a rescue service that keeps track of animals needing new homes.

The AKC also has a list of dog shows and obedience trials that are held throughout the country all year long. Going to a show is a good way to meet Irish Setter owners and see the dogs that live in your area. Some shows draw exhibitors from many states, but most of them are fairly local and can direct you to breeders in the region.

Once you find one or more breeders that you like, you may have to put your name on a waiting list, because it is not likely that you will find just the right puppy at just the right age the first time you inquire.

There is no doubt that however long it takes to find that special addition to your family, it will be worth the wait. When you consider that an Irish Setter will be part of your family for at least a dozen years, a few months of anticipation will only make the new arrival that much sweeter. There is nothing like a fun-loving redheaded puppy to enliven your life and brighten your days.

If your family doesn't have the time to care for a puppy, an adult dog from a breeder or rescue group may be a perfect choice. This beautiful mother and child are owned by Pat Cox.

The Growing Puppy

Irish Setter puppies go through dramatic stages of growth. The average puppy weighs between 12 ounces and a pound at birth, and within 2 weeks, if he is healthy and well nourished, he will double his weight and size. He will continue to gain steadily, with the majority of his growth occurring in the first six months. Puppies will continue to grow at a slower rate until they are 11 months to a year of age. By that time, most will have attained their full height, but they will still look like gawky teens. They will not achieve full maturity of bone, muscle, rib spring, and head configuration until they are about two years old. Some lines mature faster than others. At two, some are totally mature. Other lines develop much more slowly, and it is not uncommon for males, especially, to reach three years of age before they appear to be adults. Females mature faster, and if they come into their first heat before a year of age, which many do, that process hastens maturity.

Buying and owning an Irish Setter puppy has its wonderful moments, but it also can have its trying ones. It's like raising a child and seeing him through the "terrible twos" and all the years until maturity. With a puppy, however, you don't have to send him to college, and it takes much less time to see him mature into a delightful adult.

Red Barn Her Nibs Georgia Gibbs, owned by Karolynne McAteer, at five weeks of age.

Georgia at six weeks of age.

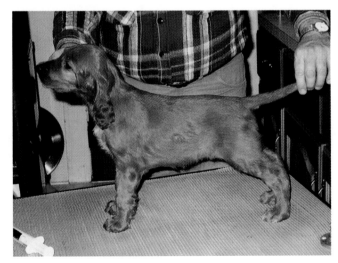

Georgia at eight weeks of age.

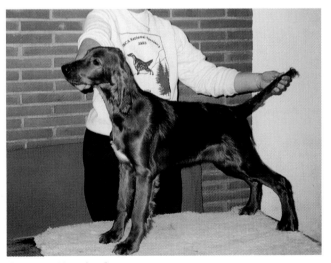

Georgia at 16 weeks of age.

ISGR—A Breeder's Tool

Sandy Novocin

The Past and the Present

ISGR stands for the Irish Setter Genetic Registry. The registry has been around for more than 20 years. Its purpose is to aid breeders in their efforts to follow a standardized method of test breeding or in documenting the steps that have been taken to verify that each Irish Setter is genetically clear of progressive retinal atrophy (PRA).

Today, Irish Setter breeders are lucky in that they can take their dog to the veterinarian and send a blood sample to the testing site. The testing site will determine if the dog has PRA, carries the gene for PRA, or is genetically clear. Ten years ago, if the breeder wanted to know that information, he or she had to breed the dog to a dog with PRA, keep the pups until four months of age (although some did histological studies that required the pups to be put down at six weeks), then take the pups to a board-certified ophthalmologist, who examined the pups to determine if they showed signs of PRA. To top this off, there had to be at least six pups in a litter for the litter to qualify for a complete test-breeding. In other words, some people had to do this twice. This whole procedure was expensive, both monetarily and emotionally, and the techniques used for diagnosis were not failsafe.

If the dog passed this test-breeding and the breeder followed all procedures set down by the Irish Setter Genetic Registry, then the dog was issued a number. If two test-mated dogs were bred together, the offspring were also eligible to be registered, and so forth down the line. PRA is carried in a recessive gene. If the parents did not carry the gene, then the offspring would not carry it either.

The advent of the blood test did present two problems—the early blood tests were expensive, and the registry that was registering the dogs would only issue numbers to dogs that were actually blood-tested. But for those that had done the test-matings in the past, the expense was still less. You did not have to locate a blind male or female and pay to lease it. You did not have to whelp the litter and hope there were no problems. You did not have to raise the pups until they were four months old and give them all the same love and health care as your others. You did not have to travel to the specialist and pay the specialist's fee for examining the entire litter, and you did not have to keep the pups until you found suitable pet homes for the pups, which were all carriers because one parent carried the gene.

The ISGR considered the possibility that it was no longer needed until it looked at the situation from the breeder's point of view. A breeder wants to know what is behind their dog and that what is said can be verified. Since CERF (Canine Eye Registry Foundation) only gives numbers to actual blood-tested dogs, the offspring had no proof of their background—and the descendants farther down the line had even less proof. People were selling their pups and claiming they were from genetically clear backgrounds. Some of these puppy buyers wanted proof. They wanted to be able to register their dog with a registry to verify that their dog had come from those genetically clear lines. And if they were breeding, they wanted to sell their pups so that they could also claim they were from genetically clear lines and have the paperwork to back it up.

277

After considering the breed as a whole and the offspring of these blood-tested Irish Setters, the ISGR made the decision to keep functioning. We made a few changes and incorporated the blood-tested Irish Setters into our registry by giving them the same status as test-bred dogs. That means that if these breeders registered their blood-tested dog, we would also give their offspring a number if both parents were blood-tested or from test-mated ancestry. We also altered our numbers so that we could keep track of which system was used for each dog entering the registry, whether it was from a blood test or a test-mating: GT refers to gene-tested, while TM refers to test-mated. We added an "A" after each to include the word Ancestry (e.g., GTA = Gene-Tested Ancestry).

The Future

The breeders of today can help the breeders of tomorrow. When breeders do the blood test, they are automatically given a permanent number from CERF (that is part of your fee when you do the test). The ISGR is not part of CERF. It is a separate entity, although CERF does send us a list of dogs that pass the blood test so that we can verify each dog that wants to become part of our registry. If you want to join the ISGR registry, there is a small fee for each blood-tested dog and his or her offspring.

The ISGR is beginning to see problems facing newer breeders who want to register their pups. They have been told that their line is genetically clear, but they don't have any verification. They sometimes have to go back two or three generations to contact people who never registered with the ISGR. Then they have to move down the pedigree and see if they can get all the others involved to register so they can give their puppies numbers.

Not everyone needs to register with the ISGR, but if you are using your dog for public stud, it certainly would be of great benefit to the people that use him to be able to have the option to register his offspring if they wish. Any top stud dog or foundation bitch should have the blood test done, because they can influence the breed so easily. We do not need to blood-test every dog if we can follow the genetic path of his ancestors. The ISGR allows you and your puppy buyers, the next generation of breeders, to do this.

ISGR is a tool for you, as a breeder, to use. Whether to use this tool is up to each individual.

Irish Setter Rescue

Marilee Larson, ISCA Rescue Chairperson

The Irish Setter Rescue became a part of the ISCA in 1992. Prior to that, local clubs and individuals handled rescue situations independently, with one exception. For years, Nonda Jones in Ohio tried to help as many Irish in the Midwest and on the East Coast as she could on her own. She was the forerunner of a national rescue service.

When we started, the first goal was to get a rescue volunteer in every state and for all the volunteers to be on the same track. We encouraged volunteers to use adoption contracts, to spay and neuter all dogs, to check out potential new homes, to secure foster homes, to find veterinarians to work for reduced fees for the rescue dogs, and to charge an adoption fee for each adoption. Money was raised through raffles and donations to get a fund started to help the rescue volunteers that did not have a local club to help them. The monies in the ISCA rescue fund can only be used for veterinary bills or boarding expenses. We now have at least one rescue volunteer in all but two states. Those two states are covered by volunteers in neighboring states.

The ISCA has one national coordinator who keeps a list of all the dogs that need homes and of homes willing to take in rescue dogs. This information is passed on to the local rescue groups in hopes that a match can be made. The local Irish Setter Clubs and their rescue volunteers are the backbone of ISCA rescue. Without their hard work—driving miles to pick up a dog, finding veterinarians who will work at discounted prices, and having foster homes in which to place these dogs until new homes can be found—we would not be as successful as we are. The Internet has been a wonderful tool for all of us to keep in touch about the location of rescue dogs and possible homes. We are listed with the AKC and we are on the ISCA web page.

Rescue obtains dogs in many ways. They come from animal shelters as strays or "owner surrenders," from owners who can no longer keep the dogs, and from breeders who have taken a dog back and come to us to help find a home for the dog. Irish Setters are not for everyone. People see these cute red puppies and expect them to grow into wonderful dogs without any training. They put them in the backyard and expect them to turn out to be perfect adults. This does not work. Irish Setters need to be part of the family; a house dog. They need a gentle but firm hand. Most of our adoption homes have had Irish before and they know just what to do to get that rescue to become a good canine citizen. Most of the people we have heard from say that their rescue dogs are the best they have ever had.

Once a dog is placed, it does not necessarily mean that that is the last we see of the new owners. Some clubs offer one-year memberships and invite the families and their dogs to club events. They participate in St. Patrick's Day parades, hospital visits, club picnics, training, and information events. At their local specialties, some clubs offer a rescue parade where the dogs and their families are introduced and a ribbon is bestowed on the dog. The dogs seem to know that they are in the limelight, and they show off as if they were seasoned show dogs. The ISCA now offers a rescue parade at the National Specialty. Because the show is held in different regions of the country each year, everyone has a chance to participate.

Rescued Irish Setters and their owners frequently assemble at specialty shows for rescue parades. This parade was held by the Irish Setter Club of the Pacific.

Almost none of the dogs we rescue come with registration papers. For most people, that is fine. But for some who would like to compete in different events with their dogs, it can be a problem. The AKC has realized that purebred rescue has become popular, so now one may apply for an Indefinite Listing Privilege (ILP) number. This does not allow the dog to be bred, but he is registered so that the dog's accomplishments in obedience, field, or other performance events can be recorded. An ILP dog must be spayed or neutered to qualify for a number.

For example, Marion Pahy is a longtime member and officer of the ISCA. Not too long ago, Marion thought her dog-owning days were over. Many of her friends in

San Antonio, Texas, knew she was devastated after the loss of the last of her Irish Setters in mid-1994, but no one quite knew how to console her. Then, suddenly, a small bundle of red fur came on the scene. At the age of 12 weeks, "Cinnamon" was found on the side of the road. Since Marion is very active in rescue, it was not surprising that the dog was brought to her attention. Marion fell instantly in love with this redhead and decided to endure the agonies of raising yet another energetic puppy.

Marion applied for and received an ILP number, and in the tradition of all her previous dogs, named her Faith Farm Cinnamon Toast. Marion is an avid lover of

Marion Pahy with Faith Farm Cinnamon Toast JH, an Irish Setter that was rescued from a roadside at the age of 12 weeks. "Cinnamon" became the first Irish Setter with an Indefinite Listing Privilege (ILP) number to receive the Junior Hunter title.

Kilban's Kimage JH CGC, or "Keri," was adopted by foster parents Rick and Chris Cerelli.

hunting and field trials, and because Cinnamon was now registered with the AKC, she could compete in Hunting Tests. In a two-month period, Cinnamon passed all four tests required to become a Junior Hunter. She became the first Irish Setter with an ILP number in the country to receive this title and the first Junior Hunter Irish Setter in Texas.

Then there is "Keri," who came to the rescue group in California. He was placed in a foster home with Rick and Chris Cerelli, who were to bring him to an adoption day where a family was expected to come and adopt him. He had spent several days with Rick and Chris, and it became obvious on the appointed day that Rick and Keri had developed quite an attachment to one another. All of a sudden, Keri's adoption papers were "missing," and Rick finally had to confess that he had them. Keri went home to live with Rick and Chris and their two other Irish. Because the other dogs were show dogs, Rick wanted to

be able to do things with Keri, too. They applied for and received his ILP listing, and Keri became Kilban's Kimage JH CGC. Rick and Chris are still involved with rescue and have adopted another dog that would have been almost impossible to place. "Scarlett" is very advanced in age and could hardly get around. With the love and care she has received from the Cerellis, she has a new lease on life.

Rick and Chris were also the foster parents for "Buddy." Buddy was a dog with very special needs. Not only was he older, but he was also blind. He had ear infections and embedded foxtails in his feet. His coat was a mess. After a few trips to the veterinarian and lots of love and care, he was ready to be adopted. A home for an old, blind dog is not easy to find, but a retired couple looking for that special case answered the prayer. Buddy went to live in the Santa Cruz mountains and quickly adjusted to his new home. He knows his way around the house and yard, and because of the advanced age of his new owner, Buddy goes for walks with a young neighbor. As long as he stays by her leg, he can jog right along.

The Irish we rescue come in ages from puppies to 11 years. We are sure they all have their sad stories to tell, but fortunately most wind up with happy endings, like "Rusty" in Illinois. He was placed with a family that had a two-year-old son with cerebral palsy. Rusty became this

Scarlett Missy O'Hara CGC, an elderly Irish Setter adopted by Rick and Chris Cerelli, has a new lease on life thanks to Irish Setter Rescue.

boy's balancing act, allowing the youngster to ride him like a pony.

Then there is "Rosie," a very high-energy dog. A call came from a woman who ran a retirement home for six elderly and fragile women. We really thought that Rosie was too active for this placement, but the woman insisted that she would be just fine. Rosie became Miss Dignified. She knew that her job was to be a companion to these special ladies. They all loved her so—in fact, one of the ladies who would not participate with other residents really came out of her shell when Rosie arrived.

One of the oldest dogs we placed is "Dodger," who was in foster care for many months. Here is his story, as told by his new family: "Cailan has a new friend and almost constant companion, an 11-year-old Irish Setter named Dodger. Cailan, although in most ways a typical 13-year-old, was born with spina bifida. Having this birth defect has affected Cailan in many ways. He has undergone 23 surgeries and relies on a wheelchair for mobility. His opportunities for socialization are limited because the homes of his friends are not handicapped-accessible. He

is not able to play on sports teams with his friends. Some time ago, we saw a picture of an Irish Setter in our weekly newspaper, with a short story stating that the dog was up for adoption through the Irish Setter Rescue League. This caught my husband's eye, since he raised and showed Irish Setters as a teenager. We called the Rescue League, but they had placed the dog in the ad. After several weeks, Dodger entered the rescue system, and when we went to pick him up, Dodger decided almost from the first minute that he was going to be Cailan's dog. Dodger sleeps next to Cailan's bed, will only eat and take treats from him, and constantly follows him around the house.

"When Cailan is not home, Dodger lies beside the front door waiting for him to come back. On school days, Dodger accompanies us to the school bus so that he can watch Cailan get on and off. When Cailan went to summer camp, Dodger was most unhappy until he returned. He protects Cailan from possible harm by putting himself between other children and his boy if he perceives a threat. He has learned that baseball is all right for Cailan to play.

"The addition of Dodger to the family has had a very beneficial effect on the boy. He takes the dog for walks, feeds him, brushes him, and even takes him to the veterinarian. Most important, he has made Cailan happy and increased his self-esteem and sense of independence."

Elizabeth Michaud, another rescue volunteer, has this story to tell: "In 1992, we received a call from the local humane society about a seven-year-old male that had been turned in, complete with original blue slip and a copy of the pedigree by his owners. My husband and I went to take a look. The dog was a pitiful sight. He was a tall male with protruding hip bones and a coat that was completed matted to the skin. He was very subdued and quite disinterested in us. We decided we had to do something for this dog.

"A friend arrived at the house with grooming tools. We had to shave most of his body to remove the mats. He stood patiently on the grooming table while we worked. He was quiet, but not intimidated by our household of Irish Setters and German Shorthaired Pointers. The dog's name was 'Rowdy,' so blatantly inappropriate that we immediately renamed him 'Rusty.'

"I contacted the owner, who said the dog barked all the time and wasn't clean in the house, so he lived in the garage. He was willing to let the dog go and had even asked the humane society to contact our rescue.

"We took Rusty to the veterinarian who found he weighed only 49 pounds but declared him to be basically healthy. He warned us to increase his food intake gradually. Rusty was a perfect gentleman in the house. Within a week, his Irish spirit returned, and he took every opportunity to tell us how happy he was. It was obvious Rusty had come to stay. He loves us passionately and, quite obviously, we reciprocate. Rusty is not an 'extra' dog. He is our gift from the rescue gods and we are grateful."

From North Carolina and Texas rescue, we have the following story: "My husband and I came to California from South Africa with our 14-year-old Irish Setter whom we had adopted when she was 9 months old. We lost her when she was 15. When we relocated to Atlanta and bought our home, we decided to get another Irish Setter, so we contacted the rescue program in North Carolina. Since there was nothing available locally, Claudia, the rescue person, contacted clubs in Florida and Texas. The rescue in Texas had three Irish, and within three days we drove from Atlanta to Houston to the foster home where the dogs were being housed. 'Paddy' took to my husband, sitting right at his feet. We passed muster with the foster parents, who welcomed us as if we were long-lost friends. They decided we would be good to Paddy, and she came home with us. She loves to come on the boat water-skiing, and we always take her for long walks in the forest. Our family is now, once again, complete.

"We want to thank the people involved in Irish Setter Rescue for what they do and all their help in making this story possible."

"Little Orphan Annie" was in the care of the Irish Setter Club of Western New York rescue. She was in sad shape, very thin and matted, and had a huge cyst on her back. She spent three weeks with her foster parents getting back in shape. When she was healthy, a home was found for her in North Carolina. It took Annie a long time to recuperate fully, but she has adjusted to her new home with three other Irish Setters to play with and squirrels to chase. Not only did Annie get a wonderful home, the rescue got a wonderful volunteer. Her owner Judy is there to help with whatever is needed.

The next story is told by "Rocky" and "Brandy," as told to their owner: "Hi! My name is Brandy. My original owners wanted to put me to sleep when I turned four years old. I don't know why, nor do I even know what they really meant. They kept me in the bathroom but did take me outside for walks. A man working on their house said he would find a good home for me. He brought me to his house, and although they looked for a home, the wife decided to keep me. She let me sleep in her bed and even took me to the park twice a day. When it got hot, she taught me how to swim by coming right into the water with me. We have so much fun together; this sure is better than living in a bathroom.

"About four years after I arrived, my folks decided to get a playmate for me. They contacted Irish Setter Rescue

Annie was in sad shape when she was rescued, but she is now thriving in her new North Carolina home.

in Connecticut, who had just the right dog for us. He was a really big dog named 'Spike.' He was huge, but skin and bones. He had been in the pound twice, was covered with burrs, and full of worms. My folks changed his name to Rocky, and they worked hard to get him in shape. Now we hunt quail, march in parades, and go to shows. We sure like staying in hotels."

Brandy and Rocky are wonderful examples of the need for rescue. Because of them, their owners Phil and Dana Cuchiaro have become one of our most active rescue volunteers.

A rescue story by Nancy Conner follows: "In April, I received a call about a six-year-old purebred Irish Setter male hit by a car who suffered multiple breaks in a hind leg. After getting a very high quote on the cost of treatment, the owners gave the shelter instructions to put him down. The shelter worker called me to ask if our rescue effort would be interested or able to take care of this dog. She said he was a very sweet dog and otherwise

"Rocky" Cuchiaro, now a contented sports fan, was rescued in very poor physical condition from a Connecticut pound.

healthy. She even offered to help by doing fundraising in her own community to save the dog. She checked with her veterinarian to see if a discount could be offered for the needed surgery.

"The image of that redhead patiently lying there in pain was torture. By morning, I had decided to raise the money in a nationwide campaign if necessary, but we were going to see that he was fixed up. I had already received support from people who heard the story.

"We bought 'Red' some time. The second vet was willing to do the surgery for much less money than the original estimate. Red's family really loved him and somehow found the money to pay off the bill. I feel that just because rescue exists and someone knew other people cared, this Irish Setter's life was saved."

From California, we meet "Darby." Jessie heard about an Irish Setter in need that was with some kind of rescue group. She contacted the group, who refused to give up the dog because they were told he was purebred and therefore valuable. (Irish Setter Rescue does not buy dogs.) Jessie asked to see him, and when she went to the place,

what she saw was beyond belief. There were all kinds of dogs tied all over the property. It was raining, and they had no shelter. Darby was tied to a bush and had dug a hole to keep himself warm. He stood in mud and feces, limping badly on his rear leg. When asked about this, the people said he had jumped a fence and hurt it. They would not give up the dog.

Jessie said, "I could not get this boy out of my mind. So one night a friend and I decided to go back, not really having anything in mind except to help Darby. When we got to the place, the lights were on. We sat for just about a second and jumped out of the pickup and headed for Darby. My friend said, 'What if he bites?' 'He's an Irish!' was my assurance. We unchained Darby and threw him in the truck and took off. Not being thieves at heart, we were both shaking like leaves. Darby was wet and muddy, stinking with mud and feces, but deliriously happy.

"When we were safely away, I called the people and told them I had the dog. His leg was broken, they had given him no aid, and I was ready to press charges. With the threat of the law, and they decided not to pursue this and agreed we could have the dog.

"Darby went into the bathtub immediately and the next day to the veterinarian. He was diagnosed with torn ligaments that had atrophied from neglect. After months of nursing following extensive surgery, Darby went with me to a show and met his future owner, Steve. They bonded at once, and Darby went home with Steve and his other rescue dog."

"Clancy" saw a lot of faces and places in his short life. Born in Kansas and shipped to a store in New Jersey, he was bought by a lady who swore she had a big fenced yard, but really lived in an apartment. When he barked, she tried to get him to run away by opening the door and letting him out. When, by four months old, he wouldn't leave, she found a girl who worked for a veterinarian to take him, give him shots, worm him, and have him neutered. He lived with her family for two weeks, but one more animal was too much, so Clancy was once again looking for a new home. He was driven from New Jersey to Connecticut on one dreary day to be given to a new family. These were Irish Setter people and they knew how to treat a puppy. Clancy finally arrived in a safe and happy home. He doesn't like to ride in cars, though. He probably thinks he'll be taken somewhere else.

Rescue can be a very emotional endeavor. It can also be the most rewarding thing that any of us can do. Taking a dog that most people would give up on and bringing it back to become a wonderful pet says it all. The years of dedication by many people, the tears, the laughs, and the hard work have saved more Irish Setter lives than can be counted. It is our hope that someday we will not need rescue. But until that time, we know that every dog in need will be taken care of. We will always see to it that all of our Irish Setters find wonderful and loving homes. To this end, we are forever committed.

The first National Specialty rescue parade, pictured here, was held in 1998.

The Irish Setter Rescue has a definite list of requirements for rescue chairpeople. There are contracts for those who wish to rescue a dog and for those who are giving up a dog (if they are known). Included here are the guidelines that local rescue systems may adopt for their own use. National Irish Setter Rescue strongly encourages local clubs to follow these guidelines.

Guidelines for Rescue Chairperson

1. The chairperson should maintain all records of dogs needing homes and all homes needing dogs.

2. Get support from your local club for the following:
a) People willing to foster a dog.
b) People willing to check out dogs at local shelters to make sure dogs are purebred, have a good temperament, and are adoptable. Remember, we cannot save them all.
c) Check with local vets to see if they would provide discounts on services for rescue dogs.
d) Be sure all dogs are spayed/neutered and current on all shots before being placed. Puppies too young to alter must be placed with a spay/neuter contract. All reasonable costs should be included in the adoption fees.
e) If there are no foster homes available, check with local boarding kennels. Some of them might board a rescue dog at a reduced rate.
f) If getting a dog that is altered and current on all shots, charge an adoption fee anyway. The adoption fee should be $100.00 to $150.00. *Never* place a dog free of charge.

3. Be sure to list your name as Irish Setter Rescue with your local animal shelter.

4. Be sure to let breeders in your area know about the rescue. They get calls from people who might want an older dog instead of a puppy.

5. Ask local breeders to let you know when they have litters. You will be getting calls from people wanting puppies.

6. Use your local newspaper to place ads. Always put a price in your ad.

7. Network with other rescue groups. They can be of valuable assistance. Keep your National Rescue apprised of dogs that you have for national listings.

8. Start out slow. The ideal way is to have a list of homes waiting. Update your waiting list often so that you know you have a home waiting when that dog comes in.

9. Be sure to drop off the rescue brochures, with your phone number listed, to all shelters and vet offices.

10. Last but not least, when you receive a dog with papers, or you know who the breeder is, be sure to contact them. It is their responsibility to take that dog back or to help in placement. This should also be the first question to ask anyone giving up a dog: Who was the breeder?

For Sale to a Good Home

I was born in the summer a few years ago.
Quite why I was born, I'll never know.
Some folks owned my mother, decided to breed.
No reason I know of except for their greed.
I know I was hungry. I know I was cold.
They sold me quite early, at just five weeks old.
My number one owners seemed friendly at first,
And life was quite good 'til my bubble burst.
They started to argue, their marriage split up.
An ad in the paper read: "For Sale—four-month pup."
Some folks arrived, the next ones in line.
They treated me kindly and life was just fine.
But master dropped dead, and she couldn't cope.
So she sold me again (I'll soon give up hope).
I now had a new home right up in the sky.
We went up in life, 14 floors high!
The new ones were kind but they left me all day.
I was bursting to wee and had nowhere to play.
It was boredom, I think, when I chewed up the chair.
They agreed I should go, as it just wasn't fair.
The next home was good and I thought, "This is it!"
They started to show me and I won, well, a bit.
Then somebody told them that I had "no bone."
So in went the ad: "For sale to a good home."
The next lot were dreadful; they wanted a guard,
But I didn't know how, although I tried hard.
One night they were burgled and I didn't bark.
Tied up in that shed, alone in the dark.
For four months I lay in that cold and dark shed
With only an old paper sack for a bed;
A small dish of water, all slimy and green.
The state I was in, well, it had to be seen.
I longed for destruction, an end to the pain,
But some new people came and I went off again.
Now I'm with rescue, and this home is good.
There's walks in the country and lots of good food.
There's kisses and cuddles to greet me each day.
But I dread the time they will send me away.
For now here I stand, skin and bone on all fours.
Please, don't let "me" happen to any of yours.

The above poem was submitted to the rescue committee by Anna Jones, courtesy of the 1989 Irish Setter Breeders Club Newsletter, England.

Health, Care, and Management

All puppies, like all children, need care and management. Some people think that a puppy can be compared to the average two-year-old child, full of energy and curiosity, ready to soak up all the information he can about the world around him. Puppies go through many stages of development, and the bewildered owner may find that what seems to have been learned one day is forgotten the next.

There are many good books on dog care that will provide the essentials of proper management and basic manners. The breeder from whom you purchase your puppy should be able to provide you with advice and suggestions. From the time a puppy is born, he begins to learn, first about his immediate environment in the whelping box with his mother and siblings, then about the wider world as he begins to explore his surroundings.

Am. Can. Ch. Allegro Farm Quintessence at play, demonstrating why exercise is so important to the health and happiness of each Irish Setter.

Irish Setter puppies, like this seven-week-old Bryfield litter bred by Helen Calvin, are slow to mature and develop. They can still be considered to be puppies at two years of age.

From the time a puppy enters a household, he is gathering impressions. How he is introduced to the family, to children, to other pets, and to the people who will be responsible for his care and well-being can set the tone for the rest of his life.

Each breed of dog has its own characteristics, and raising an Irish Setter presents challenges and subtle differences that are important to understand in order to raise a happy, well-adjusted, and rewarding companion. The Irish Setter is a slow developer. He remains a puppy both mentally and physically until he is at least two years old. He is an energetic dog, full of intelligence and love. He is not generally wild and hardheaded, though at some point in his growth, he may challenge authority, just like a child testing his parents. However, if the dog has learned his place in the household early on, behavioral problems can be eliminated or drastically reduced.

The cute puppy with the beguiling manner certainly wins the hearts of everyone, but it is useful to remember that he is an *Irish* Setter, with the rollicking nature and the gift of "blarney" that he brought from his native land. The picture of the adult dog maturing into a lovely, sedate, and elegant Irish gentleman or lady will not happen without certain critical management techniques.

The single most important thing in raising a happy, well-adjusted Irish Setter is exercise. A fenced yard or a supervised, safe area in which the puppy can get out and run freely several times during the day is essential. This does not mean opening the door and letting the puppy or older dog out to run by himself, annoying the neighbors and possibly getting hit by a passing motorist. It does not mean attaching the dog to a tie-out stake or pulley. Tie-out stakes provide no exercise and maximum frustration for any dog restrained in this manner. The myth

290

that a dog needs to be at liberty to run all day and night should be dispelled. That is simply an excuse for the owner who does not want to take the responsibility of caring for a dog properly. A fenced yard of adequate size for the dog to stretch its legs and run around, with a fence that is high enough to discourage jumping, will simplify the owner's life in managing the Irish Setter. At the same time, a fenced yard will provide the dog with a safe environment in which to grow. If circumstances prevent having a fenced yard, walking the dog several times during the day is essential.

Puppies should never be forced to exercise by roadwork, bicycle, or treadmill. Roadworking an Irish Setter is dangerous and can be cruel to an immature dog. Controlled road exercise can be useful to condition a mature dog for show or field, but it should not be used to compel a growing dog to exercise. Growing bones, joints, and tendons could be permanently damaged by overexertion. The Irish Setter should be allowed to exercise himself until he is at least two years old. Even then, roadwork should never be undertaken on hard surfaces, such as concrete or asphalt.

As in all aspects of training or conditioning, knowing what to do and how to do it will help avoid costly

The Irish Setter should be allowed to exercise himself until he is at least two years old. This litter, owned by Peter and Arlene Pilcer, is keeping busy by playing on the agility ramp.

Sandyhill Stormy Rose, pregnant with a litter of 12, enjoys a float around the pool with her sister, Sandyhill Windy Rose, pushing. Make sure to supervise your Irish Setter's playtime for safety's sake. Owned by Terry A. Moberg.

mistakes. It is best to let your puppy play as hard as he wants for as long as he wants and then let him enjoy uninterrupted sleep. Self-limiting exercise will go a long way toward turning an unruly puppy into an easily manageable pet that is a joy to have around. More dogs are given away or end up in pounds because they are unmanageable than for any other reason. Usually, the owners admit that the dog has been confined for long periods of time without exercise. A family that cannot provide the proper environment for this breed should not own an Irish Setter.

Irish Setters are intelligent and inquisitive. Consequently, they get bored easily. They are companion dogs that like to share time and space with their masters. For this reason, basic obedience is useful for the boisterous redhead to channel his energy. This can be done at home with the help of a good book or video, or at classes especially for puppies called puppy kindergarten classes. If there is a local Irish Setter club or an obedience club near you, its members will get you started.

Even though most people spend a lot of time with their pets, there are occasions when the dog must be left alone. The best way to manage under those circumstances is with a crate. Dogs easily learn to adjust to their crates both at home and while traveling. A crate, however, should not be used as a prison to keep the dog confined for hours at a time while the owner is away. If you must be away for long periods of time, a large exercise pen can be used to confine the dog safely. That said, a crate, whether wire, fiberglass, or wood, is the most useful piece of equipment you can purchase for your dog. It can be his home while you are out, a safe place for confinement while traveling, and his home away from home if you are visiting or at shows or trials. A crate can be invaluable in housetraining because puppies are generally fastidious about keeping their "nest" or sleeping area clean. If a puppy is confined to sleep at night or after exercise and is taken outside immediately after awakening or after eating, housetraining should be a quick and easy task. Common sense, consistency, and routine on the part of the owner will enable the puppy to learn what is expected without any harsh reprimand. The results will be gratifying.

A crate should be large enough for the full-grown dog to stand in, turn around, and lie down comfortably. Puppies should be introduced to the crate by making it a pleasant experience. A soft rug, some toys, and a snack will entice the puppy to go in of his own accord. Most dogs find their crates to be a safe and quiet refuge from the noise and confusion of a household. Many owners put the crate in the bedroom at night so that a new puppy can be secure and out of trouble and yet does not feel abandoned and alone.

Tempted by a chew toy, seven-month-old Kimberlin's Emerald Charm is quiet for the moment. Owned by Kathe and Dale McFarlane.

To accustom a dog to ride in a crate in the car, start with short trips on smooth terrain. Take the dog for enjoyable rides. If the only car trip a dog ever goes on is to the veterinarian for shots, he will soon associate the car with an unpleasant experience. On the other hand, if a trip in the car means going to a park or a shopping center where lots of activity takes place and attention will be paid to him, travel will be associated with a good time. Many puppies get carsick, which has little to do with the length of the trip or the bumpiness of the road. It does have to do with the development of the inner ear, and this condition will resolve itself automatically as the dog matures. However, if bad associations have been established before that, there may be a more difficult time of adjustment. Short rides, even just up and down the driveway, will help the dog overcome the fear of getting sick.

Health Care

It hardly seems necessary to advise anyone to keep a clean dog, yet many pet owners actually never attend to their Irish Setter's ears, nails, skin or internal environment.

Ears

It is essential to keep the ears clean and dry. Because of his long ears that are folded close to the head, the Irish Setter is liable to develop ear infections or pick up parasites such as ear mites. Regular attention to the ears will prevent problems from starting. Ears should be wiped out with a piece of sterile cotton soaked in a cleansing

Your Irish Setter's ears should be cleaned regularly.

agent, such as one of the commercial preparations sold for dogs. Even plain water can be used. The saturated cotton can be wrapped around a finger and inserted gently into the ear. This should be done at least every two weeks. If the ears exude a dark or smelly substance, infection should be suspected and veterinary attention sought.

Nails

Keeping the nails short is essential for both the appearance and comfort of the Irish Setter. Long nails can cause splayed feet and broken-down pasterns. If you start when the puppy is small and maintain a regular schedule of cutting nails—every two weeks, or at least every month—your dog will become accustomed to this routine. Nail cutting is usually a chore that is not welcomed by dogs or owners, but when care is taken not to cut into the quick of the nail, the stress can be minimized. Advice from either a veterinarian or a knowledgeable owner is

Keeping the nails short is essential for both the appearance and comfort of the Irish Setter.

useful to get started. Some dogs' nails are easier to cut than others, but knowing where to snip and how much to take off without hurting the dog is useful information. If a new owner gets practical help the first few times, problems can be avoided. Another technique is the use of a portable nail grinder to file the nails back just in front of the quick.

Skin

The skin of the dog is one of the best indicators of health. Dogs with dry, flaky, scaly skin or oily, smelly skin are showing the outside signs of internal problems. Various kinds of dermatitis have many different causes, some of which are easy to diagnose while others are more difficult. Veterinary care is a must to treat the majority of skin diseases, with the exception of the most common—irritation caused by the presence of fleas. Some Irish Setters are sensitive to fleas. One flea bite can begin all kinds of chronic skin problems in a susceptible dog. Prevention is the key to avoiding misery for the dog and expense for the owner. Simple but rigid and consistent care of the coat and skin and a clean environment can prevent your dog from ever having fleas. Talk to your veterinarian about the best flea control system to use on your dog, in the house, and in the yard. Over-the-counter products are often ineffective and may even cause harm.

Routine bathing and grooming can uncover skin problems and parasites before they can cause too much damage. Owners should observe their dogs carefully. If the dog scratches or chews on himself, it is a safe bet to

Routine grooming can uncover skin problems and parasites before they cause too much damage.

293

assume that fleas or other parasites are present, although allergies can also cause skin problems.

In some areas of the country, ticks present a major problem. There are several kinds of ticks, all carrying different diseases. An epidemic of a tick-borne disease called Lyme disease has occurred in several regions. Ticks can be detected by close examination, although one variety, the deer tick, is so small as to be almost invisible. Lyme disease can cause fever, lameness, and general malaise. It is very responsive to antibiotic treatment, especially if treated early. If you live in an area infested with Lyme-carrying deer ticks, dogs should be examined daily during the warm months. If symptoms appear, a veterinarian should be consulted. Discuss with your veterinarian the benefits and drawbacks of vaccination against Lyme disease.

Internal Parasites

Internal parasites are a major concern for dog owners in most parts of the country. Roundworms are particularly prevalent in puppies. Hookworms and whipworms are two other debilitating and sometimes fatal intestinal parasites. Your Irish Setter should be checked periodically for worms—annually at least, but preferably every six months, especially if the dog has been out of his home territory. Two stool samples should be taken to your veterinarian for examination under a microscope. Worm eggs do not appear in every fecal sample, so you have a better chance of getting an accurate diagnosis with two. If worm eggs are found, the dog should be given appropriate medication. Do not use over-the-counter worming pills, and only treat for the specific parasite that has infested your dog.

In addition to the most common intestinal parasites, puppies and adult dogs should be tested for the presence of heartworm. This is done with a blood test, usually in the spring. Heartworm is a devastating disease that is transmitted by the bite of mosquitoes, but it is easily prevented with the administration of daily or monthly heartworm medication. Even dogs on a year-round preventive regimen should be tested annually.

Diet

The diet of a growing puppy, as well as of the adult Irish Setter, is very important in maintaining optimum health. A good, balanced commercial diet is best for your dog. Some breeders and owners prefer to cook their own diets, and that is perfectly fine as long as the diets contain all the necessary vitamins, minerals, and trace elements needed to maintain a healthy dog. Irish Setter puppies should be firm, solid, and sturdy, without being fat. They should be fed a diet that will help them maintain a steady

Crunchy treats along with regular dental cleaning can help prevent the buildup of tartar. Here, Ch. Sallynoggin the Graduate CD and her babies, owned by Marsha Henkel, enjoy a chew.

growth pattern without the addition of supplements, especially calcium. Some Irish Setters go through a skinny, gangly stage in which they appear to be all bones and yet seem to eat practically nothing. Once you have determined that your puppy is in good health and free from parasites, feeding him a high-quality diet and providing plenty of water and exercise will ensure that he will go through the various stages of development with little trouble. The "diet wars" among the dog food companies can be very confusing for the average dog owner. Once you find a diet that works for your dog, it is best to stick with it. You can tell if the dog is getting what he needs from his diet by the shine and texture of the coat, the elasticity of the skin, and the firmness of the body. Diet and exercise go together in maintaining optimum health for your dog.

Another important aspect of good health is care of the teeth. Because dogs no longer get their food by chewing bones and tearing meat, the modern dog does not eat the type of diet that scrubs the teeth clean of tartar. Dogs are just as prone to gingivitis and other gum and tooth diseases as humans. They don't develop cavities, however. A regimen of regular brushing, using either a toothbrush or a finger covered with a washcloth, will help prevent the buildup of tartar. Crunchy treats or biscuits can also help, but most dogs will not chew enough of those to prevent all tartar from developing.

Health Problems

Owners of Irish Setters should be aware that there are certain problems that occur in the breed. Some are genetic, and others appear to be familial in nature. Some are associated with large, fast-growing breeds. Among these are diseases of the bones and joints. Hyperosteodystrophy (HOD) affects the joints, especially

An Irish Setter with healthy joints can remain active well into old age. Ch. Courtwood Easy Living AX AD CGC, nine years young, enjoys the agility weave poles. Owned by Linda Schindler.

the carpal, stifle, elbow, and shoulders of growing puppies, usually from the age of three months to seven months. It is characterized by extreme pain, high fever, and sudden onset. Puppies who show any of the symptoms should be treated immediately and vigorously by a veterinarian. Other bone and cartilage diseases are panosteitis and osteochondritis dissecans (OCD). The former is a self-limiting disease, sometimes called "shifting leg lameness." The latter is a genetically predisposed disease of the cartilage that often requires corrective surgery.

Hip dysplasia is a malformation of the hip joints that is found in many large-breed dogs. It is a progressive disease that can be identified fairly early. In one test, called the PennHIP™ method, predisposition to hip dysplasia can be detected as early as four months of age. In another, radiographs taken at six months can give an indication of whether a dog will develop the disease later in life. Although the mode of inheritance is unclear and many factors appear to be involved in the development of hip dysplasia, breeding dogs with normal hip conformation

from families with a history of normal hips gives greater assurance that the offspring will be free of this disease. The Orthopedic Foundation for Animals (OFA) in Columbia, Missouri, is a registry body that will certify hips by reading radiographs sent to them from veterinarians. Many breeders rely on OFA certification or on the diagnosis of PennHIP™ specialists to determine the breeding potential of their dogs.

Progressive retinal atrophy (PRA) is an eye disease that is carried recessively (meaning that both parents must carry the gene for the defect that causes the disease) which causes Irish Setters, as well as other breeds, to go blind. Fortunately for Irish Setter owners and breeders, a DNA test exists that can determine whether a dog is normal, is a carrier, or will be afflicted with PRA. After years of scientific research supported by the Irish Setter Club of America, the test was developed so that no Irish Setter need be born with the risk of blindness.

Idiopathic epilepsy is a disease found in Irish Setters. It usually occurs between the ages of 18 months and 2 years, although younger and older dogs have been known to develop it. The mode of inheritance is unknown at this point, but genetic research, supported by the Irish Setter Club of America and other organizations, has begun with the hope that the genetic structure of this disease will be found so that it can be eliminated from the breeding pool, just as PRA has been.

Globoid cell leukodystrophy is a wasting disease that seems to affect a small number of related Irish Setters. It has been shown to be an autosomal-recessive disease (two parents required) and appears as a neurological syndrome as early as six weeks of age. It has not been identified as a widespread problem in the breed, and a test exists to determine carriers of this disease.

Gastric dilatation volvulus (GDV), also known as bloat, is a sudden-onset, often fatal disease in which the stomach fills with gas and rotates in the abdomen, cutting off the blood supply to the stomach and surrounding organs. Irish Setters, along with many other large-breed dogs, are prone to bloat. There appears to be a familial relationship, but no direct genetic link has been found. Symptoms of bloat are restlessness, attempting to vomit or defecate without success, and swelling of the abdomen. In advanced cases, a tap on the side will sound and feel like a drum. The animal often paces, tries to lie down, and immediately gets up because of the discomfort. Bloat is a medical emergency. It must be treated immediately by a veterinarian. The Irish Setter Club of America has supported a large research project on this disease at Purdue University School of Veterinary Medicine. Eleven other breeds are involved, and the results of the study are available from Purdue.

Older dogs may sleep more and need less exercise. Pictured is Ch. Courtwood Book Mark, owned by Bob Iversen.

Hypothyroidism is a common disease of Irish Setters. Symptoms are usually mild and can be detected early—dry skin, poor hair quality, lethargy, weight gain, and sometimes irregular heat seasons in bitches or lack of libido in males. Blood tests are available to determine whether the dog has this deficiency and how much medication should be given to correct it. It is assumed to have a hereditary component, but the mode of inheritance is unknown. If it is undiagnosed, more severe but less obvious symptoms might be present.

Allergies often accompany hypothyroidism, but not always. Allergies often take the form of skin diseases and irritations. Food allergies, especially intolerance of wheat products, are sometimes seen. Allergies can be controlled in many cases, but never cured. There is a genetic component to many allergy-prone dogs.

Temperament abnormalities are not a disease, but there is a hereditary predisposition toward a certain temperament. Environment plays a large role in how a puppy develops, but basic traits are transmitted from parents to offspring. Shyness, excessive timidity, and fear are traits that can be inherited. Aggressiveness is another inheritable and undesirable trait in the Irish Setter. Hyperactivity, extreme nervousness, and flightiness are other traits that may have medical origins but may also be genetic. Only by eliminating animals that display these traits from breeding programs can they be bred out. It is absolutely essential to preserve the good nature of the Irish Setter by using only dogs and bitches with good, sound, typically Irish temperaments for breeding. One must always keep in mind that for a family pet and hunting companion, a friendly, outgoing nature is the hallmark of the breed.

Fortunately for the Irish Setter, these afflictions are only in the minority, but breeders, owners, and buyers of the breed should be aware that they exist and that dedicated breeders are committed to eradicating them.

The Older Dog

With good care, exercise, and a sound genetic background, the Irish Setter can enjoy a long, healthy life. Statistics show that the average life span of an Irish Setter is 10 to 12 years. However, dogs of 14 and 15 years of age are not

With good care, exercise, and a sound genetic background, the Irish Setter can enjoy a long, healthy life. Mandy, owned by Kathe and Dale McFarlane, is a happy senior citizen at 19 years of age.

veterinary products that can help them live long and happy lives. A large-breed dog like the Irish Setter is considered to be a senior citizen at about the age of eight. At that time, it is useful to have a complete physical checkup of the dog to determine baseline health concerns. Many dogs begin to show signs of slowing down, possibly due to arthritis in the joints or spine, or possibly just because the metabolism of the geriatric dog is slower.

Care of the teeth in the older dog can play a major role in his health. Dentistry is extremely important, and regularly scheduled cleaning by your veterinarian can prevent infection and tooth decay.

Adjustments to the diet might be needed as the dog sleeps more and exercises less. It is not always advisable to change a diet that has worked well over the life of the dog, but feeding less might keep his weight in check.

As important as keeping the dog in good physical health is to keep him active mentally. Walks or rides in the car become especially important to the older dog. Stimulation and enthusiasm for life keep older dogs young. Many outstanding dogs have continued their activities well into their senior years. One of the outstanding field trial champions attained her title at the age of nine, and one of our agility dogs was flying through the hoops at the age of ten. In the absence of life-threatening diseases, such as cancer, which affects all breeds, the quality of life of the older Irish Setter can be maintained with good mental and physical habits. No faithful Irish Setter should be condemned to a life home alone when the family leaves for a pleasant outing.

Older dogs have earned a special place in our hearts. They have given us their best years, and their offspring carry on their tradition. They have brought up our children and our grandchildren. They have taught us wisdom and patience. They deserve the same from us.

uncommon in this breed. They age gracefully, especially if their owners are attentive to geriatric problems that might arise. Dogs are prone to the same types of aging diseases as humans, but fortunately, there are many

Grooming
the
Irish Setter

The Irish Setter is a dog that requires a moderate amount of grooming to keep his coat healthy, shiny, and free of mats and tangles. Whether you keep your Irish as a pet or a show dog should make little difference in your devotion to his good care. Show dogs require more careful attention to trimming and brushing than a pet, but beyond these considerations, the conditioning, which includes exercising, bathing, and veterinary care, is the same.

Not all Irish Setter coats are alike. Some are flat with a moderate amount of undercoat that requires a modest effort to maintain. Others inherit a profuse coat with a short, thick, soft undercoat. For the dog to be properly groomed, this should be stripped out so that the top coat lies flat. Any animal that is kept in optimum condition and trimmed to conform to breed type provides visual pleasure. No matter what grooming products or practices are employed, the goal remains the same. The dog should look as natural as possible without a shaved appearance. The ultimate compliment is having someone remark, "Isn't it nice you don't have to trim that dog?" If you have just spent four hours to achieve the natural look, you may join the ranks of expert groomers.

Grooming for Show

Grooming the Irish Setter for show requires knowledge of the standard for the breed and the correct use of various types of scissors, strippers, brushes, combs, conditioners, and shampoos. Those who intend to take their dogs into the show ring will require more hands-on experience than can be presented in this book, plus the help of a talented exhibitor or professional handler. There are many ways to groom an Irish Setter for show. The techniques presented here are one way to achieve the desired effect. Most pet groomers do not know how to deal with an Irish Setter coat, and if a professional groomer is the only option, be sure that you go to one that understands the techniques of proper trimming and grooming for this breed. Good grooming can never turn a poor or even an average specimen into an outstanding one, but an average dog in optimum condition with every hair in place can and does, on occasion, defeat a superior animal shown in poor condition.

Knowledge of the standard and the ability to accurately and objectively evaluate one's own dog is necessary to trim him properly for the show ring. Trimming can enhance the strengths and minimize the weaknesses of some structural aspects of the dog. Grooming will not hide all faults, but various techniques can camouflage them and draw the eye to the best parts of the animal.

Grooming is a slow process that must be practiced in order to achieve the desired results. A last-minute swoosh with clippers and brush will never produce the finished results of trimming done in stages over a period of weeks. Novices, in particular, should not attempt to use electric clippers or sharp-edged scissors just before a show. Mistakes are bound to happen, some of them resulting in the dog appearing as if he were trimmed with a hedge clipper. Practice well ahead of any public appearance in order to give the hair time to grow back in. Also, no amount of grooming and bathing will correct problems that result from poor health and maintenance. Most coat problems come from the inside and are related to parasites, hormone imbalance, allergies (often flea-related), poor diet, lack of exercise, or improper routine care.

A word about puppy coats is appropriate here. Irish Setter puppies are born with short, blondish coats. Some are flat, with little "fuzz." Others are furry almost from birth. The dark mahogany color of the mature dog starts to appear as a stripe down the back at about eight weeks. The whole coat changes two or three times before the dog matures. Some puppies grow long top coats all over their backs at about six or eight months. Leave it alone! Don't clip it. It will shed out of its own accord after a few months. Some puppies also grow a top coat on their backs and sides that appears to have a silvery tone. This, too, will disappear.

Many Irish Setters develop light hair on the tops of the head and ears, while the rest of the body coat remains dark. This is normal. Long hair on top of the skull can be hand-stripped or carefully scissored or pulled to give a sleek and neat appearance. The Irish Setter is rarely a solid color. The burnished top coat is often accompanied by lighter furnishings, not only on the head and ears but also on the feathering on the belly, backs of the legs, and tail. Shading is perfectly normal and acceptable, as are shades of red from dark mahogany to chestnut.

Most Irish Setters enjoy their grooming sessions if they are introduced to it early. An eight-week-old puppy can be put on a table for a few minutes while being stroked and petted. This is also a good time to acquaint them with ear cleaning and with the sound of an electric clipper. Run the clipper near the puppy's head without touching the hair. If the puppy remains still, lots of praise will assure him that everything is fine. Don't overdo it and never harshly correct the puppy if he squirms around at the unfamiliar sounds or seems frightened at being off the ground. Run a soft brush over his back. Pick up each foot and put it down. Go through all the motions as if you had tools in your hand, but don't use them for the first few sessions.

Equipment

High-quality tools are a must for any project, and purchasing good grooming equipment for your dog is no exception. Good grades of scissors, clippers that hold an edge, strippers that are correct for the purpose for which they are used, and combs and brushes that will not tear the hair all contribute to the finished product. Most grooming tools can be purchased at pet shops, from concessions found at dog shows, from mail order catalogs, or on the Web through pet supply houses.

Clippers

There are two or three makers of electric clippers. You should choose one that feels comfortable in your hand and that is easy to use. Before buying, try to find someone with the brands you are looking at, or if you buy at a pet store, ask to hear the clipper run. Some are much quieter than others and work with less vibration. This is more comfortable for your dog, so he is less likely to try to wiggle away, especially when you clip around the sensitive areas of the ear. The blade that you will use almost exclusively is the Number 10. Some people like to use a Number 15, but this gives a very close cut. Sometimes this is used several days in advance of a show so that the hair can grow out. Blades are interchangeable between one or two clipper manufacturers.

Scissors

Purchase high-quality scissors recommended by someone who has had extensive experience grooming Irish Setters. A pair of scissors should hold an edge and cut cleanly. They will last longer if they are kept clean and dry and not dropped. Three pairs of scissors should be enough. A straight blade is used for trimming around the feet and around the pads, but not for much else. A blunt-ended curved pair of scissors adds safety for trimming whiskers on the muzzle or eyebrows. The scissors you will use most are thinning shears. These are available in single or double-blade. The greater the number of teeth, the more hair can be removed in a single cut. Thinners are used for blending the neck, head, shoulders, hocks, feet, and tail, and for removing excess coat that may have grown down the outer side of the back leg.

Strippers

These come in a wide variety of types and prices. Strippers are used to remove undercoat, dead hair on the head, body, and flank, and for blending hair on the neck and sides. Some have single-edged razors that are used to blend hair.

Pumice Stone

The stone is used to remove unwanted hair and to blend hair. It is used by dragging the stone over the coat or by pulling hair between the stone and the fingers.

Brushes

A natural-bristle brush is best because it will not tear the coat the way synthetic bristles do. A wooden-handled brush helps absorb the natural oil that is deposited on the bristles. The brush should be wide enough to lie flat against the hair to smooth the top coat. The other type of brush you will need is a pin brush. This has flexible wire pins

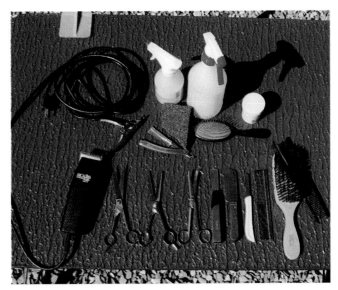

To groom your Irish Setter, the following high-quality equipment is recommended: a sturdy, slip-proof table, electric clippers, nail clippers, styptic powder, a single-edge razor, spray bottles, straight-edge scissors, curved-end scissors, thinning shears, stripping blades, a pumice stone, a pin brush, a bristle brush, and a comb.

Spray Bottles

Small spray bottles, one containing plain water and one containing diluted conditioner, are useful to dampen the bristle brush when you brush through the coat or the feathering when you use the pin brush. Some people like to spray light conditioner on the dog's feathers after grooming is finished or just before going into the show ring.

Blanket Towel and Blanket Pins

After you have bathed your dog, instead of drying the dog completely, you can put a towel over the back and fasten it around the neck and under the belly with pins used for horse blankets. You can get these at tack shops.

Dryer

A standard hair dryer can be used to dry the dog after a bath, making sure to brush the feathering down. You can also take a dryer to a show to touch the dog up before going into the ring. This, of course, necessitates a generator, complicating your life quite a bit. Standing dryers can be obtained from pet supply or grooming supply houses. These are for use at home and are very efficient because they leave both hands free to use the brush and hold the dog in the position most favorable to you. Do not leave a dog unattended in a crate with the dryer turned on. Dogs in this situation have been known to die of heatstroke and dehydration.

Grooming Table

This is probably the most significant piece of equipment you can own, because it makes the entire grooming process so much easier. Any type of sturdy table will do as long as it is covered with non-slip material. However, commercially made grooming tables exist, and they are made in many styles and sizes. You will want one that is at a comfortable height for you to groom the full-grown dog when he is standing up. A collapsible type of table allows you to take it on the road. You can purchase a grooming arm that enables you to put the dog's head in a noose and keep him from leaping away from you while you are working. One very important word of caution: *Never* leave a dog alone on a grooming table with his head in the noose. Dogs have been known to hang themselves by jumping or falling off the table while unattended. Some tables come with wheels so that when folded up they double as dollies for carrying show items.

Tackle Box

Any type of box in which you can store all your grooming equipment in one place is the most useful. You will want to take some equipment to shows, so the box

set in rubber. It is used to separate the long hair on the feathering. Never pull this or any brush through the feathers when you meet resistance, because you will pull out the hair. Brush the coat in sections from the skin out to the ends, dampening the coat with a fine spray of water or water mixed with light conditioner. Do not brush or comb a completely dry coat, or split ends will result.

Combs

A comb with graduated teeth can be used to comb out the feathers. Use the wide half first, and then go through with the narrow teeth. Combs that are coated with static-resistant materials or Teflon slip through the hair more easily without breaking the ends. Combs can be used to separate tangles or mats after they have been soaked in conditioner and worked with your fingers to loosen them. Many people take a comb into the ring for a final touch-up, although using a brush for this purpose works just as well.

Nail Cutters

There are two basic types of nail cutters. One is a clipper that you squeeze to nip off the end of the nail. The other is a pliers-type that has a guard at the end that can be set in order to avoid cutting into the quick. It is purely a matter of preference which one you choose. Along with the nail cutters, you should have a bottle of styptic powder. This powder stops the nail from bleeding if you cut into the quick by mistake.

A simple fishing tackle box will make an excellent place to store grooming supplies.

should have handles and compartments. Some people use a fishing tackle box as their grooming box. Others have much more elaborate storage boxes into which they put not only grooming stuff, but a selection of collars, leads, loose change, medications, and whatever else one might need to go to a show.

Bathing

There are so many different shampoos and conditioners on the market that the poor owner can become bewildered by the choices. What you use will be dictated in part by the type of coat your dog has. We will assume that the dog has a healthy coat and healthy skin. Medicated shampoos are useful for skin disorders but not for routine bathing. You might find that what works in some seasons of the year does not work in others. Where you live will also affect the quality and quantity of coat that your dog carries. Seasonal changes will also play a role, as will hormonal changes, such as when bitches are in heat. Ask the advice of those who have dogs whose coats and skin you consistently admire. Find out what their secrets are. Try small bottles of shampoo and conditioner until you find those that work best. There's no sense in buying gallon jugs if the stuff doesn't suit your dog's coat.

Bathing is much easier if you have a spray or shower nozzle on a hose connected to the faucet. Thoroughly wet the coat and apply the shampoo according to manufacturer's directions from the head to the tail, not forgetting the feet, belly, and feathering. After thoroughly

lathering the dog, rinse out all the shampoo with warm water. When you are finished, the rinse water should be completely clear. Mix a little conditioner with water and pour over the dog, again rinsing thoroughly. Squeeze excess water out of the coat in the tub and then towel the dog off on the grooming table. If you elect to dry the dog completely with a dryer, use a medium heat setting and brush the hair down. If the dog is not thoroughly dry, the coat will wrinkle when he lies down. If you decide to blanket the dog, rub the top coat and the feathering with a towel to remove excess water. Gently brush the coat with a pin brush so that it lies flat. Use a towel that is big enough to reach from the top of the neck to mid-tail and that can be fastened comfortably around the dog's middle. A beach towel or large bath sheet works well. Pin the towel under the neck with a horse blanket pin and pull it back and down. Fasten under the belly just behind the ribcage with a second pin. Some people leave the towels until just before showing. Others prefer to leave them on

Blanketing your dog after a bath or to keep the coat clean is easy. Pin the blanket around the neck first and then under the belly.

until the dog is completely dry and then remove them. You can then brush the dog out with a bristle or pin brush, taking care to remove gently any mats that may have developed under the elbows as a result of the bath.

The before picture: An ungroomed Irish Setter.

Step-by-Step Grooming

We are now ready to begin our grooming process.

One should always groom a clean dog. The clippers will go through the fur more easily and you will not ruin a good pair of scissors on a dirty dog. Weekly or biweekly bathing assures you that your dog is in good shape to be trimmed.

Take care when clipping your dog's nails not to cut into the quick.

The first thing you will want to do is cut the nails. Dogs being shown usually have their nails cut weekly, along with a bath and grooming. Do the nails first, because that is the part of the process that most dogs dislike the most. Once that is over and done with they will relax, because they will know you are not going to come after them with the cutters in some surprise move. Puppies should have their nails trimmed regularly from the time they can stand. They should be accustomed to having their feet held and touched so that they realize it is not a painful process.

Trimming

The most difficult problem in trimming an Irish Setter is the color change resulting from exposing the undercoat. That is why trimming should be done several weeks ahead of a show and kept up consistently, even when the dog is not being shown. The degree of color change is directly related to the type of coat. A dog with heavy undercoat and little top coat will have proportionately more color change than the dog with a straight, flat coat with little undercoat. When trimming any kind of coat, stop when the color change becomes apparent.

As you work, keep the dog in a standing position. Begin by trimming under the neck. Hold the electric clippers like a pencil with one hand while the other hand

Hold the muzzle up, exposing the neck to the clipper blades as you trim with the grain of the hair.

Trim to just above the breast bone.

Trim the top of the ear with the grain about one-third of the way down the ear. Leave the hair that covers the fold at the front of the ear.

Hold ear up, taking care not to catch the feathering.

The most difficult part of trimming the Irish Setter is blending the hair along the side of the neck so that there is not a blunt line.

props the dog's muzzle up to expose the neck to the blades. Start at the chin and clip down the middle of the underside of the neck to about two fingers above the breast bone. Do not rush with the clippers. Try to keep them steady in one straight line from chin to chest. Although some groomers prefer to start at the breast bone and clip up against the grain, the usual way is to go with the grain of the hair.

Trim with the grain of the hair to an imaginary line drawn parallel to the lower edge of the jaw, under the ear to the side of the neck. Hold the ear away from the neck, taking care not to catch any of the ear feathering in the clippers. Trim from where the hair changes direction under the ear to the point where the neck joins the shoulder. The most difficult part of trimming the Irish Setter is blending the hair along the side of the neck so that there is not a blunt line. This will be done with the thinning shears and pumice stone.

Next, you will trim the ear. Begin at the top of the ear where it meets the skull and trim about a third of the way down the ear. Trim with the grain of the hair, leaving the hair that covers the fold at the front of the ear. Some people prefer to trim the entire top third of the ear, including the fold, but leaving that fringe softens the expression and gives a more natural appearance. Turn the ear out and clean the hair from the inner surface close to the ear canal. This allows air to circulate and helps reduce the chance of infection. Raise the ear and trim the ear burr, taking care not to nick the sensitive small split area on the underside. Make sure that when the ear hangs naturally, the long hair under the ear is trimmed equal to the top of the ear.

304

Shape the hair on the side of the muzzle by holding the clipper on the flattest part of the face sideways to the grain. You may be able to take off most of the whiskers with the clippers, but dogs have a canny ability to hide them, only to have them spring out just when you think you've gotten them all. You can cut the rest later with your blunt-edged scissors.

That is all you will do with the electric clipper. Next, take your thinning shears and, with the grain of the hair, blend the hair you have clipped along the side of the neck with the long hair you have left. Work slowly and take time to view your handiwork after each cut. It is better to cut too little than too much at first. Try to layer the hair evenly and gradually so that there is a smooth transition from the longer hair on the side of the neck to the short, clipped hair on the front of the neck. Blend the hair under the ear with the hair on the side of the head. If your dog has a long topknot, use your thinning shears to cut and shape the hair to the skull. Blend the hair on the side of the head where it meets the ear. Brush the coat frequently to remove cut hair and to see the results of your handiwork, step by step. After you have scissored the top of the head, use the pumice stone to smooth

Turn ear out and clean hair from inner surface close to ear canal.

Raise ear and trim ear burr.

Shape hair on the side of muzzle by holding the clipper on the flattest part of the face sideways to the grain.

Use thinning shears to shape the hair to the skull.

305

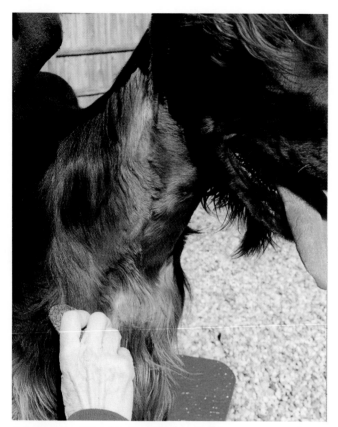

A pumice stone will help blend your Irish Setter's hair.

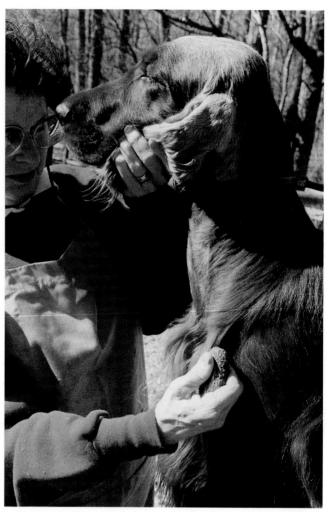

Use stone to blend long hair with clippered hair.

Drag the pumice stone over the top of the head to remove the "fuzzies" and blend the scissored and clipped edges.

the hair and remove any remaining fuzzies by pulling it through the hair. Use the stone along the side of the neck to pull any long hairs remaining and blend with the clipped hair.

Next, take your stripper and drag it with the grain of the hair from the top of the head to the tail, removing the dead hair as you work down the body. Use long, smooth strokes with the stripper lying flat against the coat. You do not want to cut into the hair or you will break it off. Work from head to tip of tail along the back and sides of the dog. Where the coat begins to flow rather than lie flat on the back, work with the grain to where the feathering starts to fall free of the body. Carefully blend the hair where the neck meets the shoulder. This is where you need to know the structure of your dog. You may want to take more hair off in some places than in others. As an example, if your dog dips behind the shoulder, you will

Pull long hair and fuzzies from sides of back and front legs with stone.

Trim the tip of the tail with thinning shears to form a triangle from root to tip.

want to leave the hair to hide the dip. If, however, your dog has a firm topline from shoulder to tail, you can take the dead hair out evenly.

With your thinning shears, trim the hair just under the tail and at the tip of the tail so that it forms a triangle from base of tail to tip. It should appear natural and not as if it was cut with a straight blade. How much you take off the rump and the area where the tail is set onto the back will depend on the topline of your dog.

Drag the strippers along the coat from the head all the way down to the tail, taking care to keep them flat against the hair.

Edge around the feet and toes with thinning shears.

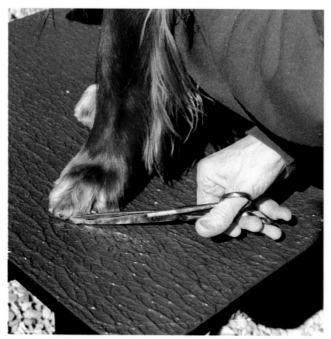

Finish edging the feet and toes with the straight blade.

Trim the feathering on the ankle with thinning shears held at an angle.

Trimming the feet is time-consuming if it is done correctly. The goal is to shape the foot to give a clean, compact look. First, using the straight blade, take out the hair under the pads and between the pads on the bottom of the foot. Be careful not to cut the pads or the toes while you are working. Keeping the hair short allows the pads to touch the ground so that the dog is not walking on hair instead of on his feet. This also minimizes the chance of foot infections and keeps the house cleaner because the dog will drag in less dirt. Then, with the dog's foot on the table, use your trimming shears to edge around the foot and toes, combing the hair between the toes upward before cutting it off. Leave *some* hair between the toes. You do not want the foot to look like a hare's, with individual toes sticking out. If there are mats between the toes, work them loose with your fingers and comb. With your thinning shears, trim the sides of the front feet and the feathering on the back of the leg to the ankle so that it is natural-looking but not touching the ground. Use your scissors at an angle to the foot to accomplish this. Excess hair or fuzz on the front legs can be stripped out with your stripper or pumice stone. Trim the back feet the same way. Hair on the hocks should be combed up and out and then trimmed with the thinning shears, angling the scissors toward the dog's heel and cutting at some distance from the bone. How much hair you leave will depend on how much bone the dog has. After you have thinned and trimmed with the shears, you can neaten the

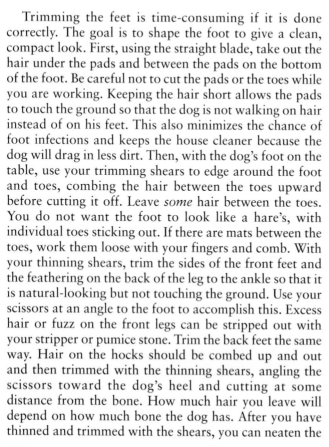

The hair on the hocks should be trimmed with thinning shears.

ragged edges with a straight blade. Some Irish Setters grow fuzzy hair along the sides of the upper rear legs. This should be stripped down with the stripper or pumice stone. Excess hair on the sides of the lower leg can be taken down with the thinning shears.

As you trim, inspect your dog from a distance. You might ask someone to hold the dog in a show pose on the ground after you are finished so that you can see if what you have done makes the dog appear smooth and stylish. Have someone gait the dog so you can see if there is a lot

Excess hair on sides of lower legs should be taken down with thinning shears.

Blanketing after a bath or to keep the coat clean. Pin the blanket around the neck first, then around the body behind the rib cage.

Pin both thicknesses, keeping your hand between the pin and the dog.

of flyaway hair as he trots along. You might have to strip more off the sides in order for the feathering to lie flat and not to be a distraction as the dog moves.

Whether or not you are preparing a dog to be shown, grooming and bathing is an integral part of general maintenance for any Irish Setter. Grooming has other advantages, too. It provides a quiet time for you and your dog to be together, just the two of you, without distractions. If your dog associates grooming with pleasure, it will be a relaxing experience for both of you. Dogs know when they look terrific. When they look their best, they feel good, too. You will be proud of your work, and that feeling is not lost on your dog. Grooming becomes a shared experience between the dog and his best friend. It is one way for you and your dog to become a team and at the same time create a work of art.

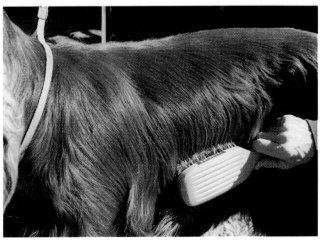

Brush out coat with a bristle brush, sprayed with water or light conditioner.

Use a pin brush on ears and feathering.

The after picture: A beautiful, well-groomed Irish Setter.

Appendix

Useful Addresses and Information

The American Kennel Club

260 Madison Avenue
New York, NY 10016
Phone: 212-696-8200

This is the headquarters of the AKC. Executive offices, publication offices, and the library are housed here. It is well worth visiting, if only to see the exquisite collection of art and books.

or: 5580 Centerview Drive
Raleigh, NC 27606
919-233-3600—executive offices
919-233-9767—customer service

This facility houses all of the departments concerning registration, show plans, records, and information concerning almost anything to do with purebred dogs. The AKC also maintains an extensive Web site at *www.akc.org*. Through this site, you can be connected to the Irish Setter Club of America and reach its current officers and directors.

Companion Animal Recovery

919-233-3706

This AKC program keeps track of dogs that are either microchipped or permanently tattooed. This is a 24-hour service designed to reunite owners with lost dogs.

Canine Eye Registry Foundation (CERF)

765-494-8179

This is the organization that maintains the database for all dogs that are DNA-tested for progressive retinal atrophy (PRA).

Irish Setter Genetic Registry (ISGR)

Sandra Novicin
301-831-5969
e-mail: bandi@erols.com

This is a list of all dogs tested either by test-mating or by a DNA blood test to determine the PRA status of every dog. CERF sends its list of PRA-normal dogs to the ISGR.

Optigen

607-796-0557
www.optigen.com.

This laboratory has been authorized to analyze the blood tests sent by owners of Irish Setters wishing to test for PRA.

Orthopedic Foundation for Animals (OFA)

2300 Nifong Blvd.
Columbia, MO 65201
1-800-442-0418
www.offa.org

This organization is the prime resource for owners to obtain scientific readings of x-rays submitted to determine the presence or absence of hip dysplasia. Preliminary x-rays may be taken at six months, but in order to obtain a rating from OFA, the dog must be two years old. X-rays will determine whether a dog has normal, sound hips or whether the hip joint is not formed properly, which will cause the dog to develop degenerative joint disease later in life. X-rays are taken by a veterinarian and submitted to OFA. They are read by three orthopedic specialists and assigned a rating of excellent, good, fair, or dysplastic. Breeders use these evaluations to determine whether a dog is of sound stock for breeding. Hip dysplasia is a common fault in large-breed dogs and is at least partially genetically based.

PennHIP™

www.vet.upenn.edu/pennhip

An alternative means of evaluating the status of a dog's hips is through a process that involves x-rays, but that is done in a different way and can be performed as early as four months of age. Veterinarians licensed in this procedure perform the tests.

E. I. Eldredge Memorial Award

The E. I. Eldredge Memorial Award was established in 1985 by George and Mary Ann Alston, longtime friends of Ted Eldredge and professional handlers who were closely associated with Ted. They offered this trophy in his memory to be given at the annual awards banquet of the Irish Setter Club of America. The wording of the award is as follows: "To the person who best exemplifies those attributes most closely associated with Ted Eldredge: good sportsmanship, compassion, kindliness, integrity, courtesy, devotion to the welfare of the breed. The trophy need not be awarded every year and its recipient is not required to be a member of the ISCA."

To be selected as a recipient of the E. I. Eldredge Award is considered the highest accolade offered by the ISCA.

Irish Setter Rescue

Rescue Chairperson, Marilee Larson
e-mail: mlarson@volcano.net

The Irish Setter Club of America supports a national rescue effort that works in cooperation with local clubs nationwide.

Principles of Integrity

The Irish Setter Club of America publishes an annual Breeders' Directory. In order to be listed in the directory, breeders must sign and adhere to the Principles of Integrity, as set forth here:

Members of the Irish Setter Club of America, Inc., agree to abide by the Constitutional objectives of the Club. Among these are provisions to protect and advance the interests of the breed, and to do all that is possible to bring the natural qualities of the Irish Setter to perfection.

To further these objectives, members listed in the Breeders' Directory agree to follow these principles of integrity:

1. Comply with all American Kennel Club rules and regulations.

2. Maintain a high standard of health, care, and cleanliness for our dogs.

3. Act in a sportsmanlike manner and not deliberately degrade other exhibitors/breeders or their dogs.

4. Make every effort to learn about the structure, anatomy, action, behavior, and other inheritable traits of the Irish Setter. To use this information to adhere to the breed standard and produce sound, healthy dogs with good temperament.

5. To use or give service only to registered stock that is believed to be free of serious abnormalities that are considered inheritable.

6. To provide a written contract/agreement for each sale or service that includes all special conditions related to the sale.

7. Provide each buyer with accurate records regarding health and pedigree for the Irish Setter being purchased.

8. Truthfully and realistically represent the Irish Setter being sold in terms of quality, health, and genetic history.

9. Refuse to sell to commercial wholesalers, retailers, or to research laboratories.

10. When selling an Irish Setter known to manifest hereditary defects considered to be detrimental to the breed, use written contracts or spay-neuter agreements to prevent the dog from being bred.

Irish Setter Club of America, Inc. Constitution and By-Laws

Constitution

ARTICLE I
Name and Objects

Section 1. The name of the club shall be The Irish Setter Club of America, Inc.

Section 2. The objectives of the Club shall be:

(a) to encourage and promote the breeding of purebred Irish Setters and to do all possible to bring their natural qualities to perfection;

(b) to encourage the organization of independent local Irish Setter Specialty Clubs in those localities where there are sufficient fanciers of the breed to meet the requirements of the American Kennel Club;

(c) to propose, amend and define a Standard for the breed, subject to approval of the American Kennel Club;

(d) to urge members and breeders to accept the Standard of the breed as approved by the American Kennel Club as the only Standard of excellence by which Irish Setters shall be judged;

(e) to do all in its power to protect and advance the interests of the breed and to encourage sportsmanlike competition at dog shows, field trials and obedience trials;

(f) to conduct specialty shows, field trials, obedience trials and sanctioned matches under the rules of the American Kennel Club.

Section 3. The Club shall not be conducted or operated for profit and no part of any profits or remainder or residue from dues or donations to the Club shall inure to the benefit of any member or individual.

Section 4. The members of the Club shall adopt and may from time to time revise such by-laws as may be required to carry out these objects.

By-Laws

ARTICLE I
Membership

Section 1. Eligibility. The following shall be eligible for membership:

(a) Individual Members, open to all persons eighteen years of age and older.

(b) Family Members, open to any two related or unrelated adults living in the same household and any minor children, ages ten to eighteen, of either, residing with them. All are eligible to compete for Annual Trophy Awards. Children under eighteen years of age are not eligible to vote or hold office as an Officer, Director, or Delegate. Only one copy of the Memo To Members will be sent per Family Membership.

(c) Junior Members, open to all persons ten to eighteen years of age. Junior members are eligible to compete for the Annual Trophy Awards, but are not eligible to vote or hold office as an Officer, Director, or Delegate.

(d) Senior Citizen Members, open to all persons, age sixty-two or over, at their option.

All members must be in good standing with the American Kennel Club and subscribe to the purposes of the Irish Setter Club of America, Inc.

Section 2. Dues. Annual membership dues for each type membership, payable on or before the first day of February each year, shall be established by a majority vote

of the Officers and Directors of the Club not later than October of the preceding year. During the month of November, the Treasurer shall send to each member a statement of their dues for the ensuing year. Only qualified members in good standing and whose dues are paid for the current year may vote.

Section 3. Election to membership. Each applicant for membership shall apply on a form approved by the Board of Directors which shall provide that the applicant agrees to abide by this constitution and by-laws and the rules of the American Kennel Club. The application shall state the name, address and occupation of the applicant and it shall carry the endorsement of two members (unless the endorsement requirement is waived by the Board). Accompanying the application the prospective member shall submit dues payment for the current year.

Applicants may be elected at any meeting of the Board of Directors or by written vote of the Directors by mail. Affirmative votes of 3/4 of the Directors present at a meeting of the Board or of 3/4 of the entire Board voting by mail, shall be required to elect an applicant.

An application which has received a negative vote by the Board may be presented by one of the applicant's endorsers at the next meeting of the Club and the Club may elect such applicant by favorable vote of 90% of the members present.

Section 4. Termination of Membership. Memberships may be terminated:

(a) by resignation. Any member in good standing may resign from the Club upon written notice to the Secretary; but no member may resign when in debt to the Club. Dues obligations are considered a debt to the Club and they become incurred on the first day of each fiscal year.

(b) by lapsing. A membership will be considered as lapsed and automatically terminated if such member's dues remain unpaid 90 days after the first day of the fiscal year; however, the Board may grant an additional 90 days of grace to such delinquent members in meritorious cases. In no case may a person be entitled to vote at any Club meeting whose dues are unpaid as of the date of that meeting.

(c) by expulsion. A membership may be terminated by expulsion as provided in Article VI of these constitution and by-laws.

ARTICLE II
Meetings

Section 1. Annual Meeting. The annual meeting of the Club shall be held at the time of the National Specialty Show, if practical, at a place, date, and hour designated by the Board of Directors. Written notice of the annual meeting shall be mailed by the Secretary to each member at least 30 days prior to the date of the meeting. The quorum for the annual meeting shall be 10% of the members in good standing or 50 members, whichever is less.

Section 2. Special Club Meetings. Special Club meetings may be called by the President or by a majority vote of the members of the Board who are present at a meeting of the Board or who vote by mail, and shall be called by the Secretary upon receipt of a petition signed by 10% of the members of the Club who are in good standing. Such meetings shall be held at such place, date and hour as may be designated by the Board of Directors. Written notice of such meetings shall be mailed by the Secretary at least 14 days and not more than 30 days prior to the meeting. The notice of the meeting shall state the purpose of the meeting and no other Club business may be transacted. The quorum for such a meeting shall be 10% of the members in good standing or 50 members, whichever is less. In the case of a special meeting called solely for the purpose of electing officers in accordance with Article IV, Section 4, the requirement for a quorum may be waived.

Section 3. Board Meetings. There shall be three meetings per year with a simple majority present. The fourth meeting, if necessary, may be conducted in person, by facsimile, by mail, or electronic teleconferencing. However, if possible at least one meeting of the Board shall be held in each of the four or more Regions of the United States each year. The number of Regions and the area included in each shall be determined by the Board. Written notice of each meeting shall be mailed by the Secretary to each member of the Board at least 10 days prior to the date of the meeting. A quorum for a Board Meeting shall be determined by simple majority and voting may be in person, by mail, facsimile, or electronic conferencing.

Section 4. The Board of Directors may conduct its business by mail through the Secretary.

ARTICLE III
Directors and Officers

Section 1. Board of Directors. The Board shall be comprised of the President, 1st Vice-President, 2nd Vice-President, Recording Secretary, Corresponding Secretary, Treasurer, immediate Past President and three (3) other persons from each of the four or more Regions of the United States, as defined by the Board plus the Delegate to the American Kennel Club, all of whom shall be members in good standing and who are residents of the

United States. They shall be elected as provided in Article IV, and shall serve until their successors are elected. The immediate Past President shall serve as a voting member without election for the period of one year beginning with the election of his successor and continuing until the next regularly elected President takes office. In the event that the office of Past President is vacated by death, resignation or for any other reason, it shall remain vacant until regularly filled by succession to this office. General management of the Club's affairs shall be entrusted to the Board of Directors.

In the interest of continuity and assurance of varied representation, the Officers, Delegate to the American Kennel Club and Directors shall be elected to the following terms and shall be subject to the following conditions: The Officers and Delegate to the American Kennel Club shall be elected to one year terms. The Directors shall be elected to three (3) year terms. The President and 1st Vice-President shall not be eligible for more than three (3) successive terms. The other Officers and Directors and Delegate to the American Kennel Club as such shall be eligible for successive terms without limitation.

Section 2. Officers. The Club's officers, consisting of President, 1st Vice-President, 2nd Vice-President, Recording Secretary, Corresponding Secretary, and Treasurer shall serve in their respective capacities both with regard to the Club and its meetings.

(a) The President shall preside at all meetings of the Club and the Board, and shall have the duties and powers normally appurtenant to the Office of President in addition to those particularly specified in these by-laws.

(b) The 1st Vice-President shall have the duties and exercise the powers of the President in case of the President's death, absence, or incapability.

(c) The 2nd Vice-President shall have the duties and exercise the powers of the President and the 1st Vice-President in case of the death, absence, or incapability of the President and the 1st Vice-President.

(d) The Recording Secretary shall keep a record of all meetings of the Club and of the Board and of all votes taken by mail, and of all matters of which a record shall be ordered by the Club. The Recording Secretary shall have charge of the correspondence, notify members of meeting, notify officers and Directors of their election to office, keep a roll of the members of the Club with their addresses, and carry out other such duties as are prescribed in these by-laws.

(e) The Corresponding Secretary shall be responsible for general Club correspondence and shall carry out such other duties as prescribed by the Board.

(f) The Treasurer shall collect and receive all moneys due or belonging to the Club. The Treasurer shall deposit the same in a bank approved by the Board, in the name of the Club. The Treasurer's books shall at all times be open to inspection of the members. The Treasurer shall report to the Board at every meeting the condition of the Club's finances and every item of receipt or payment not before reported. At the annual meeting the Treasurer shall render an account of all moneys received and expended during the previous fiscal year. The Treasurer shall be bonded in such amount as the Board of Directors shall determine. The Club's accounts shall be subject to such audits and disbursement regulations as prescribed by the Board.

Section 3. Vacancies. Any vacancies occurring on the Board or among the officers during the year shall be filled until the next election by a majority vote of all the members of the Board if the terms of the vacancies are three months or more and may be filled for a shorter time.

ARTICLE IV
The Club Year, Voting, Nominations, Elections

Section 1. Club Year. The Club's fiscal year shall begin on the 1st day of January and end on the 31st day of December.

The Club's official year shall also be the calendar year. The elected officers and directors shall take office on January 1st, and each retiring officer shall turn over to his successor in office all properties and records relating to that office within 30 days.

Section 2. Voting. At the annual meeting of the Club, voting shall be limited to those members in good standing who are present at the meeting, except that on the following matters voting shall be by written ballot either cast by mail and received by the Secretary prior to the meeting or delivered in person by the voting member present at the meeting:

(a) Amendments to this constitution and by-laws of the Club.

(b) Amendments to the Standard for the breed.

Voting on amendments to this constitution and by-laws and to the Standard for the breed may be at an annual meeting or special meeting of the Club as provided above or by mail ballot only as provided in Article VII.

The Board of Directors in its discretion may submit other specific questions for decision of the members by written ballot cast by mail.

Except as otherwise in this constitution and by-laws, all decisions shall be made by a simple majority of votes cast. Each member, other than Junior members, is entitled to one vote.

Section 3. Nominations and Ballots. No person may be a candidate in a Club election who has not been nominated in accordance with these by-laws. A Nominating Committee shall be chosen by the Board of Directors on or before September 1st. The Committee shall consist of five members and two alternatives, all members in good standing, no more than one of whom shall be a member of the current Board of Directors. The Board shall name a Chairman for the Committee. At least one and not more than two members of the Nominating Committee shall be chosen from each of the four Regions of the United States, as defined by the Board. The Nominating Committee may conduct its business by mail, or any other means of communication.

(a) The Nominating Committee shall nominate from among the eligible members of the Club, one candidate for each office and for each other position on the Board of Directors and a candidate for the Delegate to the American Kennel Club and shall procure the acceptance of each nominee so chosen. The Committee shall then submit its slate of candidates to the Secretary who shall mail the list to each member of the Club on or before October 1st, so that additional nominees may be made by the members if they so desire.

(b) Additional nominations of eligible members may be made by written petition addressed to the Secretary and received at his or her regular address on or before November 1st, signed by twenty-five (25) members and accompanied by the written acceptance of each such additional nominee signifying his willingness to be a candidate. No person shall be a candidate for more than one position, and the additional nominations which are provided for herein may be made only from among those members who have not accepted a nomination of the Nominating Committee and which meet all the requirements of Article III, Section 1.

Section 4. Elections.

(a) If no valid additional nominations are received by the Secretary on or before November 1st, the Nominating Committee's slate shall be declared elected, and no balloting will be required. The newly elected officers, directors and the delegate to the American Kennel Club shall be notified by the Secretary by mail, and they shall assume office on January 1st next.

(b) If one or more valid additional nominations are received by the Secretary on or before November 1st, he shall, on or before November 15, mail to each member in good standing a ballot listing all of the nominees for each position in alphabetical order, together with a blank envelope and a return envelope addressed to the Secretary marked "Ballot" and bearing the name of the member to whom it was sent. So that the ballots may remain secret, each voter, after marking his ballot, shall seal it in the blank envelope which in turn shall be placed in the second envelope addressed to the Secretary. At a special meeting of the membership, at a place and at a time designated by the Board of Directors between December 15th and 31st the ballots shall be counted at the meeting by three inspectors of election to be chosen by the members present at the meeting. Ballots to be valid must be received by the Secretary on or before December 15. The inspectors of election shall check the returns against the list of members whose dues are paid for the current year prior to opening the outer envelopes and removing the blank envelopes, and shall certify the eligibility of the voters as well as the results of the voting which shall be announced at the special meeting. The persons receiving the largest number of votes for each position shall be declared elected. If any nominee, at the time of the meeting, is unable to serve for any reason, such nominee shall not be elected and the vacancy so created shall be filled by the new Board of Directors in the manner provided by Article III, Section 3.

(c) Nominations cannot be made at the special meeting or in any manner other than as provided above. A member to be eligible for any Irish Setter Club of America, Inc., office shall have been a member in good standing for the previous five (5) consecutive years.

ARTICLE V
Committees

Section 1. The Board may each year appoint standing committees to advance the work of the Club in such matters as dog shows, field trials, obedience trials, trophies, annual prizes, membership or other fields which may well be served by committees. Such committees shall always be subject to the final authority of the Board. Special Committees may also be appointed by the Board to aid it on particular projects.

Section 2. Any committee appointment may be terminated by a Majority vote of the full membership of the Board upon written notice to the appointee; and the Board may appoint successors to those persons whose service has been terminated.

ARTICLE VI
Discipline

Section 1. American Kennel Club Suspension. Any member who is suspended from the privileges of the American Kennel Club automatically shall be suspended from this Club for a like period.

Section 2. Charges. Any member may prefer charges against a member for alleged misconduct prejudicial to the best interests of the Club or the breed. Written charges with specifications must be filed in duplicate with the Secretary together with a deposit of $50, which shall be forfeited if such charges are not sustained by the Board following a hearing. The Secretary shall promptly send a copy of the charges to each member of the Board or present them at a Board meeting. The Board shall appoint, by majority, a Disciplinary Committee of not less than three members of the Board. One member shall be appointed Chair and shall be responsible for committee minutes. The Board, sitting as a whole or in Committee, shall first consider whether the actions alleged in the charges, if proven, might constitute conduct prejudicial to the best interests of the Club or the breed. If the Committee considers that the charges do not allege conduct which would be prejudicial to the best interests of the Club or of the breed it may recommend that the Board vote by majority to refuse to entertain jurisdiction. All minutes of the Disciplinary Committee shall be made available to the Board. If the Board entertains jurisdiction of the charges it shall fix a date of a hearing by the Board not less than three (3) weeks nor more than six (6) weeks thereafter. The Secretary shall promptly send one copy of the charges to the accused member by registered mail together with a notice of the Board hearing and an assurance that the defendant may personally appear in their own defense and bring witnesses if they wish.

Section 3. Board Hearing. The Board shall have complete authority to decide whether counsel may attend the hearing, but both complainant and defendant shall be treated uniformly in that regard. Should the charges be sustained after hearing all the evidence and testimony presented by complainant and defendant, the Board may by a majority vote of those present suspend the defendant from all privileges of the Club for not more than six months from the date of the hearing, or until the next annual meeting, if that will occur after six months. If the Board deems punishment insufficient, it may also recommend to the membership that the penalty be expulsion. In such case the suspension shall not restrict the defendant's right to appear before his fellow members at the ensuing Club meeting which considers the recommendation of the Board. Immediately after the Board has reached a decision, its findings shall be put in written form and filed with the Secretary. The Secretary, in turn, shall notify each of the parties of the decision and penalty, if any.

Section 4. Expulsion. Expulsion of a member of the Club may be accomplished only at the annual meeting of the Club following a hearing and upon recommendation of the Board as provided in Section 3 of this Article. The defendant shall have the privilege of appearing in his own behalf though no evidence shall be taken at this meeting.

The President shall read the charges and the findings and recommendations, and shall invite the defendant, if present, to speak on his own behalf. The meeting shall then vote by secret written ballot on the proposed expulsion. A 2/3 vote of those present and voting at the annual meeting shall be necessary for expulsion. If expulsion is not so voted the suspension shall stand.

ARTICLE VII
Amendments

Section 1. Amendments to the constitution and by-laws and the Standard for the breed may be proposed by the Board of Directors or by written petition addressed to the Secretary signed by twenty percent of the membership in good standing. Amendments proposed by such petition shall be promptly considered by the Board of Directors and must be submitted to the recommendations of the Board by the Secretary for a vote within three months of the date when the petition was received by the Secretary.

Section 2. The constitution and by-laws, and the standard for the breed may be amended at any time provided a copy of the proposed amendments has been mailed by the Secretary to each member accompanied by a ballot on which he may indicate his choice for or against the action to be taken. The notice shall specify a date not less than 30 days after the date of the mailing by which date the ballot must be returned to the Secretary to be counted. The favorable vote of 2/3 of the members in good standing whose ballots are returned within the time limit shall be required to effect any such amendment.

Section 3. No amendment to the constitution and by-laws, or the Standard for the breed that is adopted by the Club shall become effective until it has been approved by the Board of Directors of the American Kennel Club.

ARTICLE VIII
Dissolution

Section 1. The Club may be dissolved at any time by the written consent of not less than 2/3 of the members. In the event of the dissolution of the Club, whether voluntary or involuntary or by operation of law, none of the property of the Club nor any proceeds thereof nor any assets of the Club shall be distributed to any members of the Club but after payment of debts of the Club the Board of Directors shall distribute all assets exclusively to an organization or organizations for the benefit of dogs that qualify as an exempt organization or organizations under Section 501 (c) (3) of the Internal Revenue Code as it now exists or as it may be hereafter amended from time to time.

ARTICLE IX
Order of Business

Section 1. At meeting of the Club, the order of business so far as the character and nature of the meeting may permit, shall be as follows:
Roll Call
Minutes of the last meeting
Report of last meeting
Report of Secretary
Report of Treasurer
Reports of Committees
Election of Officers and Board (at a special meeting if called)
Unfinished business
New business
Adjournment

Section 2. At meetings of the Board, the order of business, unless otherwise directed by majority vote of those present, shall be as follows:
Reading of Minutes of last meeting
Report of Secretary
Report of Treasurer
Reports of Committees
Unfinished business
Election of new members
New business
Adjournment
ADOPTED BY THE
IRISH SETTER CLUB OF AMERICA, INC.
February 12, 1972
Approved by The American Kennel Club, Inc.
April 13, 1972
Effective April 19, 1972
Amended February 27, 1980
Effective June 1, 1980
Amended October 20, 1981
Effective January 1, 1982
Amended April 4, 1987
Effective January 1, 1988
Amended June 16, 1997
Effective February 28, 1998

About the Author

Connie Vanacore is an award-winning author of six previous books. She has written articles and columns for newspapers and magazines in the United States and Canada for the past 25 years. She also wrote the canine section of the 1994 edition of the *Encyclopedia Britannica,* as well as the North American chapter of the British book, *Irish Setters Today,* published in 1998 by Howell Book House.

She is past president of the Irish Setter Club of America (ISCA) and currently serves as their delegate to the American Kennel Club. She is also past president of the Eastern Irish Setter Association and has served both clubs in many capacities. She is the recipient of ISCA's prestigious E. I. Eldredge Memorial Award.

Connie and her husband, Fred, have two children and seven grandchildren. They currently share their home with one Irish Setter. They have occasionally bred Irish Setters since 1956, producing several champions, including a Best in Show dog.

Index

Photo Credits

Acme Dog Studios: p. 245, right

Alex Smith Photography, Ltd.: p. 127, top left; p. 177, right; p. 253, right

Alexander: p.19; p. 20, bottom left;

Alverson Photography: p. 31, bottom; p.39; p. 44, top right; p. 48, top left; p.54, right; p. 56, top left; p. 84, bottom left; p. 89, left and top right; p. 91, top; p.102, top left; p.103, top and bottom right; p. 104; p. 110, bottom right; p.113, left; p. 123, left and right; p. 134, top and bottom left; p. 135, top right; p. 138, left; p. 244, top right; p. 246, right, p. 250, bottom right; p. 253, left; p. 258, top right

American Kennel Club: p. 8; p. 9; p. 10, left; p. 12; p. 13; p. 14

Animal Pics: p. 169, left; p. 173, bottom left

Animal World Studio: p. 121, right; p. 249, bottom right

Ashbey Photography: p. 24; p. 31, top; p. 36, bottom; p.40; bottom left; p. 46, middle right; p. 47, right; p. 48, bottom left and top and bottom right; p. 60, bottom right; p.63, top and bottom right; p.66, top right; p.72, bottom left; p. 76, left and bottom right; p. 78, left; p. 84, top and bottom right; p. 86, bottom; p. 90, left; p. 101, right; p. 116, right; p. 127, right; p. 129, bottom left; p. 130, right; p. 132, top and bottom right

Bleiman Photo: p. 43

Booth Photography: p. 36, top left; p.49, right; p.52, right; p.53, p. 58, top right; left; p. 71, bottom right; p. 95, left; p. 97; p.105, left; p.108, right; p. 109, right; p.111, top left and bottom right; p. 119, top and bottom right; p.122, bottom right; p. 179, bottom right; p. 258, left and bottom right

Booth, Susan: p. 92, left

Bruni Photography: p. 110, top right

Callea Photo: p.54, top left; p.64, right; p. 87, bottom left; p. 99, top right and bottom left; p. 138, right

Chuck Tatham: p. 101, bottom left

Collins Photo: p. 180, left

Cott/Francis: p. 107, left

Cox, Pat: p.6

Dalton, David: p. 146, right

Daniels Photography: p. 296, right

David L. Whitfield Photography: p. 250, left

Dog Ads: p. 124, right

Don Petrulis Photography: p. 62, top left; p. 85

Downey Dog Show Photography: p. 62, top right, bottom left and right; p. 115, bottom left

Freeze Frame Photography: p. 248, right

GC Photo: p. 46, bottom right

Gilbert, William: p. 23, bottom right; p. 25, top left; p. 55, left and top right; p. 71, top right

Graham, Earl: p. 22, bottom left; p. 34, bottom left; p. 73, right

Gray Photo: p. 136, right

Gray, Bonnie: p. 111, top right

Haga Photo: p. 79, left

Harkins, Bruce: p. 40, bottom right; p. 75, bottom right; p. 120, left; p. 129, top left

Hauta, Ellice: p. 120, right; p. 180, top right

Henrie, Marc: p. 160, bottom left

Holvenstot, P.: p. 22, top

ISCA archives: p. 26

Jansken: p. 17, top left; p. 23, top left

JC Photo: p. 41; p.46, top right; p.50, bottom left; p. 80, top left; p.86, top; p. 134, right

Joe Rinehart Photography: p.126, left

Johnson, Carol Ann: p. 155, top right

Kernan, Bernard: p. 47, left; p. 69, bottom right; p. 87, right; p. 88, left; p. 89, bottom right

Kernan, J. Kay: p. 74, right

Klein Photo: p. 103, bottom left; p. 133; p. 137, right

Kohler: p.51; p.71, left; p. 114, bottom right; p.115, top left; p. 139, right; p. 241, top right

Kurtis, B.: p. 55, bottom right

Langdon, Jayne: p. 99, top left

Linda Lindt Photo Studio: p. 176, bottom; p. 177, left

Lindemaier, Carl: p. 83, top right

Little, Jeff and Mary: p. 42, bottom right

Ludwig Photo: p. 100, left; p. 130, top left

Meyer Photos: p. 83, bottom right; p. 106, top left; p. 108, left

Mike Johnson Photo: p.64, left

Mikron Photos: p. 81, bottom

Nugent Photo: p. 139, left

Nugent, Sara: p. 66, left

Orin Paul Trademan Photography: p. 49, left; p. 141, top right

Paul's Studio: p. 77, right; p.124, top left

Perlmutter, Michele: p. 90, top right

Phillips, Perry: p. 66, bottom right; p. 76, top right; p. 127, bottom left

Photos Today: p. 122, left

Pike, David: p. 152, left

Prangle, Claire: p. 147, right; p. 149, left; p.151, left and right; p. 152, bottom right; p. 155, left; p. 156, top and bottom right; p. 158; p. 160, top left; p. 161, top and bottom; p. 163, top and bottom left and right; p. 164, inside left and right

Rich Bergman Photos: p. 52, left; p. 131, right; p. 246, left

Rich Black's Photography: p. 117, right

Rinehart and Allen: p. 34, top right; p.96, top

Ritter Photo: p. 125, bottom left

Ross Photography: p. 135, left

Ross, Steven: p. 87, top left; p.180, bottom right

Rustic Originals: p. 240, left

Sabrina: p. 115, right

Savory-Bolus, Anne: p.10, right

Skipper Productions: p. 262, top

Sosa, Luis S.: p. 38

Standard Image, The: p.32; p.40, top left; p. 59, right; p. 72, top right; p. 77, left; p. 95, right; p.112, top right; p. 140; p. 243, left

Stoneham Photography: p. 68, left

Swan Photography: p. 94, left

Tara Darling/Paw Prints: p. 182

Tauskey: p.17, top right

Tien Tran Photography: p.118, bottom left; p. 141, bottom right; p.242, right; p. 247, left; p. 259; p. 261, bottom left; p. 295

Trafford, Michael M.: p. 172, left

Twomey, Morry: p.243, right

Vanacore, Fred: p. 293, left and right; pp. 299-308

Varva, Jerry: p. 93, bottom right

Watters, M. T.: p.27

William Secord Gallery, Inc., NY: p.7

Yuhl, Missy: p.34, bottom right; p.59, top left

Yvonne Kent/Libra Photographic: p. 148, right